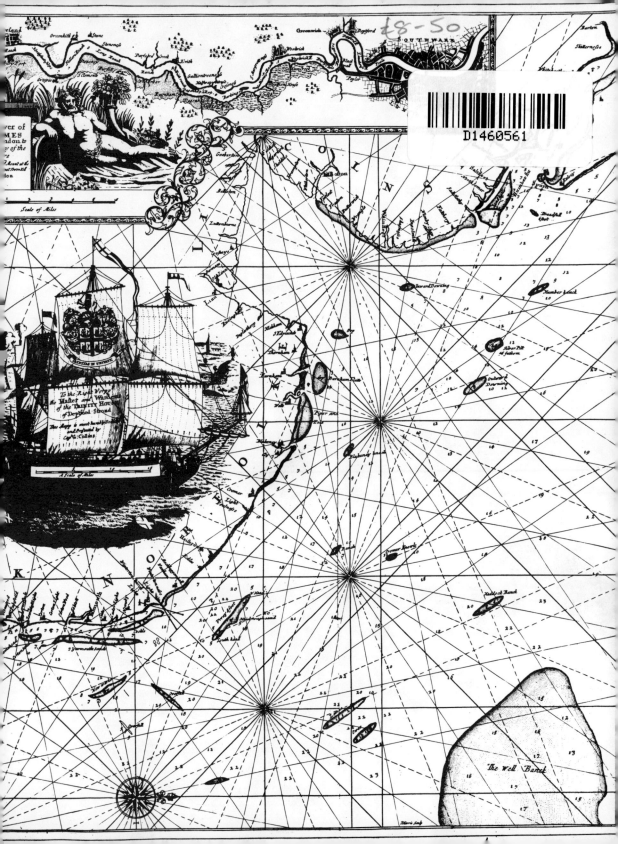

THE NORTHSEAMEN

To Susan and David

THE NORTHSEAMEN

The story of the fishermen, yachtsmen and shipbuilders of the
Colne and Blackwater Rivers

by

JOHN LEATHER

TERENCE DALTON LIMITED

LAVENHAM   SUFFOLK

1971

Published by

TERENCE DALTON LIMITED

S B N 900963 22 0

First impression 1971

Reprinted 1978

Printed in Great Britain at

THE LAVENHAM PRESS LIMITED

LAVENHAM   SUFFOLK

CONTENTS

INDEX OF ILLUSTRATIONS

ACKNOWLEDGEMENTS

THE AUTHOR wishes to thank the many relatives and friends who have contributed to the research on which this book is based.

I am particularly grateful to my mother for many recollections; to Hervey Benham for encouragement and for publishing, in the *Essex County Standard* newspaper, material of mine upon which many chapters in this book are based; and to my wife for enthusiastically enduring the household chaos of authorship, with its accumulation of data.

Others have supplied considerable reminiscence, including Captain Harold Cranfield, Norman Turff, F. Mills, Jess Carter, and Steven Cranfield of Rowhedge; Captain H. Chamberlain of Brightlingsea; W. Woodward, Ernest Lee and Charles Barr, of Wivenhoe; and A. E. South, of Tollesbury.

Unfortunately many others who provided valuable information have passed on. They included Captain Jack Carter, James Theobald, Edward Taylor, Captain William Wadley, C. Cook, William Cole, Thomas Ennew, A. Spinks, Orlando Lay and O. Springett, of Rowhedge; Howard Goodwin, Charles Wadley, Fred Firmin and Archie Turner, of Wivenhoe; Captain Hayzell Polley and E. Cook, of Brightlingsea; Jack Owen, of West Mersea; and Ted Pitt, of Maldon.

The source of photographs is individually acknowledged but I am particularly glad to have been able to include examples of the work of the late Howard Goodwin of Wivenhoe and Douglas Went of Brightlingsea.

John Leather
Tideways
Wivenhoe
1971

8

INTRODUCTION

THIS IS the story of the fishermen, salvagers, professional yachtsmen and ship and yacht builders of the Colne and Blackwater rivers, and of their vessels. It is mainly concerned with events after 1700, but sometimes extends back to the 16th century. The men and craft studied hailed principally from the small communities of Brightlingsea, Wivenhoe, Rowhedge and Colchester, on the river Colne; and from West Mersea, Tollesbury and Maldon, on the river Blackwater. It is an adventurous, varied, and often harsh story, through which runs much social change and many now little known facts illustrating the high regard in which these Essexmen were held in some branches of seafaring and shipbuilding.

I have collected information on which this book is based from first hand account and considerable research during the past 25 years. The contents have been checked and verified to present, with the greatest possible accuracy, a record of Essex seafaring which often reaches well beyond the North Sea, to the Baltic, the Mediterranean, the Atlantic, America and elsewhere.

My mother's family, the Barnards, were directly concerned in much of this history. My grandfather, great-grandfather, and his father, were smack owners, fishermen, salvagers and yacht captains from Rowhedge, and my grandmother connects me with the Cranfield family of similar background, who were also noted as captains of several of the large British yachts which raced for the America's Cup; while other relatives worked at shipbuilding; my own profession.

During the time I have gathered these tales the tradition of earning a living under sail has completely died on the Colne and Blackwater, as it had, earlier, elsewhere. There are now few active seafarers who were brought up in the local tradition of winters fishing and summers yachting; and most who participated in that maritime heyday are gone.

Their conversation and correspondence has clothed many facts with human interest and detail. From them I have heard at first hand how it felt to face the winter with a sailing smack, her nets and dredges, with perhaps three or more men depending on the skipper's skill and 'luck' at the fisheries to ensure food and housing for four families during the winter. Or how a salvaging smack laid-to in the screaming snow curtains of a winter gale, halyards frozen in the blocks and a merchantman ashore on the sands roaring under her lee. What it was like to sail a "Valkyrie" or a "Shamrock" and share with thirty other Colnesiders, the thrill of racing a yacht setting 13,000 square feet of canvas on one mast.

They were sailors of the sail. All men of humble origin but proud of their skill and the craft they commanded and sailed in. All of them sincerely wished the story to be recorded and I have tried to do this as accurately as possible, always verifying verbal statements against contemporary records.

The period was far from the 'good old days' of romantic imagination. The fisheries were often depressed and always at the mercy of fickle demand, without cold storage to regulate supplies, but with expensive transport and poor distribution.

Lack of capital was the principal weakness of the Colne and Blackwater fisheries. But even had it been generously available it is extremely doubtful that the fiercely independent Essexmen would have wished to skipper and man smacks owned by companies, and be ordered which fishing they were to work. They preferred to struggle on independently, however poor the returns, and often poverty was never far from the watersides. However, their lives must be considered against that of the hinterland. They were infinitely better off compared to the agricultural workers who then suffered malnutrition and social injustice which is almost incredible, though it was widespread only sixty years ago.

Yachting was the salvation of Colneside and the foundation of what little prosperity it knew during the 19th and early 20th centuries; besides being a cornerstone of local pride. This is an undeniable fact which, strangely, many students of local history find distasteful. Not so the Colnesiders! When yachting blossomed early in the 19th century the river's seamen and shipbuilders eagerly seized the wonderful opportunities for advancement the sport offered, with its profitable employment throughout the summers, and chance of saving something to help tide them over the often profitless voyages of the winter fisheries. It was the income from yachting, and particularly from yacht racing which was the Colne men's pride and art, on an international scale, which founded the building of much of 19th century and early 20th century Rowhedge, Wivenhoe and Brightlingsea; and of most of the large fleets of smacks working from those places. It improved the living standards of their inhabitants and advanced the scope of their seamanship and voyaging.

The great yachts, and large numbers of yachts of all types, existed throughout this time, when the rich were extremely wealthy and the poor terribly impoverished. Against this social paradox commenced the local tradition of summers yachting and winters fishing, which lasted until 1939. The fisheries became complementary to professional yachting; providing the best school of fore and aft seamanship in the smart cutter smacks with their widespread voyaging and constant sail trimming when handling the gear.

Seventy-five years ago men from Tollesbury and West Mersea were also taken on in yachts fitting out from the Colne villages and later they began to establish their own, similar tradition.

On both rivers, much of that tradition ended in 1914, and the 1939-45 war finished most of what survived the earlier conflict.

The Colne and Blackwater shipbuilders were early accustomed to building fast vessels; though after the 18th century the Blackwater yards never achieved the same size or output as those on the Colne, where large wooden ships continued to be built until 1962, and steel shipbuilding was introduced in 1890 and continues to flourish.

Colneside shipbuilding has contracted since 1962 from five shipyards to two; at Wivenhoe and Brightlingsea, both virile and versatile. In the closures the Colne has lost an asset in the only dry dock which existed between Sheerness and Lowestoft, and several large slipways.

Local wooden boatbuilding, an accumulated skill of centuries, has declined rapidly with the coming of the plastic yacht and small boat. At Brightlingsea, typically, the challenge of new material has been met and mastered; principally with that revived and interesting type, the sailing catamaran, with which, during the past decade, Brightlingsea designers, builders and crews have become internationally successful, vigorously carrying traditional versatility into a new age.

The Colne and Blackwater are not dramatic rivers. They share a common estuary and have similar mud and sand flanked shores. Both are shoal in their upper reaches at low water, with many winding creeks probing finger-like into the surrounding marshes and low, wooded hinterland. The Colne runs approximately south east to north west and is eleven miles long from the Bar buoy to Colchester Hythe, its limit of navigation. It is a gradually narrowing, winding river with wooded shores, but the uppermost reaches are beginning to be lined with commercial quays and fouled with the dunnage of trade.

But the Colne remains as interesting and inspiring to me as when I first remember it as a child, alive with the sun-glitter of high water and shadowed by the brown-sailed spritsail barges which swept past Rowhedge quays; where the masts of vessels newly launched from the shipyard reared above the rooftops, and the population was wholly maritime.

The Blackwater is a comparatively noble stretch of water; fourteen and a half miles from the Bench Head at its mouth, to Maldon. The river stretches broadly, approximately east to west, from its mouth, to Osea Island, four and a half miles below Maldon, and is one of the best sheltered sailing waters on the east coast. Man has known and used the rivers for many centuries. Ancient British settled on their shores; Romans created ports and savoured the native oysters; Saxons and other Europeans invaded and colonised; Norsemen raided and plundered, and all the subsequent crowding generations of English history have sailed from and lived by them. The shoal-strewn Essex coast, a western border of the North Sea subject to strong tides and short seas, bred a race who became justifiably included amongst the world's greatest fore and aft sailors, and builders of fast sailing craft.

Such history should be inspiring rather than nostalgic; all things change and none more than seafaring. With the passing of sail went the grinding toil of the fisheries and the sailing merchant ships. The dozens of barquentines, brigs and sailing barges have been replaced by a few coasters which chug up and down at tide time; the haulage lorries of the sea; often lacking in grace—and sometimes in maritime manners.

Much of the pride and spirit is gone. The tall-sparred cutter smacks no longer thrash up Colne in a breeze to round up, head to wind, alongside the crowded quays of Rowhedge or Wivenhoe, their canvas like thunder; or big yachts fit out in spring for the season's racing which might take them all round the British coasts, and to many foreign countries. But smaller yachts and dinghies multiply, to give many the pleasurable glories of sailing and a reminder of real seamanship, now almost vanished from the working world.

Since 1945 the local maritime scene has been much less heroic but probably more profitable. The fisheries have declined to what is their basic form; a minor part of contemporary seafaring, but remain vigorous at West Mersea and Brightlingsea, with a few boats still working from Tollesbury and Maldon where the last little cutter smacks still trawled and dredged under sail into the 1950's.

Spratting is no longer predominantly important as a winter fishery. Bottom fish and shrimps are trawled, and oysters dredged, while the ancient inshore herring fishery of the Wallet and Blackwater has been revived by the Merseamen, to their profit, while some of their boats often work as far from home as the Wash.

The Colne oyster fishery collapsed during the severe winter of 1962 but has since been revived by enterprise of a private company. Oysters remain cultivated in the Blackwater, principally at West Mersea, but the Brightlingsea oystermen gave up after 1962.

Only a handful of local professional hands are now employed in yachts, but the tremendous growth of modern sailing has brought many thousands of amateurs afloat. West Mersea boasts the largest fleet of offshore racing yachts on the East Coast, and its creeks are filled with small yachts of all kinds. Three boatyards minister to their needs and the West Mersea sailmakers send yacht sails all over the world.

Tollesbury, up its winding, shallow creek, dreamed of its former activity for thirty years and is now reviving with a new yacht harbour, wood and plastic boatbuilding, a sailmaking business achieving international reputation in the small racing classes, and a flourishing sailing club.

Across the Blackwater, Bradwell Creek is overshadowed by a bulky nuclear power station and is crowded with small craft in summer, as is Lawling Creek; while hundreds of dinghies throng the once deserted foreshore at Steeple Stone.

Spritsail barges line Maldon quay, under the low hill with its distinctive church and the 'Jolly Sailor' at its foot; but they are pleasure craft now, and the timber cargoes entering the ancient port arrive in coasters which have to pick their way through the scores of small yacht moorings lining the narrow channel.

Of all the waterfronts, Rowhedge has had the most tragic transformation; its deserted quays and vanished shipyard are shadows of the bustling past, relieved only by an enterprising yacht yard at the lower end of the village, where high quality craftmanship still flourishes, adjacent to a new commercial quay.

Wivenhoe puts on a bold maritime front with a busy and expanding steel shipyard, while small yachts and racing dinghies bring week-end life to its mellowed quayside where fitting out never seems to end.

Brightlingsea still builds specialised steel ships, small wood and plastic yachts and boats. It remains a Customs and pilot boarding station for ships using the Colne and a commercial quay is projected on the site of Aldous' once noted shipyard.

In summer Brightlingsea creek is a crowded haven for small yachts and fleets of sailing dinghies, with a large modern yacht club and two sailing clubs providing racing and shore facilities.

The movement of population into north east Essex and the consequently increasing importance of facilities for the greater leisure stemming from social progress will soon force a fresh look at the future of the Colne and Blackwater. These waters and shores could well become protected; orientated towards recreational use and conserved for oyster and other minor fisheries at the expense of general commerce; for if the projected giant port complex is built at the mouth of the Thames, its road and rail arteries will make obsolete the little adjacent ports with limited cargo handling facilities and distribution. In thirty years they will be as much a memory as the sailing barges.

When this comes about, the Colne and Blackwater will assume yet another role in their long history and new generations will continue to regard them with the affection of the earlier mariners and shipbuilders whose story I have tried to tell in this book.

CHAPTER ONE

The Stowboaters

SPRAT SLIME and bilge ran oily smears down "Beatrice's" topsides until the pump lost suction with loud sucking noises. The boy let go the handle to smear a mittened hand across a runny nose, then beat arms and hands which had no feeling against his cracking stiff oilskins. The freshening easterly, bitterest wind that ever blew, sent searching icy fingers through his thickest guernsey and strummed through the shrouds.

The Colneside and Tollesbury smacks lay spratting off Reculvers and, when the December moon gleamed through the scud it lit, gloriously, the northern face of the Kentish shore and the contrastingly dismal line of the Essex coast. The sea was restive and the moonlight set the surface of the Thames estuary into tossing, scintillating lakes of light which showed around them the black shapes and sails of smacks. Away seaward a long line of lanterns, flashing, revolving, stationary, marked the course of the deeper channels and silhouetted the shapes of great steamers.

As the boy minded these things, watching the occasional play of light from the North Foreland and the twinkling lamps in the distant villages of Kent, Jim Barnard, the owner's son, straightened his back from trying the pinion line for signs of the stow nets filling. A smart seaman Jim, who like the rest of the crew was a crack hand aboard a racing yacht. However, it was now three months since the yachts had laid up, crowding the river's mud berths, and the greater number of their crews were soon busy seeking winter employment. Most of them took on in the "stowboaters", as smacks engaged in the winter spratting were called.

Some took the train for the docks of London and Southampton seeking berths in foreign bound steamers or, if possible, aboard the great white troopships bound for India or the Cape. A handy trade trooping as it lasted until the troopers conveniently returned to lay up for the summer. But the smacks proved the winter mainstay for there was little else, and 30 or 40 of them annually fitted out from Rowhedge to join the scores sailing from Brightlingsea and Wivenhoe, and from Tollesbury, the only Blackwater village to participate in the spratting.

Autumnal springs saw smack after smack floated from her summer berth to lay on the hards, which resounded all day long with the ring of caulking irons and the chaff of seamen bending canvas, rigging gear and tarring hulls. Along the shore roads men bore on their shoulders the great stow nets and their cumbersome wooden beams. The delicate mesh of the long, brown, funnel-shaped nets had been expertly bated by village women before they were dressed in bubbling quayside caldrons.

Then they were laid aboard, triced up by the fish tackles to air; the half-inch mesh of the sleeve giving them a solid look, very different from the coarser trawls. The

The smack's boy. A finishing touch to autumn fitting out on Brightlingsea hard.   *Douglas Went* square spars of the upper and lower beams, each some 30 feet long, were shipped, together with a powerful, longlimbed stowboat anchor and many fathoms of stout cable.

The anchor had to hold both net and vessel against strong tides, wind and sea, the net riding to it, mouth to tide, under the smack's bottom and away astern by a leg of cable made fast to the lower beam. This beam was ballasted with iron to steady the net's mouth, while the upper was held horizontally above it by the "templines", ropes which, made fast to the ends, passed up to belay on either side of the smack's forward rail.

When the net was streamed and fishing its mouth might be 30 feet square. It was closed by a chain, the winchain, which started from the lower beam and passed through a ring on the upper one, over a sheave at the end of the stow-davit, fitted in winter on the opposite side of the stem to the gammon iron, and round the windlass barrel. To get the net this chain was hauled in bringing the two beams together and to the surface, where the net's sleeve was griped in with ropes and boarded.

It was an old gear dating back to the middle ages and, because of the Thames estuary's comparatively shallow channels and heavy ship traffic, was employed by the Essexmen in preference to the drift nets used elsewhere. The "stall boats", as they were originally called, were banned in 1488 by an Act of Parliament which was perpetuated in 1491. However, it must have been repealed, as many stall boats were working again by 1547, when boats from Colchester, Fingringhoe, East Mersea, St. Osyth, Maldon and Harwich were landing sprats near the Tower of London.

Traditionally, from about mid-November until mid-February, the stowboaters worked their nets by day or night as the tides served. The skippers watched for the paths of the great sprat shoals, their experience guided by the chase of flocks of gulls and other sea birds. Once located they let go, down tide from them, and waited for the net to do its work. Sometimes it took only three or four hours, sometimes a couple of days, to get a good haul which was reckoned at 300-400 bushels for a smack of about 13 tons, such as "Beatrice", though the big Brightlingsea "Masonic" once landed 3,000 bushels in a week!

Sometimes days or even weeks went by without a worthwhile landing, and during that time the fishermen earned nothing, and there were no unemployment benefits in those days. It was a fickle living and all depended on the movement of the shoals. The Wallet and Swin were the usual spratting grounds with Shoe Hole, on the Maplin's edge, proving a favourite area.

Sometimes, as now, the fleet worked the Kentish shore and, at others, the various channels between the estuary sands where they were sometimes run down and sunk in thick weather or in darkness. Occasional hauls were made "down the Sunk" and in the Whittaker channel, and exceptional schooling of the shoals or extreme bad weather would even lead them to fish in the rivers themselves; such as under the Blackwater's Bradwell shore or Collier's reach in the Orwell, though this was most unusual.

Besides the 12 to 15 tonners such as "Beatrice", many of the large first-class smacks, which were becoming fewer by the turn of the century, regularly worked the winter sprat fishery. They were joined, at rare intervals, by small coasting vessels engaging in stowboating sprats solely for farm manure. These often swung to their anchors for weeks before holds were filled with the rapidly decomposing cargo which announced their coming from afar during the passage home.

In rough weather the stowboaters dreaded a full net. This sometimes happened very suddenly, and the net would float only as long as there was life in the fish. Then the crew wasted no time in getting the net slung alongside, for if it sank they might never raise it again without damage. Often a full net had to be parted at the lacings to start the fish out of it, enabling the smacksmen, by baling out or even losing some fish, to save the net and the rest of the catch.

However, there seemed little chance of that happening to "Beatrice" tonight, as young Jim let the pinion sink back gently with an encouraging "She's fillin' boy, but

Smacks discharging sprats into skiffs, for landing at Brightlingsea hard.

I reckon that look like a real blow". He took the deck watch and the boy lumbered below through the cabin slide, to enter another world where warmth beat out of the stove's glow to thaw frozen, almost helpless, hands and body with a tingling intensity which brought tears to his eyes.

The fug was choking, the bite of old James' pipe almost made him retch and, before long, wish for air. But every chink was sealed and the owner-skipper lay snug on a locker top wreathed in clouds of his favourite tobacco. The earflaps of a round sealskin cap met under his beard but his oilskin lay open as a concession to temperature. Sea-booted feet were crossed by the stove, and the smell of warming tallow from them mingled with the fouler stench of sprat slime swilling in the bilge below.

You could always tell a stowboater; the oily slime draining from tons of sprats in her hold over the years left a fishy smell about her from which no amount of paint or tar could rid her. A gimballed oil lamp set long shadows sweeping up the bulkhead, where pegged coats swung in arcs as the smack lurched uneasily to the splash and heave of waves. The boy swigged a mug of scalding tea before squirming, fully dressed, into his dark cupboard of a berth, to be lulled to sleep by Jack Cudmore's snores, reverberating from the opposite bunk above the rattle and clatter of gear in the seaway.

James jammed a handspike savagely into the windlass barrel and felt the icy water filling his boots at every swoop of "Beatrice's" bow. Beside him Jack panted hard to keep up his skipper's fierce pace which rattled the taut cable through the davit sheave. Young Jim dodged between them, fleeting the chain and shouting for the boy to clear the tackle, ready to get the gear.

All of them reeled and swung on the bucking deck. Spray stung the skipper's face, streaming down over his beard to freeze there in the biting wind, unheeded.

"Should a been out o' this hours ago", he grunted, and would have been, he reflected, if only the price of sprats hadn't risen so this past week due to extreme weather and small landings. They were 2s. 3d. a bushel when they sailed yesterday and, as a typical owner-skipper, he was anxious to make as much as possible from the fleet's strike along the Kentish shore.

But it was no anchorage for a stowboater in an easterly gale of wind such as was making up with the wild light of dawn. "Ellen", "Wonder", "Elise" and the rest could barely have quarter filled before clearing out for Colne over an hour before, and many others were getting their gear. Now, still riding to her great stowboat anchor, "Beatrice" was swept by the seas and often hidden by the snow squalls which kept screaming in.

The thin early light dimmed almost to blackness in the squalls and the air stiffened with sleet, stinging their eyes and rattling along the deck. Crash! Her bow smashed into a sea which seemed half as high as a house. It shook her ageing frame and the chain

A Brightlingsea sprat curing yard during the 1920s. Barrelled sprats prepared for shipment to Russia, Scandinavia and the Continent. One of several similar yards at Brightlingsea. *Douglas Went*

bit into the windlass barrel with a jerk. They staggered, struggled, and held hard. The net seemed miles under them instead of only a few fathoms.

Old James was angry: it was hurried work which might easily end in a torn net, and that enraged him still more. He hated slovenly work of any kind and the desire to do well as a skipper, to find the best grounds, the elusive shoals, and to land a good catch, was always strong with him as it had been with his forebears.

Another big sea rolled down. The smack's bow rose and they held hard once more, helping to hold the deadweight strain on the pawl as she picked up. The old wooden windlass was crude; "Armstrong's patent" the Colnesiders called it. They were fishing as their forefathers had fished for centuries before them; with only muscle power to work their smacks and gear, for it was the turn of the century and compact internal combustion engines were only dreamed of and few had thought of fitting them to ships, still less to fishing vessels. Even the steam capstan, then in common use by the sailing trawlers and drifters of the larger ports, was denied to the Essexmen who lacked the capital available with organised marketing systems.

Gradually the smack's head felt the weight of her net and she curtseyed to it, shovelling up each fresh sea with a sliding dip which swirled icy water knee deep about her crew. She snubbed hard and swooped again. They panted until the brutish labour was rewarded by an increased strain on the winchain, telling of the lower baulk picking up the upper and closing the net's mouth. Soon both were awash by the bow.

Old James hung over with the jib halliard block while the others took the weight. "Beatrice" wallowed and strained; the grey water washed heavily aboard burying him as she plunged, bowsprit under. The baulks swept clear and they hove in blindly, dragging them up the bow. Jack grabbed the templines to swing them fore and aft. "Hold all!" shouted the skipper, slipping the block hook into the upper baulk strop as she lifted.

The stowboaters. Repairing a sprat net aboard a smack in Brightlingsea creek.

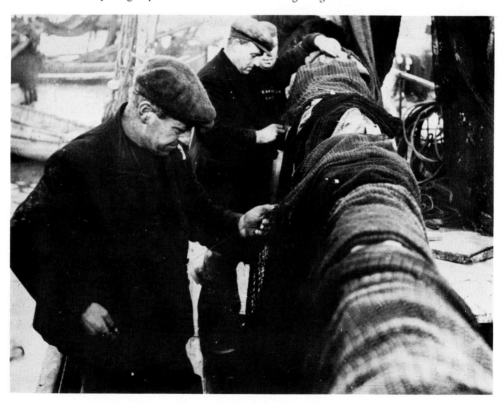

He straightened. "Now, hup with her. Haa aay yo!" The baulks swayed up to the rail and were lashed there. All hands pelted aft and ranged the leeward rail where the net's silver belly rose sluggishly in the seas alongside like a sea monster. They reached down to it, roping it in, and hooked in heaving fingers "Haaaay hi!" Soon they strained in the long tapering sleeve, dragging it up to the rail.

No time to part the net now, and they risked splitting it as young Jim slipped a strop round it and they hove the tail on deck. The skipper fetched the big wooden mingle to cut the first measure or "cod" when his son pulled the cod-end lacing. The boy cleared away the hatch and tumbled down the hold, groping for the trimming shovel as the first few bushels of silver fish shot down over him.

"Beatrice's" fine form felt the net's weight dragging at her and she canted to the sleet and spray which drove over her as the next sea slopped the length of the deck, snatching some of the hard won catch with it, despite their frantic efforts. A great watery dollup sprayed down the hold where the boy, now wretchedly sick in that slimy, reeking cavern, shovelled the slippery catch out into the wings. Another sea swilled and the blur of a big Brightlingseaman grew from a squall to roar past under short canvas. The deck gang dug split, raw fingers which had no feeling into the net and hugged it close aboard.

So they laboured on the bucking smack until at last the final cod was shaken down the hatch and trimmed. Skipper and mate made the net up under the rail, leaving Jack to clamber into the reeling smelly hold and drag the seasick boy out after him. He kicked the swollen hatchboards into place and tied the cover down tightly.

The Barnards fought flailing canvas to change the working jib for a well-roped rag of spitfire, muttering as they worked, then set about getting the anchor, wrestling, straining at the hand-spikes again, oilies discarded now for greater freedom of movement. The seas as they rode past towered high and ghastly on either side and sometimes broke, spilling their tops in a welter of white lather.

Once, James struggling to free his spike, slipped, ripping his sleeve on the bitts. His whole body throbbed with the fury of their haste and he breathed in great gulps of air, mixed with the driving spray which matted his hair in a soggy face-fringe. Thrusting the bar savagely into the barrel he threw his weight upon it, helped by the boy. The mixture of anger and anxiety in his mind gave him great strength; the thick ask spike bent under the powerful heaves and cracked off short, flinging him down on top of Jack.

The pawl took the strain. They struggled up panting and too vicious to swear. He struck the broken butt back. "And again!" The bars slid into fresh holes; all four reaching high to strain them down as the smack dipped again, loaded and slightly sluggish. "Ah haaaay! Hey ooooh!" Their call whipped away downwind and the sea smashed over the stemhead as the spikes came slowly down in a muscle-cracking pull. She was lifting now; they held on as she tossed her long bowsprit high in the air to come down again with a plunge which buried the bow in the next wave.

They paused when the big iron link which held the handfleets jammed in the snatch. The skipper worked at the shackles with a rusty spike. Would they never give, greased though they were? Old James gritted his teeth and jerked savagely at the last one. It gave suddenly, tearing skin from his hand and he flung the lines down to suck his fist.

The hull trembled again, lifting. The crew held against the pawl with sweat-soaked bodies. She reared high, sweeping a ton of frothing sea aft along her deck and shot it out over the quarters as the cable's jarring snub shook her to the keel.

The cable links bit sharply into the windlass barrel. This was the toughest part of all. "An' again boys!" They ground it in; link by link; foot by foot; fathom by fathom; heads bowed in the teeth of the squalls. Toil was timeless and the gale's icy breath chilled them, sweating hot though they were.

"Hold all!" The skipper was fumbling at the taut cable, feeling for the wire-bound joining shackle which told him another length was in. He straightened, shaking his head curtly, and the labour continued for a while. "Git yr mainsail!" Jack and young Jim dropped spikes to scramble for lift and halliards; swigging away heedless of blistered, raw hands.

Slowly the luff stretched taut beneath the throat blocks and the gaff sagged, rucked, thrashing to and fro against the lift. Young Jim leaned on the tiller, giving her a cast away. With reefed mainsail sheeted well home "Beatrice" hesitated, then the thundering sail part filled to thrust her slowly ahead, crab-wise, on her tethering cable. They hove in frantically before she snubbed to fall off on another board and, in this way she jumped, rather than sailed, to her anchor.

Scope shortened. They ground in until the cable came suddenly taut, slipping and racing out over the barrel turns with a jerk which flung them down. "Beatrice" checked, then forged on gathering way slowly. "She's clear!"

Old James started away aft at a run to keep her filled away. The others tailed on to the jib halliard and bounced the luff up in a semi-smart curve. The smack rose to the next wave, still dragging her slack of cable swinging below like a giant pendulum.

Old James nursed her easily and hailed them to get the anchor aboard and the bobstay set up. A last burst of energy dragged the slack up until the anchor lay frothing at the forefoot. Young Jim waved to windward and the skipper luffed to let him slip a bight down over the shank. Spray drove in his face but he succeeded at the second attempt. He jumped back over the rail panting. "Got yer, you beauty—heave up mates!"

Smacks fitting out for stowboating on the hard. *Sunbeam* at left.

Jack hooked in the fish tackle and they hauled. A sea boarded heavily, pounding the anchor stock cruelly against the planking. Then it was deck high and the last of the cable rattled home by hand.

She filled away as the catted anchor was lashed and, with a big jump which sent her bowsprit whipping up, "Beatrice" smashed heavily into the next ridge of foam, rising to shake herself free before staggering on, lying well to her canvas.

With the bowsprit well bowsed down, setting the jib luff hard and smart, the saturated crew rolled aft where the boy slipped on the streaming deck and slid to leeward, grabbing wildly at the capstan which broke his progress. Grinning sheepishly he tumbled down the cabin hatch, shaking himself like a dog. Young Jim pulled the slide over, "Never mind, soon be Christmas." He grinned to his father.

Two days to Christmas! The wintry waters of Brightlingsea creek were filled with stowboaters; 90 sail or more crammed the smack anchorage, and latecomers barely found swinging room in the south channel. Afloat, ice was everywhere. It caved tinklingly in the rills as the new ebb left the saltings, piled up in thin floes which bent the oyster withies, crunched and slid along the spratters topsides, and coated their decks and rigging.

Ashore, Brightlingsea was transformed into a sugar-cake town; its roofs still wrapped in the morning's snowfall, which presaged by the bitter easterly, had laid its tablecloth on Colneside and whirled in dizzy flurries over the dark sea, blinding the homeward-bounders fumbling through the squalls for the Bar buoy, the leadsman's shouted call their only guide to the river's mouth. As each made the overfalls of the Bar they cracked on, emboldened in such familiar surroundings, roaring and dodging past the looming blurs of anchored barges, finally to rush pell-mell up the creek, a crazy procession of rucking peaks and board-stiff staysails, whose frozen folds were dragged and beaten down in the rush to anchor.

"Beatrice" was a late arrival with 150 bushels of prime to show for a day and night of toil. No sooner had the anchor plunged from its lashing than James and his son were sculling swiftly ashore, their dinghy jerking along in company with those from the still anchoring fleet whose skippers hastened to the causeway, bound for a long haggle with the merchants. Jack and the boy remained aboard, occasionally wielding a sweep to poke large floes clear when they swirled round threateningly, cut by the cable.

Sprats! The waterside world revolved around them. The little silver fish occupied the thoughts of the town's merchants and curers, and the stowboaters' skippers and hands. Brightlingsea, handling half the east coast landings, was the centre of the industry and barometer of its fickle rewards. If prices were low there, smacks from other villages usually sailed their catches home to sell off as manure, though a certain amount of prime fish was landed at Wivenhoe's railway quay where the Bellmans, father and son, hooked it up in baskets to load the waiting vans. Occasionally the larger smacks landed at Chatham and, if prices were good, at Billingsgate itself. Often three of them would work in partnership, each acting runner smack in turn to land the combined catch.

Much of Brightlingsea's landings were pickled in barrels with bay leaves, salt and spices, for export to Germany, Russia, Holland and Norway; from whence some returned in tins as sardines! A good deal of prime fish was smoked by the curers, and some skippers also smoked their own in tall wooden smokehouses set on the quays or in their gardens.

There, over a slow fire of damped oak chips and sawdust which gave off acrid smoke, row upon row of tiny fish dangled on the spits, slowly mellowing to the gourmet's taste. James was an acknowledged master of this art, even troubling to make his own boxes in which the sprats were packed head to tail in fine tissue paper, ready for display on the London fishmonger's slab when opened.

The piercing wind relented as the day advanced and, easing, brought a chill mist to soften outlines and brood over the frostbound marshes, but more snow was on the way. Sleepy-eyed and frozen-fingered, the fishermen fended mechanically, answering newcomers' hails as they passed and bandying speculation on prices.

The frigid peace was shattered when a small Brightlingsea dredgerman missed stays turning over the tide and fouled a big Tollesbury smack, dragging heavily along her side to a rattle of blocks and a slowly mounting crescendo of oaths from both crews as they tried frantically to heave clear. A crunch as their quarters met and the oysterman's jib filled, canting her head off. She gathered way, pursued by shouted abuse.

Jack chuckled and laid aside his sweep to beat arms against his sides. They kept a sharp lookout for the lumbering square-bowed flats, 30-foot sprat-laden scows sculled by two men toiling at long sweeps to force the awkward brutes across tide for discharge.

Bad signs these, but to be expected with the fleet in. Big landings always meant a glutted market and, as the Barnards were finding out ashore, prices had fallen rapidly when merchants found their orders filled and buyers stocked their curing houses to capacity. Then all the skill was to no avail; large the catch and prime the fish might be, yet the hard-earned bushel plunged from shillings to mere pence in a matter of hours.

Fourpence a bushel for 150 bushels! Two pounds ten to share between three men and a boy, with a share for the smack; it would seem incredible for two days' hard work had it not happened so often to be commonplace to the "Beatrice's" crew.

One after the other ruddy-faced and angry skippers turned disgustedly from the merchants and crunched back through the icy pools on the hard; past the steaming horses drawing farm tumbrils and the greedy gulls fighting over the sprat heaps before flying off to rest and digest on the strangely black ribbons of the tidelines.

Afloat, the embittered crews, their hopes dashed, thought of and cursed those hours of keen-eyed hopeful search, scanning the icy sea for signs of feeding gulls, the cunning set downtide, with backbreaking toil heaving in; the frozen, wild dash for market, driving recklessly for the forlorn hope of being early in and securing a good price.

That day, as so often happened, dozens were disappointed; even the usually lucky "Wonder" had not made it in time. Little did any of them realise the fateful winter of 1914 would see the bushel boom to 22s. 6d., or that 70 years later the smacks which remained would search an almost barren sea.

The boat grated back alongside and the Barnards jumped aboard with cheerless faces. Jack and the boy knew only too well what that meant. Their hands were at the halliards when James' "Get your mainsail! We'll go an' see what Tom Pitt offer at home," confirmed their fears.

The night's early flood bore "Beatrice" into the reach where Rowhedge loomed darkly through heavy flakes, with deserted smacks lying canted by its quays. The helm went down and, with jib gently aflap, the smack responded falteringly, shooting halfway towards her berth before slouching her heel on the ground with a shudder which threw them all half down.

"She's on, the old box!" The skipper muttered softly as the still moving dinghy caught up and smashed into the counter, before reeling back on its painter as though stunned.

Young Jim leapt for a sweep. "C'mon boys, gimme a hand on this!" They heaved on the frozen foredeck, boots sliding for foothold with each thrust at the bending sweep. Panting breath arose in steaming clouds, dim seen in a street lamp's glow, "Hay hi, together now!" But she was firm. "The ole pig, on that hump again!" muttered Jack. Old James sounded with the boathook which grated hard bottom at four feet, as near as could be judged. "So near an' yet so far," he grumbled, a trifle more good temperedly. Young Jim flung down the sweep in disgust. The smack lay grounded broadside to the black flood swirling by her with an urgent gurgle which belied its sluggish rise.

The jib racketed down as a gust stirred the snow drizzle into a whirling curtain of flakes. Grabbing the bow warp the boy sculled off in the boat, snow water lopping about his boots with every shoreward stroke. Catching a turn on the iron ladder he clambered up the quay face as a group of Christmas singers crunched ponderous footsteps on High Street's white carpet.

Soon the lilting melody of a carol quavered out, stiffened by a cornet's blast; but the Christmas message brought little joy or goodwill into the smack's boy's heart. Cold and angry he struggled with the ring set solid in the packed snow, and damned the frozen warp which would hardly bend into the bow-line turned by mittened fingers.

At last! He hailed "Hey! Yo!" and they made fast aboard. He heard them pounding the mainsail's stiff folds into a loose stow. A lantern's gleaming circle hung from the rigging, emphasising the flaky curtains; "Hildegarde" was close astern of them and other vessels might be running up half seen; James was taking no chances.

Soon the rising flood let them warp in alongside quays already piled high with gleaming heaps of unwanted silver sprats discharged by the day tide's arrivals – prime sea food saleable only as manure. Under cover of darkness numbers of poorer villagers had already furtively picked them over for the larger sprats and the small dabs mixed with them, as a fry-up for families who knew well enough the hardships of trying to earn a living from the sea, but nothing of social security.

Thank God for the yachting, thought Jim; it had proved the mainstay of Colneside and enabled its seamen to display their ability and advance themselves. However, it was still three months to fitting out and next morning would find them shovelling the three and three quarter ton catch on to the quay, probably for 4d. a bushel, unless Tom Pitt could get 6d. from Pertwee, whose tumbrils would lumber over from the Langenhoe farms.

The fishermen rigged the mast-head tackle which would need tending on the ebb, when the smack settled in her berth. Gloomily they doused the glim and climbed ashore to swing up street, their seaboots muted in the snow.

The Rowhedge smack *Wonder*, built in 1876. Owned by Captain James Carter, she was a typical Colne smack of medium size. *Howard Goodwin*

CHAPTER TWO

The Deep Sea Smacksmen

THE QUALITY of the Colne's deep sea fishing smacks and the daring and enterprise of their crews was not excelled by any of the famous fishing fleets of the latter days of sail and their activities were stimulated by the building of railways towards the Essex coast during the early 1860's, which initiated a period of expansion and change in the area. The iron road which caused the decline of many small ports also served to revive some marine industries, especially the fisheries which had hitherto relied for market on local buyers, or on sailing the catch to London.

This was the time when everyday existence on Colne and Blackwater depended on fishing, yachting and shipbuilding. There were almost four hundred smacks working from Colne alone, manned by some 2000 hands, all of course, under sail.

At Wivenhoe a first effect of the arrival of the railway was to encourage the landing there of sprats for distribution by rail as manure. Rumours of an extension to Brightlingsea opened up still rosier prospects—the solution of the marketing problem by rapid despatch to Billingsgate without even having to work tides to Wivenhoe. Grimsby and Lowestoft had been developed by the railway companies during the previous ten years from insignificant villages into huge fishing ports. If harbours could be made out of such unpromising sites, who knew what might develop at Brightlingsea? When the railway did reach Brightlingsea in 1866 that golden dream was never realised, any more than the building of Tollesbury pier attracted the packet trade from Harwich, but it is a curious thought that Brightlingsea might today be a miniature of the great, grimy fishing ports had the capital been forthcoming.

In fact the capital was lacking but not the enterprise. Emboldened by the optimistic spirit of the age, many smacksmen who had money to venture placed orders for new craft of a size which had never before been owned locally in such numbers. No companies were created, for the thought of skippering smacks owned by others, a system common at the larger fishing ports, was horrifying to the vigorously independent Essexmen of those times who especially wished to develop the long established dredging of sea oysters, which then held a high place in the diet of the ordinary people and were in great demand.

The result was a type of powerful cutter with glorious sheer and rakish rig. Almost all were designed and built in local yards with the exception of a small number constructed at the Channel Island port of Gorey, Jersey; then a noted centre of the shellfish industry much frequented by Essexmen, and a great building place for small wooden

The Brightlingsea first class ketch smack *Hilda* in Mounts Bay, Cornwall, on passage down channel. Built as a cutter in 1886, this 65 footer was working until 1935.

craft. Aldous of Brightlingsea built no fewer than thirty six of these big smacks between 1857 and 1867, whilst Harris of Rowhedge, and Harvey, Barr and Husk at Wivenhoe, accounted for a good number; with some also built on the Blackwater. These twenty and forty tonners dwarfed the little ten ton estuary oyster dredgers, and between them existed as great a difference in purpose and voyagings as between the deep sea trawler and motor bawley of the present day. Those who recall the ketch "Fiona", which survived until recently as a Sea Scout guardship in Colne, will be able to visualise the size of these craft, remembering too that most of them were cutter rigged with spars of giant size.

The Rowhedge "Aquiline" owned by Captain Harry Mills Cook, was typical of these. A bold-sheered cutter of twenty one registered tons, she was launched from Harris' yard in 1856 where her sixty five foot hull was well and truly built, and finely formed, having a beam of fifteen feet and drawing eight feet six when loaded to her capacity of twenty one tons, and a little less when light. She carried a sail area of about two thousand square feet in her working canvas. Spars were sizeable then as her main boom was forty five feet long and the bowsprit was some thirty feet outboard. When sea-dredging the mainsail was handed and its boom stowed in a crutch and a large

29

trysail having its own gaff was set in its place, sheeted by tackles to the quarters. The mainsheet was of bass as it stretched well and was easy on the gear.

The arrangement of these big vessels differed greatly from the smaller smacks which survive today. Forward, the usual handspike windlass handled the anchor cable, which ran out clear of the stem on a short "davit", and, in season, the stowboat gear. A large geared hand winch having four barrels was fitted immediately forward of the mast for use in working halliards, running out the bowsprit, working fishing gear or whipping out cargo. A winch or geared hand capstan stood amidships and could be worked by two or more hands when dredging or working trawl warps, all of which were hauled by muscle power as, unlike the specialised trawling smacks from the big fishing ports which were equipped with steam capstans, the Essex boats relied solely on "Armstrong's patent" to get their gear, a feature of working which they seem to have endured until the eclipse of sail. A clincher built boat about fifteen feet long was carried on deck or lashed, capsized, over the main hatch in foul weather. In port on Sundays and regatta days most of them sported a long masthead pennant emblazoned with the smack's name or initial and other fancy work. Many had signal letters allotted to them which is proof of their varied sea work, but few had shroud channels as these interfered with the boarding of heavy stowboat gear. Sometimes local customs went into the hulls for you could always tell a Wivenhoe built smack from one launched across the river by the round rubbing strakes her builders fitted; the Rowhedge smacks having flat ones.

Below decks the fore peak was a cable locker and abaft this the "mast room", as the space between the peak bulkhead and the mast was called, housed a large scuttle-butt for drinking water and racks for bread and vegetable stores on extended voyaging. Partial bulkheads set it off from the hold which occupied about one third of the ship's length and had a capacity of twenty one tons on her ballast, which was clean beach shingle with a proportion of iron pigs covered by a wood ceiling. All hands berthed in the cabin aft, entered by a sliding hatch in the deck. In this space of perhaps fourteen by nine feet, six men lived for months on end. Locker seats ran down each side and the four bunks lining the topsides behind them each had sliding panels which could be closed by the occupant to shut himself off for sleep or from his noisy mates; imagine the old sea-dogs relaxing with a pipe, like be-whiskered walruses, wreathed in choking clouds of their own enjoyment! A big double berth across the counter was known as the "Yarmouth Roads" berth and could hold a couple of apprentices, who were lulled to sleep by the rudder's groan and kick in the trunk near their heads. Corner lockers held provisions and navigating equipment and on the black coal stove stood a blacker kettle and a huge teapot which was only emptied when it would no longer hold six mugfuls of water! Knives and forks were stuck in cracks of the deck beams overhead, and saucepan lids made good plates in a seaway when, rested on the knees, they could be gripped between them by the handles and the rims held the gravy from spilling!

These craft formed the finest fleet of fishing vessels ever to work from the county, and they gave nothing in size, ability or appearance to the smacks from Brixham, Ramsgate or Yarmouth, many of whom with some Essexmen, "colonised" Grimsby and Hull.

In them the great-grandfathers of many of us found their living and learnt or displayed their seamanship.

There is no point in attempting to glamourise the fisheries, which were always hard, often dangerous, and usually miserably rewarding financially; but that they bred men of strong and independent character there is no doubt. Theirs was none of the comparatively idyllic life of the estuary dredgers, but a thrusting existence, alive to any and every opportunity which came their way.

Most skippers began as apprentices serving aboard their master's smack and living in his house when in port. These boys were often sent to sea at the age of ten or twelve, being bound for five, seven or nine years to the owner who might have two such boys serving aboard his smack. This system was one of some antiquity and existed in the seventeenth century, but seemed to die out at the end of the nineteenth.

Strict rules were laid down for apprentices' behaviour when ashore. Pubs were barred, as were playing at cards or dice; and they were not allowed to marry; though this would have been pretty hopeless anyway on a yearly wage of £10. to £12.! The owner found them in food but the apprentices kept themselves in their favourite rig

Deep sea smacksmen in old age. A group at Rowhedge about 1890.

of "cheesecutter" cap, white canvas jumper or smock over a thick guernsey, and thick duffle trousers tucked into leather sea boots with cobbled soles.

It was a way of life which produced smart seamen and gave fair promise of advancement for those times. There was little of the "by guess and by God" style of navigation amongst these smacks' competent skippers, most of whom were progressive enough to obtain fishing masters' certificates when these were introduced in the 1870's. Their quest for oysters and scallops led them, at various seasons, to work the following grounds; the Inner Dowsing and Dudgeon banks, landing at Grimsby or Blakeney; the Ness grounds, stretching from Orfordness to Cromer; the Galloper and Kentish Knock areas of the North Sea and the Terschelling and Hinder banks off the Dutch coast, landing at Brightlingsea. In the Channel they dredged the Goodwin, Sandettié and Varne grounds, with those off the French coast at Caen Bay, Dieppe, St. Valery-sur-Somme, Fecamp, Calais and Dunkirk; using Ramsgate, Dover or Shoreham as ports. Down channel West Bay provided some work, landing at Weymouth and, in earlier times, the Cornish Fal and Helford rivers were visited—one almost writes raided—by the Essexmen, while the Channel Island of Jersey attracted large numbers of Essex smacks to its fishery for seventy years. Many sailed round the land to work on the south Pembrokeshire coast, based at Swansea; and Bangor, Western Ireland, and the Solway Firth also regularly saw the rakish Colne topmasts.

Work aboard was hard when dredging. On the grounds the topmast was often struck and a reef tucked in the mainsail, or the trysail would be set to ease speed and motion in a seaway and keep the boom clear of unwary heads. After this they worked almost continuously, day and night, with only occasional spells for mugs of tea and a bite to eat. It must have been muscle-cracking toil winding up those huge sea dredges with their six-foot hoeing edges from twenty-five fathoms, by hand. Often six were worked at a time on sixty-five fathom, three inch bass warps leading in through multiple rollers on the rail or through a port in the bulwark. Each weary foot of it cranked home with one man keeping tension on the slack which jerked back on every sea to etch new scars into hands already torn by the tiny shell picked up by the warp. So it would go on hour after hour without even the respite of sorting between hauls which trawling gives. At about three a.m. the gear would be laid in and the crew took half hour watches, before recommencing at six and this might go on for five or six days! They must have been heartily sick of oysters by the time the voyage ended for, after spending all day and half the night hauling dredges from the heaving sea, they tumbled below to be confronted by dishes of steaming oyster soup!

Hard as they were the fisheries flourished and by 1874 there were 132 of these first class smacks of fifteen to fifty tons, registered at Colchester; in addition to 250 second class of under fifteen tons and 40 third class vessels.

By far the largest proportion of these were owned at Brightlingsea, with Rowhedge accounting for twenty-nine and Wivenhoe and Tollesbury about a dozen each. Few of these large vessels were owned by West Mersea fishermen whose interests were chiefly centred in the Blackwater oyster fisheries, and none in the latter days of sail.

Rich oyster beds were discovered by the big smacks off Jersey in 1797, and news travelled fast even then for within a few months a fleet of over three hundred smacks from Essex, Shoreham, Emsworth and Faversham, manned by two thousand men, were working there. From the quiet port of a few months before, Gorey became a boom town with scenes ashore which must have rivalled the gold rush days that were to come.

A fleet of sixty Essex smacks sailed there each spring and carried on dredging these waters despite the hazards of the Napoleonic wars; the crew of one smack were captured in the Channel by a French warship and imprisoned for seven years. Released when the war ended these half starved but still tough seamen hiked to Gravelines, where they stole a boat and rowed to Portsmouth, a feat in itself; but they capped that by walking home to Brightlingsea!

Friction with the French continued long after the war as the best grounds extended into their territorial waters, and the English boats were often arrested as poachers. The limit went up to six miles in 1824 and violence flared four years later when a number of smacks, including many from Essex, were attacked while dredging off Chausey, in French waters. Men from two French warships boarded one and took her as a prize into a French port. When this became known to the whole fleet of 300 they sailed for the French coast, where the men-of-war were boarded at night by hundreds of enraged smacksmen armed with hatchets and windlass staves, who swarmed aboard the Frenchmen, killing many of their crews and re-taking the captured smack to sail her back in triumph; but with many dead, and leaving a number in irons aboard the warships. After this things went from bad to worse and, in 1832, the Colne boats returned home complaining of lack of naval protection when dredging, and the next year the Brightlingsea "Hebe" was seized by a French gunboat and her crew set adrift in the channel, alleging that the British gunboat "Seaflower" made no attempt to interfere or to assist them.

By 1845 the beds were in a depleted condition and delay by the authorities in opening the re-stocked grounds in Grouville bay led to serious disorders at Gorey where it took a regiment of the island garrison to control the rioting smacksmen. Afterwards the masters of ninety-six smacks were fined by the Jersey government and fifteen of the Essexmen turned their attentions to the grounds off Dieppe, where they dredged around Cape D'ailly despite French protests. After some revival the Jersey fishery became exhausted by 1871.

Wherever there were oysters the far ranging Essexmen would find them. By the 1830s they were participating in the flourishing fishery worked by the fishermen of Mumbles, in Swansea and Cardigan bays, Pembrokeshire. In 1844 the heavy dredging of local grounds was arousing protests from the Mayor of Swansea who suggested the council should interfere before the beds were entirely destroyed. But, as usual, little was done, and during the following twenty years a total of 9,000,000 oysters were dredged each year by a fleet of smacks two hundred strong, and many thousands of spat oysters were taken to restock the beds in Colne and Blackwater, and at Whitstable and Faversham.

However antagonised they felt, the Welsh fishermen were so impressed by the graceful and handy Essex cutters which were so much abler than their own lug rigged 'skiffs', that, about 1855, a delegation of them travelled to Colneside to study local smacks and methods—an early and enterprising example of work study. As a result many orders were placed with the Colne yards for small vessels of around twelve tons which cost about £300 complete; and there was great rejoicing at Mumbles when the first of these, the "Seven Sisters", arrived there. She was followed by many more, but later Mumbles, 'Skiffs', as the Welshmen called them, were constructed by Bristol channel builders who copied the lines and arrangement of the Essex built boats; and were in turn copied by the Brixham men for their "Mumble Bees", as they called their smaller cutters.

A few years later the Welsh fishery was becoming impoverished and declined thereafter; finally becoming extinct just after the First World War.

Another example of overfishing occurred in the oyster fishery which developed from Blakeney, Wells and Cley on the north coast of Norfolk during the middle part of the nineteenth century. Numbers of small local smacks were working a profitable fishery on the Dudgeon, which flourished until 1834 when sixty or so Colne smacks suddenly arrived and began to work the grounds, to the amazed resentment of the Norfolk men. Having almost cleared the fishery, which never really recovered, they disappeared, except for five or six who remained dredging and landed their catches at Lynn, Wells or Blakeney, where the nineteen ton "Thorn", once owned by the renowned Jack Spitty, was wrecked on the bar with the loss of all hands when entering that treacherous and unlit haven before a north easterly gale.

Largo bay on the north shore of the Firth of Forth was another area dredged by a fleet from Colne one season. Here they met spirited local opposition from the Scots fishermen who attacked them in their boats, armed with stones. They received a hiding, and when crowded in the tiny harbour of Newhaven, the Essexmen slept under police protection with axes and windlass spikes laid handy. Eventually the navy sent a gunboat to keep the peace.

Many readers will already know of the dredging of sea oysters on the Terschelling bank, off the Dutch coast, which has led to all the big smacks being dubbed "Skillingers" in recent times. But it should be remembered that this fishery, important and arduous as it was, formed but a part of the very many grounds and trades worked by these versatile seamen and their craft.

Jack Spitty of Rowhedge. A noted fisherman, salvager and smuggler who in later life fished from Bradwell.

This fishery lies off the island of Terschelling, about 112 miles to the eastward of Orfordness, from which point the smacks usually took their departure. Trips averaged twelve days during which a haul of about 10,000 oysters could generally be expected.

Some queer things happened to smacks in this fishery, almost as though the sea was more than usually reluctant to yield its harvest.

The 58 ton Brightlingsea ketch "Hawthorn" was so hammered by the North Sea that her crosstrees lay in the water and some of her ballast went through the deck. Eventually she was clean swept, with only the bitts and wink posts standing. She was towed into Ymuiden, where her crew sold her for £20.

A fine winter's morning in 1900 found the powerful Brightlingsea ketch smack "Emma" running eastwards across the North Sea before a light breeze, bound for Terschelling. The log spun off sixty miles since it was streamed off the Suffolk coast and skipper Bob Crickmar hummed a tune at the tiller while the crew cursed the price of shellfish; suddenly, with no warning from the placid sea, a huge freak wave rose up astern and broke aboard her. Tons of water smashed down along her decks, badly injuring all the crew except one apprentice. The dinghy lay shattered in its gripes and the hatches were gone leaving her half full of water. Painfully the crew pumped her out and, under their direction, the boy brought the wreck on the wind; but it took two days and nights to beat slowly back to the Essex coast and by that time the crew, many with broken limbs, were almost exhausted; and the boy was little better. That night as he nodded at the tiller she gently grounded on the Shipwash sand, where the Harwich lifeboat found her and towed them in. "Emma" was one of the last smacks to work at Terschelling.

In common with the smaller smacks, "Stowboating" for sprats formed a regular part of the first class boats' winter employment. Often four of them would work as partners, taking turns to land the catches which were transferred to the carrier by towing the "sleeve" of the net with the smacks' boats; a tough job in a tideway.

Apart from the more usual activities already described, many smacks were employed on contract for £12 per week as fish carriers for the great fleets of lumbering Grimsby, Hull, Yarmouth and Lowestoft ketches which spent the year round trawling the Dogger bank. They were ideal for this work, being fast and capable of being driven through the foulest weather by their crews and, blow high or low, they usually got to Barking or Billingsgate before the cargo turned; for, though ice was used aboard them to preserve the fish, a protracted calm might mean running things pretty close and all sorts of big jibs and topsails, not to mention spinnakers, were set to keep going. The boy was sent to the masthead to "skeat" the sails with water drawn from overside with the scuttlebut dipper, hauled up with the leadline.

Colne smacks were also employed, with some from Jersey, in another, lesser known aspect of the fish carrying business; the seasonal running of fresh salmon from the western Irish ports of Sligo and Westport, on the coast of County Mayo, round the northern tip of Ireland, to the Liverpool market. This was, perhaps, the hardest trade of all for the coast is exposed to the full sweep and fury of the North Atlantic, and most smacks took the precaution of reeving chain reef pendants to stand the hard driving which usually made the round voyage to Liverpool and back in four days, no mean feat in such small ships. They must have made stirring sights, cracking on and plunging bowsprit under in the seaway off Malin head or the Bloody Foreland, with the precious freight of one hundred boxes full of fresh salmon chocked off in the hold.

The Rowhedge "New Unity", owned by Tom Barnard, my great-grandfather, was one of several Colne smacks engaged at times in the equally unrecorded and arduous voyages to the German and other Baltic ports with barrelled herring shipped from Stornoway.

In fact there was nothing these boys wouldn't or couldn't tackle to get a living when the fishing was dull. One of them, the Rowhedge "Young Pheasant", owned by Sam Mills, even became the first torpedo boat! During the 1870s the Whitehead company were experimenting with the first propelled torpedoes and selected the Wallet as a suitable trials area for the new weapon. A local craft was required for the experiments and Sam Mills got the job; the "Young Pheasant" being fitted with a form of dropping gear (tubes had not then been perfected) and, for some time, she presented the unique sight of a sailing smack carrying a "tinfish"!

Many smacks were in the cattle trade from the Channel Islands to Weymouth, at certain times of the year. The Brightlingsea "Globe" was typical in being licensed to carry nineteen swine in the hold and two cows on deck. The poor beasts must have suffered in the race off Alderney, especially the cows; for it was the boys' job to truss up the boom to clear their backs when going about! However, conditions in that trade were a picnic compared with those existing aboard the Mersea smack "Essex" which in 1839 discharged a cargo of no less than forty one Norwegian ponies on Brightlingsea hard, for auction!

The Rowhedge "Aquiline" and "New Blossom", Charles Crosby's 33 ton ketch, were often employed in the French spring potato trade from St. Malo and St. Michaels to Colchester; shipments being made for Baxter and Co. "New Blossom" also often shipped the village's coal from Shields and frequently voyaged to the Baltic with cargoes of coal or barrelled herring, prior to the 1880's.

When Wivenhoe shipyard drydock was built in 1889, "Aquiline's" owner contracted to supply all the shingle needed for the cement and this was dug by hand from

Colne beach, sailed upstream, and discharged, also by hand, twenty two tons per trip; and it needed several hundred tons to complete the job. "Aquiline" and her sisters were no strangers to the London river either, for, apart from landing fish at Billingsgate and Gravesend, they often sailed up to Deadmans Creek, Rotherhithe, to load imported oysters from the steamers shipping them from the Tagus, Brittany, or Chesapeake Bay; sailing home to lay them, usually, at West Mersea, in the extensive layings then owned by the Heaths of Wivenhoe. It was warm work humping out twenty two tons of oysters from the smack's deep hold, and just as brisk when they dredged "Culch", or clean shell for use on the oyster layings. "Aquiline" and "Quiver" sometimes engaged in this for the large oyster companies.

In the latter years of the 19th century yachting rivalled and then eclipsed the Essex deep sea fisheries; and the smaller twelve and thirteen tonners became popular for working the Thames estuary, as these could be more economically laid up all summer while their crews made more colourful pages of sailing history. The days of the big smacks were numbered, though as late as 1890 Brightlingsea boasted a fleet of 52. Twelve years later several poisoning scares killed the demand for sea oysters and the remaining fleet took to working down Channel from January to March, usually dredging from the French ports, notably Boulogne, and sending the catch to London by the night steamer. Shoreham was also used when dredging the extensive grounds off Beachy Head in company with some very fine smacks from Emsworth, Hampshire, some skippered and manned from Brightlingsea; and, sometimes, Newhaven, where, about 1910, extreme weather conditions kept a dozen Brightlingsea boats in port for seven weeks as the dredges could not be kept on the ground in the terrific seas running. All that time the crews earned nothing and ended in debt for their food. The sea-oyster dredges were also used for scalloping, with the addition of wicked looking spikes on the hoeing edge, added in imitation of the Frenchmen also working the same waters and a feature which did much to wreck the fishery.

The Colne smacks often poached inside French waters, fitting black boards over their fishing numbers. The French sailing revenue cruisers, intercepting them, were fast off the wind but the Essexmen easily beat them to windward and eventually the French had to patrol this fishery with steam torpedo boats. These sometimes fired on the smacks, aiming at the main halyards, and several smacks carried bullets in their masts. During these attacks only the smack's helmsman remained on deck, with fishboxes piled round him as "armour"!

The First World War dealt a great blow to the big smacks and, though fish prices were high, several were sold away to Lowestoft and elsewhere while others were working on government fishing contracts, mainly stowboating. After it, a few carried on in the traditional ways, supplemented by a few old Lowestoft steam drifters; though with the exception of these and four or five paddle dredgers owned by the Colne and Burnham oyster fisheries, steam found no place in the Essex fleet.

"Fiona" made the last of the old style dredging voyages about 1931, and of the long story nothing now remains beyond the memories of a few aged mariners and the hulks of "Quiver" and others in the Colne, and "Pioneer" at Mersea. Yet it formed a chapter in national as well as local maritime history which, for sheer enterprise, seamanship and courage, would be hard to equal.

The 18 ton Brightlingsea cutter smack *Globe* entering Newhaven, Sussex, dredging down channel about 1900. Owned by Captain Jabez Polley she was typical of the Colne first class smacks. Note boat on deck.

CHAPTER THREE

Oysterman's Journal

ONE HUNDRED and sixty-eight years ago William Sanford, oyster merchant, quietly penned his accounts and observations by Wivenhoe's waterside. The bowed windows of Trinity House, his quayside home, overlooked oyster pits and the berths where his smacks and skiffs stirred gently each high water.

Recently, by courtesy of Mr. Bartlett, its present owner, I was privileged to read the long thick ledger, and the entries, written in a flowing hand, unconsciously capture the unsophisticated spirit of early nineteenth century Colneside; a quiet world of fishermen, traders, and wooden shipbuilders. Smacks and brigs worked to its quays and the hillsides were unscarred by sand workings. Steamships were unknown, but the riverside communities stood on the threshold of yachting's grand era which was to bring fame, comparative prosperity, and relief from often widespread poverty.

The ordered records of oysters bought and sold, of cargoes landed, of repairs to smacks, spars and sails; all incidental to oyster cultivation, that most peaceful of sea-faring occupations, make it seem incredible that when he wrote the whole of Europe was locked in war and Trafalgar and Waterloo were yet to be fought. Sanford owned, jointly with his brother Thomas, a smack, a skiff, a packing house, oyster pits and all the gear for working and retailing oysters, which the brothers cultivated largely on three layings at Tollesbury. William Sanford also owned Horned Heath farm at Fingringhoe, which was let to Daniel Smith; and another in the same parish hired by John Pertwee. In Wivenhoe he owned, besides his house, granaries, a coal yard, a wharf, and three warehouses, which were probably smack's stores. If these interests were not enough he dabbled in stocks through the Colchester bankers and also occasionally carried out valuations of boats and maritime equipment.

But Sanford's heart was in the oyster trade which in those times, with oysters a food of the working man, occupied an important place in the national economy. Between the years 1810 and 1828 the brothers 'haled', to use his expression, 9022 wash of market-able oysters from the layings, the price varying from 1/2d to 1/9d a wash. This total was approximately twice the quantity of brood oysters laid. For re-stocking the layings Sanford bought oysters from the Colne company, Burnham, Orford, Seasalter, Paglesham and Chatham, and the smack owners and dredgermen employed by him at various times included Robert Harvey, Robert Blyth, Thomas Taylor, James Heath, William Heath, Robert Munson, William Kepple and Jacob Turner; all names of old Wivenhoe families. He also often received stock dredged from other parts of the coast. In 1821 Colne smacks had a summer season dredging off north Norfolk and Sanford records buying brood from Samuel Wade of the smack "Mary" and from Thomas Harlow, at 1/- per wash. At this time Harlow was also supplying North country brood for re-laying at Tollesbury where the stock seems to have been maintained at a value of around £400. Sanford gives the costs of working these layings for the year 1827, which seems to have been typical. The brothers bought 842 ½ wash of oysters for re-laying, at a cost of £184-19-0. Haling 958 wash of marketable oysters from the laying cost £52-12-0, while rent, taxes, poor rate, stock laid, and sundry expenses came to £79-12-0; the total being £317-3-0. Oyster merchants were men of substance and during the years 1816 to 1827 the Sanfords cleared £1450 from the oyster trade, the average yearly profit being £130. In 1802 a bushel of marketable oysters sold at six shillings and the price had risen to eight shillings by 1817. Their quality was variously described as White, Small Green and Best Green. An entry for 1822 has a surprisingly modern touch. Sanford complains of "the price of oysters and oyster barrels which must appear very strange for barrels to be more than the oysters that are put into them". Oysters to fill a barrel cost 7½d. and an empty barrel 10d! 1809 appears as the "finest winter for the oyster trade ever remembered, considering the stock oysters being at the price of 11d. a wash—6d. small." Seven years later, by contrast, the smacks had to stop working in Colne because of the exceptionally heavy frosts.

In an age of slow communications, having no railways, bad roads and costly and delayed postal services, it is interesting to find how developed was the oyster marketing system. Sea transport being then quickest and cheapest, Sanford's oysters, in common with those of most Essex and Kentish merchants, were sailed round to London in smacks, for sale, mainly through fishmongers; though his distinguished London customers included Lord Howe, then first Lord of the Admiralty, and Colonel Rebow, whose family had considerable connections with Wivenhoe. Many of Sanford's oysters were carried by Mr. Jolly's smack which earned freights averaging £3-3-0 per trip at 6d. a wash in 1803, rising to 9d. by 1806. Others were also employed in the carrying trade and reference is made to "Mondays, Tuesdays, and Fridays boats". These Wivenhoe smacks, together with those from other Colne and Blackwater villages, would join smacks from Whitstable, the Medway and the Channel Islands in the annual opening of the oyster season at Billingsgate, which took place at midnight on August 4th, each year. As the hour struck a crowd of two thousand or so would scramble aboard the sixty or more smacks alongside the wharf, each with its white coated salesman shouting above the din and keeping tally with a blackboard on deck. However, the trade was not always so prosperous; in 1817 Sanford remarks on it being depressed owing to the high price of 14d. a wash, and many smacks returned from London with their freights unsold and their crews forced to live on credit.

Consignments also reached regular customers "by land conveyance". Sanford's standing orders for 1803 read; "Oysters to go weekly according to the following day and direction. Every Tuesday one barrel to the Marquis of Salisbury at W. Sparrow's, Nr. Ipswich. Thursday two barrels to the Earl Waldegrave to be left at Mr. Checkers, Chelmsford. Saturday one barrel to the Marquis of Salisbury and a double barrel to the Countess of Waldegrave, to be left at the Lion and Lamb, Brentwood, until called for, carriage paid. Likewise Thursday one barrel to the Hon. William Fitzroy to be left at the King's Head, Norwich and forwarded to him at Gt. Wickingham, by the Ipswich coach, from Colchester". Other orders were despatched to Mansfield, Nottinghamshire; Boyton Park,"By the male" (coach); Lord Sherborne, New Bow, Glaston by Harris' Gloster waggon from London". Large quantities of oysters were sent to local personalities, who figure in his accounts. George Round, the Colchester banker, and John Bawtree, banker and brewer, share a page with Joseph Simpson who farmed "Munk Wick". Captain Stacey of the revenue cutter "Repulse", Philip Sainty the shipbuilder, and the Wivenhoe parson were other regular customers.

Another was Daniel Sutton, Colchester's town clerk from 1813 to 1818, whom Sanford huffily records as a bad payer! This colourful character who lived at Wivenhoe, where he constructed a quay and took his pleasure in several boats, is reputed to have brought to the district its first news of the victory at Waterloo by hoisting a large masthead pendant as he roared up Colne, bound home from Ostende. He also owned a lugger, an unusual rig for the Essex coast and one liable to suspicion in that era of smuggling. Indeed, this lugger of Sutton's was credited with both smuggling and salvaging activities. Daniel seems to have been a live wire by all accounts and Sanford carried out various valuations of boats and seafaring equipment for him, the last in 1820, the occasion of the impecunious town clerk's emigration to Tasmania—with the aid of relatives of course!

Wivenhoe waterfront after the Essex earthquake, 1884. The small smacks at extreme right are lying in berths earlier occupied by William Sanford's smacks. His old house is partly obscured by the shed on adjacent quay. Note schooner yacht, smacks, barge and damage to buildings.

In 1821 Sanford records; "Our small vessel the "Sisters" sailed from Wivenhoe on the 6th. February for a voyage with oysters at four o'clock in the morning and got home the same day at 10 o'clock at night. Brought home 23 1/4 bushels, 93 wash natives from Whitstable". That would be good sailing today for a forty foot flag cutter and the times given, allowing for discharge and re-loading which was, presumably, carried out with skiffs provide an interesting mental exercise in Thames estuary tides and courses. Despite her ability the "Sisters" was exchanged in 1826 for James Wiseman's Paglesham smack "Providence", to which Robert Sainty carried out some repairs and S. Goodwin, the village sailmaker, supplied new cut sails. The "Providence", which would be of about 12 tons, was valued at £80 as the "Property of Wm. and Thomas Sanford, share and share alike". It is interesting to speculate whether she was a traditional bold sheered, chubby bowed and lute sterned, clench built cutter or one of the leaner, carvel planked flyers then coming into vogue and developing the beautifully proportioned counter stern which became a hallmark of the Essex smacks in their ultimate perfection of form eighty years later.

Sometimes the oyster trade could be hazardous, as in 1823 when the journal records that "Capt. Tranham was lost coming from Jersey with oysters for Milton (then a centre of the Kentish oyster cultivation) on the 8th day May. All hands lost, himself, son, and brother, etc. All belonged to Brightlingsea. Gave his widow £1". What a grim little sea tragedy lies in that paragraph. Other traditional Essex fisheries were carried on despite the Napoleonic wars. In the year of Trafalgar encouragement was given to local fishermen by payment of a sprat bounty, paid by government order. An entry for 1820 remarks on the "Quantity herring catched in Colne as high as the gard boat (probably off East Mersea stone) from Nov. 10th to 19th William Cole of the "Liberty" brought up a vessel full and a net alongside his vessel which he could not take in—such a circumstance as no man can remember". The "Liberty" may have been working the traditional Colne-Blackwater estuary herring fishery, which was revived recently by West Mersea fishermen, though more probably he was stowboating for sprats. Mackerel provided another surprise in June and July of the following year when "Such a quantity mackrel catched and brought to Wivenhoe as was never known. Mackrel selling on the 30th June for 8d. a hundred, falling to 2d. a hundred two days later when over 15000 had been landed".

Sanford lived in shipbuilding's age of oak and hemp and it is not surprising to find him planting 100 oaks and 50 ash trees on a "small piece land going up Fingringhoe hill". He measured the growth of these as it increased each year and eventually sold some of them to Philip Sainty. They wasted nothing in those times as most of the oak bark was sold for tanning. During 1809 much locally grown timber was regularly shipped from Fingringhoe wharf, with coal and chalk forming inward freights for such vessels as the ship rigged "Venice", and the "William", Capt. Green. Sanford appears to have received dues based on the value of these cargoes and may have owned the wharf, which might have been the one built in 1760, whose remains are still on the riverbank opposite Cook's shipyard. Frequent reference is made to vessels repairing on the "Town bridge", which must have meant the old town hard whose site is now occupied by the Wivenhoe Sailing Club. Again, he received sums when craft were hauled out there; as in 1826 when B. Stacey's vessel went on to have a new keelson fitted, and again the following year when Nathaniel Harvey and James Nash laid their smacks on for repair.

The journal tells of launches from Sainty's shipyard. On June 3rd 1829 a ship of 220 tons went down the ways—"a very fine and burdensome vessel". We may smile at Sanford's description of a three masted merchantman probably no longer than 100 feet, but it should be remembered that a 160 footer was a monster at that time when the merchant service was made up of very large numbers of small ships, representing capital investment by shipowners in scores of small ports, instead of a few big centres as now. A few weeks later, on June 25th, Sainty launched a 12 ton smack for James Wiseman, the Paglesham oyster merchant with whom Sanford did so much business. Sainty also carried out ship repairs. In April 1823 he re-launched a 250 tonner which was brought up to the village as a salvaged wreck, to be almost rebuilt. Her re-launch suggests he may have possessed a 'hauling up slipway' of the type patented not long before by Morton of Leith, though, more likely, she was got out on temporary ways. An entry for March 3rd 1828 records the launch of the 600 tons, three masted sloop of war "Pearl", described in another chapter. She stuck on the ways during launching and was not got off until next tides, a fortnight later. Admiralty contracts were not easily won in those newly peaceful years and one can picture the abortive launch with the flag bedecked hull jammed on the ways while the be-whiskered builder alternated between a fury of encouragement to all hands straining at the starting jacks, and re-assuring asides to the Board of Admiralty representative and the overseer. An event such as this would attract as much attention as a regatta does now, bringing crowds thronging the Fingringhoe shore, opposite. Strangely enough no mention is made of the famous yacht "Pearl", but Sanford refers to the launch on July 8th 1830, of the 60 tonner "Water Witch" for Sir Thomas Ormsby. Yacht stores are mentioned in 1818 when Philip Sainty rented one of Sanford's warehouses for six months to store the gear of "Earl Anglesey's yacht". Sanford seems to have dabbled in everything along the waterside, selling dredges and booms, and a spar to "make Mr. Parrish's smack a spread yard for her squaresail"—the 1807 equivalent of our spinnakers. An entry for 1826 refers to Thomas Harvey, carpenter; probably the same Thomas who was to take over Philip Sainty's yard in 1832 and later become a noted ship-builder. It is known that he was originally a general carpenter working jointly with an old man named Todd, and was then also landlord of the "Black Buoy".

Then, as now, tides could sometimes be a nuisance. Sanford notes that on 4th Feb. 1825 "A very large tide flow'd all our lower rooms and the marshes boath sides water, which had not been the case for this 27 years past. It will be attended with considerable loss. With a hard gale wind at N x W and North, and had been so for several days with high tide four large tides, one after the other, which was never known for many years". By contrast, in 1820, he recorded "the smallest tide ever known —never came near the vessels". Those who still attribute our normal rainy summers to "Them atom bombs" would be interested to read Sanford's entry for 1828 when he wrote "rain every day, except 16th, from 25th June to August 17th. Such quantity of rain was hardly ever known". In July 1824 "a severe tempest with torrential rain and hail stones in some parts fell as big as dove's eggs!" 1816 was the "most memorable summer ever remembered for cold and rain-hay was not in by 31st August". However, by contrast, some summers were "Very worme and fine", as in 1818, when June, July and August were rainless months. 1814 saw the "finest haysel and harvest ever known", and 1821 the "mildest winter ever known". A curious entry is that for 1826 whose summer was exceptionally fine, with the result that "scarcely a house but there

An oyster idyll. The Bartlett family of Wivenhoe aboard the smack *Diamond*, dredging oysters in Geeton creek about 1910.

is not 2 or 3 abed with agues and fevers, and many people have died". The whole countryside was dry as tinder and there occurred a "great fire within 7 miles (of here) burning farms and crops. Loss amounting to £22,000. Many families homeless".

The terrifying impressions of storm at sea conveyed by nineteenth century engravings were probably well founded in those days of heavily sparred and undermanned shipping, often lying in exposed and crowded coastal anchorages and riding to the unreliable hemp cables used before chain became general. The words "a great many ships and lives lost, likewise anchors and cables" recur with Sanford's record of every winter gale, when the Colne salvagers reaped grim harvests. In December 1815 Sanford records the smack "Good Intent", John Kent master, in company with Mr. Willet's smack and one from Harwich, brought in the Berwick smack "Lord Huntley", bound from Aberdeen for London. The Berwick smacks were contemporary with those from Leith in being the fastest method of travel for passengers and mails between London and Edinburgh; and often the safest in those days of highwaymen infested roads. These large cutters, which were such a feature of the East Coast scene until steamers displaced them in the 1840's, carried a lot of sail under the worst conditions and nothing stopped them except shipwreck or a shot from a French privateer. With this reputation it is not surprising the three salvaging crews were awarded a total of £230, a large sum in the values of those times.

December 1822 came in with a very heavy north westerly gale with "several ships lost on the Gunfleet sand and a Scotch sloop taken off the Bucksey sand and brought to Brightlingsea by John Kent of the "Good Intent" and four Brightlingsea smacks. The foresaid sloop loaded with oats and wheat, 560 quarters, bound for London". Sometimes local craft were the victims and a blow to the waterside was the loss, during a severe north east gale in September 1816, of "Mr. Blyth's yacht", which foundered coming out of Ostende with the loss of all hands; "three brothers, with three men and one boy". This is an early reference to a Colne yacht, which must have been of some size to judge by the number of hands.

A severe north easterly gale on February 18th 1807 brought one of the greatest disasters in Wivenhoe's long maritime history by the loss of the village's revenue cutter "Repulse", with Captain Stacey, her commander, and all 27 of her crew. Scarcity and lack of luxuries brought smuggling and the revenue service to a peak during the Napoleonic wars and afterwards, especially along the East and South coasts. Although sometimes hazardous it was generally a much more matter of fact business than is popularly supposed and very large profits were made from it. Several cutters besides the "Repulse" were stationed in the Colne and Blackwater areas at that time. They usually carried enormous sail areas, sometimes in excess of 3000 square feet and when in chase before a favouring wind, could set square topsails, studdingsails, and sometimes ringtails; a narrow strip of sail set as additional area on the leach of the mainsail, between gaff and boom. They would ghost in the lightest air and, when becalmed, could be rowed with six or eight huge sweeps.

Because of their speed and handiness these 60 to 80 feet cutters set the style for yachts of that period. They were clench-built, like huge dinghies, the hull being planked first on moulds and the sawn frames fitted afterwards, carefully notched over the lands. The Saintys built many of them at Colchester and Wivenhoe, though it does not necessarily follow that the "Repulse" was built locally. One can imagine her in pursuit of a luckless yet speedy smuggler: the hemp rigging cracking and straining under a press of sail which kept the crew hard at it trimming sheets to the mate's shouted orders. The intermittent crack of the bow chasers when the range closed, almost lost in the bow wave's thunder as the chase roared up Swin, the grey seas plumed with the splash of falling six-pounder balls.

The journal contains some odd entries; as when Sanford's house had a "new fence of iron by Mr. Coleman of Colchester, White smith".* I have no idea what a white smith was. Perhaps he was an ironfounder or, maybe, a smith who worked iron cold as distinct from a blacksmith? Contrasts in costs were afforded by a jib bought for £10-0-0 and a grey mare sold for £7-0-0. The notes contain several other asides; such as the payment of £5 to his servant as a year's wages, and the purchase of a new Wilton carpet for £2-4-0. However, even today's travellers, hardened to continual increases, would revolt at a £7-4-0 return fare paid from Wivenhoe to London for a two day business visit; and heaven knows how much it would represent in present currency. Sanford oddly remarks on "certain people coming to reside here as house-holders and called 'men of flight' not birds of flight, by their continuing so short a time at Wivenhoe. Some continued four or five years, some two, others not above one, and some not so long". I wonder what he would make of today's incessant comings and goings?

In 1827 Sanford sold out half his shares in oyster stock, the smack, the skiffs and the packing house, to Thomas Sanford; and thereafter his wine bills rose sharply! I know nothing further of William beyond his journal which ends in 1830. His brother must have been the Thomas Sanford whose name appears on the copestone of the village's old Congregational Church. Trinity House, Sanford's home, had a long association with the oyster trade being occupied for many years by the Bartlett family, and is now the home of Mr. Philip Finney who, with a touch which would please William Sanford, keeps his yacht in the old oysterman's berth.

*I have recently discovered that a White smith was a turnsmith or sheet metal worker.

CHAPTER FOUR

Portrait of a Salvager

A SIGNAL gun's crack whipped downwind from the storm torn bulwarks of the steamer "Battalion". The harsh easterly gale which had set the labouring ship on the Longsand a few hours previously still raged unabated and furious upon the Thames estuary shoal, driving the luckless steamer further on despite all the churning of her screw. A topsail had been set as a last recourse in an attempt to drive her over; but it split in a mass of thundering rags. Now it was past high water and, with each sea crashing her iron hull hard on the sand, all hands knew she was there for good.

There was no wireless in 1870 and officers' glasses searched desperately for a ship, or towards the low Essex coast for assistance. Hopeless hours passed and the gale increased with next flood until the "Battalion" lay like a half tide rock. Storm-swept foam flung with rain from the racing, low hung clouds, lashed her crew. Great heaps of water boomed at her stern with hissing crests, and voices sounded faint in the wind when all hands clung to anything handy before the seas broke aboard. Hull rivets and hatchcloths started and the holds began to flood. Boilers were blown down for fear of an explosion and the anchors were let go to stop her driving off and sinking. Then the desperate crew lashed themselves in the lee of the superstructure and all hope centred in a passing vessel attempting to take them off. But no ship sighted them and before long darkness held down on the sea. All that fearsome night they kept watch and fired the gun at intervals, until the last cartridge banged out a vain message. The whiplash of the rent topsail drummed in their frozen ears with the roar of seas breaking over the wreck. Attempts were made to light a tar barrel as a flare, but no flame could burn in that hurricane of spray.

Night dragged on and the sense of helplessness and isolation of storm at sea gripped them all. The ship was swept; her boats smashed and useless. Some prayed, some cursed, all hoped; and when the grey dawn spread to a wicked, flaring red, all hands strained salt rimmed eyes inshore, over the surging and shipless waters, towards the Mouse and Sheers lights and the unseen Essex shore, where roaring elms bent over marsh farms and blown sea-spume drove up the green sea walls. No sign: and all on board cursed the day they ever saw the sea. But hope was not from seaward. A sailor spied a sail. A blur of black tumbling down from the north, to leeward of the sands, with suggestions of others following.

Sight of a sail set the will to live pulsing strong in them again. Even the grey faced master, exhausted with anxiety and knowing he would never get another ship, shouted with the rest when the newcomer, a cutter smack, ran up a flag as if in answer to their tattered distress ensign. The smack beat slowly to windward of the shoal and hove to. Within two hours she was joined by others until six close-reefed, black-hulled

Thomas Barnard of Rowhedge, 1816-1896. The author's great-grandfather. A noted fisherman, salvager and life saver.

cutters, C.K. and H.H. prefixing fishing numbers on their mainsails, lay rising and falling in the seas like superb birds. Old hands in the crew knew them for salvagers and cheered others with comments on their daring rescues. In a short time one smack ran to leeward of the sand and, just afterwards, another ran up a flag and sent a boat with three men in it: two rowing and one steering with an oar. Had a ship launched a lifeboat in the sea running it would have been marvellous seamanship, but the Essex smacksmen bundled the boat into the water and handled it with an ease that had all the beauty of perfect co-ordination. They pulled with method and skill, keeping the fifteen foot boat dart before wind and sea, riding the crests and hollows of great waves thundering shoreward from the deep beyond to break on the shoal's edge, spouting and raging. Now they were in the surf and making down towards the steamer, alternately seen and lost by the anxious watchers. The steamer's men flung ropes over her sides and shouted useless encouragement into the roaring wind. Then, with a crash, the smacksmen were alongside, their boat stove and sinking underfoot as they clawed with bleeding fingers at the steamer's side and were dragged to safety by the crew they had tried to aid. Within two hours they were joined by others as boat after boat was swamped and smashed trying to board and aid the shipwrecked crew. One was less lucky; it capsized alongside the wreck, flinging the smacksmen out to be whirled astern, their drowning screams heard even above the gale.

Aboard the big Rowhedge smack "New Unity" Tom Barnard, her owner and skipper, looked on grimly. He had seen five boats' crews, one his eldest son and two hands, leap aboard from stove boats. Now he lay to windward fuming like the other skippers at this desperate situation. But not for long. The short winter day was waning and his experience told him there was no hope of ever moving that ship now, and slim chance of saving her crew and their own men. There was only one way out; he must run "New Unity" alongside and shipwrecked and salvagers must jump for it. The risk was great for it was still only half flood and surf roared over the shoal, which had barely enough water for the smack to sail over. It was a grim decision but one with prospect of a grimmer alternative. Tom signed to his hands and she was off, graceful and splendid in the lunging seas, her well reefed mainsail shining black with spray as she turned and ran into the surf stretched out before her in a grey-white thundering mass, streaked brown with upflung shoal sand. Clouds of wind driven water flew about her like smoke but Tom knew his craft was able enough and felt proud and grateful at each sea's surmounting. His two remaining hands hung on grimly, lines ready to throw as they boarded. They knew well how desperate was this chance and oilskins were flung off to speed the work of rescue. The smack drove on with plunges which set their hearts racing lest she struck; rolling wildly in the troughs towards the blur of wreck which seemed to fly towards her. Tom knew he must take the lee side and risk any wreckage piercing her bottom; if it did they would lose not only the smack, but their lives as well. "Battalion's" crew and the trapped salvagers stood ready as they closed. The smack missed the wreck's stern by inches and splintered her bulwarks to nothing as she crashed alongside. Everyone was shouting and jumping across the watery gap between the hulls which, in those few seconds, erratically opened and closed, sometimes at the height of the rail, sometimes many feet below. The last few were about to leap when they hung back as "New Unity" fell away on a frothing sea which spurted up between the hulls and hurled itself along the wreck's bulwark, flinging the smack clear to leeward, her boom end dragging fountains of spray.

Somehow they brought her on the wind and beat back over the bank, foot by foot, board by board, fearing at each big sea that she would strike. As she thrashed past the wreck the anxious watchers saw her forefoot pitching clear to hang poised on the crests, before falling with the crunch of her lean bow spitting another sea to leeward. The shivering sliver of a jib crack-rattling for the moments of impact which surged foam from her lee rail. What a ship! She was alive, magnificent; a straining picture of motion to make any seaman's heart tingle. Strong and efficient alow and aloft, her big mainsail clawing her out to windward in clouds of bursting spray and over all old Tom's masthead fly, bright as his courage, licked a scarlet tongue across the flying, leaden clouds. Tom's seamanship and doggedness won. Again the cutter swooped downwind and battered alongside, the remaining men jumping as she recoiled. All except the mate who hung in the fore chains, a bag in hand. Unperturbed he waited the seconds until the hulls again lumped together before flinging his little bundle of posessions to the exasperated smacksmen and followed it as "New Unity" dragged clear of the doomed wreck for the last time and ran to leeward over the sand to safety.

The hazardous rescue of the "Battalion's" crew was one of scores carried out between the 1830's and 1881 by my great-grandfather, Captain Thomas Barnard of Rowhedge. By all accounts he typified the far-faring Colneside mariners of the Victorian era; hard as the salty timbers of their smacks; fiercely independent; and quick as gulls to seize any chance the sea brought. A stocky seaman with hands like hams thrust into the deep pockets of his pilot coat and fearnaught trousers tucked into the tops of long leather sea boots, he wore, fair weather or foul in the fashion of that day, a tarry sou' wester, shading a face weathered to a mahogany tan. His long swinging walk reflected the motion of the graceful cutters in which he bucked about, across seas; on his business and at sea or ashore he was enterprising, combining fishing salvaging and pilotage with wide interests in the oyster trade. Born at Rowhedge in 1816, when it was a handful of waterside cottages also often known as Hedge-Row, young Tom first went to sea as boy in one of the village's smacks. Little is now known of his early years but the life evidently suited him for he rose to become, as a young man, master and owner of the smack "Prince of Orange", a husky 17 tonner built at Tollesbury in 1788. In her he worked the North Sea sprat and oyster fisheries described in another chapter, with, tradition has it, a bit of smuggling thrown in. But it was at salvaging that he became well known.

In these days of well buoyed fairways and elaborate navigational aids it is difficult to picture the appalling conditions which existed for coastwise shipping during the

Wreck of the North German Lloyd liner *Deutschland* on the Kentish Knock, December, 1875.

earlier part of the nineteenth century. Most of the world's trade was then carried in unhandy and often ill-kept square rigged vessels, and there were, of course, few lifeboats or licensed pilots. No navigation light, load line or life saving regulations were in general use and it is not surprising that the collier brigs, Baltic timber ships, emigrant packets and general traders were driven ashore in dozens during an average winter gale. Colnesiders, in common with many Harwich and some Leigh men, were not slow to seize these opportunities and, until the 1880's, receivers of wreck on the Essex coast had a busy time. Customs warehouses were crammed with salvaged goods, as were many smacksmen's cellars! The spars, equipment and even hulls of wrecked and refloated vessels were regularly being brought in, advertised in the press, and auctioned. This work, with the life saving it so often entailed, was known on this coast as 'salvaging'; always, for some obscure reason, pronounced with accent on the V. The reckless nature of it seems to have suited Tom Barnard's spirit for it was written of him that "no weather was too dirty for him to venture out to the help of others, he was strong as a lion, resolute as a bull, he feared nothing and he wanted nothing for his services in life saving". Throughout his career, until his retirement in 1881, he rescued over 900 lives from the sea with his smacks; without the loss of any member of their crews. His seamanship was typical of the daring of the "Swin Rangers", as the Colne salvagers liked to style themselves. They were seamen of the old school, bred to sail and taught to handle it from boyhood; learning the hardest way of all in fishing the treacherous North Sea. Ranging the death-trap shoals for whatever luckless ship the winter gales brought, they possessed a courage born, not of impetuousness, but from a calculated knowledge of the sea. Each knew it well, as men grow to know a foe. All respected it for its power, but none would admit that they loved the life. These salvagers have frequently been represented as sharks, luring vessels ashore before plundering the helpless wrecks, but there is no concrete evidence of this. Those terrible gales of the age of sail needed little human aid to accomplish fearful and abundant wrecks. Be that as it may these men were prime seamen and few sailors of any nation will stand by while others drown without trying to help in some way. So it was with these old Colnesiders who frequently risked lives, smacks and livelihoods to take off the shipwrecked crews in the foulest weather.

Salvage work was profitable as well as heroic. The sprat fishery, in those days a staple winter industry, was frequently depressed and, with poverty widespread, salvage presented heaven-sent chances for bolstering up the local economy. News of a well laden wreck spread fast and brought crowds of mariners thronging the village water-sides, eager to be taken on as extra hands aboard the salt-rimmed smacks already discharging salved cargo. To help in this work the salvagers devised special tools and, in winter, most large smacks carried a wide variety of gear including grapnells, mauls, crowbars, and tomahawks, as the axes used for smashing open cased goods or chopping wreckage clear, were called. Cant hooks were used for slinging casks from the holds, dighels, as iron framed nets were called, dredged up coal or small articles from water-logged holds, whilst barbed spears on long shafts with lanyards attached were used to recover sunken timber.

Salvaged cargoes ranged from the usual coal, timber and general goods to the fabulous freight of the Knock John ship of 1856; a German vessel which stranded on the Knock John sand when China-bound with barter goods. Great-grandfather and many others were at her wreck which was first boarded by a Brightlingsea smack. From her they took the richest haul ever made on this coast and the yarn is worth telling. The Brightlingseaman, a 30 tonner, was one of three smacks spratting in partnership and caught by a hard easterly gale. She found 13 colliers driven ashore on the sands but, as they declined assistance she beat down Swin, close reefed, to bring up in the bight of the Barrow sands looking for casualties seawards, or as they used to say, "Lower down". Shortly before midnight the lookout reported a flare to the south east. Getting under weigh she beat down to bring up near the Heaps sand at daybreak, which revealed the wreck burning tar barrels as flares. The smack made the north edge of the Barrows and was almost through the broken water when she had to stand back.

When the tide eased she got across the flat of the sand, passing two empty boats from the wreck and a lot of flotsam. Sails of other salvagers appeared as she fetched the north side of the Knock John shoal and stood as close to the wreck as possible.

She was a fine ship, lying with her head southwest, listing to starboard, with all her masts and spars washing at her lee side. The other smacks were coming up fast and the Brightlingsea skipper and two hands leaped desperately aboard as their smack luffed under the wreck's quarter, before trying to send off her boat. They had just boarded when another smack crashed alongside, putting her skipper and hands aboard. It was a tense moment in that waste of sea fury when the two skippers faced each other in unspoken rivalry on that swept and canted deck. First aboard had the right of salvage but how could one smack's crew work such a large cargo, still less keep others at bay? Glowering they toured the wreck together, finding but a cat, a dog, and a cockerel. One damaged lifeboat hung overside, the rest were gone; there were no survivors. Dragging off a hatch cover they found large quantities of clocks in cases, women's hats, and hundreds of beaver hats which the smacksmen could not, even in those desperate minutes, resist trying on—"Gentlemen's longshore felt toppers" they called them! All these finds were stowed in the boats alongside. By now other smacks were joining the wreck, putting hordes of hairy Swin Rangers aboard, armed with axes. Things began to look ugly when the Brightlingsea skipper abruptly refused partnership with the second to board. An instant later he was forced to agree when a sea broke under the wreck and stove his boat's side in against a topgallant yard. It sank immediately, flinging one hand into the water.

So salvage started. They found the main hatch jammed with pianos in large wooden crates. Unable to rig tackles to clear them they smashed them up with axes, out of the way. Below them the hold was full of bales of canvas and cloth, much of it intended for soldiers' uniforms. Lower tiers were stowed with cheeses in cases; wines and liqueurs; spirits and perfumes; whilst barrels of gunpowder formed the bottom freight. All hands sweated willingly to shift this amazing haul and the weather fined down during the night, allowing yet more salvagers to come aboard. Some of them sampled the spirits which were cleared and stacked on deck for transhipment. Case after case was smashed open and the ship became a mass of men fighting with fists and bottles until the whole deck rang with their shouts and the crash of breaking glass. Drunken seamen battled crew against crew, village against village, while the more disciplined crews attempted to keep some sort of order for salvage to continue. Before long the weather worsened, fighting died down, and the hatches were battened again on the gale-wracked wreck.

It took four weeks of intermittent toil before the salvagers cleared the wreck's fantastic cargo which also included cases of guns, pistols, daggers, swords, bags of shot, pocket knives by the ton, bales of cotton fabric, rolls of silk, china ornaments, oil paintings, copper plates and hosiery. The smacksmen said; "She's got everything except a pulpit"! The richness of the cargo sparked off trouble ashore as well as afloat; receivers of wreck and customs authorities, accustomed as they were to spoils of the sea, were completely overwhelmed by the amount and value landed from the "Knock John Ship", as the wreck became known. Much of the cargo was run ashore unknown to the authorities and smacks from many local villages were engaged, leading to rivalry and a good deal of bitterness which flared when someone, said to have been a woman, informed on some concealed goods and was burned in effigy in Brightlingsea High Street. Intervention by the coastguards started a fight which grew to a near riot, though no lives were lost.

In contrast with this fabulous freight there are several Rowhedgers who recall the wreck of a luckless cattle ship. After it the salvaged carcasses of drowned bullocks lay, with horns roped together, stinkingly stranded on the mud above the village,

Brightlingsea from St. Osyth Stone, about 1885. First class cutter smacks and a ketch in the creek. Others crowd the hard, where the coastguard hulk lies just below the old Anchor Inn. Large yachts hauled up in Aldous yard, beyond, and yacht stores line the saltings.

awaiting the tackle which dragged them, bloated and bulging, up over the marsh wall to the gory, oilskinned smacksmen who cut the valued hides from them with sheath knives, before kicking the rotting flesh into the fleets.

During the early 1800's smacks' crews might be awarded as much as £80 each for salving a small vessel such as a sloop or a brig and, for larger ships, sums of £500 are recorded. Successful salvaging meant big money in the values of those times and, within a few years, Tom Barnard was married and owned a new smack, the "Thomas and Mary". He kept her at Cat Island quay, which he then owned, and lived nearby in one of a pair of houses which are now a paint shop of the Lower Yard. These stood, conveniently, over large cellars of which he made good use, and looked out over a Rowhedge waterfront, showing a hundred masts against the sky, which stirred briskly at each tide time. The quays would be thronged with the village's fleet of sixty smacks. Big, fast and handsome; tall topmasts soaring from their lower sticks and cutter rigs weaving a web of rigging fit to swing a cloud of canvas. As they lifted on each flood, gently groaning, rail to rail, bold sheer to shapely quarter, there would be no mistaking these craft. The logic and appropriateness of every fitting told that these twenty and thirty tonners were vessels rigged by men who had to contend with the sullen grey North Sea, and were accustomed to its winter fury.

One of the toughest jobs Great-Grandfather ever tackled was at the wreck of a ship when not only his boat, but the boats of all the other smacks attempting to aid the vessel were smashed in boarding. He was one of the half-dozen salvagers trapped aboard the fast breaking up ship with a crew almost mad with fear. The gale screamed above the thunder of seas breeching clean over her and, away to windward, the three smacks hovered, powerless to get near in the shoal water. Tom set to work and drove the others to make a crude 'boat' from one of the wreck's topsails and some spars. Awaiting a smooth they launched it over the lee side and it floated; driving clear of the shoal with 27 furiously baling survivors in it, until they were picked up by one of the smacks.

The Longsand was notorious for wrecks and at one, Great-Grandfather, together with a dozen other smacks, hovered around, unable to approach for lack of water. The gale worsened and eventually the others sailed off except "New Unity". At 11 o'clock that night the ship lifted on the flood, drove across the sand, and quickly sank; but not before Tom had taken off all hands. From another victim of the Longsand, a Spanish schooner, he took off the crew of six, one of whom died from the vicious exposure. Beating out to the Kentish Knock one wild winter night he found a great German barque crowded with emigrants, bound for New York, but pounding her bottom out on the sands. No time could be lost if all were to be saved and, manoeuvering alongside in heavy seas, the terrified passengers were bundled over from the doomed ship to the wildly pitching smack. It was not until "New Unity" had made three voyages to Walton and others to a steamer which hove to nearby, that the whole complement of two hundred or more were saved from the splendid barque which was matchwood 48 hours later.

Great-Grandfather, his sons and crew, were several times 'chaired' round Harwich after particularly spectacular and hazardous rescues of shipwrecked crews. This form of spontaneous civic reception consisted of being borne through the old town's narrow streets on the shoulders of cheering crowds, sometimes with a band leading the way. The East Mersea "Dog and Pheasant" was a favourite haunt of Great-Grandfather and other salvagers; which is not surprising as the landlord was also owner of the big smack "Pheasant". Smack crews sometimes foregathered there for a sing-song and often, after settlement of a successful salvage, a crowd of them would come clumping up the road from Mersea Stone to go thronging in the pub's doors, singing and joking, blue eyed and bristly, dark eyed and gaunt, crowding the taproom and filling it to the beams with their shoulders, some bowed a little by years at sea yet even the least of them looking capable of cracking a gale. The rattle of coin on counters was soon drowned by choruses roared to the lilt of a concertina as leather sea boots stirred the sawdust in the step dances of those times.

Great-Grandfather was a most powerful swimmer and personally rescued many lives from drowning; notably in 1851 when two Rowhedge boys who were swimming got into difficulties. Tom, who had gone to bed, was roused by the shouting and nipped out in his nightshirt to dive repeatedly into the river; eventually bringing them out; though one was dead. His brand of humour once led to an elaborate practical joke. It was well known that he could swim for some distance underwater and he said he would dive at Fingringhoe mill and re-appear at the ferry. Tom dived before a knot of sceptical onlookers whose grins and jibes faded as quickly as the bubbles trailing rapidly towards the first bend of Mill creek. Swimming fast for a distance Tom hauled himself out under some overhanging bushes and, waiting until the crowd passed on along the wall, ran hard ahead, avoiding them, and dived again near the ferry, to emerge dripping and with a triumphant wink for the disbelievers! The customs men once wished to interview Great-Grandfather but, strangely enough, he was not at home so they kept watch. After a few hours the village coal cart arrived on its rounds, laden with the peculiar tall sacks then in use. The coalman heaved up a heavy sack and staggered across to the cellar flap. Down it went; and into the cellar shot a rather coal-dusty Tom!

Sometime during the 1850's Great-Grandfather moved to Emsworth near Chichester, and for several years carried on an extensive business in the channel oyster trade; but eventually returned to Rowhedge and a new smack which embodied all his previous experience. The "New Unity", as she was named, was a fine example of a big, first class cutter fit to range the seas in all weathers. In her Tom fished the usual grounds around the British and French coasts and, occasionally, also shipped cargoes of barrelled herring from Stornoway to the Eastern Baltic, a seasonal trade sometimes favoured by Colne smacks at that time. She proved a fine sea boat and with her he rescued many shipwrecked seamen from almost certain death, receiving several medals from life-saving societies, and the British and foreign governments.* During the 1860's, Trinity House, recognising his ability and thorough knowledge of the Thames estuary, chartered

*He is reputed to have been the first to receive the Stanhope Medal for saving life at sea, for one of his rescues.

him and his smack for pilotage work off the East coast; and even in this employment he found time to take off the crews of six stranded ships. Crews presented no problems to Great-Grandfather for his eight sons, Turner, Arthur, John, Robert, Thomas, William, Ben, and James, my grandfather, all served in her at various times before becoming well known yacht skippers and smack owners themselves.

"New Unity" was one of several Colne, Harwich and Kentish smacks which attempted to render assistance to the North German Lloyd liner "Deutschland", wrecked on the Kentish Knock in December 1875. Many fallacies have grown up around this terrible wreck and much has been made of the smacks' failure to get to her in time to prevent great loss of life. The "Deutschland" struck in the sleet and snow of a howling north easterly gale and 57 passengers were swept from her before help arrived. The salvagers were aware of her plight but the weather was, as the Swin Rangers used to put it, 'too coarse' for even their stout smacks to beat over the sands, and those who attempted it were forced to lay to under the lee of the shoals, or run for shelter. Their determination to reach the wreck was typified by the action of Captain Harry Cook of the Rowhedge "Aquiline". Forced to put back into Walton backwaters with

A first class smack leaving Brightlingsea creek, 1890. Two reefs in the mainsail and boat on deck indicate a hard breeze outside. Yachts and stack barges in Colne.

a sprung boom he brought up and the crew fished it. Whilst waiting for the gale to ease he rowed ashore to Ramsey and walked to Harwich intending to give warning of the wreck. However the coastguards had just received news of it from Sheerness, where lifebelts were picked up, but he was in time to go off in the steam tug "Liverpool", a great rival of the salvagers, which was the first to reach the ill fated ship and take off the 173 survivors.

The powerful "New Unity" was to have an unusual and violent end which is best described in Great-Grandfather's own words, as told to a reporter just after the wreck. He said; "We were lying in Colne water, and, fearing the floating ice was likely to injure the vessel's bottom, we resolved to put to sea, and after crossing the Wallet we brought up under the Buxey and reefed our sails and made all snug for the rough night we saw coming. Just as we were going below to make some tea, we saw a schooner go ashore on the Whittaker spit; so tea had to wait, and we got under way as quickly as possible to go to her assistance but the gale kept increasing so that it was quite impossible to board her, the daylight being gone, and as the best we could do, all things considered, we brought up as near to her as we could and let go our anchor with fifty-five or sixty fathoms of chain cable out; hoping to be able to assist her at daybreak.

"All night the gale kept increasing, and at 9.30 a.m. our cable parted and our stow-boat anchor, with fifty fathoms of chain, was lost. As soon as we got the remainder of the cable in we made the Sheers light and shaped a course for Sheerness. Within ten minutes every stitch of canvas we had set was blown into ribbons, and we drove before the blast in such a snowstorm that we could not see the end of the bowsprit, and we had to get under the lee of the boat or the mast or anything we could hold on to, for to stand on deck was an impossibility, and had you attempted to get on your legs it would be at the risk of being blown overboard like an old swab, for our foresail, a brand new one, was blown clean away from everything, and as long as we could see it it never did touch the water. It did blow then. After that, though we could not see twenty fathoms ahead, we made the Mouse light, and then we knew we were on the right course for Sheerness. After this we kept feeling our way with the lead as opportunity offered, and could find we were going right away up the Medway. I was for'ard, holding on for dear life, and the wind enabled me to hear my son at the helm ask me if he was steering the right course. I said, "Keep her straight, for no sand is in our way". The "New Unity" could sail as well as most of them, and I knew that if we did not run into an ironclad or some other obstacle we should ultimately run into the mud on the banks of the Medway, and escape with little further damage.

"But so it was not to be, and bang we went on the Grain Spit, perhaps the first instance of one of the strongest forts in the world being boarded by a fishing smack.

"Quicker than I can tell you, our vessel was then blown right up against the out-works of the fort, and my son at once off boots and socks and walked along the bowsprit, which he could not have done had we not struck on the weatherside of the fort, for under other circumstances he would have been blown off like a butterfly.

"I have seen some strange scenes in my time, for I am an old Swin Ranger, but never in my life did I feel as I did when I saw the dear old craft, the pride of my life, in which so much good work had been done, come broadside on to the fort and crack up like an old cheese box. Not that she was not in good order, for as we watched her break up, and I don't mind telling you I could not help shedding a tear when I saw the old craft in which, by God's help, I had been instrumental in saving hundreds of persons' lives, tossed about like an old broken match-box, but in all this I had the satisfaction of observing as she went to pieces that she was as sound as ever a vessel of her class was".

The loss of this fine smack was a great blow to Great-Grandfather who afterwards retired from the sea, though not from its company. From his cottage windows he watched his sons' sturdy smacks sail to the winter spratting and, each spring, saw the sleek yachts they commanded fit out for the sport which brought fame to the Colne and its seamen.

At the age of eighty the old seaman passed on, mourned by a great gathering of skippers and the half-masted ensigns of every vessel in the river. True to his wish they buried him in a sea lavender lined coffin—and his sou'wester.

Oyster dredging smacks hove-to on the Colne fishery at end of a day's work in 1901. Note foreman's smack with flag at mast-head. The catch is being transferred to the Colne Oyster Fishery Company's steam paddle dredger *Pyefleet*, built by Forrestt and Co. Wivenhoe, about 1895. This steel 50 footer steamed at 8 miles per hour and was the only powered fishing vessel owned on the Colne before 1914.

CHAPTER FIVE

Trawlers, Dredgermen and Wildfowlers

THE COLNE and Blackwater fishermen's prime interest in shell fish dredging and spratting has historically over-shadowed the many other minor fisheries which were of seasonal importance to local communities.

Traditionally fish trawling was a short, seasonal fishery for most Colne and Blackwater smacks, many of which trawled for roker and soles in spring and roker and dabs in autumn, at the ends of the stowboating season, with occasional bursts of winter activity trawling codling in the colder water offshore. Some smacks continued trawling through the winter and a very few all year round, but these were exceptions, for spratting and shellfish dredging were the winter staples.

Most works on fisheries have it that trawling was "invented" by the Brixham or Barking fishermen during the late eighteenth century. However, in April, 1377, fishermen from Brightlingsea, St. Osyth, Fingringhoe, Alresford, Tollesbury, East and West Mersea, Salcote, Peldon and Heybridge, were before an inquiry of Colchester justices, accused of causing damage to fisheries in the Colne, Blackwater and Wallet by using primitive trawls called "wonderthons". These had been in use for sixteen years and were said to be causing severe damage by overfishing. Certainly, the wonderthon was a great advance on lines and drift nets, and fishermen were trawling "plaise and buttes" in great numbers, being accused of burying 20,000 fish which remained unsold!

Richard Clarke of Brightlingsea was trawling the Wallet with a wonderthon having an eight foot beam and a net four fathoms long with a mesh "so close that no fish can escape, however small". Another wonderthon was described as having a ten foot beam and a three fathom net with two inch meshes and a leaded groundrope with stone rollers. These new trawls promised spectacular returns and it was recorded that a "great quantity of labourers have withdrawn from the business of agriculture, such as carters, ploughmen, and shepherds, plying these nets because of the gain and excessive wages they receive, to the no small damage of the whole people".

The inquiry condemned the wonderthon for inshore fishing but recommended its use for deep sea fishing. What would the justices and fishermen think of the gear now worked by the 250 feet stern trawlers?

Other early mention of trawls occurred in the Ipswich court rolls of 1566 where trawl heads are described; and some of the fishing "Engines" condemned at Orford in 1491 were probably wonderthons. This early evidence refutes the sudden "invention" of trawling two centuries ago. It is possible that the Brixham or Barking men first used trawls extensively in deep water, but the adventurous Essexmen would surely have worked their trawls offshore before the late eighteenth century.

The beam trawl has now been almost completely superseded by the faster towing "otter" type, of greater catching power, though beams are still used by some shrimpers. Beam trawls were most efficient for the slow speed of sailing craft. The beam's length was determined by the distance from the smack's main shrouds to her counter and, when at work, it was supported by an iron "head" at each end which kept it a few feet above the sea bottom on which they rode like sledges. A slack "ground rope" stretched between the heads and varied in construction with the type of ground worked; heavy rope "wouldings" and bobbins being used on soft mud when a "tickler" chain was often needed to stir the soles from their burrows. The net was held to the beam and ground rope and stretched away in a great tapering cone of mesh terminated by the "cod end" which was closed by a special knot and protected underneath against chafe by either old netting or hides. Fish entered the trawl, jumping against its "back" to escape the ground rope and going down its tapering sleeve to the cod end, where cunningly worked net traps in the wings stopped them working back to the mouth.

A rope towing bridle stretched from each trawl head. A large wooden block on this carried the trawl warp, one end of which was made fast forward and the other to the capstan or wink, amidships. When towing, the warp was pinned in by wooden tholes set in holes along the rail and adjusted to lead the warps astern, to suit wind and tide. With her trawl down and a fair tide, a smack could be made to steer herself. In case of a bad "fast" on an underwater obstruction the tholes were drawn and the smack came head to net, which could be recovered with the windlass. Most Colne and Tollesbury smacks of twelve tons and upwards had a double-handed iron capstan, or a "wink" amidships. Older smacks, such as the Wivenhoe "Eliza", often had a wooden barrel capstan with deck treads, round which the crew walked pushing the bars. Recovery of the trawl was aided by the "fish tackle" purchase leading from the hounds and also serving as a backstay when required.

Local smacks needed two, or at most three, hands for fish trawling, and the proceeds of the catch, like most Essex fishing, were divided into shares. A smack with two men and a skipper/owner would produce one share for each man, one for the net, and two for the skipper. If for some reason the skipper was not the owner, he received one share and the owner another.

The Wallet was a favourite trawling ground of the Rowhedge smacks. One trip Captain Simons' "Hildegarde" trawled with the ebb off the then unspoiled and rural Clacton. His mate spotted a keg floating nearby and brought it aboard where it sat, tight and inviting. They broached it and found rum. As it was a cold day, a few nips were in order and each haul called for further cheer. That evening, the coastguard tramping his beat at Holland Low came on the "Hildegarde" ashore at low water,

The cutter smack *Dove*, owned by J. Pearce of Tollesbury.

with all sails set and drawing. The crew were asleep on deck and the trawl spread out astern on the sands with fish still flapping in the cod end!

The one fishing song sung by the Colne seamen was about trawling.

Songs which were really sung and enjoyed by sailors of the sail usually had an interesting background and this East Anglian ballad originated in the harsh toil of the North Sea fisheries, amongst the Yarmouth smacks which worked on a system of "fleeting" until seventy years ago. In common with fleets from Lowestoft, Hull and Grimsby, the Yarmouthmen were usually away from port for an eight week trip; each fleet trawling the grounds under its own "admiral" and using carrier smacks, and later steam cutters, to rush its catches to market.

Many of Campbell's Yarmouth smacks were skippered and manned from Brightlingsea, and the Wringe family, also from Brightlingsea, owned and commanded several large Grimsby smacks. These probably provided the link.

The song has survived for over one hundred years without its words or tune being written; passing from generation to generation in the villages. My grandfather, Captain James Barnard of Rowhedge, was fond of singing its lively tune, which ran;

"Oh once I was a schoolboy and lived at home at ease,
But now I am a fishing lad who ploughs the raging seas.
I thought I'd like seafaring life but very soon I found,
It was not all plain sailing when we reached the fishing ground. It was

Chorus.

Heave away on the trawl warp boys and let's heave up our trawl,
For when we get our fish on deck we'll have another haul.
So heave away on the trawl warp boys and merrily heave away,
For it's just as light when the moon shines bright as it is at the break of day.

2.

Oh, every night in winter, as reg'lar as the clock,
On goes sou'wester, deep sea boots and oilskin smock.
Then straight away to the capstan boys and merrily heave away,
For it's just as light in the middle of the night as 'tis at the break of day.
                                                                    It was ...

3.

Oh, when the eight weeks are over, hard up the tiller goes,
Sou'west by west for Yarmouth Roads with the big jib on her nose,
And when we reach the pierhead all the lassies they will say.
Here comes our jolly fishing lads that's been so long away."

The other favourites which gladdened many a smoke shrouded gathering in the captain's rooms of the "Anchor", the "Ship" and the "Albion" were, peculiarly, "Jim the Carrier's Lad" and "Under the British Flag", pronounced "flaig" by the Essex vocalists.

Most Colne and Tollesbury smacks laid up for the summer while their crews went "yachting", which was their pride, art, and financial salvation. However a few carried on with shrimping. The development of East Coast seaside resorts during the Victorian period brought a demand for seafoods, especially shrimps. Leigh fishermen were shrimping before 1840 and when the railway reached Harwich twenty years later, that port took to the trade in a large scale. After about 1870, Leigh bawleys started working out of Harwich during the summer and were a familiar sight amongst the cutter rigged smacks from the Colne and Blackwater, and others from the Kentish ports, joining in the trade. One day during the 1880's a record fleet of 118 shrimpers sailed from Harwich for the grounds, which varied but included the Goldmer Gat off Walton, the Sledway, the Sunk, and the Swin.

Until the beginning of this century the Leigh bawleys towed as many as four shrimp nets of their own peculiar pattern, while the Harwich bawleys and the Colne and

Blackwater smacks preferred the beam trawl. A crew of two was normal for shrimping under sail, which always seemed to need finer adjustment of canvas than fish trawling, hence part of the Harwich and Leigh men's preference for their brailing and boomless mainsails. Shrimp nets are of fine mesh which, though extremely efficient in catching shrimps, are also very destructive to immature fish, especially soles, which could usually escape from the larger meshed fish trawls and live to become a marketable catch. The amazing thing about shrimping on good ground is the prodigious quantities caught compared with the comparatively small amount fit to market. Decks are filled to the bulwarks with a writhing mass of grey shrimps. The crew stand knee deep in them or in the well, rapidly riddling them through a sieve and culling a stream of offal overside, which attracts a cloud of gulls about each smack. Quality of the catch is frequently checked by a "tell tale", or small net on a dredge-like frame towed ahead of the trawl. The culled shrimps are tipped into a large domestic copper filled with clean salt water, with salt added to taste, and kept boiling in the hold. When cooked, the Essex coastal shrimp turns pink, while Thames shrimps go brown. The catch is dispatched to market in wicker baskets called "pads" and is sold by capacity measure. Like all fishing under sail shrimping was an ill rewarded trade.

Shrimping smacks from Rowhedge and Wivenhoe drifting up-river on a summer evening, about 1900. Pleasure party aboard smack in foreground.   *Howard Goodwin*

Billy Bartlett of Wivenhoe. A well known fisherman, photographed about 1890.

Harry Myall of Tollesbury at the helm of the family smack *S.W.H.*

Few Rowhedge smacks went shrimping because of that village's prime interest in yacht racing. The two or three which did often managed to land sixty gallons daily, usually at Clacton for dispatch by rail to the merchants. The Rowhedge "Lily" was let by Captain Jonathan Cranfield during the racing season to either Mr. Gunn or Mr. Glozier of Wivenhoe. After one hard day's shrimping, Mr. Gunn landed his catch on Clacton beach during Army manoeuvres. As the smacksmen trundled half the catch to the station some soldiers helped themselves from pads left in the dinghy. When the enraged smack skipper discovered his loss, British Army manoeuvres were interrupted while the Colonel of the regiment paid for his shrimps!

Shrimping gave its name to a local summer weather phenomenon known as "shrimper's winds". These occur during our finest local weather and the old term is still used to describe them. It apparently originated about 1904 when the Colne smacks enjoyed fair winds to and from the shrimping grounds almost every day. Mr. Archie Turner of Wivenhoe recalls a typical day's work that year as, leaving Wivenhoe with a light northerly wind which carried the shrimpers out through the Spitway to the Swin middle, where two hauls of the trawl brought a fair catch. Meanwhile, the wind was veering round through east to south east before settling at south and freshening, sending the smacks bowling home before it with smoke from their copper fires streaming out ahead through the clouds of gulls. By evening the catch was landed and dispatched to Beare's the Colchester fishmongers.

At that time, several Colne smacks regularly went shrimping out of Grimsby in summer, working the Haile sands in company with the Yorkshire cutters from Paull. Notable amongst these migrants were Captain Green's "Elise" of Wivenhoe and the Rowhedge "Ellen", chartered by the Glozier family from Walter Leavett, who then owned Rowhedge Ferry. The "Ellen's" origin was unusual in that Leavett had her built by Harris as a near sister of the Wivenhoe "Jane" and "Maria", but specially for letting to fishermen in winter, and yachting parties in summer; the only known local instance of such speculation. The Gloziers often took her for shrimping, and for party sailing a skylight was fitted over the hatch, and berths fitted in the hold. She made several "yachting" trips to the Continent with a Rowhedge crew. Leavett sold her to Zac Burch, who resold her to Captain Richard Cranfield for about £250, the average cost of a fifteen ton smack in the nineties, and she paid for herself in eighteen months of good, skilful fishing. After half a century with the Rowhedge smack fleet, and being a spectacular performer on regatta days, she was sold to Harry Death of Brightlingsea and was hulked there during the war.

Amongst the "Ellen's" crew was one of the Welham family, some of whom were victims of a cruel trick of fate. The saltings and beach above Alresford creek have long been known as the "White House". During the 19th century, the spot was known as Welham's hard, after the family of fishermen who lived in the White House which

West Mersea smacks, 1935. From left; *Unity*, *Kingfisher* (in background) *Gracie*, two Maldon smacks and the *Boadicea*.

stood there, adjacent to the railway line. During the 1880's the brothers Welham worked a smack from there and, one tide, she got beneaped in her berth. Faced with a fortnight's loss of earnings they dug round her desperately, to deepen the rill, but tragically the smack slipped and fell over, crushing one brother to death.

In the past smacks were owned in what would now be thought unlikely places. Bradwell had at least two; the "David and Eliza" owned by the noted fisherman and smuggler Jack Spitty, who at one time hailed from Rowhedge; and a smack, now named "Taffy", and a yacht at Tollesbury, then worked by "Fan" Hewes and his son, who had earlier sailed in the "Fiddle". Apart from general fishing Jack Spitty also engaged in the age-old Blackwater and Colne herring fishing which with the May-July mackerel drifting in earlier times, often provided work for a few smacks from Mersea, Bradwell and Wivenhoe, which were the only places to work it as far as I know.

In those days before chemical fertilisers, early spring found many local smacks dredging five fingers for manuring the farmers' fields. Usually each smack worked four to six dredges with the net slacked back from the hoeing edge to avoid rubbish. Favourite grounds were on the Kentish Shore and in the Wallet. The trade was largely carried on at Tollesbury, though Tom Pitt handled the many tons landed at Wivenhoe railway quay by a few Rowhedge and other Colne smacks. He bought by weight and big scales were rigged on deck for the skips. Sharp as Tom Pitt was, his eagle eye did not detect the frequently rigged wire leading from the scale pan, below deck; pulled by the smack's boy at the right moment when the skip was nearly filled!

Mr. Jack Owen, that veteran West Mersea seaman who lived through more Essex maritime history than most can discover, recalled dredging five fingers in Jack Spitty's "David and Eliza", landing at £1 per ton. Spitty chanced on a thick patch of them off Frinton, just below the telegraph cable to the Old Gunfleet Lighthouse. Word went round and a few days later, a score of Rowhedge, Wivenhoe and Tollesbury smacks appeared to reap this harvest. However, the cunning Spitty anchored a skin buoy right over the cable and dredged around it with dredges hanging just below the surface. Down came the others, some with 16 dredges apiece and, with warps straining, fouled the cable and each other, losing many dredges and their tempers. With a satisfied grin Jack Spitty retrieved his buoy and sailed off to Harwich, returning early next morning when he filled his hold without another smack in sight.

When there was no sale for five fingers some Wivenhoe and Rowhedge smacks went dredging brood oysters on the Priory Spit and the Knoll, for sale to Bartlett, the Wivenhoe oyster merchant. This trade was known as "little dredging" and had been carried on locally since at least 1377, when John De Heerde (Heard) of Salcote was recorded as dredging brood oysters and laying them in fleets to fatten.

Dredging culch for oyster layings also employed smacks at odd times. Even this peaceful occupation could lead to disputes. During the 1890's about forty Tollesbury

Tollesbury and Mersea oystermen at the oyster pits and packing sheds, West Mersea, about 1913. Group includes; A Carter, Joe Pearce, Jack Pearce, Isiah Binks, Nehemiah Ward, A. Rice, John Redgewell, R. Page, William Collins, James Heard, Joseph Heard, Michael Heard, Peter Frost, J. Pettican and some of the Mole family of Mersea.

and Mersea smacks were dredging culch on common ground in the estuary when four Burnham smacks joined in, to the rage of the locals who sent a score of their largest men aboard four Tollesbury smacks, armed with shovels and hidden in the holds. The Burnham cutters dredged on, filling their holds and indifferent to the four Tollesbury-men whose topsails shadowed their decks and blanketed them to windward. Suddenly the smacks were alongside amidst mutual cursing, the Tollesbury men emerged with a great shout and, after a fight, shovelled the Burnham fishermen's hard gained culch back into the Blackwater, sending them back to the Crouch with empty holds! The subsequent court case was, apparently, won by Mersea and Tollesbury.

In winter, smacks, especially from Tollesbury, favoured sailing with topmast housed and the heel lashed to the rigging, ready to send up when required. Others sometimes laid the topmast ashore for the winter and sailed with a short topmast aloft known as a "Chocker Pole". On this they often set a topsail with a spar on its luff. In winter the Tollesbury smacks could generally be recognised at some distance by their topmast shrouds which were coiled up and lashed, swaying like giant earrings from each crosstree. One Tollesbury smack caused a ribald sensation by arriving at Wivenhoe railway quay to discharge sprats with "Beechams Pills" painted in white letters across her mainsail!

Dredging mussels for manure was another trade occasionally worked by a few local smacks. The Rowhedge "Elizabeth Ann" and "Lily" had the hoeing edges of their dredges moused with brass rings, made by twisting wire round a stick; an occupation of fishermen's families, or their sick. The Kentish shore off Reculvers was a favourite ground for mussel dredging, though some good hauls were had off the Knoll by Wivenhoe smacks.

Winkling provided something of a living for the owners of the little gaff rigged bumkins (now called winkle-brigs) from Mersea, and the small smacks from Maldon and Mersea which lay in the outfalls along the Dengle flats, where their crews walked the soft mud in "splatchers", as the boards strapped over their feet were called. The few Colne winklers hailed from Brightlingsea and Wivenhoe, where the winter of 1908 saw the biggest boom in these humble shellfish. Occasionally, one of the smaller Brightlingsea smacks made a winkling voyage, the Brightlingsea "Frolic" making some of the last to the flats off Canvey Island about 1912.

The long nosed gorbills or guardfish were fished in season with a form of seine having an exaggerated cod in its middle, and seines and peter nets were used to catch mullet on the Dengie shore by the little transom sterned Maldon smacks which also regularly trawled eels on the grassy Mersea flats in company with a dozen or so Merseamen, before 1914. Counters do not seem to have become fashionable in Maldon smacks until after the first World War, when several, such as the fast little "Polly", had counters built on over their transoms to add deck space for oyster dredging. Transom sterns featured in some old Colne smacks such as the "Juan Fernandez", worked from Rowhedge by Ephraim Fisher, an old skipper with a jet black beard and a "voice like a thunderstorm". The ancient "Amelia" was another contemporary Rowhedge smack nicknamed the "Giant's Shoe" and owned by a woman, who sold her to John Woodward of West Mersea. With a delightful mixture of pride and candour she told Woodward that the "Amelia's" motions were beautiful but she was slow in "turning round"; added to which she leaked like a sieve and after a season's dredging was "put in a creek to die" as the expression had it.

The few Colne fishing craft smaller than smacks were referred to as "bumkins"; a name also used in the Blackwater for the sloop rigged open boats used for dredging and winkling. The "Elizabeth Mary Ann" owned by Elijah Wade of Rowhedge, was, perhaps, the best example of a Colne bumkin. Her shapely 28 foot hull was built by Harris to suit her owners' brief specification; that she should be sailed by one man and must be capable of "poking up-river in a calm with the mop handle!" Elijah always sailed and worked her single handed, and her modest draught enabled him to fish the shallows, besides working well beyond the Estuary. She was one of the few Colne craft to engage in cockling, working the once extensive beds at the head of the Geeton creeks in Fingringhoe marshes. The "Elizabeth Mary Ann" is still remembered as well sailed and well kept—a tribute to any fishing vessel. I would like to know what happened to her.

Bumkins were versatile craft. One owned by a publican named Wade, who kept the "Ship at Launch" on Wivenhoe Quay went salvaging potatoes from a wreck on the Buxey in the nineties. The Brightlingsea "Ant" was for half a century the quaintest of the Colne's small craft. Built in his garden for one of the Francis family, she came out in the mid-nineties when yachts were popularising the well rounded stem they still affect. The little "Ant" was duly given a similar head, complete with spike bowsprit, though her thirty feet length ended in a plumb transom and it was said "she had two ends and no middle". Despite her odd appearance and short draught she earned her living under sail for many years, dredging and trawling and even, I believe, working a miniature stowboat net in winter. The "Ant" fished from Brightlingsea until about 1950 and is still sailed for pleasure from Maldon.

Each summer from 1875 until 1906 the old yacht "Glimpse" was a familiar sight lying under Mersea Stone or cruising and fishing about the East Coast and its rivers with Captain Mark Cutts of Rowhedge at the tiller while her owner, Dr. Sorby, eagerly

Sailing smacks at Maldon, 1952. Oyster dredges on deck and peter nets drying in the sun.

Douglas Went

George Peggs of Brightlingsea in a typical gun punt, 1895.

waited the hauling of her trawl. On deck she was just an outdated yawl of the "sixties" but below she was a floating laboratory devoted to her owner's lifelong microscopial research into minute sea creatures, which brought him international fame. The doctor considered the Colne and Stour the two English rivers richest in marine life. He insisted that the "Glimpse" was in Colne each Sunday, when he was rowed ashore for morning service at Brightlingsea. Captain Cutts, a veteran fisherman and salvager, was fascinated by the minute creatures revealed by the microscope from which, as he remarked, they "glouted at ye, cruel".

Wildfowling was hardly ever considered part of a fisherman's living in the Colne, though on the Blackwater the reverse was often true. At least one Mersea smack, the "Phantom", is reputed to have been built mainly for "gunning". Many of the Bright-lingsea yachtmasters, local farmers, and others were fond of wildfowling which, in its heyday during the seventy years prior to 1914, attracted as many gentleman gunners as the turf did jockeys.

Special gunning yachts were occasionally built, and one steam launch; owned by Colonel Davis of New House Farm, Walton-on-Naze and skippered by one of the Brightlingsea Griggs family, perhaps the most noted of Colneside fowlers. The heavily armed launch cruised from Walton backwaters on the winter high-waters, with funnel lowered, seaward to where the birds gathered while their feeding grounds were underwater. The launch cruised round them in decreasing circles until the $1\frac{1}{4}''$ swivelling muzzle loader boomed out, before the rising birds were raked by the $2''$ breech-loading swivel firing 2lbs of shot! That launch must have been a profitable investment!

Seabirds have prompted some strange legends. One of the most incredible, but true, incidents occurred during the 1870's when a Brightlingsea smack was overwhelmed during a North Sea gale. The waterlogged cutter lay on her beam-ends in the trough of great seas, with the belly of her reefed mainsail submerged. The crew were lashed the the bulwarks, saturated and blinded by the stinging spindrift, and deafened by the roaring seas. There was nothing they could do to save themselves and none expected to live. In the heart of the storm, a tremendous flock of gulls suddenly appeared on the seas to weather and created a momentary "smooth" which enabled the smack to lift. William Cross, lashed to the capstan, managed to throw his knife into the mainsail and split it, releasing the water and enabling them to get her under control again. We may smile at the black skies and tremendous seas of the old sea prints and woodcuts but, in many ways, they convey the true terror of a North Sea gale in winter under sail, in the small ships which did much to mould the character of the Colne and Blackwater seamen.

A professional fowler and wildlife author, J. Wentworth Day, at West Mersea with their armament and equipment, about 1938.   *Douglas Went*

CHAPTER SIX

Regatta Day

WITH THE big yachts tucked safely in their mud berths on the high springs of autumn, regatta day was eagerly anticipated as the gayest in the waterside villages' calendar. Its races for small yachts, gigs, cutters, shells, sculling, pulling, watersports and general horseplay, not to mention the fairs, were all overshadowed by the highlight of that day—the smack race—annual tussle between the champions of the various local villages, competing for the first prize of £8, and the greater honour of being crack smack of the fast and able Colne and Blackwater fleets.

In Rowhedge, and at Wivenhoe, Brightlingsea, and Tollesbury, great pains were taken to fit out the fastest smacks for racing; a task made easier on the pocket by the regatta coinciding with the fleets' annual fit out for the winter spratting season.

A typical regatta eve at Rowhedge found the crew of "Sunbeam" busy adjusting her ballast. When she trimmed just right they stopped and, after a beer, set about black-leading her bottom, going over it afterwards with tallowed rags. All this was done with much banter from the crew of "Ellen" at the next quay, slushing down her bottom with a bucketful of cold porter, Richard Cranfield's recipe for speed. When the biggest sails which would possibly fit the spars were all aboard and the smart crews shipped, "Neva", "Wonder", "Ellen", "Sunbeam", and "Xanthe", Rowhedge's competitors, dropped down on the night ebb to lie in Pyefleet with some of their rivals.

Early morning found all astir and the chirrup of throat and peak halyards carried on the chilly autumn air as mainsails went up and the glistening hulls lay to the last of the ebb. Soon the dregs of faint northerly breeze sent catspaws scurrying across the limpid surface, wafting mist wraiths about the crews absorbed in their work at the halyards. "Old Jim's carryin' a clout today!" The white jerseyed, racing slippered, Lemon Cranfield paused from stopping a spinnaker to jerk a thumb towards James Carter's big "Wonder", head of the line and a fine sight griping gently on her cable as a gigantic mainsail, surely white enough to be the pride of any yacht, creaked up, half hoisted, to swing lazily in the lifts until the topsail was ready. Bill Cranfield's wool capped crew sang as they worked about "Xanthe's" decks, and soon the long-yarded topsails were on deck. Hands aloft poking them clear as they were mastheaded and laced, to be broken out, board stiff, to the high peaked gaffs.

"Sunbeam's" slick crew were getting her mainsail up under William Cranfield's eagle eye. "Now then HUP with it boys!" He squinted up the towering luff. "Hold her at that." They belayed and slipped the buoy rope. His figure bore against the handsome, carved tiller and "Sunbeam" forged ahead under the stern of "Elise". "We've got th' legs o' you already Cap'n," called the irrepressible skipper Green, sweating heartily at the handspikes with his Wivenhoe crew, heaving the straining bowsprit tackle down until it pointed the spar to the water like a finger of doom. The "Sunbeams" laughed and soon Pyefleet presented a spirited scene when, with the windlass pawls clinking, all the racers got under weigh. The rivals' gibes flying back and forth, providing amusement for the crews of other smacks just mustering, and for whom it was just another workday.

Joined by entries from Brightlingsea and Tollesbury the whole clutter worked into the river's mouth and manœuvered for the start. The breeze swung southerly and freshened as the sun strengthened to a summer-like morning. Stop watches were checked for the five minute gun when the day's work would begin in earnest; old stuff this to these crews accustomed to international contests, yet given a keener flavour by its homeliness. "Ten minutes and watch out for William!" said Lemon, his "Lee oh!" slamming "Neva" round as "Sunbeam" cut fine across her bow. Gear rattled and the voices of both crews came on the wind. After that the scene became blurred; every smack seemed to be thrashing up and down the line, churning the river in a fever to obtain a weather berth. Crews leapt like cats as the sheets were worked while the minutes ticked by. Lemon crouched on deck, one hand on the tiller. A puff of white smoke drifted from the committee smack anchored off Mersea stone. "Five minutes. See if you can just get another pound on that jib halyard." The luff seemed bar taut already but a scuffle ensued at the mast. "Well if she don't go now she never will," commented Lemon, and left it at that to take stock of his competitors' tactics. Steve Redgewell's "Bertha", with a big crew of young Tollesburymen determined that the rival Row-hedgers should be taught a lesson, was performing exciting evolutions on the line. "Sunbeam" circled warily with an eye to "Neva's" weather. "Ellen" was to leeward and working clear of "Elise" and "Foxhound", whilst "Wonder" was in trouble with her mainsheet. Suddenly "Bertha" developed a scuffle with "Elise" who bore away with "Neva" luffing under her stern to steal the Tollesburyman's wind and cover her as she neared the committee boat. But William bore down from windward and pipped her to it. The mainsheet swigged in as "Neva" luffed for the start. Neck and neck, now slightly ahead—perhaps too far? They tore for the line almost rail to rail, topsides echoing the bow waves frothing rumble and crews shouting as they hauled, the skippers pretending not to notice each other. Seconds seemed minutes as timekeepers sang them out. "Four, three, two, one, GUN!" Bang! it went and "Sunbeam" was first over with "Neva" second and the others following. Sheets were hardened for the beat to the Colne's entrance and the deck crowds sweated to make the lean hulls leap and quiver like spirited ponies under their straining spars. "Ole William's got the edge on 'em already," drawled a smacksman leaning on the sheerpole of his anchored craft. "Ah! He wants to watch out. They black-leaded "Bertha's" bottom yesterday," came the reply in Tollesbury's defence. But, sure enough, "Sunbeam" was drawing slowly clear, with "Neva" to leeward and "Bertha" romping third in her back-draught. "Wonder", "Foxhound", "Elise" and "Ellen" followed, with others in their wake. The breeze freshened as they neared shoal water. "Ready about!" crews scrabbled about the heeling decks.

Rowhedge smacks racing in the village regatta. From left; *Sunbeam*, Captain William Cranfield. *Neva*, Captain Lemon Cranfield. *Xanthe*, Captain 'Bill' Cranfield. The graceful sheer and rakish rig of the Colne cutters is well shown.   *Howard Goodwin*

"Lee oh!" and round they came. Jibs and staysails flacking once, and only once; you could be slick with hands who had, probably, just spent the summer trimming the sheets of some crack forty rater, or one of the big cutters.

So the racers thrashed out towards the bar and, after a few boards, the slippery "Neva" slowly crept up on "Sunbeam" till they were bow to bow, rigging strumming in the breeze, their covering boards awash with the white water playing between the hulls. As slowly "Neva" drew away despite William's luffing, until the bar buoy slipped by and they met the Wallet tide. The race was won or lost here with a long and a short to the Wallet Spitway buoy, for the wind had drawn to the east. The fleet split up. "Sunbeam" and "Bertha" stood inshore while the others ranged to the south. "Bertha" seemed to be weathering "Sunbeam", and "Elise" and "Foxhound" were having a luffing match, joined by "Maria". Aboard "Neva" Lemon sent up a larger staysail which drew well but required careful sheeting. The gang laboured at it till it trimmed to his satisfaction. She approached the Spitway buoy on the starboard tack; "Sunbeam" converging with her, footing fast with the wind fine on her port bow. "Neva's" crowd wondered if they'd weather her. The mainsheet was got in a trifle and even Lemon crouched perhaps a little tenser. William was intending to just scrape in under his bow before flinging round on the other tack to cut in on "Neva" at the turn. Closer and closer, until they could hear the quiet orders aboard each other. But William had not reckoned his tide quite finely enough. The swilling flood was setting fast to the west and, with his bowsprit almost at the belly of "Neva's" big jib he was forced to bear away fine under her stern. The rival brothers exchanged no signs, but "Neva's" crew were jubilant. Her bow was at the buoy. Suddenly they flung themselves on the mainsheet, heaving it in. Then, Crash! The boom was over and paying off. "Neva" was round, taking the lead and setting a huge bowsprit spinnaker which urged her on with a cascade of foam thundering about her lean forefoot. Runner tackles were hardened up and, with the Bar astern in no time, the spinnaker sheet was eased and five hands dragged on the thirty foot boom, yet it still skied. So Lemon lay away up Colne with hardly a glance for the long yellow tongue of the beach which spun by the rhythmically rolling smack. The others were strung out astern, flashing past an inward bound barge as though she were anchored.

Soon they were off Brightlingsea and up beyond Pyefleet. The oyster dredgers straightened their backs and spared ten minutes of the company's time to relish this, the finest sight of working craft in contest. Eight fine hulls, white canvas and tanned bellying to the fresh breeze, each carrying a great white triangular spinnaker pulling

A close finish! Captain Green's *Elise* of Wivenhoe and Captain Richard Cranfield's *Ellen* of Rowhedge pass Harris' shipyard to finish within six feet of each other after racing a 22 mile course in a pre-1914 Rowhedge regatta.

like a racehorse on the weather side. Then they were by, driving hard for Aldboro point and leaving the Binnaker buoy rolling in the foam swaths cut by black stems.

Meanwhile, upstream, Rowhedge was going gay and strings of yacht's flags and bunting had been airing since early morning. Newly laid up yachts and the dozens of smacks not racing wore masthead ensigns and were dressed overall. "Aquiline" sported her long, royal blue pendant, emblazoned with her name in white letters, and everyone's decks had been cleared of moveables in anticipation of the quayside crowds of afternoon, to whom no deck was sacred when the watersports were in full swing.

With dinner over and the yards closed, the quays began to fill with spectators. Special trains brought hundreds more sightseers from Colchester attracted by black and white posters displayed in shop windows. They swelled crowds on the Wivenhoe bank where the old committee smack lay anchored, carrying her yearly freight of good wines, smart skippers, and the hardly less important shipbuilders; plus a timekeeper and his mate with the starting twelve bore. Soon the reach began to fill with the boats of sightseers and competitors; overcanvassed yacht's cutters, new gigs, old gigs, raters, dinghies, steam launches and small yachts. As the Alresford Silver Prize band struck up "On the Quarterdeck" the pulling and sailing races began on the rising flood.

Opening with a few sedate rowing events the spectators were soon treated to the sight of two dozen brawny smack's boys, each furiously sculling a heavy boat two hundred yards downstream, to round a cork float in a welter of wildly rocking boats, before streaking back to cross the line, where each flourished his oar with a cheer at the finish. The wool capped ladies pulled next and, meanwhile, a gang on the ferry hard launched the whiffs and rum-tums; pair and single oared sculls of the local rowing clubs. Two fours were pushed off and paddled lazily to the committee boat. Frail shells these, more suited to the placid upper Thames than the muddy, tidal Colne. There was great interest in this race for the Rowhedge club's Mistley rivals were matched against them in a championship that day, and much shouted encouragement greeted the white singleted crews; rising to jeers as a Mistleyman fumbled and splashed his scull on the line. A few preliminary jiggles and they were off to the sudden shotgun crack which always seems to take the tensest crowds by surprise. The eager crews were away pulling a fast stroke, sending twin silvery feathers up the tiny bows. The click-clicking of sliding seats was drowned in the swelling roar as the heavier Mistley crew hurled themselves half a length ahead by sheer muscle power, to lead as the rivals jerked like demented water beetles, away out of sight beyond the bend into Wivenhoe reach.

The dainty little raters started to waltz lightly down over the flood as a new number appeared in the committee boat's shrouds. Officer of the day picked up his megaphone and bawled; the crowds muttering subdued to a murmur. "Race numbah ten! Numbah ten! Shipwrights crew aginst the sailors!" Two long black gigs drew out from the anchor quay to a roar of greeting for the day's most popular rowing race. They levelled up in mid-stream, backing and filling under the starter's orders. The brawny, tanned

Regatta committee aboard committee smack at Wivenhoe regatta about 1910. Refreshment for members visible down main hatch.

young seamen pulling "Phantom's" gig looked more than a match for the lighter shipwrights, practised though they were. However, they had "Namara's" new gig that year and looked confident enough with their varnished oar looms bright against the black planking, the dripping spoon blades poised ready to bite into the flood. A few more jiggles and they were off, gunwhales whipping under powerful strokes slicing thrust and drive from the rivers' surface. Bow waves spurted up to the squadron bow-badges on both hulls and clean wakes sprang from the finely moulded quarters. Cheer upon cheer   dash and spirit were in that sport.

So the watersports went with a swing until, with the raters just finishing, the first big topsail was sighted down in the bight. Excitement grew when a second and third appeared, followed, after a pause, by others racing hard upstream. A tense atmosphere settled on everything with all eyes focussed on the smacks downstream until they disappeared behind the sheds of Wivenhoe. Five minutes later a white cloud appeared. Three together! Interest in the watersports flagged immediately. The racers were coming! They were through Wivenhoe reach. "Neva's" leading!" The shout went up from some boys at a yacht's masthead. Shouts and cheers, and it seemed only seconds before the whole reach was filled with urgent black hulls, three of them so close that the boom end of one almost touched the spinnaker guy of the next. The band almost burst itself and the spectators went wild, each and every one caught up in the intense spirit of this annual rivalry. Children were held up to see and dozens of youngsters

Spectators at Rowhedge regatta about 1900. Captain John Cranfield's smack *Lily* in foreground. Ketch barge alongside Crosby's coal yard in distance, right.

raced along the quays cheering the leaders on. The crews tensed as the smacks drove hard in a puff. Then, in a flash it was all over, the gun almost unheard in the din, but everyone knew that "Neva" had won again this year, as she had so many times before. Her mastheadsman was up on the gantline immediately, jamming a gilt cock in place of the racing flag when the Alresford boys blared out "See the Conquering Hero Comes" and old Lemon, more pleased than ever with his success, waved his cap to acknowledge hats and handkerchiefs. "Sunbeam" was second with "Elise" third, and the others creamed home one by one. As the headsails came down they luffed for their berths, cheering each other as they went.

Now there was fresh excitement, the gigs were back and had come well up by the lower yard almost unnoticed in the uproar. But there was little doubt over this result; the sailors had held a good lead and the plucky shipwrights had to be content with second, much to coxswain Springett's disappointment. As the black gig flashed across the finish he hurled his cap at the bottom boards and raised a bigger roar than ever. It seemed only minutes later when the yacht's cutters came in, "Moina's" and "Baka-loum's" fighting it out under immense spinnakers, with the crews hanging outboard on the guys. But a great disappointment was to come. Not long after the tub race; that ancient and hilarious spectacle of a dozen seamen paddling hard downstream in big barrels, the leading four shot into view—alone. Consternation! The terrible realisation swept over the Rowhedgers; the Mistleymen were leading—and what a lead! They were a good seven or eight lengths ahead and pulling as furiously as at the start. There was no hope now. Village pride suffered a great blow and the polite cheers and handclaps for the victors were given as half-heartedly as those for the defeated natives.

The greasy pole and pull devil-pull baker, two uproarious favourites, finished up the watersports. The greasy pole was a long, well greased spar rigged out at right angles from the committee smack's side. One at a time all the liveliest young sparks stood on it, balancing themselves by the shrouds before trying to make their way along it to grab the flagged stick tacked to its end—a grab which would bring the prize of a leg of mutton. It was like walking the plank but the spar was round and slippery and the delighted crowds might see a score or so heroes skid off and splash into the river before the prize was won. Each competitor had his own method. Some approached it with a cautious science which almost came off, others took off with a whoop which sent them two thirds along it before taking a topple. Some gave thrills by taking a backwards somersault when they slipped, bringing shrieks of applause. To everyone's surprise, and the Rowhedgers' chagrin, a Wivenhoe apprentice took the mutton, skidding the full

"Champion of Champions". Captain Lemon Cranfield's *Neva* sets a larger staysail, with Captain William Cranfield's *Sunbeam* to windward. Photo taken about 1902. Note hand capstan amidships, typical of Colne smacks.   *Howard Goodwin*

Rowhedge shipwrights' gig crew racing at Wivenhoe regatta about 1899. From bow; George Barnard, John Cheek, James Theobald, Fred Rose, Arthur Springett.

length of the pole, snapping off the stick, and disappearing into the river with it, yelling his head off.

In no time the comically dressed devil and bakers crews were fighting it out all over the tideway. Three each in big dinghies, the devils armed with bags of soot, the bakers with bags of chalk, and both boats fast by the transoms with a good length of bass. The rowers sat forward, pulling against each other while their mates pelted the opposite crew with the bags. The bakers' rower stopped a faceful of soot and toppled over, leaving the two boats to drift in circles. They pelted each other; dived, swam, and boarded each other, exchanging roles again and again, plastering black on white and white on black. The crowds were roaring. It ended when the bakers capsized both boats and they all drifted downstream, raising their bowlers and shouting. The band struck up, the spectators dispersed for tea, took an early look at the fair, or clapped the winners at the prizegiving in the "Ship".

As soon as darkness fell the village's firework display began. Giant rockets spluttered into the sky to burst in clouds of coloured stars drawing prolonged "Aaah's" from the crowds and shouts from the children allowed up late on regatta night. Maroons sent crashing echoes around the hillsides and scores of roman candles and whirling catherine wheels reflected their flaring in the bright lit, hurrying ebb, before the man from Brocks dodged, half seen, behind the setwork, to touch off the giant portrait of the queen flanked by fiery union jacks, and the silver band broke into the national anthem. Drifting powdersmoke half obscured the waterfront as the crowds turned upstreet once more towards the two fairgrounds. One, owned by raucous voiced Mrs. Ross, occupied the Lion Quay; the larger spread over the marsh. There the strident voice of the steam organ beckoned and shouts of stallholders competed with the ground-shuddering throb of gleaming traction engines whose snaky black tentacles drove glaringly lit roundabouts and hobby horses, all crowded with shipwrights, yacht hands, and their girl friends, spending the prize money. Everything was noisy and gay. The swingboats went higher than ever and money faster than ever, but who cared? It was regatta night—only came once a year. In High Street's five pubs the smoke filled bars were packed with roistering seamen and shipwrights gathered round tinkling pianos. Pint after pint, round after round, the bar tills clanked away the cash. They sang as they drank; all the old sea songs and all the patriotic ones. "Heave away on the trawl", "The British Flag", and the "Carrier's Lad" were favourites, and they stamped to the tunes until well after midnight. They'd have heads of the year in the morning but who cared? Regatta night only came once a year!

Gradually the revelry died, pubs closed and the fairs shut, and, in the small hours, when the flags stirred to the night breeze, the streets were left to the last drunks and couples finding a long way home.

Rowhedge regatta, about 1895. Committee smack, spectator crowds and firework setpieces on Wivenhoe wall. A race for 'fours' finishing in foreground.

The King's *Britannia*, 1894. Sailed by Captain John Carter of Rowhedge.

CHAPTER SEVEN

The Cutter Sailors

THE COLNE and Blackwater have a long association with the sport of yacht racing, but perhaps few now realise why this arose, or how the sport made such an important contribution to the district's past economy and evolution. To understand these things is to share the high esteem in which the racing skippers and hands from Rowhedge, Wivenhoe, Brightlingsea and, later, also Tollesbury, were held in the yachting world, and the great pride which these villages had in their achievements. During the nineteenth and early twentieth centuries these places, always the homes of seafarers and shipbuilders, became transformed by the skill of their inhabitants to centres of yachting only equalled in influence and activity by the Solent and Clyde. Most of this past glory has departed but the old Essex racing tradition survives in a more democratic age of small yachts and amateur sailors to produce boats and crews like the Brightlingsea built and manned catamarans, which have beaten the best of America and Australia during recent seasons.

The first English yacht race was supposed to have been sailed on the Thames between the royal yacht "Catherine" and the Duke of York's "Anne" in 1661, a year after the sport, and name, of yachting had been imported from Holland by Charles II on his return from exile there. For over 100 years the ownership and racing of yachts was localised and spasmodic due to the frequent state of war, and only kings or their wealthiest subjects could afford them. Although the first recorded open race for a cup took place on the Thames in 1749, regularly organised racing was not introduced until 1775 when the "Cumberland Fleet" was founded in London as the first English yacht club, to race cutters above and below bridges. Its members were inspired by the numbers of yachts present at what is reputed to have been Britain's first regatta, held for rowing craft on London river that year.

The exact origin of local participation in yacht racing is now impossible to trace accurately but, in 1783, a sailing race for Essex fishing smacks was organised by Bradwell's parson Bate-Dudley, held in the Blackwater, and won by a Burnham cutter. The regatta craze caught on and a few months later, Captain Hopkins of Wivenhoe organised a similar event for smacks belonging to Wivenhoe, Rowhedge, Brightlingsea and Mersea, which raced for a silver cup and suit of colours which were respectively won by Captain Cooke's "Mayflower" of Rowhedge and George Wheatly's "Two Sisters" of Wivenhoe. The race had become established by the following July when six smacks competed for "the annual silver cup and suit of colours" won by the Brightlingsea cutter "Cleverly", Captain Tabor, with Captain Worrel's "Mayflower" of Mersea, second. The event seems to have lapsed next year but was certainly held in 1786 when the "Essex Chronicle" published the following spirited account so typical of these early Essex races:

"By nine o'clock on Monday morning the sea between Mersea and Bradwell was crowded with pleasure yachts, sloops etc. decorated with various colours. At ten the Bradwell yacht (aboard which were several of the principal gentlemen of the county) got under weigh and fired a signal for the commanders of the cutters entered for the prize to go on board the yacht, draw lots for the weather gauge, and receive their distinguishing colours.

"As soon as their several pendants were hoisted and the cutters got into their destined stations, a second gun was fired as the signal for starting, when eleven fine, well trimmed vessels got under weigh, and with clouds of sail stood out to sea under a salute of guns from the surrounding yachts etc. the whole forming a very striking naval spectacle.

"The contest lay principally between the "Two Brothers" of Rowhedge, Captain Shakeshaft, and the "Batchelor" of Mersea, Captain Overall, which was very sharply disputed, till the last time doubling the Eagle buoy, when a heavy squall coming on, the "Batchelor" found it prudent to strike some of her sail, which at this moment unfortunately going overboard threw her so much to leeward that she was unable to recover her station.

"About five o'clock the "Two Brothers" passed the starting flag on the middle buoy, and, receiving a general salute, went on board the yacht where being drank to by the donor, received the cup . . . . . "The 'Pink' of Burnham, Captain Richmond, coming in second, received the second prize, viz. a full suit of St. George's colours; the "Friendship" of Paglesham, Captain Wiseman, was the third vessel; but the others came in so close that it was impossible to class them."

The cup and colours for the 1787 sailing match were donated by gentlemen members of the Colchester King's Head Club and ten smacks sailed the usual estuary course for them, the Burnham "Friendship" winning with the "Batchelor" of Mersea, second. No regattas appear to have been held in 1788 but next year the "White Hart Club" of Colchester put up the prizes and invited contestants from Rowhedge, Wivenhoe, Brightlingsea, Mersea, Bradwell, Tollesbury, Burnham and Paglesham to meet at the Mersea "White Hart" to discuss holding a race that September; however, there is no record of its having taken place.

Thus local fishermen had, by inclination and working necessity, a sound knowledge of racing under sail, and similar local regattas were also organised along the Devon coast and in the Solent, with Cowes holding its first in 1776 and Southampton shortly afterwards. In Suffolk, Woodbridge held a regatta in 1784 and there were sailing matches at Ipswich in 1791 and 1792 which were probably for commercial craft. Apparently it was then common for pubs to organise sailing matches for in 1816 the Fountain Inn at Ipswich sponsored one.

86

In all these events yachts were present as a minority of the onlookers and few existed before 1800 when there were probably not more than seventy in the country, mostly used for cruising. An early reference to a Colne yacht was the loss with all hands of "Mr. Blyth's yacht", which foundered off Ostende during a severe north east gale in September, 1816. Such vessels were generally built without thought of racing and to no arbitrary limits of size or rig, most owners requiring comfortable boats of imposing appearance with ample accommodation for cruising coastwise and to the continent and Baltic; and often to Bordeaux or Lisbon, to stock up with wines for the season. Their crews were largely drawn from the Colne, Orwell, Thames or Solent seamen sailing the similarly built and rigged smacks and other small craft. These men of the narrow seas were always the best yacht sailors, and for racing they were unequalled. Accustomed to lives of toil hauling the dredge or trawl, and stowboating or salvaging in the winter gales amongst the myriad shoals they brought a wonderful knowledge of tides and pilotage, coupled with an alertness and skill in getting to windward quickly, denied to the deepwater sailor. Their impression of gentlemen who took their leisure sailing in small craft can be imagined. However, the early amateurs were keen to learn, and some were probably more competent than we realise. For instance, Joseph Weld, the squire of Lulworth and a noted early owner of racing yachts, took a personal part in their design and, like his rivals, was always aboard lending a hand when racing, a spirit which was often lacking in owners of the greater yachts of later years. In 1800 Weld sailed one of the earliest yacht races on the open sea, off Weymouth, against a Bridport yacht for a heavy wager. Occasional matches for wagers formed the early phase of yacht racing and seem to have been confined to the South Coast where, in the Solent, the wealthy and leisured visitors who had just discovered waterside pleasures were content to leave the developing sport of yachting to a few enthusiasts, for even then Society overshadowed the sails at Cowes, which was changing from a smuggling haunt to a resort where bathing machines lined the castle beach in summer and fashionables paraded the narrow streets.

At this time a few yachts sailed from the Menai Straits which, oddly enough, had long had oystering connections with the Colne and produced good sailors. One of them was Lord Uxbridge, better known as the Marquis of Anglesey, a pioneer racing yachtsman well known on the Colne and, in 1815, a founder-member of the Royal Yacht Club, forerunner of the Royal Yacht Squadron. The Marquis was a remarkable man in an age of characters and a pillar of early nineteenth century sailing. As a cavalry commander, he served with distinction in the Peninsular War and later lost a leg at Waterloo, but a wooden leg did not quench his love of yachting. Although spending much time in the Irish Sea and the waters of the Wight he, at first alone amongst members of the Royal Club, patronised Colneside shipbuilders. Sometime before 1809 he ordered from Philip John Sainty, then shipbuilding at Colchester Hythe (probably in the yard then recently vacated by William Stuttles) a yacht named "Emerald" which, with a local crew, proved unbeatable by yachts of her own size, and often raced the Holyhead—Howth packet cutters across the Irish Sea. On leaving for the Peninsular War he presented her to the Prince of Wales and in later years she was sometimes used by the Princess, afterwards Queen Victoria. However, in 1819 she appeared again being raced by the Marquis in a match against the 60 ton "Charlotte" and the 52 ton "Sylph", when the "Emerald" won two of the three heats in light airs and the Marquis won £800. Alas, the following day he lost some of it by sailing his 42 ton "Liberty" against Mr. Weld's "Julia", losing the match and 300 guineas. The "Liberty" was also built by Sainty at Colchester especially for racing and her early success prompted the Marquis publicly to remark of him that as a builder of fast sailing vessels "He has a capacity beyond what I ever met with". This reputation attracted an order for a racer from Owen Williams of Beaumaris, a prominent Welsh yachtsman for whom the quaintly named and locally manned 39 tonner "Blue-Eyed Maid" was launched at the Hythe.

The cutter yacht *Gazelle* off Cowes. A 64 footer built in 1820 by Philip John Sainty. Painted by J. C. Schetky.
National Maritime Museum

Having owned such fast yachts it is not surprising that with newly proclaimed peace encouraging yachting, the Marquis' thoughts turned to a new, larger cutter and he journeyed to Colchester to discuss her design with Sainty. The story of the building of the "Pearl" has been told many times and, traditionally, Sainty is supposed to have built her in 1815 at Wivenhoe on a site just north of the present Cooks' Shipyard, but the following eye witness account by a Colchester Customs Officer disproves this:—

"It was in 1814 that I came into the excise and was ordered to Colchester (Buonaparte had been sent to Elba, and the short peace that took place led many to go abroad). There was in Colchester at that time a man by the name of Brown, a whip-maker by trade; he left Colchester and went over to Holland, and took with him a vast many counterfeit guineas, and after a while he was detected. I, with many others, watched the newspapers every day, expecting to see an account of his death for his crime.

"At that time Sainty used to sail backwards and forwards to Holland, and did a vast deal of trade in contraband goods; he had a vessel with false sides. Sainty had great interest in Holland, and through this he got Brown off and brought him home in his vessel. As soon as they landed Brown went and informed against Sainty, and told where the smuggled goods were to be found. (It was supposed Brown got a vast sum of money for his information, as he came to Colchester and took a public house in Barrack Street. I have several times been in it and seen him, but he did not prosper long, he had to leave it, went to his trade again, but could not do; and I forget now what became of him. Sainty's vessel was condemned; and Sainty, his son, and his brother were sent to Chelmsford gaol (it was stated for life). In 1815 Buonaparte made his return to France, and soon after the Marquis of Anglesea lost one of his legs at the battle of Waterloo. After the war was over (it was in 1816 or 1817, I cannot say the year exactly) the Marquis came to Colchester to inquire about John Sainty; and they told him he was in Chelmsford gaol for life; and I heard the report that the Marquis should say "that if he were in hell, he would have him out". The Marquis went out and saw Sainty, and asked him if he was the man who built him a yacht some years ago (the "Emerald"). He said he had. He then asked Sainty if he could build him one that would beat that one. He said he could, and one that no other could beat. In consequence the Marquis either went or wrote to the Prince Regent, and an order was sent down to the Governor to liberate John Sainty. Old Sainty knew what he was about, and his son's name being John, he let him get out. When the Marquis saw him, he found they had let the son out instead of the father. He then wrote for the father's liberation, which soon took place, and when he saw the Marquis he told him he had a brother in gaol that he could not do without, and in a few days all three were in Colchester. In a little time, the yacht was commenced about a mile out of Colchester and during its building there were shipbuilders from all parts come to see its progress. One Mr. Dorrell, a glazier, furnished the ballast for it, which were all cast iron balls, and they were all behind the mast. The cabin had three large frames, one 8 ft. long and

4 ft. wide, the Marquis having ordered the frames to be caned. The day came when the vessel was to be tried and she surpassed all expectation. After the Marquis' first trip in her she came again to Colchester, and he ordered the large frame to be made shorter and narrower. After this the Marquis settled £100 a year on Sainty, on condition that he did not build a vessel for any other person; but after a time he broke his contract, and when I left Colchester, in 1831, he was a large shipbuilder at Wivenhoe . . ."

The "Pearl" was launched in 1819 and registered in 1820 with a tonnage of 113, making her a giant amongst most yachts of the day which averaged between 20 - 70 tons. She displaced 127.5 tons on a draft of 11.5 ft., with a waterline length of 65.3' and 19.5' beam. Her lines were beautifully easy and fair, as I found when redrafting a copy of them. In an era of bluff bows she was notable for a fine entrance which blended almost imperceptibly into a long run, terminating in a delicately proportioned counter. Her form was typical of much of Sainty's other work and was to influence South Coast builders for many years. The hull was clench-built below the wales and carvel above, as was then fashionable for fast craft, and her construction combined lightness with strength and was of remarkable finish, the whole confirms history's high opinion of Sainty as a builder of fast sailing craft. The caned frames referred to were partition bulkheads thus made for lightness.

We may picture her trial sail down Colne under easy canvas, past the admiring waterside villages which were the homes of her crew. The aged builder chatting to the top-hatted Marquis, who broke his wooden leg during the day's sailing and, at the tiller, Captain William Ham of Wivenhoe probably cursing the stretch of her hempen rigging, and anybody who marked her spotless decks. When Lord Fitzclarence came aboard with varnished boots which marked the white pine, Charlie Bates, the Wivenhoe mate, told a hand off to follow him and remove each stain with a swab! Captain Ham was a thorough seaman who later spent his winters in command of the carrier-cutters "Lady Elizabeth" and "Volcanic" in the fish and fruit carrying trades to the London markets. On the Marquis' death in 1854 he received an annuity of £100 and went off to skipper a French transport running supplies through the blockade to the beleaguered Crimean garrison at Sevastopol. The "Pearl's" crew were all, with one exception, reputed to have later become masters of yachts. They were trained in small arms and cutlass drill as a defence against the privateers and corsairs still prevalent, and the yacht also carried six brass cannon, for gun salutes were common and gunpowder freely used when meeting other yachts, though club commodores were entitled to a dipped topsail.

In contrast to her hull, the vast cutter rig would excite little comment from seamen seeking their living in fishing smacks and smugglers so rigged, and frequently being chased by revenue cutters of similar appearance but often inferior speed. The "Pearl's" flax canvas totalled 3,218 square feet comprising loose-footed mainsail, staysail, and jib, but excluding the triangular gaff-topsail. Off the wind she set a square topsail spread by a barren yard below it, which was lowered to the bulwarks when not in use. For racing she set a long-yarded gaff topsail and added studdingsails to the square topsail and a ringtail to the mainsail leach. In light weather the sail luffs were drenched with water to hold a better wind, some yachts being specially fitted with pumps and canvas hoses to aid in "skeating", as this practice was called.

At the time of her launch only one other cutter yacht was larger than the "Pearl", the 116 ton "Atlanta" owned by John Fitzgerald of Boulge, Suffolk, grandfather of the poet Fitzgerald and another founder-member of the Royal Yacht Club at Cowes, which for the first eleven years of its existence did nothing to encourage racing, preferring to stage Solent regattas which consisted of processions of pilot boats and yachts taking orders from the commodore's yacht which signalled evolutions by flags and gunfire. Such pompous displays were too tame for some spirited members and by the 1820's match sailing for wagers became common, with proud owners challenging each other with arrogant provocation for stakes which now seem fabulous. Sometimes jealousy and quarrels tainted the sporting atmosphere but, for the few East and South Coast builders beginning to specialise in yacht construction, this increasing rivalry was good for trade and a spur for improved design.

Although the "Pearl's" memory has become enshrined in a tradition of successful racing, actual records of it are scanty and she does not appear to have competed often. The event of the 1821 season was a match round the Isle of Wight between her and Captain Bacon's 120 ton schooner "Hussar", which the "Pearl" won easily. But her principal early rivals were the smaller South Coast cutters "Charlotte" and "Elizabeth", sixty tonners owned by Joseph Weld and Assheton-Smith, both noted racing owners of the period. That the 113 ton "Pearl" invariably beat them is not surprising and her racing reputation seems to have laid in her superior size and she was for many years cock of the racing fleet for this reason. The real contests of the day lay, as always, between yachts of similar size such as "Charlotte" and "Elizabeth", but, incredible as it seems now, no allowance was made for the great disparity in tonnage and the "Pearl" went on winning. In 1825 the 85 ton Lymington built "Arrow" designed three years earlier by her owner, Joseph Weld, challenged the "Pearl" to a race from Cowes to Swanage and return for £500. The Marquis was so certain of victory that in accepting he vowed, "If the "Pearl" should be beaten I will burn her as soon as we get back". He must have regretted the words early in the race when the "Arrow" led, but the "Pearl" eventually won by 10½ minutes and escaped a fiery end!

By this time owners had discovered that a good big yacht repeatedly beat a good little one and accordingly a number of large yachts were laid down on the South Coast to beat the Essex flier, whose bow they had copied. At Southampton Rubie built the 147 ton "Miranda", at Hastings the "Menai" of 163 tons left Ransom's ways and in Cowes Joseph White launched the 121 ton "Therese" for Lord Belfast who later the same season took delivery of the 96 ton "Harriet". There was now no chance for small yachts or small men for these yachts were surprisingly costly for their day. Large racers such as the "Pearl" left little change out of £8,000 each, and in 1828 the larger "Lulworth" cost £14,000 and about £1,200 in annual upkeep. More modest yachts of about 30 tons only cost a guinea a day to run and, as ever, wiser men bought good boats second-hand for ridiculous prices, the famous "Louisa" going for £3,000 when her racing days ended.

The day of the big cutter had dawned and in 1826 the "Pearl" and "Arrow" met their match racing against the 103 ton "Nautilus", built by Lynn Ratsey at Cowes, which completely outsailed them for a prize of £500, although never again did the "Nautilus" distinguish herself in racing for they "fished her mast and killed her", as the old sailors said. "Pearl's" defeat conflicts with the delightful but evidently untrue story that when the new iron-hulled "Mosquito" came out in 1848 with Southampton's John Nicholls at the helm she sailed through the "Pearl's" lee and emerged on her weather, at which the Marquis is reputed to have dipped his ensign to the first yacht to have accomplished the feat. In 1826 the captain of the Cowes-built 100 ton revenue cutter "Vigilant" challenged three yachts, including the "Pearl" to a race round the Needles and back to Cowes, which the new Government cutter won by such a margin that her cheering crew sailed her back to circle the yachts before they finished. Even the East Coast revenue cutters were not above an occasional race and in 1824 the "Scout" beat the "Lively", "New Charter", "Eagle", "Fly", "Sea Hawk" and "Desmond", over a sea course from the Cork ledge buoy off Harwich, round the Kentish Knock, to Margate Roads. As proof of the similarity then existing between yachts, smacks, smuggling cutters and revenue cruisers, in 1840 this same "Scout" captured the Ipswich smack "Rosabelle" smuggling tobacco, snuff, and spices. Built at Portsmouth as a yacht in 1825 for a member of the Royal Yacht Club, the "Rosabelle" had been advertised for sale in 1838 as a pleasure yacht with "Stowboat gear" as fishing for pleasure was even then reckoned part of the East Coast yachtsman's year, and that same season three yachts from Colne were almost overwhelmed by a waterspout when trawling off St. Osyth.

There seems to have been no regular racing for yachts on the East Coast at this time, apart from the annual regattas which were beginning to offer a race for yachts, besides the various classes of working craft for which they were primarily organised at most of the large and small ports from Yarmouth to the Thames. But yachts were increasing in numbers and the rivers Colne, Stour and Orwell became centres for building and manning them. Yards at Colchester Hythe, Wivenhoe, Mistley and Ipswich were busy launching racing and cruising yachts of all sizes and yachtbuilding skill matured early in those places which only Lymington, Southampton, Cowes, and Hastings could rival. Few of them could approach the subtle draughtsmanship or clientele of old Philip Sainty whose yards at Colchester, and later Wivenhoe, usually had the frames of a sleek racer rising alongside the hulls of ships and smacks.

In 1820 he launched for Owen Williams the 64' racing cutter "Gazelle", which was still sailing 66 years later, and the following year built the graceful 124 ton cutter "Swallow" for the Duke of Norfolk, a yacht described as "sumptuously fitted and ornamented with, amongst other things, a profusion of glass". The "Flower of Yarrow", for the Duke of Beccleuch, was a handsome 100 tonner while other products of his yards were smaller, like the 36 ton "Gulnare", the 21 ton "Hind", the 26 ton "Gipsy", the 53 foot "Ruby" and the 63 ton "Witch", all built for members of the Royal Yacht Club who were beginning to patronise the East and South Coast regattas as part of the season's regular round, although it was not until 1826 that the Royal Yacht Club at last awakened to racing at Cowes and presented cups for competition in its annual regatta.

Instead of the flying start we use today, these early races started with the yachts anchored about a cable apart, usually with all sail lowered, but sometimes with only headsails down. At the second gun canvas was hoisted and anchors rattled home in a frenzy of activity still to be seen in the oyster cutters at the Fal River regattas. At that time booming out of headsails was not allowed, a regulation which survives in the West Mersea, Maldon and Rowhedge smack races. Two other now familiar rules were introduced during the 1820's; port tack gave way to starboard, and an adequate

The Marquis of Anglesey's cutter yacht *Pearl* built at Colchester by Philip John Sainty, 1818/1819. Two views with single reefed mainsail and squaresail yard stowed.   *National Maritime Museum*

dinghy had to be carried in case of accident. As the sport became more organised the inevitable arguments began—and have continued ever since! Racing fever gripped yacht owners and sail areas increased alarmingly, accentuated by the 1826 ban on extra sails which led to ordinary rigs of immense size, and consequently large hulls to carry them. Ballast was increased and a proportion of it shifted to windward when racing, a practice frowned on by many owners. So the evils of racing in the form of excessive canvas, ballast and expense arrived early in the sport and protesting, but unheeded, voices were raised against regatta racing, in favour of the open sea.

All these early racers were sailed by professional crews hailing, mainly, from the Colne or Solent areas and great was their rivalry. They took racing seriously and there were incidents such as the fouling of the "Arrow" by the "Miranda", when the crews set about each other with windlass handspikes and axes! By 1825, 500 of these hands in their glazed top hats manned the 100 yachts of the Royal Yacht Club alone, and berths in racers were eagerly sought as their crews' weekly wage was 25 shillings if they found their own food, and £3 monthly if food was provided by the owner; either being a good wage for the time, with the odd chance of a guinea being thrown in after a successful race. The early Colne racing skippers had some clever Solent seamen against them, many of whom had been South Coast pilots. Principal amongst these were the brothers Corke of Cowes and typical of this robust era is the story of Edward Corke's handling of Lord Belfast's brig yacht "Waterwitch" in her heavy weather race against the Welsh-crewed schooner yacht "Galatea", from the Nab, round the Eddystone and back for £1,000. As both yachts rounded the Eddystone in roaring darkness the "Waterwitch" was being luffed ashore by the "Galatea" which Corke hailed with "Starboard your helm or I'll sink you!" The Welshman gave way and the Cowes boat eventually won a hard fought race.

In this atmosphere the high water mark of early racing rivalry dawned in 1828 with the launch of the 127 ton "Lulworth" for Squire Weld and the 162 ton "Louisa" for Lord Belfast. During the next two years, yachting interest focussed on the tussles between these two and the "Menai", all of them being stripped out internally and used for nothing but racing. Belfast challenged Weld to a match from Spithead, round the Owers and back to Cowes roads for £1,000, which "Louisa" won, which is not surprising as she was skippered by Edward Clarke, a Colnesider "whose skill as a steersman is not surpassed, if equalled, by any cutter sailor in the Kingdom", as contemporary reports put it. In the next season's King's Cup Race, "Louisa" fouled the "Lulworth", whose crew prided themselves on never giving way on the port tack, and Captain Clarke's bowspritendsman cut away the "Lulworth's" clew earing with an axe, disabling her and sparking a quarrel which led to her withdrawal from racing. Another Colne-crewed racer of the times was the 39 tonner "Blue-Eyed Maid", handled by Captain Jack Crickmar of Rowhedge who, when entered against the giant "Louisa", started and then hauled down his racing flag in disgust, a feeling then shared by many at the long overdue introduction of time allowance.

While tempers flared in the Solent, yachting elsewhere was getting established. In 1827 the Marquis of Anglesey was appointed Lord Lieutenant of Ireland and the "Pearl" became a familiar sight in Dublin Bay where regattas were held and races often won by the old Colchester-built "Liberty", which had passed to the Earl of Errol, who enjoyed spirited racing against such suggestively named Irish yachts as the "Young Paddy", "Black Dwarf", and "Wild Irish Girl", while the "Pearl" is shown as a spectator in prints of the events.

Although Belfast and Weld were not on speaking terms their rivalry continued, culminating in 1830 in the building of Weld's giant "Alarm"; queen of the South Coast and the terror of racing men for generations. This 193 tonner was one of the largest cutters ever built and she had a romantic origin as her lines were taken from a condemned French smuggler captured off the Needles and taken to Lymington for breaking up. To match her Philip Sainty's Wivenhoe yard launched the 188 ton racer "Arundel" for the Duke of Norfolk, a yacht notable in the Squadron's records of the time as "the finest seagoing cutter ever built". Occasionally the Wivenhoe boat outsailed both the "Alarm" and "Louisa", but inside the Wight the "Alarm" was supreme. Outside she was often beaten by the "Louisa", by then skippered by Ted Corke. Wager matches continued on a grand scale; a race was proposed in 1830, but never sailed, between the "Alarm" and "Pearl" for a thousand guineas. Experiment was rife and there was a craze for lengthening and rebuilding the fliers as they became outclassed by new yachts. The "Pearl's" bow was remodelled in 1832 in accordance with theories of Mr. Fincham of Portsmouth Dockyard who had made a study of the "Pearl" and her contemporaries, but the most altered yacht was her old rival, the "Arrow", whose hull was continually rebuilt and still winning prizes until 1870! The "Pearl" lived to an even greater age, being rebuilt as a 92 foot yawl by Nicholsons at Gosport in 1873 and was the oldest yacht afloat when broken up in 1902 after 83 years' service.

After a decade of hotly contested racing, these big cutters went out of favour in 1834 when many races were restricted to yachts of under 75 tons, and the most colourful period of the sport's early days was ended. Although the "Pearl" was outclassed, the ability of her builder and crew, with her owner's influence, had laid the foundations of the Colne's greatness in yacht building and racing which formed a cornerstone of local prosperity and pride for the next century.

CHAPTER EIGHT

The Racing Men—1830-1890

THE RIVER Colne had a profound influence on yachting. Its villages provided skippers, hands, designers, builders, repairers, and sail-makers for the sport from its beginnings in the late 18th century, to 1939.

As that era recedes memories fade and legends often founded on half-truths are born and eventually come to be regarded as fact. Because of this it is interesting to analyse local participation in yacht racing which contributed largely to Colneside prosperity during this period.

Until the beginning of the nineteenth century the Colne and Blackwater waterside communities depended principally on fishing and salvaging, with a certain amount of shipbuilding and smuggling. The sport of yachting expanded rapidly after the Napoleonic wars and local seamen were in great demand to sail, and especially to race, the yachts which brought comparative prosperity and, eventually, international fame to the district. It divided the year into winter fishing and summer yachting; a cycle which only ended with the outbreak of war in 1914; to be resumed again for the twenty years after 1919.

How this arose and how a sport could make such important contribution to the district's past economy and evolution, few can now realise.

The skill of building yachts matured early on the Colne and only Poole, Lymington, Cowes and Southampton could rival this experience. These small, fast types of sailing craft developed to become a separate branch of shipbuilding, requiring specialised knowledge which builders of larger ships did not necessarily possess, as they do not today, and the subtle art of designing and building yachts grew gradually away from shipbuilding.

The yachts of the 1830's had little in common with the racers of a decade later; most were still clench-built and builders turned out craft with sensible beam, despite yacht tonnage continuing to be based on a modified form of the 1794 rule for merchant ships which measured length along the keel, breadth twice, but ignored depth; just as its offspring, Thames tonnage, still does. Until the mid-1850's builders preferred to ignore the loophole of reducing beam excessively, to decrease tonnage; preferring to create yachts which sailed on their bottoms. Most yachting histories unfairly describe all British racers prior to the "America's" visit in 1851 as bluff-bowed tubs with baggy sails, and hail the Harvey-built "Amazon" and Waterman's "Mosquito" as heralds of a change in mid-century, but Philip Sainty had built many hollow bowed fast craft, including the cutter "Pearl", early in the century, and many of the Colne smacks built before the 1850's, whose form and rig were almost indistinguishable from yachts of that time, had extremely long, hollow entrances favoured by builders such as Sainty of Wivenhoe,

Aldous of Brightlingsea and Cheek of Rowhedge, who all constructed yachts. It is reasonable to suppose that the racers were at least as advanced in form as the smacks, whose windward powers were remarkable for that time.

For almost two centuries there has been considerable fluctuation in the size of racing yachts, influenced by economic and social factors. Sometimes the big yachts have flourished into large numbers and attracted much attention, then subsided for a period, but the small yachts have always been there, and always will, and in larger numbers. Some owners have always preferred to sail a small yacht which they could handle with a minimum of crew or a few friends, and in the early days of yacht racing as much attention was paid to the small classes as to the larger cutters. In London, the Arundel Yacht Club was founded in 1838 to race only small craft, under 7 tons; a limit later raised to 12.

On the East Coast early yacht racing took the form of regattas organised by committees which at a later stage often turned into a club, which would, however, continue to promote the annual regatta as its prime concern, rather than holding regular races during the season. Thus the town regattas are of older origin than most clubs and survive today in lively traditional form at West Mersea, Rowhedge, Maldon and other places.

In the Solent the Royal Yacht Club had, in 1836, become the Royal Yacht Squadron; which has always had strong East Coast connections in the building and, more especially, crewing of its yachts. Bayley of Ipswich launched a 44 tonner for a member in 1827 and several years later, a Mistley shipbuilder launched the 160 ton schooner "Xarifa" for Lord Wilton, later commodore of the Squadron, which became the world's most exclusive club.

Her size and rig was not unusual during a period when the Royal Yacht Club commodore, Lord Yarborough, took pleasure in owning a full rigged ship and a ten gun brig, both armed as 'men of war' with crews disciplined by the cat and carrying out gun drill regularly when cruising with the channel fleet. It was that spirit which granted the title 'Squadron', and the right to fly the navy's white ensign, to the club.

The Marquis of Anglesey continued to influence yachting until his death in 1854. He was often in the Solent or Thames; "sailing down Long Reach in the "Pearl" with his great mainsail set", as an observer put it. For a number of years in later life he nominally resided at Cowes Castle and after his death it was tenanted by the Royal Yacht Squadron, who have occupied it since.

The Colne seamen and yachtbuilders had strong links with the Royal Thames Yacht Club which, with the Royal Harwich, established in 1845, were the principal promoters of yacht racing on the East Coast, with craft which rivalled those of the Royal Yacht Squadron, the Royal Southern at Southampton, the Royal Western at Plymouth, the Royal Cork in Ireland, the Royal Northern at Glasgow and the Royal

Mersey at Liverpool. These were then the principal clubs in the country, when British yachting was on the threshold of the great surge of yacht clubs.

The Royal Thames racing rules and arrangements were typical of that period. The sizes of racing flags were laid down; 3 ft. hoist x 4 ft. 6 in. fly for the first class and 2 ft. x 3 ft. fly for the second. The racers drew lots for position and had to be at the starting buoys a quarter of an hour before the start, or be disqualified.

No jib was to exceed 2 ft. in the head, nor to be hoisted above the mainmast head. Headsails were not to be boomed out and if any yacht deliberately fouled another during racing its owner was expelled from the club. Yachts could not bear away to leeward on to a competitor but could hail for water if being forced on to an obstruction. If a protest was intended an ensign was to be hoisted in the rigging as protest flag. Bulkheads and cabin soles were not to be dismantled and put ashore for racing, as was often done elsewhere.

Whatever the tactics during the race the winner was always cheered by the losers, who were cheered in return as an expression of good feeling. This custom of "cheering the winner" remained in British yacht racing until 1939, and is still practised in the Colne and Blackwater smack races.

In 1844, fourteen Royal Thames cutters sailed to the Solent to challenge the South Coast fliers for a cup open to yachts under 31 tons. Prominent amongst them was Lord Alfred Paget's 25 tonner "Mystery," sailed by a crew from Wivenhoe, where she may have been built, and H. Gibson's "Gnome," whose Brightlingsea crew called her the "G-nome". Gibson also simultaneously owned the 25 ton cutter "Ino", which entered the same races as the "Gnome". The "Ino" was sailed by Captain Blackwell of Rowhedge with a village crew. Blackwell was lost with two of his hands next winter when salvaging in the Swin with his smack, named, as was the custom, after the racing yacht.

The 1844 race was sailed in stormy weather with the Thames yacht "Bluebell" losing her bowsprit and one of the "Gnome's" Brightlingseamen going overboard when trying to save the coil of the mainsheet. He was hauled back by the skipper, who left the tiller to grab him by the hair. The "Mystery" won narrowly from the Solent cutter "Champion", built at Poole. Shortly afterwards Lord Alfred Paget sold the "Mystery" for £500, then a large sum for a 25 tonner. He was a son of the Marquis of Anglesey, owner of the "Pearl", and was a close friend of Prince Albert and Queen Victoria. He had a lifelong interest in the seamen and yachtbuilders of the Colne, had several yachts built by the Harveys at Wivenhoe and regularly employed Colne crews.

The Royal Thames opened the 1845 season on April 4th with members sailing down river in company with the club steamer, hired to carry the committee when racing was in progress, and a common feature of Thames and other regattas. The "Gnome" led the way, carrying the commodore's flag, but all eyes that season were on the C.R.

Tatham's new racer "Prima Donna", a "very rakish cutter", just launched from Thomas Harvey's Wivenhoe yard and sailed by a crew from that village, keen to beat their rivals in the flourishing 25 ton class. The usual courses were from Greenwich to Gravesend, or from Gravesend, round the Nore and back with one minute of time per ton as a common handicap allowance which lasted for many years in classes all round the coast. The "Prima Donna" was a great success that season but I cannot discover who was her skipper.

In 1845 Lord Alfred Paget had the new 25 tonner "Belvedere" built in iron on the Thames. She and the iron-built "Blue Bell" sailed to the Solent to race in the Royal Yacht Squadron regatta. In a special race for "wood versus iron" they raced the Southampton built 25 tonner "Fawn", and the "Secret", built at Poole by Wanhill Brothers and sailed by them to victory, after the "Belvedere" lost her mast off Egypt point.

Contemporary carrying-on in a breeze cost many masts and spars. In that year's Royal Southern Yacht Club regatta, during a very stormy August, the "Secret" was

The 48 ton racing cutter *Volante*, sailed by Captain George Pittuck of Wivenhoe. Built in 1849 by Harvey and Son, Wivenhoe and Ipswich.

leading three other yachts in the second class when her mast went overboard off Ryde in a strong wind. Within minutes the masts of the "Tartar" and "Exquisite" were "fairly blown out of them" and the "Jilt" broke her bowsprit.

Regattas all round the coast remained heavily supported by races for local working craft. The first match of the Royal Victoria Yacht Club's 1845 regatta was for "First class Ryde Wherries", and the 15 to 31 ton class for yachts started as second race. Typifying the informality of contemporary racing, Queen Victoria and Prince Albert arrived during this regatta in the steam tender "Fairy" and stopped to watch the race for four oared galleys, in which the cutter "Pearl's" galley competed, rowed by selected hands of her Colne crew, eager to beat their Solent rivals.

Yachts' crews of the period were tough and able seamen, wearing a uniform provided by the owner. The captains wore the typical mid-victorian sea officers' "cheese-cutter" peaked cap, with club badge; blue serge jacket and trousers; collar and tie and black shoes. The hands' rig was usually a shiny black straw hat with nameband, like a man-o-war's man; called "Nab light hats" because many of them were plaited by the crews of light vessels to supplement their pay: blue guernseys having the yacht's name worked across the chest in elaborate scrolls; white duck trousers and black shoes.

In bad weather all hands wore sticky yellow oilskins, sou'westers and sea boots. The owner also provided every man with a blue serge suit and shoes for a smart "going ashore" rig; a custom which originated in the 1860's and persisted until 1939.

The rivalry amongst racing crews, particularly from different areas, sometimes caused trouble, but those serving aboard yachts of the Squadron were curbed by knowing they might get into its crew's blacklist, which was not discontinued until 1864.

The yacht crews were then regarded as a form of naval reserve and in 1845 numbered over 5,000 seamen, manning yachts of which a contemporary writer said "discipline in which is equal (if not superior) to any man of war cutter". He also commented that the eleven man crew of the 70 ton cutter "Ganymede", owned by a member of the Royal Southern Yacht Club, could fire "4 guns at six seconds time or 10 guns a minute, thus discipline as well as pleasure is observed with the southerners".

Gun salutes remained in favour amongst yachtsmen well into the nineteenth century and as late as 1862 the commodore of the Royal Harwich Yacht Club, Lord Rendlesham, was entitled to an eleven gun salute from the clubhouse as he entered the harbour, which must have been a noisy place as this was acknowledged, gun for gun, by his fine schooner "Aegidia", then newly launched from John Harvey's Wivenhoe yard.

As well as his ability in navigation, seamanship and racing, the yacht's captain had to ensure that contemporary yacht etiquette of flags, salutes, receiving boats alongside, guests, etc. was observed in the then considerable British yachting tradition which evolved during the 19th century. Their sense of order was well described by a contemporary writer:

"She is an English yacht, a cutter of fifty tons—her low sides shining with glossy blackness. Her tall and well-oiled mast contrasts well with the trim and jet black ropes, while the sails, smoothly cased up in their canvas covers, stretch along the boom and the heel of the bowsprit. A sturdy tar in short blue pea jacket and round oil skin hat keeps watch on the starboard quarter of her white pine deck .... with all the precision of a man of war's man. To such a point did he carry his notions of order that although the sun had been visible for a full ten minutes yet he would not fire the morning gun till the very moment when his nautical almanack told him it was sunrise."

40 to 50 tonners of about 55-65 feet length were the favoured sizes of large racer at the middle of the 19th century when the "Volante" or "Mosquito" were successful and desirable craft compared with some of the much larger racers such as "Alarm", which only raced a quarter as often and were heavily sparred and stripped out for match sailing.

The 55 ft., 39 ton cutter "Avalon", launched from Thomas Harvey's Ipswich shipyard in 1850, was a good example of a first class racer of the period. She was plumb stemmed, with the forefoot radiused below the waterline, into a long, straight, raking keel, ending with a well raked sternpost and moderate counter. Planking was durable red deal, copper fastened to grown oak frames and centreline. Decks were of yellow pine, with oak or mahogany covering boards, surrounded by a low bulwark capped by a varnished "rough tree rail", to use the old shipwright's term. Apart from a small iron or lead shoe, all the ballast was internal, of iron or lead, most of it stowed below the ceiling, with a proportion of lead in bags or boxes, for shifting when racing; for which purpose the maple panelled saloon would be stripped out, and ballast retaining boards fitted on each side.

The crew berthed forward in cots around the sides of the narrow, tapering foc'sle where all cooking was done on a black iron coal stove abreast the mast. In the larger racers the skippers might have a tiny private cabin and toilet, though more normally all hands used the draw bucket or, in secluded anchorages with the owner away, the main chains.

Deck fittings were simple; a handspike windlass barrel handled the chain cable and two stocked anchors were catted and stowed at the forward rail; but were stowed on the ballast in the bilge, when racing, along with the windlass barrel.

A substantial dinghy stowed on deck amidships or in davits. On larger racers a small cutter might also be slung in davits, but was, of course, not carried when racing. Sheet leads were carefully arranged, with tackle for their handling.

Tillers were of moderate length as most of these craft were well trimmed and balanced, except when really hard pressed, when the tiller tackles kept control.

Constructional lightness was appreciated as being desirable for speed but was not sacrificed to durability, and the "Avalon" and her contemporaries lasted for thirty to forty years as useful yachts, and often later as pilot boats and cargo carriers.

The arrangements and proportions of her rig typify British cutters from 1850 to 1885 as, while designers strove to improve hull form, construction and ballasting, sail plan design remained relatively stagnant. These yachts could be, and were, raced in very hard weather, when topmasts were usually housed and lower sails reefed and shifted. However, they sometimes lost their bowsprits through bursting the bobstay and occasionally topmasts were carried away; both usually from pitching in a sea.

A topsail bowline was another now forgotten piece of racing gear used in the 1840's and early 1850's; set up from the bowsprit end, it tautened the luff of the large, square headed gaff topsails.

By the 1870's materials were available to heighten rigs and steel wire came into general use for standing rigging, but change came slowly in the cutter rig.

Sails improved in cut and quality. The leading yacht sailmakers were Messrs. Lapthorn of Gosport and Charles Ratsey of Cowes, who advocated use of cotton sailcloth in Britain for many years until its superiority over flax in racing efficiency was at last recognised in the 1880's and it became universal until the 1950's.

Racers' bottoms were usually coppered and kept well burnished at every opportunity, but some skippers preferred to coat them with blacklead, which was polished before an important race.

In such craft our great-grandfathers displayed their seamanship or took their ease, depending on their position, and they seem to have enjoyed themselves much as we do now.

Space permits only an outline of racing history and, as with all racing yachts up to 1939, full credit for their success should be given to their professional captains and crews whose considerable skill, judgement and determination often made the reputations of yacht designers and builders. Captains and crews from the river Colne were prominent in racing throughout the period and the skill of skippers from Rowhedge, Brightlingsea, Wivenhoe and later Tollesbury, on the nearby river Blackwater, was pitted against rivals from Itchen, Gosport, Hythe and Cowes and other Solent ports; and others from Largs, Gourock and Port Bannantyne on the river Clyde. The Essex men found their winter living sailing their smacks, fishing all round the British isles, North Sea and Channel; breeding fine seamen skilled in helmsmanship at close quarters and the subtle handling of fore and aft craft. Racing captains rose solely by merit in a hard school and were in complete charge of these often huge racers, which might have crews of up to 35 hands. Although the crews were poorly paid, substantial money prizes were then won by yachts finishing first, and after the mid-nineteenth century, second and third; and a proportion of this was divided amongst the winning crews as "prize money". Skippers whose command showed a long string of prize flags at the season's end were well rewarded, and many on the Colne built houses and smacks from this source, usually naming them for the yachts whose skilful handling had made possible their construction.

With yachting now an almost all amateur sport it is hard to realise its social structure before 1939. "Fancy paying men to enjoy your sailing for you!" mused a retired Row-hedge professional who had spent a lifetime racing other people's boats; and certainly it seems that the captains and crews got most of the fun, as well as their living.

The owner's function was to provide money for building, equipping and manning the yacht in the best manner, and his enjoyment was pride of ownership of a smart yacht and, if a racer, in seeing her carry his colours at the topmast head and, hopefully, of seeing her win and having his name inscribed, with that of his craft, on the ornate silver trophies of the time. The yacht owner then was in the position of the present-day racehorse owner who is not expected to have the ability to ride the horse carrying his colours, and would probably look foolish if he tried.

Racing yachts starting from buoys for a Queen's Cup 1852. Headsails lowered, mainsails and topsails set. A common method of starting until the 1870's.

An owner required considerable means to stand the heavy cost of maintaining a first rate racing yacht, whose huge sail area frequently broke spars and gear in hard weather.

Each winter several racers were altered and, sometimes, completely rebuilt. Recoppering bottoms to achieve a smooth finish was frequent and often whole sail plans were scrapped after a season's use to obtain some desired improvement or rule advantage. All this could be afforded in those days of small wages, great skill and hard work, but its present cost would be immense, and even then comparatively few could or would indulge in this expensive pastime.

Many owners of 20 tonners and above were unable to be aboard during every race and some had no wish to do so. These had an owner's representative sailing aboard, usually a wealthy friend who maintained the owner's social contacts in his absence, and corresponded with him. The captain had sole charge of the yacht, her crew, and the yacht's condition and business. His opinion was respected by the owner who employed him for his ability and, in racing, the tactics and handling were his. Many skippers entered a yacht for a race on their own responsibility, in the owner's absence, emphasising the excellent relationship usually existing between them, and in some cases they became friends, in the formal manner then dictated by their differing backgrounds.

In winter the yacht laid up in a yard at or near the skipper's home, in the three principal areas of the Colne, Solent or Clyde. The captain, and often the mate in large yachts, were on a retaining payment during the winter, but unlike the skippers of cruising yachts, successful racing captains frequently changed yachts and owners, spurred on by the prospects of improved craft and the possibility of increased prize money.

Mid-Victorian racing skippers were versatile seamen; one month they would be delighting the crowds at Harwich, Cowes, or Kingstown, the next might find them racing Russian Archdukes in a Baltic regatta, as in 1852 when seven English yachts, several with Colne crews, sailed out to race at Cronsdat regatta, where warships acted as markboats on the 106 mile sea course. There was then little distinction between inshore and offshore racing; skippers and crews had to take both in their stride without fuss.

These old skippers had a very liberal interpretation of the racing rules and were especially fond of "false tacking", to force a yacht covering them to windward, to tack. The skipper sang out "Ready about!" loud enough to be heard aboard his opponent, and eased the helm down, just shooting head to wind while hands hauled up the fore sheet and took in the slack of the jib sheet. As the windward yacht put about the cunning one bore away again with a clear wind. Another favourite trick was for the yacht prevented from passing a competitor by luffing, to edge down until the bowsprit end was close aboard her rival; the mighty spar almost level with the helmsman's head, sometimes for minutes at a time, while the great cutters rumbled and frothed along at perhaps nine knots. Not a word was exchanged nor an eyelid batted in the test of nerves. All these and many more racing tricks were accepted as part of the game, unless any part of the yachts, or their rigging, touched the other, when both skippers protested, on principle!

Preparedness and seamanship were tested before the start until the 1870s when most sailing races started from buoys or anchors, which were slipped at gunfire. Usually the yachts started with after canvas hoisted but sometimes with everything lowered. The yacht was fast to the buoy by a rope and could give herself a cast to suit the wind by means of a spring from the buoy to her quarter. The gun brought feverish activity; the skipper gave her a sheer with the helm while the mate cast off the buoy rope, forward, and hoisted the jib, helped by a hand. Simultaneously two hands each tailed on to the staysail and throat and peak halyards, while the racing pilot, stationed on the counter, gave her a hearty heave ahead before slipping the spring from the quarter where, if it fouled, he cut it with the axe always kept handy in the companion hatch. A start before the wind under these conditions would cause confusion but usually all went clear. If a foul occurred there was great temptation to set about an opponent's rigging with the ever handy axe; and windlass handspikes were sometimes used to subdue a rival crew. Before the rules were amended, extra hands were engaged as "canvas hoisters" who, when everything was set, were bundled off in a boat to avoid overcrowding.

Gradually the anchored or buoyed start was superseded by the method of starting under weigh, with flags and ten, five minute and starting guns, which we use today. When introduced during the 1860's it was known as the "flying start" and was regarded as rather exciting, usually with good reason! In its early enthusiasm, tactics before the gun included coming about so the bowsprit end swept over a rival's stern, threatening his after hands and confusing the helmsman. Alternatively, the boom end could be gybed over, to a nicety, with terrifying effect as it whipped over a competitor's counter; all quite within the rules of course and without a word exchanged.

Sometimes a hard pressed racer sailed straight for the markboat, clearing her by inches at the last moment; a manoeuvre which usually caused panicked veering of chain by the markboat, resulting in a gain of precious seconds by the brazen racer. Sometimes the markboats had their revenge. At Margate regatta in 1852, Captain George Pittuck in the "Volante" was doing well against the larger "Marina" until it fell calm. When the breeze returned all the markboats had vanished because it was dinner time! What the exasperated crews thought of the race committee is not recorded, but the skippers boiled over when the race was ordered to be resailed.

Fortunately, most coastal regattas were better managed and all seem to have been carried through in a robustly cheerful atmosphere, with the visiting crack yachts providing the spectacle (and taking most of the prize money), while participation by local working craft, pulling races and other watersports, followed by a ball, made it a good day out for all, reminiscent of a present day West Mersea or Bursledon regatta.

The racing was keen, but good sense and seamanship usually prevailed. When the cutter "War Hawk", brand new and pride of the west country, was dismasted at Plymouth, Captain Pittuck, in the "Volante", gave up the race to tow his disabled rival into port under sail. When the race was resailed "Volante" was matched against the larger, iron hulled "Mosquito" in a four round, fifty mile course off Plymouth in a full gale. These old cutters displayed their speed and seamanship by slogging round under housed topmasts and single reefed mainsails in 4¼ hours; "Volante" only losing by 3 minutes, 8 seconds.

Captain George Pittuck of Wivenhoe was a noted mid-19th century racing captain who sailed the Harvey-built 48 ton cutter "Volante" against the schooner "America" in the historic 1851 race around the Isle of Wight for the cup which has since become famous as the "America's Cup". "Volante" was lying second to the "America" (which

Colne-crewed racing yachts running under squaresails, 1852. The Harvey-built *Thought* and *Avalon*, at Lowestoft regatta.   *Radio Times Hulton Picture Library*

had sailed a shorter course due to faulty instructions) when the yacht "Freak" collided with her, springing "Volante's" bowsprit and causing her to give up. The big cutter "Arrow" was fast coming up astern but got ashore, where the equally big "Alarm" stood by her, allowing the "America" to win. Even so she only finished 21 minutes ahead of the 47 ton cutter "Aurora," and as there was then no time allowance for difference in size, the 170 ton "America" won the cup.

English yachtsmen were naturally annoyed at her victory but could not forsee that the cup would be instituted as an international challenge trophy for which millions would be spent in futile efforts to regain it, and many more in its determined defence. However, the radical difference in design and rig between the "America" and the English yachts caused a flurry of imitation, in orders for new yachts and rebuilding of old.

Two years later another American racer arrived at Cowes, the New York Yacht Club sloop "Sylvie", a 205 ton centreboarder designed by George Steers on more radical lines than his "America". She was allegedly the fastest yacht afloat and her owner, Louis Depeau, challenged any English racer for "any amount of money or for the honour of the American flag". He got his wish. The "Sylvie" sailed well against three English yachts and a Swede, but was soundly beaten by the cutter "Julia" sailed by Captain John Nicholls of Southampton and returned home with little more being heard of her.

After the "America's" visit schooner rig became fashionable for racing in Britain. Many were built and some cutters, including the giant "Alarm", were converted to the rig. The Brightlingsea manned "Gloriana",* nicknamed the "champagne bottle" because of her lean bow and full stern, won a Queen's Cup in 1853 and 1856, beating the East Coast manned "Shark" and the Solent-crewed "Lallh Rookh" by 5 seconds over a 40 mile course. These schooners still carried standing bowsprits and jib-booms and when the 59 ton "Wildfire" came out in 1855 with a running bowsprit and a cutter's plumb stem, she was christened the "cutter rigged schooner", Captain John Herbert of Brightlingsea raced her with such spirit that, besides beating the schooners, she also outsailed the cutters. Amongst his crew was young Tom Diaper of Itchen, second of the name, who later also became a noted racing skipper.

Having taken the Harvey 25 tonner "Thought" to the top of the second class cutters, Captain George Pittuck also had a crack at the schooners with the 77 foot, Inman-built "Vestal", which was very successful with a Wivenhoe crew, and for a time these small schooners were fashionable.

In 1857 there were 780 British yachts, totalling 30,000 tons; including 511 cutters, 138 schooners, 75 yawls, and 37 "other rigs"; but there were only 19 steam yachts. By then most racing yachts were generally rated for racing by the Thames tonnage rule which had been introduced by the Royal Thames yacht club in 1854 and lingers on

*Glorianna was sailed by Captain James Major of Brightlingsea.

today amongst English yachtsmen, though it was outmoded for racing in 1878! In this, only length on deck from stem to sternpost, and the beam, were factors, and as beam was penalised twice in the formula and depth was not considered, builders were gradually forced to reduce beam and increase draught to compensate. Generally this was against their better judgement as they preferred craft of more moderate breadth, depth and ballasting. However, as racing became keener, sail areas, depth and length increased and lead became general for inside ballast. However, apart from a small iron shoe along the keel, racers and cruisers still carried their ballast inside and for racing about one third of the total was carried as bags of shot which were shifted to the weather side at each tack by hands who remained below throughout the race, trimming to orders shouted through the hatchway. At each tack they piled the bags behind retaining boards in each bilge of the stripped cabin.

Shifting ballast was greatly disliked but was practised by all the racers of that period which still had a fairly firm bilge to obtain a lever for its use, but there were some accidents. In 1856 one of the Colne yacht skippers' greatest rivals was Captain William Penny of Southampton, skipper of the cutter "Glance", built by Dan Hatcher in the previous year. At Kingstown regatta her rivals included the new Fife built cutter "Cymba" whose Scotch crew the Southampton men particularly wished to beat. The "Glance" won on both days but her crew became so excited that, in gybing round the last mark, they forgot to shift the shot bag ballast and the 60 footer almost capsized, showing all her keel clear of the water when the boom went over and pitching three of her crew clean overboard, to be picked up by a Brightlingsea-manned competitor, while she went on to win.

In 1860 the "Glance" was bought by a Mr. Duncan, a keen racing owner who secured Captain John Downes of Brightlingsea to race her. Downes was a smart young skipper and the "Glance" commenced a series of victories beating, besides her own class, the largest and fastest cutters of the day. Wherever a regatta was held or a cup was to be raced for during the next two years, she was successful, but did little for three years following. In 1865 she changed owners and Captain George Bartlett of Wivenhoe took the helm to continue her racing career.

Shifting ballast was banned after 1856 but the English cutter yacht continued to develop as a narrow, deep draught, plum bowed craft having a counter stern; oversparred and overcanvassed for heavy weather, wet in a seaway, but able to beat to windward through almost anything providing she was properly reefed and the crew could stand it and stay aboard. As the Thames tonnage rule disregarded sail area altogether the powerful and versatile cutter rig flourished and attained excessive area. The legend of this exaggerated type of cutter yacht has persisted and is often, wrongly, regarded as the only true breed. Outclassed racing yachts became useful cruisers with sail plans reduced and sometimes made seaworthy pilot and fishing craft. However, the contrast with working cutters designed and built by contemporary yachtbuilders is interesting, as in them was retained the healthy beam and other proportions which the rule denied the racers.

At Brightlingsea Robert Aldous built many fast cutters of both types and became noted by the windward ability of the 9 ton racer "Violet" of 1855. Three years later he built another "Violet" which, renamed "Christabel", became the most famous of his racing yachts and her story is told in chapter 20.

The small racers flourished, especially the 5 ton class which the Fife-built "Pearl" and "Torment" ruled until they were beaten by the Thames fishing smack "Arrow", which proved so fast in the shrimping trade that she was sold for a yacht, rerigged and entered the class to beat soundly the yacht designers' creations, as the Liverpool shrimper "Wonderful" was to do with the 10 tonners twenty years later.

In 1861 the 9 ton cutter "Bessie", built by John Harvey for J. Hedge, won the Prince of Wales' Cup in the Thames and was champion of the small class for a time.

Until 1865 racing cutters when running set a squaresail with a triangular raffee topsail above. That year Dan Hatcher of Southampton built the cutter "Niobe" for William Gordon, whose skipper was Captain Thomas Diaper (senior), of Itchen. Between them they devised a triangular running sail to be set from the masthead, with its clew boomed out in the manner which headsails had been boomed out for years before, except in racers, where their sheets had to be held by hand. Having tried it outside the Needles the "Niobe" first set it racing on the Thames against the cutter "Vindex", beating her by its efficiency when running. The sail became known as the "Niobe" and was called by this name in the racing fleet for two or three years until the yacht clubs wanted a different name for it and for no explicable reason, despite its later use in the racing cutter "Sphinx", it was called a "spinnaker" and has remained so.

Until 1860 racing schooners' masts raked aft, their crews reckoning it improved the lift of sails. That year Camper and Nicholson of Gosport launched the 216 ton "Aline" with plumb masts and a running bowsprit. Captain Pike of Southampton took charge with a picked crew and she was the fastest schooner afloat for five seasons until Wanhill's of Poole built the beautiful 153 ton "Egeria", perhaps the most graceful of all racers, sailed by Captain John Woods of Brightlingsea, who later moved to Southampton and was a noted racing skipper of the 'sixties and 'seventies. In 1861, aged 24, he was appointed captain of the 175 ton schooner "Shark" and left her for the "Egeria" which he first brought to the line for the Queen's Cup at Cowes against the "Aline", "Aquiline" and "Albertine", with Colne crews; and the Solent manned "Galatea," "Viking" and "Pantomime". What a sight they must have been in the confined waters between Lymington and the Nab. The power and grace of schooner rig emphasised by the thundering quarter waves and shouts of the thirty men crews getting in the main-sheets. Throughout, Captain Woods made it a personal struggle with Captain Pike and the rest were nowhere as the rivals tore through Cowes roads, boom to boom, with

Captain I. H. French of Brightlingsea. A racing skipper of the 1880's.

giant squaresails urging their black hulls towards the Squadron line which "Egeria" crossed seconds before the "Aline", to establish a supremacy she held for many years.

She won six Queen's Cups and the Prince of Wales' Cup three times, from Cowes, round the Shambles light vessel, outside the Wight, round the Nab and back to Cowes, about 130 miles; once sailed in a fog so thick that the yachts did not sight each other after the start. "Egeria" set a spinnaker from each mast, as she often did, and a guest complained of danger of collision, to which John Woods snapped "We might as well get run down with two spinnakers as with one."

In 1869 the schooners raced from Cherbourg, round the Nab and back for a cup given by the Emperor Napoleon. The American schooner "Dauntless" entered against the English "Gwenivere," "Shark", "Egeria" and the French schooners "Mystere" and "Dione". John Woods beat the "Dauntless" but could not get by the stately "Gwenivere", sailed by Captain Mildhall of St. Helens and a crew of "corkheads", as the Colne men described their rivals from the Isle of Wight; "Gwenivere" won.

Captain Woods' hardest race was off the Irish coast where the "Egeria" raced against the Irish yawl "Enid" over a fifty mile course in a gale of wind, starting off

Kingstown. The big schooner was leading, hard on the wind, when the strop of her mainsheet burst and the mainboom flew to leeward, where the lee runner broke it like a pipe stem. For a short time the schooner became almost unmanageable and John Woods thought he would lose her. Green seas broke over the foc'sle head in tons, before the 5,000 square foot mainsail, which was thrashing about with its broken boom attached, could be subdued and the schooner headed back for Kingstown under foresail and headsails, while the "Enid" went on to win.

In 1871 John Woods was offered command of the 280 ton schooner "Livonia", built for James Ashbury, a member of the Royal Harwich Yacht Club, as challenger for the America's Cup. Tuning up in the coastal racing before leaving for America, the "Livonia" took part in the Dover to Liverpool race, carrying a double reefed mainsail nearly all the way but beating the 165 ton cutter "Oimara" by 15 hours. She sailed out to America in 24 days and her racing for the cup is described in chapter 14.

The average length of course sailed by racing yachts at that time was 50 to 70 miles. Long distance races were generally disliked by racing captains for the good reason that they felt obliged to be at the tiller throughout and, as Captain John Nicholls said; "Nine hours at the tiller is quite enough to do it properly."

Two incidents from John Woods' career illustrate the pride of these racing captains. In 1872 James Ashbury had the 60 ton cutter "Iona" built by Michael Ratsey of Cowes to designs by Ratsey's chief draughtsman, William Jones, another of yacht design's unknown but brilliant men. She was sailed by John Woods but proved a failure in the Thames matches and returned to Cowes where she was altered to Captain Woods' ideas. Before she could be raced again Ashbury telegraphed for him to fit out the "Livonia" for racing but John Woods tendered his resignation because, as he put it; "I did not like the chance of my reputation being injured by not racing the "Iona" after she had been altered according to my ideas." Leaving his owner on amicable terms he took charge of the big cutter "Kriemhilda" and raced her with success in the South Coast regattas. When she was hauled up for the winter at Southampton the owner, Count Batthyany, told the yard to strip the copper off her bottom for replacement and John Woods resigned as he had not given instructions for it to be done.

He returned to the "Egeria" and continued her success in the great schooner races of the seventies.

The "Iona" passed to the command of Captain George Pittuck of Wivenhoe, with a Colne crew. He had all the copper stripped off her bottom and had it smoothed and blackleaded. He also ordered a ringtail for racing, then an outmoded sail in racing yachts, and set it when running with a watersail below the boom and the spinnaker out to windward. She entered the season with high hopes, but could do little against crack boats such as "Neva" and "Fiona". "Iona" was entered in the Royal Yacht Squadron regatta, starting from buoys off Cowes. Her quarter spring jammed round the cavil but Captain Pittuck laconically ordered; "Don't cut it, clear it; we 'ont do no good against them schooners;" a typical racing skipper's view of the absurdity of racing sixty ton cutters against two hundred ton schooners.

The "Iona" was the unluckiest of racing yachts; she started in 56 races during 1875 and 1876 and though well sailed with the utmost determination by Captain Pittuck, she won only one prize-— a second. In the Harwich to Southend race "Iona" and the other big racers beat into the Thames at night in a thunderstorm and torrential rain with the leads going. The leadsman were calling out false depths loudly in hopes that unwary competitors would stand in too far and get ashore; a practice favoured by the Colne skippers, themselves thoroughly accustomed to wriggling to windward in shallow, confined waters in all weathers. Earlier in this race the Scottish cutter "Fiona" had her jib set upside down, resulting in a sudden explosion of oaths from Captain John Houston when he discovered the cause of her sluggishness.

Captain George Cranfield of Rowhedge was amongst the best racing captains of the 1870-1880 period. His first large command was the 153 ton racing schooner "Pantomime"; a straight stemmed, flat sheered creation of Michael Ratsey of Cowes which he skippered from 1872 until about 1876. In 1873 she beat the great "Egeria" handsomely and was the fastest British schooner. In 1874 she raced the 203 ton, South Coast schooner "Cetonia," sailed by Captain Harry Thompson of Itchen, and the "Egeria" sailed by John Woods, from Gravesend, round the Mouse light and back. At the Mouse "Egeria" luffed the "Pantomime" who was cutting it fine at the mark and George Cranfield responded so quickly that "Pantomime's" lean bow sliced the lightship's stern off. He was a man of lightning judgement and was later captain of the 40 tonner "May" which, in 1881, had a spectacular record all round the coast, where her owner followed her in his steam yacht. He was so proud of the "May's" record that at Rothesay regatta he towed her round Rothesay Bay with all her prize flags flying. Captain Cranfield was very embarrassed by this show but justified her reputation next day in beating the new 40 tonner "Annosona" sailed by Captain William O'Neill, in the hardest race ever seen on the Clyde. As the yachts were going for the Skelmorlie buoy the "May" was close hauled and the "Annasona" was reaching in hope of going through her lee. George Cranfield bore away to cover her but the "Annasona" was going so fast and so close that her weather wash swept the Essexman's deck of everything moveable and her crew had to cling on, but the "May" went on to win.

John Harvey built the "Sea Belle" in 1874 to beat the "Pantomime". At first the "Sea Belle" was sailed by Captain Harry Harlow of Wivenhoe, later by Captain John Downes of Brightlingsea and then by Captain Wadley of Wivenhoe. She was successful but in 1876 John Harvey launched his masterpiece, the 110 ft. racing schooner "Miranda", designed to reach faster than the "Sea Belle". She had a magnificent hull shape with a graceful clipper bow, and set 7,700 square feet of working canvas, with a spinnaker of over 5,000 square feet. Her mainmast was almost amidships and her crew of 15 hands were hard worked when racing. Captain John Downes brought her out and she first raced in 1877, emerging triumphantly as top boat of the big schooner class with 10 prizes worth £540. By 1878 she had spoiled the class for a time and at the Thames matches "Egeria" and "Corinne" refused to sail against her and at Harwich regatta she had to lie at anchor for want of competition. The schooner "Corinne", sailed by Captain Embling of Gosport, beat her twice that season in the Solent, but during Cowes week she beat seven other schooners including the American "Enchantress", and after it she laid up as the schooner class had collapsed. From 1878 to 1881 she was sailed by Captain J. Barnes of Wivenhoe with a village crew, and remained the crack racing schooner, often racing against the cutters for lack of competition. She was to achieve even greater success later.

The period 1850 to 1870 saw the golden age of Wivenhoe's yachtbuilding and manning. During it Harvey's berths were seldom without a racer, large or small, building alongside the dozens of yachts and other craft under construction or repairing there.

Across the river a few yachts then found winter berths at Rowhedge, a village which awaited the great fame its racing yachtsmen were to achieve in later years. Although several early yachtmasters and crews hailed from Rowhedge, it did not fully awaken to the possibilities of racing until about 1865, when its seamen began to seriously challenge the eminent position in racing previously held by crews from Wivenhoe, Brightlingsea, Southampton, Cowes and the Clyde. At the same time Harris Brothers' yard blossomed into great activity and began to rival Harvey's in the number and quality of yachts built and laid up there.

After 1865 the Colne and Solent yachtbuilders had increasingly to reckon with competition from Clyde builders. The first William Fife was a Scottish wheelwright who built rowing boats in his spare time at Fairlie, Ayrshire, on the Firth of Clyde. His boatbuilding prospered and eclipsed his wheelwright trade. He established a yard which built small commercial craft and yachts, principally cutters. Fairlie was a most unpromising site for what became a noted yacht yard. For many years yachts were built in the open on the rocky, shallow foreshore which made launching of anything but small craft very difficult, and the anchorage was exposed.

Fife's son William (II) joined the business bringing a flair for design. The 55 ft. cutter "Cymba", launched from the yard in 1852, won many prizes but young Fife's masterpiece was the "Fiona" of 1865, the most noted cutter of her day when sailed by Captain John Houston of Largs, with a crew of local hands, most of whom, surprisingly, turned to weaving rather than seafaring for a winter living. For a time the "Fiona" turned the tide of south country racing cutters' success and the ability of Fife and other Clyde designers and builders was, paradoxically, to provide great opportunity for a generation of Colne racing skippers and crews.

Wealth was being made in Glasgow's grime and the Clyde's rich men were enthusiastic patrons of yachting, and many were determined to have a crack at the southern fliers, naturally with craft built on the river. Experienced crews were the problem, for most of Scotland's best racing men were manning the "Fiona" and a few other noted racers. National pride was pocketed and word went out to the south. On the Colne there was a young generation impatient to chance or to make their reputations with new yachts and many of those approached entrained for the north, to stand by new racers completing at Fife's, Reid's or Boag's. The debt the names of Fife, Watson, Reid and other Scottish designers owed to these soft spoken Essex men is now mostly forgotten, but was freely acknowledged in their day, when yachting correspondents wrote of the Clyde racers being "manned by smart and powerful English crews".

Captain John Carter was amongst the earliest of the Colne skippers attracted to the Scottish racers. He was born at Wivenhoe in 1850, of a seafaring family, and fished in smacks as a boy before going yachting in summer and fishing in winter, after he was 18 years old. In 1872 he first became master of a yacht and three years later took charge of his first racer; the 10 tonner "Lancer", built two years earlier by William Fife. He showed rare ability at her helm and moved on to another Clyde racer; the 10 tonner "Gondola" built by Boag of Largs. The 10 ton class was a great nursery of young racing captains who were to rise to the top of their calling. In 1876 the "Florence" came out, sailed by Captain Charles Bevis of Bursledon, Hampshire, who came top of the class and was to be a rival of the Colne men for many years. John Carter beat him at Bangor and Kingstown regattas, as these little racers sometimes made long passages for their sport. They had only a captain and two hands as crew, to handle a sail area of 3,000 square feet which drove the deep, lean hulls at amazing speeds on all points of sailing. Their hull proportions were extraordinary and John Carter's next command, the 10 ton "Merle", built by Reid of Port Glasgow, had 7 ft. 9 in. beam on 39 ft. waterline length; an average for the class. She raced principally on the South Coast where the class was strong and amongst her six or seven competitors was the "Chip", sailed by young William Cranfield, and the first racing command of that captain from Rowhedge, where John Carter had settled in 1877.

In 1879 John Carter's ability gained him command of the new 20 tonner "Sayonara", also built by Reid for a Scottish owner. Despite tough opposition from the "Vanessa", sailed by Captain George Cranfield, Carter's near neighbour from Rowhedge, and the "Enriquita", "Louise" and "Viola", the "Sayonara" finished the season with 18 prizes, and was top boat.

In 1881 William Fife built a 110 ton fast cruising cutter named "Moïna" for Robert Stewart and John Carter was offered command. This was a big step forward to a yacht of large size from the 10 tonner of three years previously, but "Moïna" did little racing, which irked her captain, though in her he mastered the handling of a yacht over 100 feet in length, and was competent and delighted when Sir Richard

The 40 rater racing cutter *Deerhound*, 1889. Sailed by Captain Tom Jay of Rowhedge with a Colne crew.

Sutton asked him to become skipper of the 100 foot racing cutter "Genesta", building in D. & W. Henderson's Glasgow yard to the design of J. B. Webb, which was to be the America's Cup challenger in 1885.

The 80 ton "Genesta" was one of John Carter's most successful commands. To meet her, designer Alexander Richardson of Liverpool had produced the big "Irex", sailed by Captain O'Neill, and the 60 ton "Marguerite". They were joined by the 68 ton "Marjorie", sailed by Scottish Captain Robert Duncan. The big cutters had a wonderful season racing around the coast, and on the Clyde their numbers increased to nine, making a splendid sight with the hills as background to the Firth, whipped by a fresh breeze, the lower canvas drenched with spray and the lean black hulls glistening as they pitched away to windward throwing out their burnished copper with an easy motion to the drive of the great sails.

John Carter used the 1884 season to get "Genesta" and her crew thoroughly tuned up for the American adventure next year. They were Colne men, almost all from Rowhedge and Wivenhoe, under Charles Pudney the mate, who started life as an orphan smack's boy and finished as captain of the 160 ton yawl "Maud". John Carter's attempt for the America's Cup, with the "Genesta", and his subsequent distinguished racing career will follow.

There was tremendous enthusiasm for racing during the 1870's, when there were commonly 10 or 12 starters in the larger classes; cutters, yawls and schooners of from 60 - 200 tons, and sometimes there were 15 or 20 racing flags aloft on a summer's morning, besides increasing numbers in the small classes which had again achieved importance.

The old style racing season around the coast was a crowded one. "Hunt's Magazine" commented on that of 1879; "..the season proper will not commence until the 30th May, when the Royal London Yacht Club sails its matches for cutters. From that date until the very end of August, every day will be occupied with racing, and anyone so inclined will be able to race his yacht almost every day during these three months, except when making a passage from one port to another. With so many clubs to give regattas it is quite impossible to arrange the various fixtures so that there should be no clashing..." Of course there was then no racing on Sundays.

The tradition of the British racing yachts competing at regattas all round the coast had its origins in the late 1840's and by the 1870's was very firmly established custom. Commencing with the Thames matches in May the racers, from 10 tons upwards, worked their way through a full programme; the Down Swin; Harwich regatta; the Up Swin; Nore to Dover; Dover/Ostende; Dover/Calais; racing in the Solent; a passage round Land's End and up the Irish Sea to Liverpool; Barrow; the Clyde fortnight; back via Belfast; Kingstown; Bangor; a long passage to Le Havre; more Solent racing; Cowes week; Weymouth; Torbay and Dartmouth, which usually finished the season. As their passage making was all under sail the yachts covered several thousand miles each summer and often had hard driving to arrive on time at some fixtures.

When racing in other than familiar waters, captains often took a 'racing pilot', usually a reliable local fisherman or perhaps a yacht captain, noted for his exact and comprehensive knowledge of depths, shoals, tides and local weather and winds; which might all be used to advantage when racing. Such men were thoroughly accustomed to racing yachts, and captains frequently used the same pilots each year in various localities, paying a fee for days' use of their knowledge.

The keeness of racing crews and the thoughts of prize money caused many incidents not covered by the rules. An 1874 Queen's Cup race was sailed in a strong breeze and the yachts racing included the crack Solent cutter "Kriemhilda" sailed by Captain Tom Diaper of Itchen and the old, rebuilt, 200 ton schooner "Shark", sailed by Captain Hayward with a Brightlingsea crew. By some fluke the old "Shark" was ahead when the "Kriemhilda" fouled her rigging in gybing, with damage to both yachts. The Brightlingseamen, rather astonished at being up with a crack boat, waved their caps and cheered ironically, at which one of "Kriemhilda's" Itchen hands angrily shouted; "How the hell did you ever get here to get in our way."

At the New Thames Yacht Club matches that season the racers assembled to start under the club's new rating rule, but the skippers and owners felt it was unfair and the cutters remained at anchor after the gun fired. When the gun for schooners went all remained at anchor except the Solent-manned "Cetonia" which "sailed over" the course for the prize, permitted by the rules but bringing derisive cheers from the Essexmen.

In 1874 the racing yachts won prizes totalling £13,264. Several of these were "sail overs" caused by yachts arriving at a coastal regatta, perhaps after a hard passage, only to find they were the only starter in their class. So they "sailed over" for the prize money; a practice which offended all hands, truly sporting desire for a race, but helped the end of season share out for the crew, which made yacht racing the most profitable aspect of the Colne's seafaring.

The practice still exists; in the 1970 'C' class International catamaran week, at Sheppey, the new "Snark II" 'sailed over' when her competitors failed to appear for the start.

Occasionally the racers had almost to fight for the prize. Captain Tom Knights of Rowhedge sailed the aptly named "Rival". In the 1874 Royal Clyde Yacht club regatta she was lying second to the Scottish "Ildegonda" who luffed the "Rival" almost ashore. Tom Knights put his bowsprit over the "Ildegonda's" weather quarter, where it fouled her warp chock and one of her crew cut the "Rival's" bobstay tackle and disabled her. The "Ildegonda" was disqualified and the prize went to the "Queen", which being a south coast manned cutter, enraged both crews.

In a Thames race of 1878 the schooner "Egeria", sailed by John Woods of Brightlingsea, met the new Scottish schooner "Fiona", sailed by Captain John Houston, on the starboard tack. The Scotchman hailed Woods to come about but the Brightling-seaman replied that he had just done so for lack of water; so Houston held on and rammed the "Egeria" amidships, smashing her bulwarks and jamming his bowsprit into her mainsail.

Occasionally the fouls were intentional; as when the cutter "Fanny" on the starboard tack met the French cutter "Zephyr" on port. At the time the "Fanny's" bowsprit-endsman was stowing the jib-topsail and, as the "Zephyr" refused to give way, the "Fanny" ran her bowsprit into her mainsail which, being light canvas, burst, and the bowsprit passed clean through it, bowsprit-endsman and all; completely demoralising the Frenchmen, who gave up.

Captain Ben Harris of Rowhedge was one of the most brilliant young skippers of that time. In 1875 he was sailing the 20 tonner "Clown" in the handicap classes, with a crew of four hands from the village. Amongst his keenest competitors was Captain Thomas Angier of Brightlingsea sailing the 35 ton yawl "Isabel".

The 1870s brought a craze for yawls, and the entry of cruisers in occasional races. In 1875 the plucky 42 ton "Surf", sailed by Captain Mason of Wivenhoe, won the New Thames yacht club match for yawls against three competitors, including the 128 ton "Dauntless", skippered by Captain James Ham of Wivenhoe and the 33 ton, Aldous-built "Mignonette", sailed by Captain Coppin of Brightlingsea. "Surf" finished only 8 minutes after the big "Dauntless" to win the hundred sovereigns prize on handicap. As she crossed the line and passed through the fleet she was loudly cheered for, as an observer wrote, "No yacht was ever better sailed". These Thames courses were generally from Gravesend, round the Mouse and back and could provide keen racing. A few weeks afterwards the schooner "Egeria" and the Harvey built "Sea Belle", sailed by Captain Wadley of Wivenhoe, raced that course in a gale. They started with double reefed mainsails, reefed foresails and staysails, second jibs, and "Sea Belle" had her bowsprit run part way in. The skippers agreed to stay round the Mouse rather than gybe, a seamanlike precaution, and covered the course in 5 hours 23 minutes.

In the Royal Yorkshire regatta off the Humber, the 88 ton yawl "Rosabelle," newly built at John Harvey's Wivenhoe yard and sailed by Captain Harry Harlow with a Wivenhoe crew, raced the "Christabel" sailed by his neighbour, Captain Forsgate. "Rosabelle" broke her topmast in a squall but, undaunted, they replaced it with the spinnaker boom, lashed aloft, and went on to win.

During 1878 Captain George Pittuck sailed the Ratsey-built yawl "Lufra" which dwarfed the rest of the class with her 222 ton, 130 foot hull; but by then time allowance had been adopted and she did not win a prize all season, although splendidly sailed.

The 110 foot "Jullanar", sailed by Captain John Downes of Brightlingsea, was the most spectacular yawl of that time and her origins are described in chapter 18. She won 12 prizes worth £795 during 1877, which was her first racing season, and next year had amazing success, despite hard racing against the big yawls "Ada" and the new Scottish "Condor", sailed by Captain William Mackie. The "Jullanar" came back into Colne in September almost dressed overall with prize flags and her crew well pleased with the £1,065 prize money they had won. Her owner, A. D. Macleay, was

The Royal Thames Yacht Club race from the Thames to Harwich, 1865. The yachts between the Kentish Knock and Sunk. The Solent *Alarm* leading, with the Wivenhoe crewed *Xanthe* second.

Radio Times Hulton Picture Library

delighted at her having beaten the big yawl "Florinda", for long cock of the class, sailed by Captain George Couzens of Weston and pride of the Solent.

The 40 ton class provided the closest racing during the 1870's and one of the crack boats was the "Coryphée", built by Reid of Glasgow and sailed by Captain Tom Aingier of Brightlingsea, with a village crew. Her greatest rival was the "Myosotis", sailed by Captain William O'Neill from Kingstown, Ireland, with a crew from Itchen, where he had settled. They raced round the coast and, at Liverpool, "Myosotis" was leading the class when her peak halyards carried away allowing the "Coryphée" to take the lead. She re-set her main and chased the "Coryphée", almost catching her, when a tug towing a ship came across the yachts' bows. Captain Aingier bore away under the ship's stern but O'Neill hailed the tug to stop, which she did and as the towrope slacked down the "Myosotis" sailed over it, between the tug and ship, and emerged to windward of the "Coryphée" to win the race.

Captain O'Neill was a character amongst the racing fleet and handled his craft in unorthodox fashion. When the newly built 40 tonner "Coralie", manned by a Rowhedge crew, raced O'Neill in the "Myosotis" and Captain Ben Harris of Itchen in the "Bloodhound" at the Thames matches of 1877, O'Neill fell overboard while the spinnaker was being set. He could not swim, but the committee steamer hailed the "Myosotis" with "Carry on, we'll pick him up"; to which the mate replied; "We can't go on, he's our captain!"; which brought cheers from the "Coralie" as she roared past.

In 1878, tonnage length was measured on the waterline and plumb stems were gradually replaced by graceful clipper bows. Of course there was at first great controversy over these "ugly" bows, and more because the proportions of length to breadth became even more freakish after another rule amendment in 1881. The 5 ton "Oona", built at Wivenhoe in 1886 was the most tragic racing yacht ever built; designed by talented, 25 year old William Payton, she had only 5 ft. 6 in. beam on a 33 ft. 10 in. waterline, yet drew 8 ft. Her displacement was 12.5 tons of which her lead keel was 9.6 tons and construction was very light and strong with double-skin planking on steel frames. She set 2,000 square feet of working canvas and sailed from Southampton for the Clyde manned by an experienced skipper, two hands, her owner and the designer. Leaving Kingstown, Ireland, she met with a heavy gale, was apparently embayed off Malahide, and attempted to beat offshore under a trysail which burst and she drove ashore, where the hull was torn from the keel and all hands drowned.

By 1881 there were 2000 British yachts afloat, having a gross tonnage of 100,000 and were worth £4,000,000, with owners spending threequarters of a million annually on maintenance and employing 6000 hands who were reckoned "the smartest seamen in the country". That season the racers competed for prizes valued at £12,000, and the big new Scotch cutter "Vanduara", sailed by Captain William Mackie, was a great rival of the Colnesiders. Racing off Belfast she tried to pass to windward of the 80 footer "Daphne", sailed by Captain John Cranfield of Rowhedge, who prevented her passing by luffing. By then the "Vanduara" was so far on "Daphne's" weather quarter that she not only could not pass her to weather, but could not bear away under her stern. Meanwhile the other two competitors were slipping away through their lee and the Colnesiders, who had no chance of a prize anyway, thought this a joke. Mackie, with a brand new boat to justify, was furious. After exhausting his vocabulary he danced with rage and finished by taking off both shoes and hurling them at his crew!

Like many of his Colneside contemporaries John Cranfield made his name in the 10 ton class; racing the Sherlock-built "Lily" all around the coast regattas with tremendous success during 1877, and building a new smack, also named "Lily", from his share of the prize money.

The "Lily's" most remarkable performance was in the race from Liverpool to Llandudno when she beat the 20 tonners "Ivanhoe" and the "Playmate" sailed by Captain Jack Wyatt of Hythe, without calling on her handicap allowance.

Two years later he jumped up to command the "Quickstep" in the 20 ton class, with a string of prize flags at the season's end, and from her he went on to the racing-cruiser "Daphne", a 61 ton yawl built on the Clyde by Elder and Co., but returned to the sporting 20 ton class with the "Amethea" of 1883, whose Lymington skipper could do nothing with her, but John soon put her into trim and in the prize lists.

John Cranfield was one of five brothers who made a tremendous reputation in yacht racing. Their father was a Rowhedge mariner; a fisherman owning his own smack, who probably also skippered yachts, but the great racing ability of the brothers reputedly stemmed from the youthful teachings of Lemon, the eldest who, with William and John, was the best known. Steven raced less than his brothers and skippered the Harvey-built 49 ton cutter "Syren" whilst Richard, the youngest, was to get his big chance with the 20 rater "Dierdre" in 1893. All of them owned smacks and fished in winter; after William and John's racing success brought prosperity in the 1890's, they often preferred their smacks to be worked by relatives.

It is interesting to follow the career of Lemon who in 1872 was appointed captain of the new 10 ton racer "Cloud", built by Boag of Fairlie. The lanky young Essexman raced her with such success that two years later he was selected to race the 62 ton cutter "Neva" which had been laid down by Fife as a speculation and was bought on the stocks by Mr. Holmes Kerr, who was determined to challenge the big class with this 68 ft. waterline cutter which had a beautifully formed hull. Lemon Cranfield brought a crew of fellow Rowhedgers with him and they made her name a legend for speed all round the coast, winning £610 prize money that season.

Captain Cranfield sailed the "Neva" for Holmes Kerr until he sold her to Mr. Borwick in 1877. During 1875 she started in 20 races, winning 11 prizes worth £495.

"Neva's" winning of the £100 prize in the Royal London race from Erith, round the Nore and return, was typical of Lemon Cranfield's tactics. She started from anchor against the cutter "Cuckoo", sailed by Captain Jack Wyatt from Hythe, and the cutter "Fiona", the pride of the Clyde, sailed by Captain John Houston of Largs. Nearing the outer mark, with "Fiona" leading, Lemon saw that the Scotchman was inside him and would emerge to windward after they rounded so he ordered 'in spinnaker" and checked his sheets, to cross her stern and cut fine inside her at the mark, emerging ahead to have a great race back, averaging 7 knots. John Houston could not get past "Neva" to windward and, as an observer put it; "To get through her lee was a task that few vessels could have successfully performed".

A typical example of a racing yacht's passage making is given by Captain Lemon Cranfield's log of the "Neva", on passage from the Clyde to Rowhedge in 1875 to lay up. "September 30th. This afternoon at 3h. p.m. we left Largs and anchored at Lamlash for the night. Next morning (Friday) we got under weigh at 6h. a.m. with a single reef in mainsail, the weather being fine, with a fine sailing breeze from S.W. About five in the afternoon the wind began to be squally and we stowed the mainsail and set trysail, having even then plenty of sail in the heavy gusts. Off the Copelands, which we passed at about 7h. p.m. the sea was running high, and as the wind was dead ahead, the prospects for the night were far from cheering, so we bore up and ran for Bangor, Belfast Lough, where we let go anchor at 9h. p.m. During the night the weather continued squally, but Saturday morning broke fine and at 6h. a.m. we again got under weigh with one reef tied. The wind was west by south and the sea was trying and nasty, but we made good headway. However, the wind freshened again and a strong squall coming down off the Mourne mountains, struck our little vessel so hard that we had to haul down staysail and slack away the mainsheet to ease her. This lasted only a short time and we went on allright until mid-day, when we were off Carlingford Lough. Here a tremendous squall struck us and we had to lower both staysail and mainsail. Fortunately, the wind was more northerley and so we bore up and ran for it, the wind was threatening to take the bowsprit away at every gust, as we had our second jib set. This lasted for about an hour, when it calmed down and we again got our main sail set, and kept on our proper course, steering about southwest. We made Baily light at sunset, and as the weather looked better made for Wicklow head, anchoring under the shelter of the headland. The glass, however, was still going down, gave warning of dirty weather, so we got under weigh again on Sunday about noon and ran to Kingstown, where we remained until Tuesday at 10 a.m. when, seeing the schooner "Leonora", 117 tons, bound for Gosport, leave the harbour, we got under weigh with trysail and snug headsail set. The wind being west by north was favourable, but when we got off Arklow it looked squally and threatening, and we had to stow our staysail, and so we put in there for the night. Next morning the glass was rising, so we got our anchor up and made a start, the "Leonora", which had also come to for shelter, doing the same. The wind was blowing fresh from W.N.W., and with trysail, reefed staysail and small jib, we kept going, although the heavy sea then running gave us plenty to do in nursing the little vessel, and had it not been for the glass rising we would have gone back again.

Two hours after starting we lost sight of the schooner astern, which had not apparently been making very good weather of it. Our little vessel was going along like a duck, shipping scarcely any water and proving herself a grand sea boat, and keeping up a steady nine knots to Lands End. All Thursday we had a fine breeze and setting mainsail off the Lizards at 4h. a.m. sailed well all day until noon, when the wind came away from W.S.W., and we set balloon-jib on a spinnaker boom and got a small topsail aloft, running about four or five knots an hour, until about 3h. a.m., on Friday, when the wind got more southerley, and our balloon-jib had to come in, and we got our sheets aboard. We were off the Isle of Wight about 7h. a.m. next morning, and as the weather looked threatening, and began to be squally, we got a reef down in the mainsail. The weather cleared again, however, so we set balloon staysail, and with a clear sky, bright

The 110ft. racing schooner *Miranda*, designed and built by John Harvey of Wivenhoe, 1876. The fastest British racing schooner until 1884.

sun, and the kind of breeze we wanted so much and so often during the racing season, we ploughed along merrily, the old ship seeming to be in a hurry to get to her winters resting place after her long summers work. At a rattling pace we came up channel, passing Ramsgate at 7h. p.m., when we reduced sail, having plenty of time to take the Colne with daylight. On Saturday morning, about nine o'clock, we got to the end of our voyage and as we came up to our winter quarters with our ten racing flags flying, we received many hearty cheers. Considering the bad weather we had nearly all the way, our passage was not by any means a slow one, and we were greatly pleased with the way the "Neva" behaved in such heavy seas and strong gales as we experienced during part of the time. It is fortunate, however, that yachts do not encounter such weather during the racing season, as the little ones, such as the ten and twenty tonners at least, would hardly be able to make passages from one regatta to the other. The "Neva" is to be hauled up high and dry and will have her copper stripped off, and be thoroughly dried for next years campaign." In considering this passage we should remember that the racing season being over, there was little urgency in arriving to lay up, in great contrast to passages made in the racing season, and that the careful preservation of spars and sails was of consequence as there was no good excuse for carrying on.

At Rothesay in 1876 the "Neva" raced the "Cuckoo", sailed by Captain Jack Wyatt of Hythe, with a Hampshire crew, and beat her by one second; Lemon using his wonderful judgement in tacking exactly to fetch the mark, within a foot.

That season she won 13 prizes in 21 starts, worth £885, and from his share as captain Lemon ordered a new cutter smack from Harris at Rowhedge. She was launched as the "Neva" and became as famous as her namesake by dominating the Essex smack races for thirty years, and was Lemon's special pride.

During 1877 he drove the "Neva" to fresh success, winning £1335 prize money, but a greater challenge was in the offing.

That winter Lemon Cranfield was offered command of the 104 ton racing cutter "Formosa", building at Michael Ratsey's Cowes yard to designs by Ratsey's draughtsman, William Jones.

"Formosa's" owner, F. S. Stanley, wanted her to beat the big class and in her first race, from Harwich to Southend, Lemon Cranfield sailed her with such skill that she finished over an hour ahead of the second boat; a then astonishing difference. She won the Queen's Cup at Cowes regatta and beat the 104 ton, Solent-manned racing cutter "Vol-au-Vent", sailed by Captain Charles Diaper of Itchen; finishing the season with 9 firsts and 4 second prizes worth £725, won in 21 starts. Her other competitors, the Scottish cutters "Oimara" and "Fiona", and the "Neptune", "Cythera" and the old "Arrow", were nowhere.

Next season was wet, cold and gale ridden, but "Formosa" emerged top of the big class with 15 prize flags, winning a Queen's Cup in the Solent, and her 12 man crew shared some of the £898 prize money of a hard season.

That winter the "Formosa" was sold to the Prince of Wales and in 1880 Lemon Cranfield was offered command of the racing schooner "Miranda", built at Wivenhoe by Harvey, which had been sailed by Captain John Barnes of Wivenhoe. She was the first schooner he had sailed and already had a remarkable reputation for speed. When he stepped aboard Lemon reckoned her rigging was too tight and ordered the riggers to slack the shroud lanyards. Her principal rivals in the very competitive racing schooner class were the "Pantomime", then sailed by Captain John Herbert of Brightlingsea and the 203 ton Solent schooner "Cetonia". "Miranda" won 9 firsts, 2 seconds and 3 thirds and finished top of the class. Next year was much the same but in 1882 Watson designed the Scottish schooner "Lenore" to beat the "Miranda". However, Lemon Cranfield kept her reputation as the fastest schooner afloat by winning 25 prizes in 30 races and a tremendous £1,415 in prize money. He stood at the top of his calling, acknowledged as the genius of yacht racing, at which no man before or since has had such phenomenal success. Her huge mainsail, set on a mainmast stepped almost amidships, intimidated her competitors and was partly responsible for her success.

In 1883 the schooner class again refused to race against her and she went off to sail with the cutters and yawls, which she frequently beat, but it reduced her prize money to 10 prizes worth £485 for 17 starts and the following season she only started 9 times, gaining three prizes.

In the autumn Lemon was approached to take command of a new racing cutter to be built on the Clyde to the design of J. B. Webb, for Lieutenant Henn, a wealthy naval officer who had retired early from the service to enjoy sailing and shooting. Mrs. Henn was an enthusiastic yachtswoman and they had cruised extensively in small craft, but knew little of racing. Henn's ambition was to win the America's Cup and he commissioned Webb to design a 90 ton cutter for the challenge he intended making in 1885. However, Sir Richard Sutton's challenge with the cutter "Genesta" was accepted first and the "Galatea" completed for racing around the coast with the British large class, to challenge in 1886, if "Genesta" was unsuccessful.

It is interesting to consider the dimensions of the yachts these men raced in the '80's; "Galatea" was built of steel by Reid of Port Glasgow; a typical long, deep, narrow cutter, 102 foot 7 inches overall, 87 foot waterline x 15 foot beam. Her mast, deck to hounds, was 53 foot; topmast, fid to sheeve, was 45 foot 6 inches; boom 73 foot; gaff 45 foot; bowsprit outboard 36 foot 6 inches and spinnaker boom 65 foot 6 inches long.

Captain and crew of the 107 ton yawl *Waterlily*, 1864. Built by John Harvey of Wivenhoe for Lord Alfred Paget.

Her rig was that of a typical racing cutter but was unusual in being the first large British racing yacht to have the mainsail foot laced to the boom.

Lemon took "Miranda's" smart crew with him; all picked men, the best in British racing. They had high hopes for the "Galatea", but were to be very disappointed. Her 60 tons of lead ballast was run inside her bottom plating and, due to a fault in pouring she never achieved great speed and it took all the skill of Lemon Cranfield and his crew to win two second prizes in 15 races. Her racing at Belfast Lough typified that heartbreak season. For once "Galatea" was managing to hold the "Irex", sailed by William O'Neill, and the Scottish cutters "Marjorie", skippered by Robert Duncan, and the "Marguerite". "Galatea" came round on the starboard tack off Grey Point but almost hung in irons. A heavy squall hit her at the time and the mast went off just above the deck and the whole lee side was buried. Luckily, the wrecked spars, sails and gear went overboard, clear of all hands, but the mate had a narrow escape from being struck by the heel of the housed topmast. "Marjorie" at once stood by, while "Irex", which had rounded the mark, spoke her disabled rival as she ran past and "Marguerite" hailed to know if anyone was hurt.

That winter "Galatea" was altered under Webb's supervision, guided by Lemon's experience and observation, but they could not alter her designed hull form which was too full in the lower sections, reducing wetted surface but not letting her point well. She emerged in spring little improved and after a few races Lemon Cranfield resigned command as he considered her unfit to challenge for the America's Cup.

After Lemon Cranfield left the "Galatea" her owner was determined to race her for the America's Cup and put his cruising skipper, Captain Dan Bradford of Dartmouth, in charge of her. Although an excellent seaman he was unused to racing yachts and the hustle needed for a first class racer to keep her racing engagements around the coast. Hard driving up the Irish sea under trysail gear the skipper, in streaming oilskins, turned a salt rimed face to the owner as a great shower of spray drove over them, saying; "If I was a gentleman, I wouldn't never turn to windward."

A few weeks later Lemon Cranfield's career was to mingle with that of Captain French, the young Brightlingsea racing skipper, and that of an owner who became a benefactor to the Colne seamen and shipbuilders.

In 1885 at the age of 32, Charles Nottage, a London business proprietor, bought his first yacht, the 40 tonner "Foxhound" built in 1870 by the Marquis of Ailsa in his own yard, for his own use. The "Foxhound" had never been successful and was utterly outclassed when Nottage bought her. Earlier experience as a guest in racing yachts owned by friends had brought Nottage into contact with skippers and crews from the Colne and he engaged for his skipper Captain I. French of Brightlingsea. Fitting out had just commenced when the death of Nottage's father caused the "Foxhound" to be laid up for the season and Captain French was released. He returned next spring when the yawl-rigged "Foxhound" was fitted with a new suit of Ratsey sails.

In 1886 the rejuvenated "Foxhound" started eleven times but won only one prize; then her skipper seriously injured a hand and left her at Dover. Charles Nottage was determined to win races and telegraphed to Rowhedge for Captain Lemon Cranfield who had just resigned command of the America's Cup challenger "Galatea" and was temporarily without a yacht in midsummer. Captain Cranfield soon sized up the old "Foxhound", against which he had often raced, and with characteristic skill instantly sailed her to win prize after prize.

Captain French resumed command in August and completed the season's racing in the west country, winning three races before leaving Nottage's service to take a yacht out to America. After further improvements the following season proved equally triumphant with Lemon Cranfield again at the tiller. The "Foxhound" had a smart crew including James Simons, the mate, (later mate of the royal cutter "Britannia)" and William Brown, later tragically killed in the collision between the yachts "Satanita" and "Valkyrie II". Both hailed from Rowhedge.

In the spring of 1888 another Rowhedger, Captain Tom Jay, took the "Foxhound" over as his first racing command. All hands tried hard but the old yacht was really outclassed and Charles Nottage decided to have built a new 40 rater. The 56 ton "Deerhound" was designed by G. L. Watson of Glasgow and built at Southampton by Black and Co. Her 72 foot hull was of the proportions of our present 12 metres, but carried 4,065 square feet of sail; twice their area.

Although she was a racer her owner insisted on comfortable accommodation, even having a large refrigerator built into the galley. Like all yachts she was completed behind schedule and Tom Jay hustled her round to compete in the season's opening matches on the Thames with unstretched sails, five days later.

She won her maiden race and her success continued, winning 22 prizes that summer and making Tom Jay's name. During the winter of 1889-90, in the Mediterranean, the "Deerhound" had phenomenal success winning first prize in every race entered, mostly against inferior French yachts. Nottage was now thoroughly immersed in racing. He became a member of the Yacht Racing Association Council and of many yacht clubs, including the Royal Thames Yacht Club, Portsmouth Corinthian, and the Imperial Yacht Squadron of Austria.

The 1890 season brought "Creole", a new rival by the same designer but built at Forrestt's Wivenhoe yard and skippered by Captain Tom Skeats of Brightlingsea, with a Colne crew. The rivalry between her and the "Deerhound" was the feature of the year in a class including "Velzie", sailed by Captain Gould of Brightlingsea.

"Deerhound" won a Queen's Cup and 64 other trophies and ended her career in home waters by beating the "Creole" by a length in a tremendous race at Torquay regatta, both yachts storming into Torbay soaked halfway up their mainsails, with the skippers and crews enjoying the rivalry between Rowhedge and Brightlingsea which spiced their racing as much as the prize.

That spring the health of Charles Nottage failed and the "Deerhound" was sold to the Italian Marquis Rodolfi. Nottage relieved his illness by commissioning an unusual design for a 130 ton, centreboard cruising schooner, fitted with steam auxiliary power and intended to be named "Boarhound". She was never built as Charles Nottage died on Christmas Eve 1894, aged 42.

Nottage was a keen social observer, with genuine concern for the welfare and future of the skippers and hands whose seamanship and skill he employed and admired. He realised in that era of Britain's greatest mercantile expansion that their future need, as a class, was the opportunity to become competent navigators. In August 1894 he had written to his first captain, I. French of Brightlingsea, who had retired from the sea to manage North's Navigation Collieries at Southampton, stating that he proposed to leave funds for the establishment on the Colne of an institute "where yachtsmen could improve themselves in navigation and generally make up their deficient skills". Thus the evening school known as The Nottage Institute was founded and continues to cater for the needs of today's amateur yachtsmen and boatbuilders in its premises at Wivenhoe.

In 1887 the Royal Thames Yacht Club provided a "handsome prize" for a race round Great Britain and Ireland, to commemorate the jubilee of Queen Victoria's reign. The eleven entries ranged from the 270 ton schooner "Selene" to the 40 ton racing cutter "Sleuthound," and included the "Genesta", sailed by Captain John Carter, and the 100 foot yawl "Vol-au-Vent", sailed by Captain William Cranfield.

To assist with tides and courses round the north of Scotland and the west coasts of Scotland and Ireland, which were waters unfamiliar to racing yacht captains, the "Genesta" carried a pilot in Captain Smith of Bosham, Sussex, the genial owner of a coasting ketch who had spent much of his life sailing those waters. Captain Smith was unused to racing yachts and, accustomed to the high bulwarks of his ketch, viewed the "Genesta's" inches-high footrail with suspicion. To humour him Captain Carter had the yacht's single-wire deck lifeline and stanchions, which had been specially made for her transatlantic passages, rigged, and received much chaff from his competitors for the "fence".

The racers were seen off "down Swin" by a fleet of spectator yachts and 18 passenger steamers, while the whole race was followed by the chartered liners "Norham Castle" and "Athenian". Large numbers of Colne smacks sailed into the Swin to cheer the racers, many of whose crews were from the river, but thick fog clamped down as the breeze freshened and the "Genesta" was soon thrashing to windward through the southbound collier fleet from the north. The yacht was tearing along under full sail in narrow waters, Captain Carter at the long, white tiller attentive to the calls of the two leadsmen forward; one for either tack. The crew were shadows in the dripping fog. The boy had to work the foghorn, forward, giving one or two blasts as she tacked through the dim-seen shapes of hooting colliers. All night they turned to windward, through shoals, past the Sunk and Inner Gabbard, clear into the North Sea, building up a lead. During darkness the yawl "Dauntless" was run into and nearly sunk by the steam yacht "Pandora", and her owner wrote an indignant letter about the collision, sealed it in a bottle and threw it overboard. It was picked up by a smack and forwarded to London, appearing in the Times two days later.

"Genesta" had no competitors in sight as she worked away up the North Sea in light weather, through the Pentland Firth, round Cape Wrath and down the Minch, where she ran before a moderate gale under spinnaker, with two hands at the tiller, sailing 202 miles in 24 hours and logging $12\frac{1}{4}$ knots for four hours. Then she was out beyond the west coast of Ireland in the long green seas of the Atlantic. All hands were terrifically enthusiastic, especially Captain Carter, whose bronzed, bearded figure was by the tiller, often discussing courses and tides with Captain Smith and giving quiet orders to the mate when his wonderfully sharp eyes caught hint of a wind shift.

"Genesta" rounded the land and beat from the Lizard up-channel, sailed as she had been all round the course, with the same verve and smartness displayed in a fifty mile day's racing inshore. The 1590 mile course ended at Dover where "Genesta" anchored just under 13 days out from Southend. She was first home and Captain Carter sent a man aloft with a glass to the crosstrees, to spot the next astern and enable a check to be made on time allowance to see if the "Genesta" had won. He was relieved at hourly intervals and, as the "Sleuthound" did not arrive for another 31 hours, all

The Rowhedge crew of the 60 ton, Scottish racing cutter *Neva*, 1874. Captain Lemon Cranfield, seated, right foreground. Probably the most successful of all racing crews.

the hands stood a watch. But by the time she hove in sight they knew "Genesta" had won the £1,000 prize money, and they received their share of it when the season ended. The recent races round Britain have been for the "Genesta" trophy, named for the winner in 1887.

One of "Genesta's" competitors in the Jubilee race was the 69 foot waterline ketch yacht "Bridesmaid". In 1888 her owner, Mr. Buller, challenged L. M. Ames, owner of the 70 foot waterline cutter "Atlantis", to a race from Southampton Water to Madeira for £1,000. Both yachts were built six years previously, for cruising. The "Bridesmaid" was skippered by my great-uncle, Captain Turner Barnard of Rowhedge, with a crew from the village. News of the match arrived aboard the "Bridesmaid" as she lay off Southampton. The mate came off with a letter from the owner to start preparations for an ocean race, and enclosing the course instructions. "Start off Hythe, leaving Calshot spit light to starboard hand and the Solent by the Needles channel" read the mate; "Proceed to Madeira to finish off the Loo rock fort, distance approximately 1,300 miles". "Hmmm" said great-uncle Turner, staring thoughtfully at the deck; "Do that say anything about luffin'?"

They had a good race in "coarse weather", according to the log. Captain Barnard was determined to win and there was considerable spar making aboard the "Bridesmaid" as she carried away topsail yards and spinnaker booms. Besides her usual sails as a gaff ketch, including main and mizzen topsails, she set, off the wind, a large squaresail, with a raffee topsail over, triangular spinnakers from each mast, a large mizzen staysail, and watersails under the main and mizzen booms. Under this press of sail she regularly logged ten knots and occasionally surpassed it when studding sails were set on the squaresail.

The yachts lost sight of each other after the first day and in 48 hours the "Bridesmaid" was off Cape Villano (Finisterre). A day later she was running before a moderate N.E. gale and heavy sea which lasted some time, but the race finished in light winds with the "Bridesmaid" winning by three hours ten minutes after 7 days 6 hours sailing; largely because of better navigation as she sailed 1,325 miles to the "Atlantis'" 1,375.

The "Bridesmaid" laid up each winter at Rowhedge and one year there was a cholera epidemic in the area. Captain Barnard hastily rigged her in makeshift fashion and sailed down river to lie off East Mersea for a few weeks with his family aboard, his children enjoying this novel holiday from school. During the first world war the "Bridesmaid" became a "Q" ship and after it she was sold to become a Barnardo training ship and, renamed "G. L. Munro", was lost on Sizewell beach, Suffolk, laden with coal in 1927.

The 50 foot cutter "Ulidia" was a noted racer in the 10 ton class: built in 1883 by Fife for a Mr. Corry, an Irishman. She was sailed by Captain James Carter, a brother of John Carter, with a Colne crew all of whom, like true British sailors of the times, were fond of a drink. The owner was a noted teetotaller and told Captain Carter that he did not permit alcoholic drink to be consumed on board. With a great effort the skipper said "No, sir." When the crew joined, the dismal news was broken that they were expected to drink only tea, cocoa or water. After a few miserable days Captain Carter had the idea of filling the teapot with beer and pouring it out in teacups for all hands. At the end of that very successful season Mr. Corry congratulated his Captain and crew on the 16 first and three other prizes they had won and said he had never seen sailors so keen to put the kettle on for a cup of tea!

Next season the "Ulidia" was faced with the Watson designed "Ulerin", but won 6 firsts and nine other prizes worth £260.

In 1885 the "Ulerin" was sold to Edgar Vincent and was sailed by Captain I. French of Brightlingsea, the son of a smack owner and yacht captain. At 18 years of age he was skipper of a 25 ton Brightlingsea smack working on the east coast of Scotland. His sailing ability was noticed and he was asked to skipper cruising yachts, which he occasionally raced during the 1870's, graduating to command of the 20 tonner "Freda" during 1883-4. His greatest achievement with the "Ulerin" was winning a Queen's Cup in the 1885 Nore to Dover race in light weather. The 10 ton "Ulerin" was by far the smallest of the nine competitors which ranged in size to the 125 ton yawl "Wendur" and included most crack yachts of the day. Captain French sailed splendidly and finished only 32 minutes after the winner, the big cutter "Irex". When she passed the fleet of yachts in Dover bay the "Ulerin" was cheered by all hands and her crew were quite hoarse with returning the cheers. The owner was so proud of this feat of handicap racing that he had a medal struck in commemoration and presented one to each of the crew.

Captain French's principal competitor in the 10 ton class was the "Queen Mab", also designed by Watson, sailed by Captain Ben Harris of Rowhedge, who in 1879 was sailing the 19 tonner "Pixie", alternatively rigged as a yawl or a cutter, in the handicap classes, where he quickly showed great ability, and was one of the most promising young racing skippers in Britain. The "Queen Mab" was his pride, and she sometimes beat the 20 tonners in mixed racing. He sailed her for three seasons with success and on the Clyde, in 1886, she won 7 firsts and 1 second in 9 starts. The class raced all round the coast regattas. They were wet at sea but were capable of being driven hard; racing or cruising.

At the season's end of 1887 the Torbay Royal Regatta brought rough weather and a keen race, which cast a shadow over Captain Harris' life for, as the "Queen Mab" stood for Brixham during the second round, leading "Melissa" and "Mabel" under housed topmasts and double reefed mainsails, her bowsprit went off short at the gammon iron and her forestay carried away, letting the mast fall. Amid warning shouts of her crew the whole rig crashed aft, falling on her skipper and a guest, seriously injuring both.

Captain John Carter of Rowhedge and the crew of the *Genesta*, 1885.

So Captain Harris came ashore for good and, buying himself a horse and cart, became Rowhedge's carrier for passengers and goods to Colchester. His equipage was kept in a little brick built stable in Chapel Street, which still stands. Thus ended a fine racing career for one of England's most accomplished skippers. How his sailor's heart must have longed for salt water and the feel of a tiller when he saw the brigs' and barges' topsails lifting above the trees as he jogged back and forth to Colchester behind his cob.

Captain William Cranfield was a contemporary of Ben Harris. In 1882, aged 26, he was skipper of the 12 tonner "Bonina" in the small class, racing her with such success that he was captain of the 40 tonner "May" four years later. She was by then reduced in sail plan and sailing in the 'C' class, winning 17 first and 11 other prizes worth £1,065 in 36 starts. His reputation was made and brought an approach to skipper the old 104 ton yawl "Vol-au-Vent" in the large class. He did well with her during 1887 taking with him his carefully picked crew from the village.

In autumn William was approached by George Watson who was designing a new 85 foot racing cutter for Paul Ralli, a London banker, to race in the large class. "Yarana", as she was named, was amongst the most elegant of racers with sweeping sheer and outreaching clipper bow setting off an efficient rig of 5,700 square feet. William and his crew soon had her tuned up for a dazzling season, winning 24 first and 6 other prizes in 38 races, against such well proved yachts as "Irex" and "May". When she came up the Colne, with prize flags flying, to lay up at Rowhedge, she was hailed and cheered by the crews of smacks and yachts, and yard workmen, as no other yacht had been. Her shapely black hull was the subject of eager scrutiny by scores of skippers when she was hauled out for the winter at Harris' yard. William Cranfield was tremendously proud of the "Yarana", and in contemporary custom named his fine new house on Church Hill after her. Regrettably the name has recently been changed; a sad fate of many Rowhedge houses named for the yachts which were the village's pride.

In 1889 William had to contend with the big, new "Valkyrie I", owned by Lord Dunraven and sailed by Captain Tom Diaper (II) of Itchen, and the "Irex", sailed by Captain O'Neill; but he sailed the "Yarana" so determinedly that she won 31 prizes to "Valkyrie's" 26, and the "Irex" was nowhere. In two seasons she won over £3,000.

William Cranfield was an especially brilliant helmsman in light weather; a most exacting aspect of racing. Men who sailed with him told how he kept a craft moving when there was no apparent wind and the racing flag drooped aloft, but there were ripples from the stem. He was a quiet man, a deep thinker, and a splendid seaman, to whom yacht racing was an art. "However quick you were, you weren't quick enough for Captain William," one of his "Valkyrie" crew remarked to me but, perhaps more than any other racing skipper, he inspired the lifelong respect and friendship of his crews.

Designer George Watson became a firm friend of William Cranfield, whom he greatly respected as a helmsman capable of getting the utmost from some of his most daring designs and a captain who, typically, was always eager to discuss or try new gear and methods for improving speed of handling.

The following season the 108 foot Scottish cutter "Thistle", America's Cup challenger of 1887, was again fitted out and dominated the class, with "Yarana" a close second, despite the difference in size, but Mr. Ralli decided that sport in the big class was dead for a while and the "Yarana" was sold, to be renamed "Maid Marion". William Cranfield was quickly sought by Lord Dunraven to sail the "Valkyrie I" and was at the commencement of the finest part of his career, described in the next chapter. In contrast, Mr. Ralli decided to take things easy and bought the spritsail barge "New Zealand", which he had converted at Cowes into a sailing summer home. She was fitted with strong davits on each side in which were carried his one-raters "Brat" and "Dee-Dee", which were to be a nursery for another Colne racing skipper in the glorious era of yachting which the 1890's brought.

The 100ft. racing cutter *Genesta* of 1884. Sailed by Captain John Carter of Rowhedge with a Colne crew. Photographed racing for the America's Cup, 1885.

CHAPTER NINE

The Racing Men—1890-1939

THE NINETIES was a period of tremendous development and expansion in yachting. It is impossible to more than skim the surface of its personalities and craft and, inevitably, some notable skippers and incidents must be omitted.

In 1891 big class racing had temporarily almost collapsed, the only competitors being "Iverna", sailed by Captain William O'Neill; "Valkyrie", sailed by Captain William Cranfield; and the "Yarana", renamed "Maid Marion", sailed by Captain Thompson of Itchen. Handicap classes flourished and, racing in Torbay in 1891, the cutter "Moina" fouled the 100ft yawl "Erycina", sailed by Captain Ned Ennew of Wivenhoe. During the scrimmage one of "Erycina's" crew jumped aboard the "Moina" and was unable to return as the yachts drifted apart. He was not missed aboard the yawl for about a quarter of an hour then, thinking he was lost, the "Erycina" gave up and returned to Torquay to find the 'drowned' man waving to them from the "Moina". Captain Garrard of Wivenhoe sailed the 95ft yawl "Columbine" that season and surprised the handicap class by winning six prizes right off, during Cowes week.

Despite the dazzling rebirth of big class racing in 1893, the 40 raters were the largest numerical class racing all round the coast in the early nineties. They were between 85 to 90 feet long and set an average of 4,000 square feet.

In 1891 Captain John Carter left the "Genesta" and took the new 40 rater cutter "Thalia", designed by Fife and built for J. Inglis of Glasgow. Tom Jay was appointed to the new "Reverie", launched by Fay of Southampton to designs by Joseph Soper. These, with the Wivenhoe built "Creole", sailed by Tom Skeats of Brightlingsea, battled all round the coast, joined by the "White Slave", a joint design of her owner and Will Fife, built on Hastings beach by Gausden and rigged with two huge lugsails. The "White Slave" was a failure but the "Thalia" won 26 prizes and spoiled the class; the "Reverie" only winning 12. At the Royal Irish regatta off Kingstown, John Carter was sailing "Thalia" in a ding dong duel against Tom Skeats in the "Creole", with the slower "White Slave" lagging astern when, at the height of the regatta, the horizon suddenly loomed with warships of the 'red squadron' on manœuvres and, under a cloud of smoke, dozens of torpedo boats raced through the racing fleet to make a mock attack on the harbour. Wash, smoke, smuts and close shaves brought shouts of protest from the racers, which were drowned when the guardship, the battleship "Bellisle", opened up with her 100 ton guns whose concussion shook the mastheads.

In 1892, at the height of the class's popularity, six of the seven 40 raters were sailed by skippers and crews from the Colne; "Creole" by Captain Skeats; "Corsair" by Captain Sycamore; "Varuna" by Captain Gould and "Irene", owned by Prince Henry of Prussia, by Captain Maskell; all of Brightlingsea; and "Reverie", Captain Jay and "Thalia" Captain John Carter. The other 40 was that season sailed by a Scottish captain and crew. As ever, the small classes often had brilliant helmsmen and served as the nursery for the giants of future yacht racing.

After 1887 the racing rules were changed from "tonnage" measurement to "linear rating", and from being called 10, 20, 40, etc. "tonners" racers were described as 10, 20, 40 etc. "raters". There were, of course, much smaller classes; 5, 2½, 1 and ½ raters being very popular. In 1889 the very competitive Solent 2½ rating class was invaded by the peculiarly shaped and rigged 30 footer named "Heathen Chinee". She was a pointed stern, shallow draught craft having a centreboard at each end and a large open cockpit amidships. She was rigged with two fully battened lugsails, like the sails of a junk; hence her name. Designed by watercolour artist Landseer MacKenzie, who had a flair for centreboard craft, she was built for him in 1878. Ten years later he sold her to W.A. Beauclerk, who also owned the 14 ton cruising cutter "Amelia", built by Puxley at Rowhedge in 1874. "Amelia's" young skipper was Edward Sycamore, who transferred to the "Heathen Chinee" when Beauclerk entered her for the Solent races in 1889. His sole 'crew' was young Roger Sparling of Wivenhoe and between them they raced her hard.

Captain Sycamore was to have a very long and notable career in yacht racing. He was born in 1856 and his parents were natives of Rowhedge. He sailed in smacks from childhood and in 1875 shipped as a hand in the schooner yacht "Lady Evelyn" owned by the Marquis of Ailsa, the noted Scottish owner of the 40 ton racing cutter "Bloodhound", sailed by Captain Ben Harris of Itchen, Hampshire. Young Sycamore often raced in her as a hand and showed promise as an exceptionally good racing man. He also cruised to the Mediterranean and West Indies in the "Lady Evelyn". In 1879 he shipped as a hand in Mr. Atkins' 20 ton cutter "Louise" under Captain Unwin and served in her until the end of 1881 when he was made skipper of the owner's 3 ton racing cutter. For several years Edward Sycamore lived at Harwich and, in winter, fished under sail in the whelking trade. In 1884 he moved to Brightlingsea and became captain of the 56 ton yawl "Amberwitch" and next winter became skipper of the "Amelia".

In Mr. Beauclerk he found a friend as well as an owner; both being very keen wildfowlers, spending many winter mornings and evenings poling their punts about the East Coast estuaries and making good bags of duck and geese. Mr. Beauclerk enjoyed the sport and success achieved by this remarkable young skipper and commissioned Arthur Payne, the brilliant Southampton designer, to produce the 30 ft, 2½ rater "Babe" to beat the keen Solent class. During her first season, in 1890, this deep keeled, miniature racing yacht, rigged with a high peaked lug and foresail in contemporary fashion, started in 27 races and won 15 first and 6 other prizes. This reflected the skill of her skipper and the meticulous attention to detail which characterised his career. His greatest rival in a class of seven was the Hampshire-manned "Humming Bird".

Next season the "Babe" had wonderful success, winning 36 first and 3 other prizes in 45 starts; well beyond the rest of the 2½ rating class. The flush decked "Babe" had only two other hands besides her skipper and they could not live aboard her cramped hull so, as it was all day sailing, they lodged ashore at night. These Solent raters were one of the greatest development classes for hull form, gear and crews, but it was a surprise to the yachting world when at the end of 1891, Edward Sycamore was approached to take command of the new 40 rater racing cutter "Corsair", building at Payne's Southampton yard for Admiral Victor Montagu. It was a long step from a 2½ rater to the 85 ft. racing cutter, but Captain Sycamore took it all in his stride and won 13 first prizes in 1892.

Rear Admiral the Honourable Victor Montagu was a great supporter of British yacht racing. His love of the sea was not quenched by long service in the Royal Navy and his introduction to yachting was aboard the old "Pearl", when owned by the Marquis of Anglesey. After sailing and owning many yachts he had the "Corsair" built to challenge the 40 rating class and, although the Watson designed "Queen Mab", sailed by Captain Ben Parker of Itchen, dominated the class, she was no match for Captain Sycamore in the "Corsair" to windward on a breezy day. The admiral's blood was now really roused and he ordered another new 40, the "Vendetta", from Payne, and Edward Sycamore and his crew transferred to her in the spring of 1893. She was a most extreme craft with a fin bulb keel and a balanced rudder; a blown up version of her designer's successful 2½ raters, but was well beaten by John Gretton's new "Lias", sailed by Captain John Cranfield of Rowhedge and also by the year-old "Varuna", sailed by Captain Edward Gould of Brightlingsea, all with crews from the Colne.

The admiral was now thoroughly determined to head the class and had yet another 40 rater built, this time to designs by George Watson. Named "Carina" she came out in 1894 sailed by Captain Sycamore and raced against the old "Corsair" and "Vendetta" under other ownership, besides racing at Kiel and the Baltic regattas, arriving back at Brightlingsea flying 31 prize flags, including 26 firsts. Some of her German experiences were peculiar; she was once taken round the wrong side of a buoy by the German pilot's instructions and on another occasion was run ashore under his direction. At the end of the season Captain Sycamore was asked to join the new "Valkyrie III", with Captain William Cranfield.

When he left the "Carina", Robert Wringe, the mate, was appointed captain and commenced a distinguished career as master of racing yachts. Born at Brightlingsea in 1861 he first went to sea in fishing smacks as a boy in 1875 and shipped in yachts in summer. He quickly rose to command some of the largest of the Brightlingsea smacks and several from Grimsby, where a branch of his family owned them; working all over the North Sea and around the British coasts. He served in the 20 rater "Velzie", under Captain Gould of Brightlingsea, during 1890 and left her to become captain of the 39 ton cutter "Alceste" before joining the "Corsair" as mate.

Robert Wringe was a man of comparatively few words but of lightning and iron nerved decisions; a temperament which suited bluff old Admiral Montagu, and his splendid sailing of the "Carina" established him as a great racing captain. Captain William Maskell was another noted Brightlingsea racing skipper who had an unusual career. Born in 1844 he followed the Colne tradition and rose to command the famous old "Lorna", a 54 tonner built by Camper and Nicholson in 1875, and a rare prize winner in a breeze. One day her crew found all the wind they wanted in a race from Harwich round the Shipwash, where the big seas made the long bowsprits of the racers plunge badly. "Lorna's" broke between the bitts and the gammon iron, and the big spar began to twist the stem head off, while the broken butt was forcing down the foredeck at each plunge. They had to saw through the bowsprit forward of the stem, and the hands told off for that job had a rough and apprehensive ride before the spar was hewed away.

In 1892 Captain Maskell became skipper of the 40 rater "Irene", owned by Prince Henry of Prussia, and raced her in Germany and Britain. Two years later he took the 40 rater "Queen Mab" out to America and remained with her as captain, before taking command of the American big class racing sloop "Vigilant," until his death in 1906.

The 1890's brought a tremendous upsurge of interest in British yachting in all classes, from tiny half raters to the largest racing cutters, four of which were ordered in the winter months of 1892. At Glasgow, George Watson designed and Henderson's

The 20 rater class starting at Brightlingsea regatta, May 1895. From left; *Inyoni* and *Audrey*, sailed by Solent crews. *Stephanie*, Captain Lemon Cranfield of Rowhedge and *Luna*, Captain Albert Turner of Wivenhoe. The only known photograph of class racing yachts competing in a Colne regatta.

built "Britannia" for the Prince of Wales and "Valkyrie II" for the Earl of Dunraven. William Fife III, at Fairlie, designed and built the unlucky "Calluna", and at Southampton, J. & G. Fay's designer, Joseph Soper, worked all through the Christmas holidays draughting the beautiful "Satanita", the fastest cutter on a reach ever built, sailing at over 16 knots on a timed course off the Isle of Wight.

The command of all four of these big class racers was offered to racing skippers from Rowhedge; such was then the fame of the Essex village of only 1,000 inhabitants, in the yachting world. Thomas Jay sailed the "Satanita", William Cranfield the "Valkyrie II", and John Carter was offered command of both "Calluna" and "Britannia", but chose the Royal cutter. So "Calluna" was sailed by Captain Archie Hogarth from Port Bannantyne on the Clyde.

The four yachts were alike in general appearance and size. "Satanita's" dimensions were 131 foot 6 inches overall, 93 foot 6 inches waterline x 24 foot 6 inches beam x 14 foot 6 inches draught. She displaced 126 tons. Her sail plan was the tallest but she typified the quartette and a few rig features are worth recording. The total sail area was 10,094 square feet comprising: mainsail 5,264; headsails 3,360 and topsail 1,470. Her boom was 91 foot long and height from deck to topmast shoulder 114 feet. "Satanita" was a very fast yacht, averaging 13.7 knots in a race from Gravesend, round the Mouse light vessel and back on a broad and close reach.

The considerable sail area and speed of these cutters resulted in many broken bowsprits and topmasts, and several sprung masts, for staying was lagging behind the rapid hull development. Considered basically their hull form was a development of progress made during the three preceding years in the small rating classes, up to 10 rating, but untried in such large craft which, despite the most careful thought, calculation and design skill, were very unknown quantities until sailing trials. Not that this deterred their captains and crews. The great strength of these Colne racing men was their versatility; if someone had brought out a boat with three keels they would have sailed her, and whatever new piece of gear was dreamed up by designers was eagerly tried in the search for speed under sail. With their cut away profiles these yachts could tack very quickly; from the order "Lee oh" to all canvas filled and drawing on the other tack, took only between 12 and 15 seconds. When one considers that in that time two sets of backstays had to be slacked and two set up; the jib, jib-topsail and staysail sheets let go and those on the opposite side got in and trimmed; the smartness of the crews can be appreciated.

Like all British racing yachts until the turn of the century, these big cutters were steered with tillers about 20 feet long, which rose waist-high at the forward end and in a breeze were controlled by tackles led to eyebolts in the port and starboard deck edges. The captain steered holding the weather or lee tiller line, which was the fall of one of these tackles. This sounds an unrefined method but in practice gave an excellent 'feel' to the helm of such a large craft. Often, to get a clear view forward, the helmsman

Captain Edward Sycamore sailing the 21/1 rater *Babe*, 1890. A typical small racing yacht of the time.

stood to leeward of his tiller, knee deep in water foaming up the lee deck in a breeze going to windward, keeping control with the tiller lines; something he could not have done with a wheel.

The captains and crews were very proud of these new yachts which were such a radical departure from anything of their size previously built, and they strove to get the very best from them. These great racing skippers were above all fine helmsmen, particularly to windward, and had wonderful judgement. They also had the ability to consider the hull and rig as a whole, and tune the yachts to perfection, besides co-ordinating the work of a crew of 35 hands. To keep their place in the prize lists they had to anticipate their equally experienced rivals; had to know the racing rules thoroughly and have calm nerves to stretch them to the utmost without flinching; as an error at the helm of one of these giants could not only shatter their reputation, but also lose the lives of several men. Captains had from £3 - 10s. to £4 per week and were all found when in commission, and most were on a winter retainer. Besides this they had a reasonable share of the prize money and a successful racing skipper could live comfortably by the standards of the times, often putting money into local housing property, besides.

The crews of the "Britannia", "Valkyrie II" and "Satanita" were principally Rowhedge men, with a few others from Wivenhoe, Brightlingsea, Tollesbury and the Lower Clyde. There were about 35 of them in each yacht and they were the very smartest racing hands it was possible to get. They well earned their 26 shilling weekly wage, with the prospect of prize money to back it up.

Apart from the captains, first and second mates, stewards and cooks, the racing hands were principally young men between 20 and 30 years old, invariably with the traditional background of winter fishing in the smacks and summer yachting; working up from smaller yachts to the big cutters. They were superb fore and aft seamen; able to work as a team with perfect drill yet also able to think and act independently, and from their knowledge of racing tactics and awareness, could anticipate orders, which were executed with lightning speed. They also possessed all the skills of the sailor, in rope, wire and canvas work, and could maintain a good varnish and paint finish after the yacht left her fitting out yard. A finish so perfect and beloved of the first mate, who was responsible to the captain for the yacht's smartness in every particular. When they set a spinnaker it was with perfect co-ordination of a practised team. When the skipper ordered "All hands on the mainsheet!", within a second there were thirty powerful men hauling in unison, and with the practised power which amateurs can never attain on a canted and heaving deck. When it was in, and those 4,000 square foot mainsails took some sheeting in a breeze, at the traditional order of "Belay, try that!", the mainsheetman cast his rope stopper round it in a twinkling and all hands melted away like cats, to lie all round the weather deck crouched intelligently into positions of the least windage with their noses over the weather rail like pointers, carefully noting the tactics of the most dangerous rivals. With never a sound amongst them, the slightest quiver of an opponent's sail, the least check on a sheet, or some half concealed movement and so many inquiring eyes were on their own boat's helmsman. Every face had the same expression; "Did you see that, skipper?" If he had, they knew, although not a word was exchanged; if he had not he knew the meaning on every face and at once traced the cause. Instinctively these men were ready at the "Lee oh!" or "Look alive boys!" The sails were all silently adjusted, tackles and leads cleared for every point of sailing, and often without a single order until the crucial one when the yacht herself seemed to answer it.

Keen on their work and good at it they were shockingly poorly paid for their ability. They were, generally speaking a fine type of man, physically and mentally alert and taking as great a pride in their yacht as though she belonged to them. If seen before she was planked up they would criticise her with wonderful judgement and, after a short trial spin, offered as sound an opinion as could be given. From their 26 shillings weekly wage the crew 'found themselves' in food. At the start of the season one of them was appointed foc'sle cook and caterer, the others paying him 5 shillings each week for their food and at the season's end expected a few shillings back. His was a difficult job as all hands had good appetites and expected plenty of food. Each morning in port or an anchorage, the caterer went ashore with his basket for fresh provisions. Usually the foc'sle cook came to an arrangement with the steward and made stews with what came from the saloon table, supplemented by plum duff and spotted dick, which were cheap and filling, and surprisingly, coffee was often preferred to tea in the foc'sle; made into a thick syrup with condensed milk and sugar.

Naturally, the smartest hands were picked for the most exacting jobs such as mast-headsmen or bowsprit-endsmen, which were reckoned posts of advancement in pay and prospects of promotion towards mate. In the days when bowsprits protruded 40 feet or more outboard and huge jibs were set and handled from their ends, the bowsprit-endsman's position was a wet and uncomfortable one, but of all jobs aboard a racer the mastheadsmen's was the most dangerous. All racers of any consequence carried at least one hand specialising in this task and larger ones had two; the first and second mast-headsmen. Their duties included being aloft anywhere to a topmast head 180 feet above the waterline, before and during racing, to clear sails and topsail yards when they were hoisted or lowered. They also laced the topsail luff to the topmast; no light task head to wind in a breeze with a 2,000 square foot topsail attempting to shake them off the gantline. At all times they were checking gear for chafe and efficiency.

A mastheadsman combined the ability of a racing seaman with the head of a steeple-jack. Quick wits and a sharp knife were his best friends when working aloft from his station on the spreaders, maybe a hundred feet or more above the yacht's foaming wake. For this work they received extra pay of a few shillings each week and certainly earned it. Many paid the price of their daring and fell to their death, others went on to become noted racing mates. The most noted of this daring breed was Jack (Pups) Cranfield, first mastheadsman of the "Valkyries" and a close second was 'Monkey' Byford of Colchester, for many years mastheadsman of the "Britannia" who, in later years, became her mate. Typically, when a contingent of local yachtsmen were travelling to Brightlingsea for their annual two weeks Royal Naval Reserve training, "Monkey" just missed the train at Wivenhoe. Seeing the "Crab and Winkle" disappearing round the bend he raced after it and swung himself on the rear buffers for a triumphant ride to Brightlingsea!

The new yachts were a tremendous success, though at first critics decried their 'ugly' bows. Looking now at a photograph of these round-bowed cutters which seem the acme of grace in hull form, it is difficult to realise that, to eyes accustomed to the clipper bows and straight stems which preceded them, these overhangs were ugly.

The 40 rater racing cutter *Thalia* wearing her prize flags in Kingstown Harbour, Ireland, 1892. Captain John Carter of Rowhedge standing by the tiller.

The four new racers soon proved their seaworthiness, racing at all the usual principal regattas and fixtures round the coast between Harwich and the Clyde, and in the height of the season the "Valkyrie II" sailed the Atlantic to race for the America's Cup, and home again the following spring. "Britannia's" owner, Edward, Prince of Wales, was fond of spending part of his winters on the Riviera and after the 1893 season's racing "Britannia" refitted and sailed for Cannes to race against the "Satanita" in a series of winter duels off the Riviera ports. Occasionally they were joined by some smaller French yachts and the "Valkyrie I", then owned by Ignazio Florio of Palermo and sailed by Captain Lemon Cranfield, with a Rowhedge crew. "Britannia" had a rough passage outward bound to the Med, meeting gales in the Bay of Biscay, when the seas kept washing her navigation sidelights out.

Racing mainsails were not generally used for serious passage making, for which the trysail was set. This smaller and stouter version of the mainsail was set without a boom, laced to its own gaff and toggled or hooped to the mast with its clew sheeting to either quarter by tackles leading over the boom, which lay securely lashed in its crutch. Coastwise passages between regattas and ocean and sea passages to and from America, the Mediterranean, and the Baltic, were usually made under trysail gear. Some of them were fast passages too. Captain Jack Carter recalled, when he was first mate of the "Britannia" under his father, returning from Cannes to Southampton during March, under trysail gear and making 13.4 knots for over two hours.

The "Valkyrie II" and "Britannia" were the best of the four new yachts and won many prizes in that splendid season of 1893. "Satanita" was the fastest on a reach, but was more tender, and Tom Jay did wonderfully to succeed so well with her. The "Calluna" proved a failure and withdrew from the class at the end of the season.

Much of the racing of "Britannia" and her contemporaries is recorded in Chapters 12 and 13, and it is sufficient to remember here that in 1894 "Valkyrie II" returned from her unsuccessful America's Cup attempt and was sunk in collision with the "Satanita" before the start of a race on the Clyde, where the American "Vigilant", her opponent in the Cup races, was to meet her for the first time in England. During 1894 Tom Jay sailed the 20 rater "Thelma" for A. B. Walker, a keen racing owner who was planning to have a first class cutter built for the big class, and the "Satanita" was raced by Captain Diaper of Itchen.

Colne racing men were also active in the smaller classes. When Paul Ralli sold the big "Yarana" and took to summer cruising in his spritsail barge yacht "New Zealand", she carried two little raters in davits for her owner's pleasure in day sailing and racing. To help in sailing them at races around the Solent and along the coast, he took in his crew Albert Turner, a young Wivenhoe hand who had served under Captain Cranfield in the "Yarana". He and Mr. Ralli were constantly sailing the raters in races and Turner showed a remarkable ability in tuning the boats. In 1892 Paul Ralli joined the very competitive Solent 2½ rating class with the 33 footer "Papoose", designed by Payne and setting 543 square feet of canvas, which with Albert Turner as hand, did well. Her success had much to do with Albert Turner being appointed skipper of the new 20 rater "Luna" in the spring of 1894, building by Fife for F. B. Jameson. It was a keen class with "Dragon", "Dierdre", sailed by Captain Richard Cranfield of Rowhedge, "Audrey", "Inyoni", "Zinita", "Asphodel", and "Stephanie", sailed by Captain Lemon Cranfield of Rowhedge. These 70 footers raced all round the coast and their crews lived on board all season. The "Luna" started in 53 races in 1894 and came top of the class, winning 20 first prizes, 9 seconds and 3 thirds; a tremendous performance which really established Albert Turner as a racing captain of great skill.

Next season the 20 raters split up and several, including the "Luna", did not go west of the Needles, while the remainder raced on the Clyde. The American 20 rater "Niagara", owned by J. Gould, was shipped over and raced against the British yachts, sailed by Captain John Barr, with his brother Charles, later a noted racing skipper, and other Scotsmen who had emigrated to America, as crew. She won many prizes and gave the Essexmen some hard fought races.

In 1896 Mr. Jameson had another 52 footer built, which he quaintly named "The Saint". Captain Albert Turner and his crew transferred to her and had the best record in the class for the year, against the American "Niagara" and the "Penitent". The "Luna" was sold and was sailed that season by Captain Richard Cranfield.

The old 5 rating class had become the 36 footers and Dan Aldrige, a young Rowhedge racing man who had been in the crew of "Britannia", was given this first chance as a racing skipper in the 36 footer "Fern", whose owner, A. B. Walker of Ailsa, intended to christen "The Sinner", but his wife made him change his mind!

In 1895 Lord Lonsdale, a supporter of all kinds of sport in a grand manner, ordered a 20 rating racing yacht by sending a typical, brief telegram to William Fife at Fairlie. Six weeks later this 65 footer stood ready to launch; her hull handsome above water but shallow below, with a deep fin and bulb keel and separate rudder developed from the smaller raters, reminiscent of modern trends in yacht design. Two other telegrams conveyed the owner's wishes to builder and captain, and Lord Lonsdale did not see the "Eucharis", as she was named, until she had raced five times! "Eucharis" was afterwards sold to the Connell brothers of the Clyde shipbuilding firm, who renamed her "Hermia" and Captain Dan Aldrige stepped up from the 36 foot class to sail her. She was unsuccessful, and in 1898 the Connells ordered a new 52 footer which was also built by Fife, and named "Viera".

There were five boats in the class that season including the "Senga" sailed by Captain Charles Bevis of Bursledon, on the Hamble, Hampshire, with a Solent crew, and the new "Eldred" sailed by Captain Robert Wringe of Brightlingsea. The closeness of their competition, which took them all round the coast, can be gauged by the finish of their race at Campbeltown regatta, Scotland, when only 57 seconds separated the first and last of the 52 footers after a fifty mile course. Dan Aldrige and his village crew did well and when they brought "Viera" to Rowhedge to lay up at Harris yard she was flying flags for 11 first, 10 second and 1 third prize, won in 35 starts.

In a typical example of passage making by a racer the new 52 footer "Eldred", fresh from Payne's Southampton yard, under the command of Captain Robert Wringe of Brightlingsea, sailed from the Solent on Sunday 26th June 1898. She made her next port at Penzance in company with the cutter "Betty", sailed by Captain John Cranfield of Rowhedge. They left there together and for three days hammered to windward up the Irish sea. The "Eldred" arrived at Hunters Quay one hour before the "Betty" on Friday 1st July and immediately went on to Robertson's slip for a bottom scrub and a brighten up for the Clyde races. Such attention to perfect finish and condition was typical.

By 1895 the Colne was at the peak of its yachting glory; its captains and hands were sailing in every class and type of racer and they brought prosperity to the river. George Watson designed a new super cutter for the Earl of Dunraven's final attempt for the America's Cup that year. The "Valkyrie III" was one of the most extreme racers ever built and her statistics are worthy of appreciation. Her dimensions were 129 foot

Racing the *Valkyrie II*, 1893. Captain William Cranfield of Rowhedge (seated at tiller). His brother, Captain Lemon Cranfield, standing. First mate William Taylor of Rowhedge, at extreme right.

overall, 88 foot 10 inches waterline x 26 foot 2 inches x 20 foot draught. She measured 187 foot from bowsprit end to boom end and had a 77¾ ton lead keel. Sail area was 13,028 square feet and she was the first large yacht to have a steel mast. The "Valkyrie III" was commanded by Captain William Cranfield with a crew of 37 hands, mostly from Rowhedge. Captain Edward Sycamore also sailed in the "Valkyrie III" and assisted when racing, the two captains taking her helm when each thought he could get the best out of the yacht on different points of sailing. Early in 1895, Fife launched the 283 ton racing cutter "Ailsa" for A. B. Walker. She was sailed by Captain Tom Jay, who took her out to the Mediterranean and raced against "Britannia" during the Riviera season, the 40 rater "Corsair" also competing on handicap. "Ailsa" was difficult to tune up, but did well when she returned to England for the home racing around the coast regattas, principally against the "Britannia" and the new, 100 foot cutter "Hester", built by Hansen's of Cowes, to Payne's design and sailed by Captain John Cranfield of Rowhedge, with a village crew. When he left the "Ailsa" at the end of the 1895 season, Tom Jay was again asked to skipper the 20 rater cutter "Thelma", and sailed her with success during 1896-7. Although skippers sometimes graduated from a smaller yacht to a first class cutter for a time, and then back to the smaller classes for a further period, this reflected the change of the most sporting classes, rather than their ability.

Captain Robert Wringe of Brightlingsea was appointed skipper of "Ailsa" that winter and took her out to the Mediterranean to race against the "Britannia". A hand was lost from her on passsage in bad weather which also delayed the 20 rater "Stephanie", sailed out by Captain Lemon Cranfield to race in the Riviera matches. Returning to Rowhedge in the spring of 1896 he took command of the 40 rater "Corsair", an 1892 boat which was thought to be outclassed, but characteristically Lemon raced her with wonderful skill and gave some of his younger opponents plenty to think about. A contemporary writer, referring to racing skippers said; "Just as I don't know all the Parkers and Diapers, I don't know all the Cranfields. I know all their records and I am proud of the supremacy, but somehow or other my heart always gives a great big jump for joy when I see Lemon. What he does not know about racing is hardly worth learning. Of the elders he is indubitably the greatest." Such was his fame—I believe the "Corsair" was his last racing command and afterwards he took principally to acting as racing pilot in yachts, fishing in his beloved smack "Neva" in winter, and racing her in the regattas until his death, about 1912.

The "Valkyrie III" was laid up after her return from America and William Cranfield was released by Lord Dunraven to skipper the 100 foot yawl "Namara" in the handicap class, though she also raced against the big cutters with a time allowance. The big class had begun to break up for a period, as it had often done throughout yachting history.

The 1896 season was notable for the German Emperor's new 236 ton cutter "Meteor," second of the name and, like her predecessor, sailed by Captain Robert

Gomes and an English crew. She was designed by Watson and built at Glasgow by Henderson. The Earl of Dunraven had the 105 foot ketch "Cariad" built by Payne in 1896 and Captain Barty Smith and a Rowhedge crew sailed her for many years. She was a cruiser, but occasionally raced. In 1898 she won the Vasco Da Gama challenge cup at Lisbon and sometimes raced in Cowes week, to support the large handicap class.

Large schooners were still being built and in February 1897, Captain James Carter of Rowhedge was appointed to the 300 ton Scottish schooner "Shamrock" which had a mainsail so large that her crew were exhausted when it was set! That year the big class was boosted by Italian Prince Louis of Savoy, Duke of the Abruzzi, who ordered the 110 foot cutter "Bona", as usual designed by Watson and built by Henderson at Glasgow. She was sailed by Captain Edward Sycamore with a Brightlingsea crew and had considerable success, partly due to the favourable handicap she received for racing against the larger "Britannia", "Meteor" and "Aurora". Although his racer was being hard sailed all season around the British coast, "Bona's" owner was away all summer on a mountain climbing expedition in America! Racing on the Clyde the 40 rater "Carina" got her bowsprit close to the "Bona's" stern and for nearly half a mile she was towed along by the big racer's suction. Captain Sycamore tried everything possible to shake her off but which ever way he put the helm the 40 rater followed, drawn away from the rest of her class at tremendous speed, until they came on the wind at the mark. Apart from her smaller size the "Bona" could easily be identified amongst the big cutters by her dark coloured mainsail made from Indian ramee cloth. She was afterwards sailed by Captain Tom Skeats of Brightlingsea and Captain Archie Hogarth from the Clyde.

The big class was further diluted during 1897 by the inclusion on handicap of the 40 raters "Isolde" and "Caress". "Isolde" was sailed by Captain Archie Hogarth with a Scottish crew and his great rival was William Cranfield racing the "Caress" with a crew of Rowhedgers. These 90 footers were matched against the "Bona", "Britannia", "Meteor" and the "Aurora", sailed by Captain Cook Diaper of Itchen. In the Southend to Harwich race the "Caress", with John Cranfield as well as William on board at the helm, only lost by 4½ minutes from the German Emperor's giant "Meteor", sailed by Captain Ben Parker of Itchen with Captain Lemon Cranfield on board as racing pilot.

At Harwich regatta, "Meteor" and "Caress" went foaming out of the harbour under full mainsails and jib headed topsails, for a dead thrash off to the Shipwash in a tearing breeze and jump of short sea. "Meteor's" mainsail foot burst from its track on her steel boom, which began to bend like a bow just as she was working off the lee shore of Felixstowe ledge. Both yachts had to reef down and lower foresails and jib headers as the wind and seas increased. "Caress" was scooping up seas and had to give up, leaving "Meteor" to go on, sailing easy round the Shipwash and the Sunk, and back to Harwich for the prize. Racing off Southsea the "Meteor's" 98 foot boom swept over the German 52 footer "Isolde" and the falling mast killed her owner, Baron von Zedwitz. Although

Captain Gomes was exonerated from blame, he was replaced by Captain Ben Parker of Itchen.

"Bona" raced in the 1898 Mediterranean matches, in spring, against the old "Satanita", sailed by Captain Charles Jewitt of Southampton, who did remarkably well, but "Bona" arrived at Brightlingsea in April after a 26 day passage from Nice flying 12 prize flags. Captain Sycamore continued to sail her during that season, when she won three Queen's Cups and an astonishing £4,455 in prize money! John Gretton sold the "Hester", which had been very successful in the handicap class and in 1898 his new cruiser-racer "Betty" was launched by Hansen's at Cowes to designs by Arthur Payne. Captain John Cranfield and his Rowhedge crew soon had her fitted out and racing where she did very well, winning a Queen's Cup in the Royal Yacht Squadron regatta of 1898. "Britannia" and "Ailsa" continued their series of winter races in the Mediterranean but when they returned in spring, the "Britannia" was laid up as first class racing had almost collapsed in England.

In 1897 C. Orr-Ewing ordered a 331 ton racing schooner to designs by George Watson. Her 150 foot hull was composite-built with a clipper bow extending her 116 foot waterline and giving her astonishing beauty. She was named "Rainbow" and was to be commanded by Captain John Carter of Rowhedge; the largest yacht he had sailed. But "Rainbow's" construction lagged and the yacht swarmed with 200 workmen rushing to complete the big black schooner. John Carter brought many of "Britannia's" crew with him to man the "Rainbow". Seven officers and stewards and 23 hands joined her as she fitted out at Partick, "As fine a looking body of yacht sailors as ever came to the Clyde" reported the Scottish newspapers. With "Rainbow's" powerful rig they were picked for strength as well as skill and none were less than 40 inches round the chest. Unfortunately Captain Carter was taken ill and sent to Rowhedge for Captain Tom Jay to superintend the "Rainbow's" fitting out. When it was complete, Captain Carter was unfit for a long period and command passed to Tom Jay who found her extremely fast, making her maiden passage from Gourock to South-hampton in 50 hours.

The "Rainbow" had the fastest timed speed of any displacement yacht. She sailed 60 miles in four hours, the log twice registering $16\frac{1}{2}$ knots. During this performance, in the Channel, her helm balance was perfect and the yacht steady. "Rainbow" was the subject of one of West's most beautiful photographs. In it can be seen her skipper to leeward of his wheel as the board stiff topsails draw her, with roaring quarter wave, and forty hands a'weather, past the steam yachts and ironclads in Cowes Roads. Her principal opponents were "Satanita" and "Ailsa", Tom Jay's old commands rerigged as yawls, and the newer cutters "Bona" and "Aurora". Although "Rainbow" finished first in many races she did not win on handicap, which dulled the sport. Like all racing schooners the "Rainbow" set a spinnaker from each mast and during the Royal Yacht Squadron race around the Isle of Wight in a strong westerly wind, she carried away both spinnaker booms as she came ranting up the Solent ahead of "Ailsa" and "Aurora".

Few large yachts raced during 1898 but on the Clyde "Rainbow" and "Bona" sailed against the gigantic, three masted schooner "Gleniffer", which George Watson had developed from the "Rainbow". Built that year, she was the largest schooner yacht which ever raced inshore; 141 feet on the waterline and 180 feet overall hull length. She was built of steel for James Coats of Glasgow. This 496 tonner proved too cumbersome for racing and was well beaten by the "Rainbow" which, as usual, lost on time to the "Bona". The "Rainbow" was Tom Jay's last racing command and he left her in 1900, a successful skipper, for the less strenuous life as master of the 141 foot steam yacht "Kempion".

By 1892 the large numbers of racing yachts sailed by captains from the Colne brought a demand for racing hands which could not be entirely fulfilled from the river's limited sailing seafaring population. Some Scottish and Southampton hands

Ailsa, sailed by Captain Tom Jay and the Royal cutter *Britannia* sailed by Captain John Carter, racing on the Clyde, 1895.

were taken into the crews of the larger yachts and each spring numbers of Tollesbury seamen walked to Rowhedge and Wivenhoe, seeking berths in the yachts fitting out there.

With the Colne surging ahead in yachting and navigation classes being held each winter at Wivenhoe and Brightlingsea, Tollesbury awoke to opportunities the sport offered to its seamen and their village. Navigation was the first essential and Captains Isaac Rice and William Frost gave classes during the winter. By arrangement with the village schoolmaster, Captain Rice taught some of the older boys navigation and when the sun served at noon, they took a sight with sextants; a bath of water forming an artificial horizon. The school realised the needs of its young community of potential seafarers and provided knitting and darning classes and, for older boys, cookery lessons.

One of the earliest Tollesbury yacht captains was Alfred Carter, born in 1837. His most noted command was the 53 ton yawl "Hyacinth," built by Payne at Southampton in 1886, which occasionally raced in the handicap class. Besides a house of their own the ambition of most Tollesbury yacht skippers was to own a pony and trap. Seventy years ago the Tollesbury yacht skippers' club was formed, largely by the energies of Captains Frost, Redhouse and Carter, and amongst other activities it promoted the village regatta, the first of which was held in 1900.

By 1901 the yard and slipways of Messrs Drake showed a good selection of moderate sized cruising yachts laid up in winter, with larger ones moored in the saltings, and W. A. Snape and Co. and Williams and Phillips were busy refitting them in spring. That year five Tollesburymen were picked for the crew of the "Shamrock II" and others were sailing in racers skippered from the Colne and elsewhere.

In 1899 Sir Thomas Lipton made his first challenge for the America's Cup with the "Shamrock I", commanded by Captain Archie Hogarth from the Clyde but sailed in the races by Captain Robert Wringe of Brightlingsea. There were many Colne hands in her crew. After the cup races Captain Wringe was approached to skipper the American racing yacht "Mineola", building by Herreshoff at Newport, Rhode Island, as one of four sisters, gigantic 'one designs', 106 feet long and 70 feet on the waterline. The owners were all millionaires and Cornelius Vanderbilt's "Rainbow" also had an English crew, skippered by Captain George Parker of Itchen, Hampshire. W. K. Vanderbuilt, Jr. had the "Virginia", sailed by Captain Hansen and a Norwegian crew and Harry Whitney sailed his "Yankee" with an Norwegian crew. The crews of the "Mineola" and "Rainbow" should have been Americans but, when wanted, the American sailors would not sail under an English captain so, to their relief, Captains Wringe and Parker were able to bring out picked English crews in the spring. "Mineola" was the best to windward and "Rainbow" off the wind, and these two dominated the class, leading to protests and charges against them by the other boats. As 'one designs' the yachts were very closely matched. Great rivalry also arose between

Rainbow in her glory. The 158ft. racing schooner sweeping through Cowes roads with Captain Tom Jay of Rowhedge at the Helm.

the Essex crew of "Mineola" and the Solent manned "Rainbow", aggravated when Captain Wringe forced the "Rainbow" about on the starboard tack. During one series of races off Newport the "Mineola" averaged 11 knots over a 30 mile course, winning by 34 seconds from the "Rainbow", but in the strong breeze the yachts' hulls were badly wrung and had to be repaired. They were fast boats, setting 7,000 square feet of working canvas and the owners spared no expense to ensure a good season's racing as each ordered an 80 foot steel steam yacht to act as tender to his racer for that year.

Unlike their English contemporaries the American owners interfered in the running of the yachts. When "Mineola" was leading in a handicap race a rain squall made up and August Belmont insisted they must give up as the yacht's sails might get wet and stretch before the following week's series of class races.

Many Colnesiders were amongst the crews of the big yawl "Sybarita" and the cutter "Kariad" during their famous race around Ailsa Craig in June 1901. The 213 ton "Sybarita" had two captains; Charles Bevis and Fred Mountifield of Gosport, with a crew of 33 hands. She was powerfully rigged with 12,000 square feet of canvas and her mast was so enormous that three large men could stand back to back inside one of her mast hoops. The "Kariad", known as the "K-Kariad" to all racing men to distinguish her from Lord Dunraven's ketch "Cariad", was sailed by Captain Archie Hogarth with a mainly Scottish crew. The yachts started off Rothesay for a stake of 500 guineas laid by another yacht owner, Mr. James Coats. He contended that "Sybarita" was the fastest yacht afloat and wagered that she would beat the "Kariad" in a race of 75 miles. They started in almost a gale of wind under double reefed mainsail and small jib, with topmasts housed, having a tremendous sail down to the island of Ailsa Craig; pounding to windward until twenty feet of "Sybarita's" copper sheathing tore from her bows with the force of the seas. Rivet heads sheared and the gear strained as she ran up the Firth at over 14 knots, with "Kariad" close aboard. Captain Bevis ordered the reef to be shaken out and a Brightlingsea hand was sent out along the heaving boom with a razor sharp knife, slashing the reef lacing as he went until he got to the clew where he cut the earing and as he regained the deck, all hands tailed on to the main and throat halyards, swaying up the mainsail. They roared across the line and "Sybarita" won, having sailed 76 miles in 6 hours 10 minutes. As old Mr. Coats left the yacht in his gig he gave each of her crew a present of 30 shillings.

Perhaps the owners who got most from the sport were those contented with less extreme and smaller craft. Such was Mr. Justice Channell, later Sir Arthur Channell, a High Court judge with a taste for cruising and racing under sail in a delightful mixture of informal seafaring throughout his summer recess. In 1890 he had the 60 foot cutter "Xanthe" designed and built by E. P. Harris at Rowhedge as a fast cruiser, which also occasionally raced with success. She was skippered by Captain Bill Cranfield of Rowhedge, unrelated to the captain of the "Valkyries", who sailed her with one hand from the village and the judge, who was a keen and practical amateur sailor. For weeks at a time "Xanthe" might be cruising on the East or South coasts, then they would put in somewhere, perhaps at Lowestoft, Deal, Weymouth or Falmouth, where a regatta was to be held. Then, up went "Xanthe's" racing flag and the big yard topsail and spinnaker came out of the sail locker and with the 'long roper' jib topsail sent up, they piled all her loose gear in the dinghy on the mooring, and swept out to the start under her 2,200 square feet, with her skipper's racing blood out for sport and the judge hauling lustily on the mainsheet. Having thrashed round the course, and perhaps won a prize, they enjoyed all the fun of the regatta. Next day might find "Xanthe" under easy sail and the judge whiffling mackerel in the channel swell, yarning to the skipper about last winter's spratting, while the hand fried steaks in the foc'sle. Each autumn "Xanthe" laid up at Rowhedge and her crew fitted out Bill Cranfield's smack, also named "Xanthe", for the winter stowboating. There was always a happy atmosphere aboard the "Xanthe", invariably pronounced "X-anthe" in Rowhedge, as with her predecessor, the 40 foot cutter of the same name which the judge bought in 1876. From that season, until he gave up yachting in 1914, Bill Cranfield and his mate sailed the "Xanthe's", the last being sold at the judge's death in 1919.

The German Emperor was an enthusiastic supporter of yachting and in the nineties established Kiel Week to rival Cowes. In 1897, to celebrate Queen Victoria's Jubilee, he presented a trophy for a race of 310 miles from Dover to Heligoland; hoping to attract British yachts to Kiel. As this excluded yachts of under 40 tons, an English cup was put up for these "little 'uns", and entries poured in for all classes.

The Colne men were active in this early offshore racing. In 1897 the 100 foot yawl "Freda", sailed by Captain William Mathewman of Rowhedge, with a village crew, won the first German Emperor's cup for the North Sea race from Dover to Heligoland. Next year his neighbour, Captain Jesse Cranfield won with the 85 foot yawl "Merry-thought", a graceful old straight stemmer; while in 1899 "Freda" repeated her success. There was no snugging down in these races, where inshore racing canvas was carried in typical North Sea conditions and, for instance, the "Freda" set 6,190 square feet, without her spinnaker.

The Rowhedgers seemed to make a habit of winning the Emperor's cup; in 1900 Captain Fred Pearman won it, sailing the old, 90 foot Scottish cutter "Fiona", which had been bought in 1898 by H. M. Rait, an ardent admirer of Fife's old racer, who loved to see her go. With everything straining and the topmast threatening to break at any time, Mr. Rait would stand by Captain Pearman, on the spray swept deck, proudly taking in the bending spars and roaring wake, replying to the skipper's warning glance; "Never mind, Frederick; let it go. God bless the old "Fiona"."

As a result of this enthusiasm, Captain Pearman drove the old cutter harder than ever and she was often seen foaming along with a smashed topmast and its brand-new gear hanging in tangles aloft. At Kiel the Emperor came aboard "Fiona" to see the men who had won his cup, and was quite impressed. The late Mr. Jack Owen, a West Mersea yachtsman and noted rigger, recalled how, at that time, he walked to Rowhedge seeking a berth aboard a yacht; a then customary spring pilgrimage for many hands from Tollesbury and, occasionally, Mersea. Referred to the "Fiona" fitting out at Harris' yard, he was interviewed by Captain Pearman, to be respectfully told he was too small to be of use aboard that heavily rigged racer whose strong gear and deep bulwarks matched her bronzed and bearded crew of giants, each with wool cap and sheath knife at belt, who drove the old racer to fresh glories in the Dover-Heligoland races, being second in 1903 and fifth a year later. She was successful in other events, winning the Nore to Dover race in 1901 and the Dover to Boulogne in 1903 and 1906, besides many other races in regattas from Rothesay Bay to Ostende.

The "Fiona" was noted for her wonderful gig's crew, in an age when racing of gigs was an exciting regatta event; especially at Dartmouth, from which port she cruised extensively. Captain Pearman last sailed her in 1906, when her owner died and willed the old "Fiona" to the Royal Thames Yacht Club, who were embarrassed rather than delighted, and she was sold to be broken up "for the vally of her lead", as her crew put it.

The 131ft. 6in. racing cutter *Satanita*, 1893. Sailed by Captain Tom Jay of Rowhedge she was capable of speeds exceeding 16 knots. Sail area 10,100 square feet.

Captain Jesse Cranfield of Rowhedge was prominent amongst the hard driving skippers of the early offshore races. A dapper, torpedo-bearded seaman he was, strangely enough, unrelated to his noted namesakes from the same village; his forebears originating from West Mersea. Rowhedge born and trained he quickly made a name in that village's glorious era of supremacy in racing big yachts. From the 80 foot yawl "Merrythought" he stepped up to command the 130 foot cruising-racing schooner "Cicely", built by Fife in 1902 for Cecil Quentin, one of the Kaiser's many English admirers.

Early offshore racing owed much to the Kaiser who was busy imitating the prestige of his English cousins. His naval and mercantile policies were the wonder of the times and to encourage his people's interest in the sea he almost commanded his courtiers, merchants and naval officers to take up yachting. Even the Empress nominally owned the fine schooner "Iduna". To assist his ideal he imported not only racing and cruising yachts designed and built in Britain, but Colne and Solent skippers and crews to sail them and teach German sailors yacht handling and racing tactics.

In 1902 he had a new schooner, named "Meteor III", built in America. She was sailed by Captain Ben Parker of Itchen, with a Southampton crew, who sailed her home to Kiel. When "Cicely" raced at Kiel week she proved much faster than the "Meteor III", pointing to windward remarkably well for a schooner. "Cicely" was very successful at Kiel, Ostend and Cowes and in 1904 her owner wagered a thousand pounds against any yacht willing to race her over a long ocean course, but the challenge was unfortunately never taken.

In 1902 the nineteen year old, big cutter "Irex" fitted out for handicap racing under Captain Charles Simons of Rowhedge, with a village crew. She won yet another German Emperor's cup, at Cowes regatta this time, beating all the big class on time allowance, including the "Cicely". The 100 foot ex-American sloop "Navahoe", rerigged as a yawl, was amongst the "Cicely's" German competitors, sailed by Captain Edward Sycamore with a Colne crew. She won the Dover to Heligoland race in 1907 when, with Robert Wringe in "Susanne", second, and Edward Gould in "Clara", third, the race was a 'Brightlingsea benefit'. Some of the "Navahoe's" adventures in the Baltic will be found in Chapter 12.

Between 1902 and 1906, British large yacht racing was at a low ebb and had become a handicap affair for craft of very varying size. There was, of course, the excitement of Sir Thomas Lipton's third challenge for the America's Cup with "Shamrock III" in 1903, sailed by Captain Robert Wringe of Brightlingsea with a Colne crew, but only the 52 foot class kept thoroughbred yacht racing alive, sailing to regattas all round the coast in the old tradition. The 52 foot class yachts were, perhaps, the most sporting class with continuity of racing from 1896 to 1906, when their type was changed to 15 metres rating by a change of rule. Before 1896 their equivalent had been the 20 raters, and before that the 20 tonners. Colne men were

Two noted Brightlingsea racing skippers. Left, Captain William Woods of the schooner *Egeria* and the America's Cup challenger *Livonia* of 1871. Right, Captain Robert Wringe.

prominent in all of them. In 1898 Captain Robert Wringe was sailing the "Eldred" for John Gretton, battling it out against Captain Dan Aldrige of Rowhedge, sailing the Scottish boat "Viera", and Captain Charles Bevis of Bursledon, on the Hamble river, racing "Senga" with a Solent crew. They also had to contend with the Scottish "Forsa", "Morning Star" and "Penitent", and races were won or lost by seconds.

In 1898 Sir Henry Seymour King had the 88 ton yawl "Heartsease" built by Camper and Nicholson and, with a Brightlingsea crew, raced her in the handicap class. He so enjoyed this that an out-and-out racer for the 52 foot class was ordered next season. Captain Fred Lungley of Brightlingsea was put in charge of the new yacht, named "Caprice", but she had to contend with the "Eldred" and the "Penitent", both also designed by Arthur Payne, and the "Caprice" was withdrawn in mid-summer.

Dan Aldrige had become skipper of the "Penitent" owned by William Burton of Ipswich, the principal of a large grocery business who had a passion for racing and had previously owned several yachts in the small handicap classes. Albert Turner was mate of the local crew of seven and for three seasons the "Penitent" never won less than £250. The racing was extremely close, often only 15 seconds separating each boat at the finish and the yachts were very lightly built for their seventy feet length. Going to windward in a breeze it was possible for a hand to sit in the foc'sle on one of the side lockers with feet on the opposite locker, and feel his knees working!

When William Burton had the new 52 footer "Gauntlet" designed and built by Payne in 1901 he lost Captain Aldrige and engaged a skipper from Burnham, Captain William Deacon. The other new boat of the season was "Magdalen", designed by Fife for a French owner and sailed by Charles Bevis. The "Gauntlet" chased the "Magdalen" all round the coast and was beaten by her almost every day in more than 30 races but Burton, who always sailed aboard his own craft and had begun to steer them too, stubbornly sailed out this disastrous season, selling the "Gauntlet" at the end of it and ordering another 52 footer to thrash the Frenchman next year. Naturally he went to Fife this time, but when the new "Lucida", as he named her, came to the line in 1902 the French yacht, which was fully fitted out with her racing crew aboard, was withdrawn from racing!

Albert Turner returned as skipper in the "Lucida" and commenced a partnership which was unique in that William Burton insisted on steering his yachts when racing, with the skipper acting as adviser; an action greatly resented by most racing captains of that time who considered the finer points of handling a racing yacht of that size was above and beyond amateur capabilities. However, for the next 12 years these two sailed several yachts up to cup defender size, in this dual manner, Burton constantly asking Turner's opinion; "What do you think Albert?"—"A little more breeze over there, sir".

In 1905 Captain Fred Stokes of Tollesbury had the distinction of sailing an English 52 footer designed and built by the famous American yachtbuilder, Nathaniel Herreshoff, who was commissioned by Mrs. Turner-Farley to build the "Sonya" because she considered British designers had exhausted their ideas in that class. Captain Stokes was present at her sailing trials off Newport, Rhode Island, with designer Herreshoff, then came home aboard the ship in which the "Sonya" was shipped to London, where her Tollesbury crew joined her and sailed her round to Tollesbury to fit out for racing. However, she lacked balance in design and was frequently altered before being laid-up in 1908 and sold in 1909. The owner was one of the two ladies ever to have actively owned a racing yacht of the larger classes, the other being Mrs. Workman with the 21 metre "Nyria", in 1920. In 1906 "Sonya" and her principal rivals "Britomart" and "Moyana" sailed 45 races in less than 12 weeks, but she was least successful due to the frequent breaking of her gaff jaws.

The big racing yawls revived after 1896 when rating changes caused the splendid large cutters "Satanita", "Ailsa", "Navahoe", "Bona", "Kariad", "Sybarita", and the German Emperor's "Meteor II", to dock their main booms and step a mizzen in order to win. Their mainsails were extremely large in proportion to the mizzen, which was almost useless on the wind causing it to be despised by yacht skippers and crews as being 'only fit to cheat the rule or fly the ensign from'. Nevertheless, some splendid yawls were afterwards built, including "White Heather I" and "Brynhild I", and the lovely "Valdora", launched by Fife in 1903; a 90 footer sailed by Captain Button from Brightlingsea with a local crew in the big handicap events of the time which took the place of first class racing until 1907.

They had tremendous rivalry with Summers and Payne's "Leander", an 80 footer which won the King's Cup in 1902, sailed by a Solent crew and these fast yawls expressed the striving of owners for more wholesome yachts than the lightly built and oversparred craft to which contemporary rule makers had driven the sport. The 110 foot yawl "Glory" was queen of them all and amongst the best and last designs of Arthur Payne of Summers and Payne. She was built for Sir Henry Seymour King and her generous rig raked the wind. With spinnaker set on its 80 foot boom, and Captain H. Chamberlain of Brightlingsea and his crew revelling in her power and grace, she sped across a sparkling Solent; a happy ship whose owner and his wife gave a dinner to the crew, on board, on their birthdays. In 1904 a hand was lost overboard and the owner vowed the "Glory" would never race again, and she was sold, becoming the "Cassopeia", owned by Miss Napier and Miss Kennedy, and sailed by Brightlingsea's Captain Tom Skeats with a Colne crew.

"Valdora" won the German Emperor's Cup from Dover to Heligoland in 1904, beating the 248 ton American schooner "Ingomar" and many other fine yachts, and the following year she finished third in the Royal London Yacht Club race from Cowes to the Clyde, won by "White Heather I".

Captain Edward Gould of Brightlingsea was amongst the earliest Colne racing captains to sail one of the big German racing yachts which blossomed prominently at the turn of the century. Most of them were German only in name and ensign, and the 183 ton "Clara" was typical in being designed by J. M. Soper and built in 1900 by J. G. Fay and Co. of Southampton. She was a most graceful, clipper bowed yacht whose 8,122 square foot rig sent her 130 foot hull along "like a trine", as one of her crew put it. Her owner, Max Von Gilleaume, sported the white cheesecutter cap beloved by German yachtsmen and took great interest in the "Clara" and her English crew, some of whom were gradually replaced by German sailors whom they trained in yacht racing, to their disgust. But the pay was good and, whatever the owner might think he had no choice, for it was the Kaiser's wish that in about ten years Germany would have a fleet of big yachts manned and sailed by Germans. Captain Gould and his Brightlingsea crew sailed the "Clara" successfully for the next ten years and her greatest rival was the "Susanne", sailed by Captain Robert Wringe. To improve speed the "Clara" had her masts heightened, which made her tender, and to their chagrin the "Susanne" went faster than ever.

In 1904, Captain Wringe of Brightlingsea took command of the new, Fife-designed racing schooner "Susanne" at Ingalls Clydeside shipyard, where she was building for another German owner, Herr Huldschinsky. In those days of giants she was called "the little "Susanne" " in the racing fleet, being only 154 tons compared with the bigger "Clara", "Meteor", "Hamburg" and "Germania", which were her principal contestants.

How the old hands loved their big yachts. One, with whom I discussed a racing captain's career, laughed when I mentioned a certain yacht; "What her! She was only a smig of a thing about 20 ton!" Large or small they handled them superbly and "Susanne" won her share of prizes, including the 1904 Dover Heligoland race for the German Emperor's Cup though, as Captain Wringe remarked to a guest: "The Kaiser's very fond of giving these 'ere long races, but he takes precious good care he don't sail in 'em himself."

At Kiel, "Susanne" raced for the £2,000 trophy presented by King Edward VII for the big class. In light and fluky winds she beat the whole fleet, leading them proudly up beautiful Kiel Fiord, sparkling in the crisp Baltic sunshine. But, alas! she had set a main staysail which should have been measured but was not, and was disqualified; the prize going to the big American "Ingomar", though Captain Wringe won it on merit. Like all her rivals "Susanne" always raced at Cowes week, of which a contemporary observer wrote: ". . .the big yacht hands cluster on the forecastle to watch the glorious duels between "Shamrock" and "White Heather", to discuss the keen matches between the 15 metre boats. It was a standing joke to chaff the great designer when the other fellow's boat was ahead, but Jack Jones, who has skinned his knuckles bringing his little ship round, was the man who stood in mute admiration of the marvellous finish of the Cowes Town cup. Almost in line, barely stemming the tide, "Meteor", "Germania", "Cetonia", "Susanne", the two "Cariads", "Julnar" and the smaller classes, all were threading their way through a maze of anchored yachts. Not a biscuit throw from the shore "Susanne" was leading "Cetonia" and "Cariad", all with spinnakers boomed out, and as they took her wind she dropped back to them without steerage way. No room on either hand, it seemed there must be a smash; but no—all were splendidly handled, and at last, in a body, they crossed the line. The judging was enough to turn a man's hair grey, but it was done, and well done; and never shall I forget that mass of golden canvas, seemingly in one, against the sapphire sea, while the shapely hulls forged their way through the cool green of the foreground water. Farther out still lay the hundreds of decorated yachts and battleships . . . ."

Perhaps 1908 was typical of "Susanne's" rather short seasons. She fitted out in May at Sandbank, on the Clyde, won the Dover-Heligoland race in June, raced at Kiel and in the Baltic, and returned to Brightlingsea at the end of July, with the German Emperor's Cup on board and wearing 11 first and 2 second prize flags won in 15 starts. She was hauled up on Stone's slip in early August, with her crew paid off. "Susanne's" finest race was the Nore to Dover in 1908, in a tremendous sea. That season she caused a sensation by setting a ringtail on the leech of her mainsail; a sail which had not been seen in yacht racing for thirty years. She sailed in the Baltic during much of 1909 and was very successful, but that November she was sold to Maurice Verstraete and was laid up at Brightlingsea.

During the depressed state of big class racing between 1897 and 1908, which reflected economic conditions as much as yachting fashion, there was great enthusiasm for rejuvenating old racing yachts, and racing in the handicap classes. The old forty raters "Creole" and "Carina" had many battles in the small handicap class. "Creole" passed to the command of Captain John Redgewell of Tollesbury when Tom Skeats left her to sail the big "Bona" in 1899. She was then long outbuilt in class racing but her owner, Col. Villiers Bagot, was very proud of his yacht and entered her in most events around the coast, where she was very successful. After Captain Redgewell's death in December 1904, the "Creole" was sailed by another Tollesburyman, Captain Charles Levett, whose great rival was the "Carina", sailed by Captain William Goff of Brightlingsea, who got his 1894 built cutter along in great style, sailing from Dover to Boulogne in 2½ hours, in 1908. Next season she also raced on the French coast and won the President's Cup and a £40 prize at Le Havre regatta.

Captain Tom Jay of Rowhedge aboard the racing cutter *Ailsa*, 1894. The owner and Mrs. A. B. Walker at right. Typical silver prize cups. Note trysail sheets and size of main and spinnaker booms.

The old 40 ton racing cutter "Bloodhound" made the most triumphant return, 34 years after her launch! She had been built by Fife for the Marquis of Ailsa, who re-purchased her in 1908, when she was long outclassed in racing of any sort. After altering her keel, adding outside ballast and giving her a taller and lighter sail plan, the old "Bloodhound" came out with her racing flag flying bravely and Captain Ben Chaplin of Brightlingsea at the tiller. He quickly justified her renaissance by winning 30 prizes in 40 races. The 90 foot yawl "L'Esperance", sailed by Captain A. Downes of Brightlingsea, was Captain Chaplin's greatest rival in the handicap class and, at the start of a race off Cowes in 1908, they were manœuvering and collided at speed, the "Bloodhound" bursting her bows open and sinking head first on the Shrape, without loss of life. She was raised after five days and taken to White's yard at Itchen for repair, her crew returning to Brightlingsea.

Two months earlier the "L'Esperance" was lying at Bridlington, Yorkshire, when a sudden gale drove a fleet of local cobles ashore on the South sands and Captain Downes and his Brightlingsea crew mustered alongshore with ropes and tackles, giving welcome assistance in beaching the battered cobles and hauling them up out of reach of the raging seas. Off the Yorkshire coast, "L'Esperance" also raced against Lord Dunraven's ketch "Cariad", sailed by Captain Barty Smith of Rowhedge with a village crew and in the Solent these big racing cruisers were often matched against Brightlingsea's Captain Ben Fenn sailing the smart yawl "Isola", and the "Moonbeam", sailed by Captain Harry Cross for owner Charles Johnson. The "Moon-beam" was always the first yacht to fit out at Brightlingsea and the owner and all hands got tremendous sport all round the coast.

The wonderfully successful combination of "Bloodhound" sailed by Ben Chaplin and his Brightlingsea crew continued each season until 1914. They started 217 times and won 143 prizes. Both yacht and captain had sad ends; the old "Bloodhound" was burnt when laid up in 1922 and Lieutenant Ben Chaplin, D.S.C., died when the armed yacht "Rhiannon" was mined.

In 1903 J. W. Leuchars joined the 52 foot class with "Moyana", designed by young Alfred Mylne, and Steven Barbrook of Tollesbury was appointed skipper. He had sailed as a hand in the crew of "Ailsa" and the schooner "Rainbow", under Captain Tom Jay, who had coached him in helmsmanship. "Moyana" was his first important racing command and he thoroughly justified the owner's confidence in a comparatively unknown skipper by ending the season with a long string of prize flags. He raced her during 1904, when "Moyana" finished the season second to the new Fife cutter "Maymon", sailed by Charles Bevis of Bursledon; but Captain Barbrook continued to race "Moyana" with considerable success in an extremely competitive class for four seasons before she was laid up during 1907.

In 1908 Captain Barbrook sailed the 23 metre cutter "Brynhild," for Sir James Pender. She had come out the previous year and was the unluckiest yacht ever built.

At her launch on a Friday the cradle killed a shipwright, and old sailors shook their heads at this omen of disaster. During her first sail in the Thames matches one of her mastheadsmen fell from aloft and was killed, and a few weeks later a hand was lost overboard and drowned. Racing, eastward of the Isle of Wight, "Brynhild" lost her topmast and when the raffle of gear had been cleared away the owner's wife suggested to Charles Nicholson, her designer, that they should give up and return to Gosport to have a new topmast made. Knowing the keen watch kept on racers built by the firm, when in sight of lookouts in the yard, he replied: "I expect it's half made by now, madam".

The 23 metre cutters were fast but very wet boats, setting 10,000 square feet of canvas and had a crew of 22 hands. They cost about £12,000 fitted out; a tremendous sum in those days.

Captain Barbrook took "Brynhild" over from her previous skipper, well knowing this background of tragedy, and set about improving her performance against the slightly smaller "Nyria", sailed by Captain Steven Ray of Gosport and the 23 metre "White Heather", built by Fife in 1907 and splendidly sailed by Captain Charles Bevis of Bursledon, with a Solent crew. All of them had a formidable competitor in the newly-launched 23 metre "Shamrock", built by Fife for Sir Thomas Lipton and sailed by Captain Edward Sycamore of Brightlingsea, with a crew from Colne. Until well into the season "Shamrock" and "White Heather" were most successful, but in a terrific spurt during Cowes week and the subsequent West country regattas, Steven Barbrook brought "Brynhild's" first prizes up to eight, against "Shamrock's" twelve and "White Heather's" five. Sir James Pender was delighted; always an enthusiastic owner, he wore a special striped guernsey for racing, woven in "Brynhild's" racing colours of red and black.

The "Brynhild" was not fitted out in 1909 and Captain Barbrook went as skipper for King Alfonso of Spain in the new 15 metre yacht "Hispania" which had been built at Pasages to designs of William Fife. He raced her at San Sebastian in July, when she won her maiden race, and sailed her in England for Cowes week, but had a Spanish crew who were poor racing hands. For several days at the beginning of the week he did not dare bring the "Hispania" to the line in the heat of class racing against William Burton's new "Ostara", with Captain Albert Turner and her Colne crew, or the new "Vanity" which Mylne had designed for Mr. Payne.

The 15 metres were the best sporting class in British racing from 1907 until 1914. These 76 footers cost £3,500 to build and the crew's expenses were generally as follows; Captain £150 per year; mate, 22 weeks at 32 shillings—£35 4s; cook and steward 22 weeks at 32 shillings—£35 4s; five hands at 26 shillings—£143; 'Grub money' at 2 shillings and six pence per head for fifty starts £50. Prize money was paid to the crew from the yacht's winnings, as follows; £2 to the captain for each first prize and £1 for each other prize; £1 to each of the crew for each first prize and 10 shillings for each

Crew of the 263 ton racing schooner *Cicely*, 1902. Captain Jesse Cranfield of Rowhedge at extreme right. First mate William Cranfield (junior) to left of wheel.

other prize; 5 shillings to each man when no prize was won—known as 'starting money'. Other expenses included; an average of 30 shillings to a racing pilot for each race where he was necessary; entrance fees and other expenses—£100; clothes for captain and crew—£68; hauling up the yacht and scrubbing for racing—£60; insurance—£35; laying up the yacht for winter and sundry items—£100. The yacht might hope to win about £250 prize money during an average season which, when depreciation is taken into account, cost the owner about £1,500; a large sum in the days when 'a sovereign was a sovereign'.

Although she did not race in England until Cowes week, "Hispania" proved to be a fast boat and her owner was well pleased.

In 1910 Captain Barbrook and his crew fitted out the "Brynhild" which had alterations carried out to her mast step, to increase the height of her sail plan. At the Orwell Corinthian Yacht Club regatta off Harwich on May 23rd, "Shamrock", "White Heather" and "Brynhild" started, and near the weather mark, the North Cutler Buoy, "Brynhild's" mast failed below deck, drove down through her bottom and sank her in fourteen minutes. She was leading at the time and the dinghy was quickly launched, her crew of 25 clinging to it until her competitors launched theirs and a destroyer came steaming up to help. The "Brynhild" filled slowly at first, then lay over on her side until her mast was lying on the surface. Sir James Pender insisted on being rowed over to cut her racing flag from the masthead and a few minutes later the fine cutter sank.

1911 was notable for the great international regatta which was to be held in the Solent and for the introduction of the 19 metre class; fine 100 ton cutters, 95 feet long and setting 6,200 square feet of canvas, handled by a skipper, mate, and 12 hands. They could race in any weather short of a strong gale and could have been the nucleus of a healthy class of large racer. Four were built; Captain Barbrook was appointed to sail Almeric Paget's and Mr. Hennesey's "Corona", designed and built by Fife, who also launched the "Mariquita" for A. K. Stothert, sailed by Captain Edward Sycamore with a Colne crew. The "Octavia" was designed by Alfred Mylne and built by McAllister at Dumbarton for William Burton who, as usual, sailed her himself, with Albert Turner as skipper. The fourth boat, "Norada", was designed and built by Nicholson for Frederick Milburn, but had a crew from the owner's cruising yacht, only one of whom had previously sailed in a racing yacht, so she had little chance. These boats were one of the finest classes of British racing yachts, sailing to Kiel, where they had keen racing, then back across the North Sea to Aberdeen, through the Caledonian Canal and round the Mull of Kintyre for the Clyde fortnight, before sailing down the Irish Sea and up channel to the Solent regattas, finishing the season along the west coast regattas. Some of their adventures are described in Chapter 12.

"Octavia" topped the class, winning 15 first prizes in 48 races, "Mariquita" being second with 12 and "Corona" third with 10. "Norada" proved an excellent design and won 9 firsts.

The class raced again in 1912 when "Mariquita" was sailed to the top by Captain Robert Wringe, as Captain Sycamore had returned to the "Shamrock", 23 metre, to continue his duels with Charles Bevis in the "White Heather". William Burton continued to sail "Octavia", with Albert Turner as skipper and Charles Wadley of Wivenhoe as mate of his very experienced crew. Burton's description of one race that season is interesting in illustrating the feeling between professional and amateur helmsmen, and the high standard he must have attained.

'It was a duel between "Mariquita" and "Octavia". The latter just had the start, and with luck, or good sailing, soon got a couple of minutes ahead. Bar accidents, it looked as if she had the thing fairly well set. However, a sudden shift in the wind brought "Mariquita" close up, and then, after rounding the middle buoy with spinnakers up, we had a rare set-to. First, she threatened one side, then the other, and it took all the knowledge I am supposed to possess to keep her behind. With a strong fair tide, however, it was a quick passage to the Solent Banks buoy. When just upon there, it looked as if "Octavia" were safe to round first, and sheets were got in for the gybe and close haul to follow; but Wringe sails a hard race, and takes every inch out of the rules; certainly more than any amateur would do in similar circumstances. Mind you, I make no complaint. He is well known for his iron nerves, and if anything is wrong it is the wording of the rules. Be that as it may, he wiped across my stern and secured an overlap, certainly before I had the buoy abreast of me, but with that tide I do not think five seconds elapsed, and what would have happened if I had been unable to bear away I hardly care to contemplate. Suffice it to say, I just did, and gave him room; he got round neatly, while I shot a hundred yards past before I could complete my gybe.

'Then commenced the windward work against the awful tide. Wringe on my weather had me fast, and evidently intended to keep me so; but I had intentions, too, and I could call the tune. So, without a moment's hesitation, I broke tack, only to be followed like a shot by "Mariquita". Break tack again was the order, and so we did again, and again and again. I think it is no exaggeration to say we made a hundred tacks in as many minutes. Each tack "Octavia" gained an inch, until at last Wringe was a trifle slow, and "Octavia" just had her wind clear, or nearly so. Then "Mariquita" was sailed along, till once again "Octavia" was smothered, and this time it did look as if it were all up. But we were nothing daunted, and my crew, still confident and obedient to my smallest whim, heard me whisper:

"Ease off jib and staysail."

This done, "Octavia" dropped back.

"All clear, Sir," cried the mate—he knew the game.

Captain Sycamore and the crew of the America's Cup challenger *Shamrock II*, 1901.

Racing the 23 metre *Shamrock* on the Clyde, 1909. Captain Edward Sycamore of Brightlingsea at the wheel. Sir Thomas Lipton (owner) centre. Col. Duncan Niell (left) and Herbert Springett of Rowhedge, a hand, right.

"Lee oh!" and "Octavia" was round like a top; "Mariquita" too, but not quick enough. We had our wind clear this time.

"Now sail her by the wind," my skipper said, "and she should draw through."

"Sail her full and cover him!" One could almost read the thoughts in Wringe's set face—and he did—yes, he did!

"She's fouled us," shouted the "Mariquita's" crew.

"Has she?" said the owner. "Where?".

"Why, his crosstrees caught our yankee sheet."

Then out came the good sportsman. "Give up," he ordered, for Mr. Stothert knows the rules. "It was our duty to keep clear," he owned.

And thus "Octavia" won what I think was the best, the hardest race I ever sailed in my life.'

Before the "Octavia", William Burton had owned the 52 footer "Britomart", of 1905 which also raced as a 15 metre when the rules changed to the international metric formula in 1906, and the 15 metre "Ostara" of 1909, which was phenomenally successful with 21 first prizes, and 20 the following year; both designed by Alfred Mylne and built at Dumbarton by McAllisters.

Alfred Mylne designed the Scottish owned 15 metre "Tritonia" in 1910. She came south for the opening races in the Thames and called at Harris' Rowhedge yard for alterations. Afterwards, John Cranfield piloted her down the Colne and the owner requested him to go with them to Harwich. The Scottish skipper could do nothing with her so John sailed her in Harwich regatta, winning a first and a second. He stayed with her until the Thames matches when an amateur helmsman sailed her, but she sulked and was last. John Cranfield itched to get his hands on the tiller and, when the amateur peevishly asked if he could do better, he took the helm and ordered the sheets to be slacked after which the "Tritona" began to pass her competitors one by one to finish second to Mr. John Payne's "Vanity". Payne chaffed John Cranfield for "not waking up until he was half round".

In 1912 the leading contemporary designer, Charles Nicholson of Gosport, produced the 15 metre cutter "Istria" for Sir Charles Allom. Always a weight saver and original thinker, Nicholson scrapped the topsail yard and increased the masthead to include topmast and topsail yard in one spar of then extraordinary height, and the topsail luff was set on this by track and slides. The elaborate rigging and height of mast caused it to be known as 'marconi' rig, after the aerials of the radio inventor, then in the news. "Istria" was sailed by Captain Alf Diaper of Itchen, who had several

Essex-manned 52 footers racing in a strong breeze, 1903. Left; *Lucinda*, owned by William Burton; Captain Dan Aldrige of Rowhedge. Right; *Moyana*, owned by J. Leuchars and sailed by Captain Steven Barbrook of Tollesbury.

Brightlingseamen amongst his crew. She dominated the class, leading most other larger racers to adopt the rig.

By then amateur helmsmen appeared occasionally in classes up to 15 metres. Many were derisively called 'Port Victoria dinner hunters' by the yacht skippers and crews; a label arising from the yacht club sited in the Medway, whose members were always hopefully looking for a chance of a day's sailing in a racer.

Fife designed and built the 15 metre "Maudrey" in 1913, for W. B. Stamp whose family had long owned cruising yachts skippered and manned from Rowhedge. True to this tradition Captain Wallace Allen, with a village crew, raced the "Maudrey" but, despite their skill, she proved a mediocre performer, winning only 12 prizes in 43 starts. "Octavia" was sold to a German owner and in the spring of 1913 Captain Albert Turner and his crew transferred to the "Norada", which was sailed that season by amateur helmsman Charles MacIver, against "Corona" and "Mariquita".

Fateful 1914 brought Sir Thomas Lipton's fourth America's Cup challenge with the Nicholson designed and built "Shamrock IV" prepared to be raced by the old combination of William Burton, Captain Albert Turner and a Colne crew, but war intervened. By then Captain Sycamore had taken to the 15 metre class, sailing the German "Sophie Elizabeth", built by Fife in 1910. He and his Colne crew were bound with her for Cowes week, 1914, under tow in company with the German Emperor's schooner "Meteor IV", when war was imminent, and they were towed back to Germany. Their subsequent adventures are described in Chapter 12.

Most yachts were quickly laid up in 1914 by owners convinced the war would soon be over, but, as the conflict deepened into 1915, many were sold, particularly the racers, mainly to buyers from the neutral Scandinavian countries, which were reaping rich profits. Many more had their huge lead keels removed for making bullets. However, several of the German racing yachts which were at Cowes at the outbreak of war were confiscated, and sold out of the country, paradoxically retaining their lead keels intact!

It was an odd collection of yachts which assembled for Cowes week in 1919. The smartest was the 42 tonner "Thanet", owned by J. Cook and sailed by Captain Zac Burch of Rowhedge, where she had been built by Harris Brothers in 1914. She was joined by the old racer "Nyria", bought by Sir Charles Allom, as she lay in Brightlingsea, without her lead keel and still in the ketch rig to which she was converted in 1912, when she was renamed "Lady Camiella". Her unstable hull was towed round to Colne beach for ballasting with tons of shingle to give her sufficient stability to sail round to Gosport under a runner crew, for refitting. Apart from this the Colne saw little sign of a racing revival. Two large racing schooners occupied Stone's slips for months; the "little" "Susanne" and the mighty "Westward", bought as a war prize by Clarence Hatry, the financier who was subsequently to commit suicide so dramatically before the court hearing his bankruptcy.

Racing hands' weekly wages had risen from the pre-war 26 shillings to £3 17s. 6d. and the cost of labour and materials for repair and maintenance of yachts had rocketed, so it is not surprising that only a score of yachts were laid up at Brightlingsea that winter. Many thought the big racers would never revive but they were soon proved wrong. That winter King George V decided he would race the "Britannia" during 1920 and this lead brought spectacular results. R. Lee ordered the powerful 115 foot cutter "Terpsichore" from White's yard at Itchen, to designs by Herbert White, and for C. Johnson, Fife designed and built the beautifully proportioned 90 foot cutter "Moonbeam", sailed by Captain Tom Skeats of Brightlingsea. Both of these were gaff rigged, but the "Nyria", which had been sold to Mrs. R. Workman, was taken to her builder's Gosport yard and re-rigged as a bermudian cutter and fitted out as a first class racing yacht, to be sailed by Captain Bob Diaper of Itchen. Sir Charles Allom bought the 23 metre 'White Heather", sailed by Captain Fred Mountifield of Gosport; Westward fitted out under Captain Edward Sycamore; "Susanne" joined in; and the "Britannia" came out with Major Hunloke in charge, with Captain Charles Leavett of Tollesbury as skipper.

They had a fine season during which the "Moonbeam" won a King's Cup. Next year the "Westward" dropped out and the "Susanne" was sold and in 1922 the big yachts did not fit out but in 1923 the class revived with "Britannia", "Nyria", "Terpsichore", "Cariad" and "Valdora".

In 1924 Sir Thomas Lipton had his 23 metre "Shamrock" fitted out to race with Captain Charles Leavett in command and Sir Charles Allom's "White Heather" joined

The 23 metre class racing at Harwich, 1909. From left; *Brynhild*, Captain Steven Barbrook of Tollesbury. *White Heather*, Captain Charles Bevis of Bursledon, Hampshire. *Shamrock*, Captain Edward Sycamore of Brightlingsea.

her. The "Terpsichore" was sold and, renamed "Lulworth", was sailed by Captain Charles Bevis. The "Britannia" came out again, rebuilt and in charge of Major Hunloke, the King's sailing master, and with Captain Albert Turner of Wivenhoe in charge of her crew. The big yachts were again racing all round the coast and the structure of yachting in Britain had regained much of its pre-war glory.

By 1926 Captain Edward Sycamore was back as skipper of the 23 metre cutter "Shamrock" which was thoroughly refitted and soon proved a competitor to be reckoned with in the big class. She was driven as hard on passage as when racing and Gus Spinks of Rowhedge recalled her, bound for Cowes from the Clyde fortnight, storming up-channel under trysail and small jib, with her deck swept and streaming as she roared past ten knot steamers.

No more gaff cutters were built for racing and in 1928 the Fife built cutter "Cambria" and the Nicholson built "Astra" arrived to finally prove the superiority of the bermudian rig in the big class.

The big handicap class also raced around the coast and during the late 1920's was dominated by two beautiful yawls built by Fife and sailed by Essex crews. Sir William Burton's "Rendezvous", launched in 1913 was an elegant 87 footer sailed by Captain James Barnard of Rowhedge and his great rival was Hugh Paul's "Sumurun", a fast 79 footer sailed by Captain Gurten of Tollesbury. Both boats set 5,500 square feet of canvas and, immaculately kept and sailed, were examples of the very best type of yacht produced by any period of the sport.

The big cutters had revived but the 12 metres, seventy foot sloops, were the class of the future which provided great racing and a chance for many racing skippers from the Colne, Tollesbury and the Solent, to show their skill. Typical of them was Edward Carrington Heard, born at Tollesbury in 1879. He fished in the village smacks and in 1899 was selected as a hand in the 52 foot class racer "Penitent", skippered by Captain Dan Aldrige of Rowhedge. In 1903 he went to America as a hand in "Shamrock III" along with Tom Sampson and William Riley, the two other Tollesbury members of her 40 man crew. In 1914 he was first mate of "Shamrock IV" under Captain Albert Turner, also racing in her postponed attempt for the America's Cup in 1920.

In 1925 the Norwegian-built 12 metre "Noresca", launched for Sir William Burton and R. G. Perry the previous year to designs by Johan Anker, was sold to R. Ellis Brown and F. G. Mitchell who engaged Edward Heard as her skipper. The "Noresca" was a big, powerful looking boat, bermudian rigged and 68 feet long, and setting 2,150 square feet in a sloop rig. Captain Heard proved himself to be a dashing tactician, with a reputation for taking great risks. "Noresca" had a remarkable season, winning two King's Cups; at the regattas of the Royal Northern Yacht Club, on the Clyde and the Royal Ulster Yacht Club, Belfast, finishing the season with 17 firsts, 3 seconds and 4 thirds in 38 races. She was hard pressed by John Payne's "Vanity" but won £500 prize money and made the name of her captain in the racing world.

From 1924 until 1939 the 12 metre class provided some of the finest sport in British yacht racing, and at the modest cost of £4,500 for a new boat, restricted to a professional crew of a captain and three hands to handle a sail area of 2,000 square feet, and a spinnaker of greater area. The class raced all round the coast in the traditional manner, besides racing at Ostende, Le Havre and Deauville.

Next season four new 12 metres were built and competition hardened. It became general for more and more gear and moveables to be left ashore on race days, to lighten the yachts; even to taking off the skylights and leaving them in the dinghy, on the mooring. The 12 metre conception had been for fast but seaworthy yachts whose owners and guests could live aboard throughout the season. But good accommodation meant weight and some owners began to live aboard a steam or motor yacht which followed the racing fleet around the coast. They arrived on board in a launch an hour before the start, and left her shortly after the finish. There was also development and decadence in the rig; the "Iris" Scottish owner designed his own 12 metre and took her mast height to the limit with a mainsail 86 feet in the hoist. The 12 metre class flourished and four other Tollesbury skippers came into the class, and for a time Drake Brothers yard had several of these sleek boats hauled up, each winter, standing high above the saltings like a badge of village pride. In 1927 Edward Heard had to contend with Sir William Burton's new "Iyruna", skippered by Captain James Barnard of Rowhedge, which beat the class.

Thomas Sopwith's remarkable 12 metre "Mouette" came out in 1928 with a Solent crew and gave "Noresca" tough competition, winning the first three matches of the season, but in the race for the King's Cup at Harwich, Captain Heard beat her by 16 seconds, despite, or perhaps because of the large headsail set by "Mouette". But "Noresca" was outclassed by the new boats and finished sixth in the class. During the four years that he sailed her Captain Heard won 116 prizes in 137 starts: a splendid record.

In 1929 Captain Heard was offered command of the "Shamrock V", the last of Sir Thomas Lipton's green hulled challengers and the first British yacht built to the 'J' class of the American universal rating rule. She was designed and built by Camper and Nicholson's at Gosport and commenced her season at Harwich. Her crew of 19 from Tollesbury, the Colne, West Mersea and the Solent, were jubilant when she proved her weatherliness by sailing clean through "Cambria's" lee and also well beating the "Candida", skippered by Captain Jim Gilbey of Emsworth, Hampshire with a Hampshire crew. This despite what many of them thought was her comparatively small sail area of 7,600 square feet and the weight of her wooden mast and elaborate rigging. "Shamrock V" was rigged as a bermudian yawl for the passage out to America, making a 24 day crossing from Brixham to New London, Connecticut.

Lipton's steam yacht "Erin" escorted her and towed the challenger whenever conditions permitted, which was not often, to the crew's relief, as the racer was much easier under her double reefed trysail and storm jib than corkscrewing along through long, steep Atlantic seas behind a towline. Sometimes the "Shamrock" lost touch with the "Erin" for days and was becalmed in mid-ocean, with the crew vainly trying to get her along with a big headsail and squaresail set; boxing about for a time before the western horizon darkened again with shrieking squalls and days of big seas and wind which forced them to crawl about the heaving deck at the change of the watch, or to tend the badly chafing running rigging. The foc'sle became almost uninhabitable in pounding seas and some hands shifted to the sail locker in the long, flat counter, whose slamming in the seas was as noisy as the booming of the long, outreaching bow, but drier. Often, at meals, the saloon skylight would darken with a green sea and cascades of water roared down over the watch below.

At last they arrived in America and raced the more lightly rigged "Enterprise", sailed by amateur, Harold Vanderbilt. "Enterprise" defeated the "Shamrock" in each of the seven races but Vanderbilt wrote of Captain Heard and his crew; "In defeat lies the test of true sportsmanship and they have proved themselves—quite the finest it has ever been our good fortune to race against." A fine tribute. Shamrock's crew received a friendly welcome in the United States. The American observer who sailed aboard during the races noticed Captain Heard was fond of bananas with his sandwich lunch, served when racing, and next morning arrived on board with a big bunch under his arm! A dinner was given for the crews of both yachts who sat opposite each other at table, under Captains Heard and Monsell, and enjoyed themselves in the friendliest spirit. "Shamrock V" returned to England and, Sir Thomas Lipton dying soon afterwards, she was sold to Thomas Sopwith.

In 1932 it was back to 12 metres; Captain Heard taking charge of the eight years old boat "Morwenna", previously "Moyana II". Although she started 37 times and was sailed with skill and verve, she won only 4 firsts, and was outclassed by "Flica", "Zoraida" and "Veronica". Captain Heard was offered command of the 23 metre "Astra" which had been designed and built by Camper and Nicholson in 1928 and was previously sailed by Captain Pound, of Gosport, with a Solent crew. In 1931 she was bought by Hugh Paul, one of the Ipswich milling family, and soon improved her fortunes with Captain Heard at the wheel.

By 1930 the composition of crews in the big racing yachts was changing; no longer did a skipper strive to keep most of his crew from his native village, or even from the same district, but accepted men from other places, provided they were smart hands. Brixham men had come into the big racing yachts as hands when King George V requested that a proportion of "Britannia's" crew be drawn from that port, in those days of meagre employment and opportunity; and later a few from Looe were added.

In the "Astra", Captain Heard had a Brixham first mate; Jack Gampton, and hands from Itchen and Southampton in his crew, besides men from Tollesbury, the Colne and West Mersea. The "Astra" was an especially happy yacht and Mr. and Mrs. Paul were keenly interested in her crew. She fitted out in her builder's yard each spring, when a pleasant little tradition was maintained; "Astra" lay on the buoy in Portsmouth harbour, the Pauls came down by rail from London and the launch met them at the harbour station. As they came alongside "Astra" Captain Heard met them at the gangway, cap in hand, to welcome them and as the owner stepped aboard the burgee was broken out at the masthead. "Astra" was painted white for many years but one season Mrs. Paul, when motoring down from London, saw a green coloured rick cover on a stack and decided the yacht would look splendid repainted to that shade, and so she remained until 1939, and Captain Heard remained her skipper. "Astra" seemed a lucky yacht; rarely suffering damage and never losing a mast like some of her larger opponents. But the season of 1935, when the curtain came down on the glorious climax of big class yacht racing, brought tragedy to the "Astra".

In June 1935, "Astra", "Endeavour", "Velsheda" and the visiting American sloop "Yankee" assembled at Southend for the Thames racing which opened the season. "Astra" was recalled at the start and returned to start again, behind the others, in the south westerly wind which was freshening to half a gale. The lee mark was the Mouse light vessel and the "Yankee" gybed at the West Oaze buoy but the British yachts continued and ran by the lee only to be forced to gybe at the Mouse, where disaster struck all three. "Velsheda" broke her boom, "Endeavour" was gybed before

The hulk of the 23 metre racing cutter *Brynhild*, beached in Brightlingsea creek for breaking up, after her dramatic sinking at Harwich, in 1910.

the backstay had been properly set up and the mast went overboard, fortunately clear of everyone aboard, but, saddest of all on the run to the Mouse, "Astra's" spinnaker went wild and its sheet took charge. George Lewis of Brightlingsea, "Astra's" steward, tried to check it but was flung into the sea. In seconds "Astra's" boat was over and searching, while the yacht circled, but there was no trace of Lewis. With sad hearts they gave up and, with an ensign in the rigging for a lost shipmate, sailed back to the Southend anchorage. Despite the gloom this cast over the season, the "Astra" was very successful, winning 8 firsts, 7 seconds and 3 thirds.

When Thomas Sopwith had the "Endeavour II" built by Camper and Nicholson in 1936, to challenge for the America's Cup during the following season he had only the old "Endeavour", "Velsheda" and "Astra" to race against. The "Britannia" had been scuttled, in accordance with the King's wishes, after his death, and "Yankee" had returned to America. The challenger tuned up in a background of depression amongst the big class but the 1937 challenge was probably the best organised there had ever been. "Endeavour II" was to be sailed by her owner, with Captain Williams of Hamble in charge of her crew of 30, and to tune her up in America, Herman Andrae, who had bought "Endeavour I", lent her to Sopwith as trial horse. Captain Heard was released by Hugh Paul to sail the "Endeavour I" against the challenger. The two racers were rigged down as yawls for the transatlantic passage but were to be towed across; "Endeavour II" astern of the Belgian trawler "John" and "Endeavour I" by the motor yacht "Viva II". The challenger had an uneventful voyage but "Viva II" lost her tow two-thirds of the way across and Captain Heard set sail and arrived unaided.

Captain Heard, sailing the "Endeavour I", beat both the American defender "Ranger" and the previous defender "Rainbow", in trial races before the start of the Cup matches in which "Endeavour II" was well beaten by the "Ranger". "Endeavour II" was towed home, safely, by her owner's new motor yacht "Philante", but during the passage her skipper, Captain Williams, was taken ill, died, and was buried at sea. The homeward bound "Endeavour I" with Captain Heard and his crew from Essex, Southampton and the West Country, again came into the headlines.

In tow of "Viva II", "Endeavour" left Newport, Rhode Island, on the afternoon of September 12, but 24 hours later, when approximately 230 miles east of the Brenton Reef light vessel, the weather, which up to then had been fine, deteriorated and a strong south south-easterly breeze brought up a heavy sea from that quarter. Because of the violent pitching, the speed of the tow was reduced, first to 9 knots and then to 5, to lessen the strain on the yacht's hull and her crew. As evening advanced the weather continued to get worse, and preparations were made to stream the sea anchor in case it became necessary to slip the tow-rope. "Viva II" was kept informed of this by wireless telephone. However, by 10 p.m. the wind reached hurricane force and, owing to the heavy seas which were constantly sweeping the decks, it was impossible for any man to go forward to slip the tow-rope. All sails, with the exception of the small mizzen,

Captain James Barnard of Rowhedge at the wheel of the 100ft. yawl *Rendezvous*.

which was later to be so important, had been stowed and everything movable on deck was securely lashed.

Just before midnight it was found that the 9 inch hemp towrope had parted and the sea anchor was streamed. In the weather conditions it was impossible to get the 70 fathoms of towrope inboard so it was left hanging from the stem head, acting as an additional sea anchor. When everything on deck was secured all hands were ordered below and the yacht battened down. For the next 12 hours the yacht lay with the mizzen set and riding to her sea anchor. The motion was extremely violent and wireless communication with the "Viva II" broke down when seas broke the skylights of the after cabin and flooded the set.

The "Endeavour" suffered no damage while hove to and by the following morning the weather fined away sufficiently to enable the towrope to be recovered. Shortly before noon there was a fair wind and the sea anchor was recovered; the yacht squared away on an east south easterly course under staysail, trysail and mizzen, with a fresh wind.

Meanwhile the "Viva II" was searching anxiously and wirelessed the American coastguard for assistance in her search. Cutters and seaplanes carried out a wide sweep, without success, and anxiety rose for the "Endeavour" and her crew.

On September 15 the "Endeavour" sighted a seaplane flying low in the distance, but of course they were unaware of the dramatic fears for their safety which the press and radio had propagated. On September 19 a schooner was sighted but not spoken, and the yacht continued to roll slowly eastwards until the wind freshened next day and she began to make knots.

On September 21 the "Endeavour's" crew, listening to the wireless receiving set which was still working, heard a broadcast which said that the American Coastguard had called off their search and that the yacht was presumed to be lost. Desperately they tried to get the transmitter to work, but this message was never picked up.

The "Endeavour" sailed on in everything from light breezes to half a gale, when the rubber mast wedging had to be reinforced with wooden wedges driven up from below. On September 27 the wind came ahead and the yacht spoke to the British tanker "Cheyenne", who reported them. For two days they beat against head winds and sighted the Bishop Rock light in the early hours of September 30, 19 days out from Newport.

The "Viva II" had crossed the Atlantic and, when she was almost at the Needles, the message that "Endeavour" was sailing home reached her and she turned back at full speed. The "Endeavour" had a triumphal return up-channel and her arrival in Portsmouth harbour on October 1 could not have been greater if she had been the returning "Victory".

By 1935 social customs and yachting fashions were changing and inshore racing in class yachts, which had been brought to near perfection in the 12 metre class, and to excess in the rig of the bigger cutters, was proving too expensive and unattractive to the rising generation of sailing men. Their enthusiasm and means were attuned to the sport of passage racing in comparatively small yachts which had been established in America before 1914, largely by the efforts of Thomas Day, and had spread to England during the 1920's, where enthusiasts established the Fastnet race and the Ocean Racing Club, later the Royal Ocean Racing Club. Although a few of these early offshore racers, such as "Halloween", carried a full professional crew, the majority were almost totally manned by amateurs, usually with one professional hand, and professional helmsmen were banned.

There was a great deal of work, at times, aboard a forty footer for one man to keep her in racing trim and be expected to do most of the cooking and generally 'nursemaid' the crew, and there was, of course, no prize money as this was regarded as an unnecessary survival of old traditions which had to be changed. So it was not surprising that professionals generally disliked the new style offshore racing. The single hand was often treated on equal terms with the amateur crew and had as keen an interest in the boat's success, but many were felt socially inferior amongst a crowd of loud-talking amateurs, whose lack of seamanship they secretly despised. However there were humorous moments; at the end of the stormy channel race of 1928, after two days and nights of wet windward work, one entry wallowed towards the finish and, as the gun fired the Brightlingsea hand turned to the tousled owner and his crew with a grinning "Twice round, sir?"

Seamen who spent their winters since childhood fishing under sail in the smacks were amused at the pose of some amateurs who assumed participation in passage racing gave them a 'tough' character. But the new style racing flourished and grew to breed a healthy type of yacht and amateur yachtsman.

After 1936 big class racing collapsed in British waters. The "Astra" fitted out in 1937 as her owner's summer home and tender to his new 12 metre "Little Astra". For the next three years the 'twelves' kept alive, in a glorious manner, the round the coast racing traditions which had been established over the previous century. The Colne contributed its share of skippers and crews to the class with Captain William Wadley of Rowhedge in Mr. Connell's "Zoraida" and "Zelita", and later Hugh Goodson's "Flica"; and Captain George Francis of Brightlingsea in Sir William Burton's "Marina" and "Jenetta"; all with four hands in each and matched against other twelves with skippers and crews from Tollesbury, the Solent and the West country. Something of their rivalry is told in Chapter 12.

With the occasional construction of a 12 metre for day-sailing in America's Cup racing now an object of wonder in the yachting world, it is well to remember that in 1939 there were eight British 12 metres racing, four of them new that season; Sir William Burton's "Jenetta"; Thomas Sopwith's "Tomahawk"; Arthur Connell's "Ornsay"; and Hugh Goodson's "Flica II". These, with "Blue Marlin", "Trivia", "Evaine" and "Little Astra", each had a professional crew and sailed against the American 'twelve' "Vim", which beat the class in a spectacular season, ending as they lay in Torbay harbour when war was declared.

It is now difficult to realise what yachting meant to Brightlingsea, Wivenhoe, Rowhedge, Tollesbury and West Mersea before 1939. Even the children felt the pride their villages had in the yachts. At Rowhedge school during the 1930's there were a number of children in the same class as the author whose fathers were away racing in 12 metres all summer, but the boy whose father was in the "Britannia" felt himself a distinct cut above the rest! Rowhedge was then still wholly maritime; we saw yachts launched from the shipyard, as well as ships, and 12 metres and other racers and motor yachts laid up in the lower yard or on the mud above the village each winter, their long snouts pointing at the road. Village talk was of yachts and ships; of who would win the America's Cup in 1937, or how an owner who had a village crew was going to order a new 12 metre. Men walked the streets or dug their gardens in blue guernseys with the names of famous yachts embroidered on them in white letters and, on village occasions, the opening of the 'rec', a wedding, or the king's coronation, Rowhedge could put a display of bunting across its streets which Cowes would envy during 'the week', the results of which caused such speculation in the village.

Indoors, the walls of every 'front room' had paintings and photos of yachts, including the inevitable two views of a favourite big cutter, schooner or steam yacht, one under all plain sail or steam, on a summer's morning, with Naples in the background, and the other showing the yacht under storm canvas in a heavy sea with lowering skies of a Biscay gale. Rooms fascinating to a child; the measured, clock-ticking silence changing to the thunder of seas and the scream of wind as young eyes stared in wonder at the "Reverie R.Y.S." on passage to the Mediterranean under trysail; or recognised, with dawning surprise, the faces of the bronzed young seamen hauling on the mainsheet in the fading photographs as those of the old men who yarned on the village hard. But the youngsters turned to shipbuilding or engineering for a living, steered in that direction by parents determined that their sons would not go to sea, as their forebears had done for generations; they knew it was the end of an era. The Colne's professional racing men died out at that generation, but the sailing urge remained, channelled into the surge of amateur sailing and racing of the 1930's and subsequent years, where the dinghies and offshore racing boats have retained the racing spirit.

1939 saw the end of the traditional sequence of professional yachtsmen, everywhere. On the Colne, the decline of the fisheries for winter employment, hastened by economic depression, coupled with the natural desire for a secure job and regular return for less arduous labour ashore and better family life, had led to a decline in the number of professionals afloat even before the second world war, and in 1970 only a very few of the breed remain to remind us of the old racing glory.

12 metres at Harwich, 1939. *Trivia* leading *Jenetta*, sailed by Sir William Burton of Ipswich with a Colne crew under Captain George Francis of Brightlingsea. The start of the last season of yacht racing around the coast in the traditional manner.   *Douglas Went*

CHAPTER TEN

Laying Up and Fitting Out—A Colneside Tradition

THE WINTRY sun shines for an hour or so and the family take the car to some
local waterside for a look at the boats. Perhaps they're disappointed or even
astonished to find the crowded anchorage of summer deserted, except for a few smacks
and a coaster or two; and the graceful yachts lying unmasted and undistinguished in
saltings, by the shining Essex mud. Probably the visitors drive off disgustedly without
realising that 'Laying up' is as much a traditional, and in some ways enjoyable, part of
the yachting year as the summer days spent cruising or racing.

In the grand period of Essex yachting, between 1820 and 1939, September lay up
was a milestone in the local year and it is interesting to discover just what went on
between that month and April, when the banks and creeks of the Colne were crammed
with yachts, providing a winter spectacle paralleled only at Cowes, Gosport and
Southampton.

The rapid growth of yachting in the early nineteenth century provided Colneside
seamen with an opportunity for their subtle skill such as comes to a community but
once in history. How well they seized this chance and their subsequent supremacy in
the sport, are now sailing history and the benefits yachting brought in relieving the
waterside villages from utter dependence on precarious fisheries, and its influence on
local progress, can never be overestimated. Summer after summer the seamen thrived
as never before and Colne shipyards, sailmakers, riggers, painters and many other trades
blossomed the year round on the upsurge of nautical activity. An improving standard
of living came in the wake of their success and, as a result, rows of new houses began
to stretch up new streets away from the watersides, remaining to testify their origins
by the yacht names they bear.

Through the early enterprise and ability of Colne skippers and crews comparative
prosperity came and stayed with the yachts and the season's end in early September
found most of them, sail and steam, bound to the skipper's home port to lay up. One
by one the elegant craft entered Colne, picking their way amongst others already arrived,
and hailed by their crews. The racers with crack skippers were dressed from bowsprit
end to topmast head and often down to the counter with prize flags, as was the custom;
each fluttering miniature of the yacht's racing colours representing a victory in the
season just ended, and the attendant 'something extra' in the shape of prize money for
the crew.

The yachts often lay in the mouth of Colne for a few days awaiting the equinoctial
springs, as the exceptionally high tides which conveniently occur in September and

March are called. With these brimming full for a few days, putting the saltings awash, the whole assembly would sail or tow, some into Brightlingsea creek, others upstream to Wivenhoe or Rowhedge which, with Tollesbury after the 1890's, formed the East Coast laying up ports for the yachting fleet. Processions of yachts came upstream on each flood, swinging round off their intended berths, carefully dug out by yard men and marked by wands stuck in the mud. The crews picked up the head lines and warped them in on the very top of the tide until their bows almost touched the saltings, when they secured them to mooring anchors dug firm into the shoreward side of the seawalls and set up sternlines running to kedges laid in the river bed.

Crews were busy in the few days remaining before they paid off. All sails had any salt carefully rinsed from them and were dried on the earliest calm and sunny day, when the river banks blossomed out like regattas at anchor, as airing canvas swung idly from every mast and stay. Topmasts were sent down and bowsprits put ashore, together with the masts of smaller craft, to lay in the spar sheds—long, strongly framed lean-to's, each holding a score or so heavy spars sewn up in sacking jackets to keep the frost from the varnish. Then there was running rigging to grease and stow in the stores in carefully labelled coils, and the standing rigging to grease down. Any lowermasts left standing were slushed down with a sticky mixture of red or white lead and tallow, to protect them from winter weather—a messy job this for the hand dangling in a bosun's stool smearing the mixture on the mast and himself, but not daring to drip it on the sacred deck below! Those same decks eventually hid their traditional hounds-

The 222 ton yawl *Lufra* hauled out at Stone's Brightlingsea yard, about 1895. The copper sheathing is being stripped from the bottom.

tooth appearance in a winter coat of thick varnish, and the skylights and hatchways stood snug under canvas jackets.

In a week or two most yards and mud berths would be filled and in some places the seawalls were almost impassable for the standing bowsprits of the great steam yachts, some of them over 1000 tons, whose length protruded graceful counters further into the stream than anyone elses. Stagings and brows reached out on spindle legs over the saltings giving access to forecastles where rope mats were ready for the muddy boots of crew or visitors. The photographs, which seem almost incredible to us now, are typical of the river banks as they appeared each winter from about 1850 until 1914, when the practice was at its height; though large numbers of yachts continued to lay up in the river well into the 1930's, as a good number of smaller ones do today.

Many yachts, especially racers, were regularly hauled out and struck over to winter, shored up on blocks in the shipyards, and the numbers wintered in this way increased with the introduction of the long ended hull form during the 1890's.

If the skipper were a popular one, the crew of larger yachts might club together, or sometimes the owner paid, to give a laying up supper, usually held in a local pub. After this and the tremendous fun of the village regattas which were purposely held at this time, the crews were busy fitting out the smacks for spratting or oystering, or were away to the London or Southampton docks seeking berths in steamers, especially the Cape and India bound troopers, whose season lasted, conveniently, until spring.

Around the turn of the century many skippers received a weekly winter retainer of 10/- from the owner and were, of course, left in complete charge of the yachts with instructions to fit out as necessary in the spring. Some had a spell at the fishing, but the skippers of larger yachts, especially racing men, were often on fairly generous winter pay, supplemented by the season's prize money; and were to some extent independent.

Yachts laid up at Harris Brothers' yard, Rowhedge, 1897. Lord Dunraven's 129 ton cruising ketch *Cariad*, alongside quay.

Little maintenance work was done aboard during the winter, and none by the owners of those times, who rarely saw the yachts between early September and mid May. A mate or a hand might be kept on to clean and paint through the bilge or do a few rigging jobs, but of course, all the yachts received a very thorough overhaul in the yards during spring fitting out.

While their crews laboured hard and ill rewarded at spratting, oystering or salvaging, the laid up fleet slumbered in their winter berths, stirring but gently to the windsong of high water, or in the winter gales whirling snow squalls about the decks. Most, as an odd conceit, wore their ensigns from halliards at the masthead during the short winter days, and many had a wisp of smoke curling from the forecastle stovepipe —signifying that the interior was airing, or that the skipper was roasting his toes, whichever way you looked at it! Perhaps the steam yachts looked most forlorn. Rain-cover topped buff funnels and boatless davits gave a dejected air to rakish hulls streaked here and there with red lead plied by a few hands on slung staging.

This use of the teather soft Essex mud for laying up was no new thing. Ships of Henry VII's Navy were wintered at Brightlingsea in the same fashion during the 16th century, and small fishing and trading craft were doubtless laid up during slack seasons in much the same way for hundreds of years before the yachts, which brought the custom to prominence, were ever dreamed of.

By 1850 laying up had become an established business locally, as the following card, typical of those sent to yacht owners each June by mud berth proprietors, indicates:

JOHN GRIGGS

Begs to inform gentlemen, owners of yachts, that he has accommodation, at Brightlingsea, at the mouth of the Colchester river, for the laying up of ten yachts, drawing not more than ten feet water.

The yachts can be laid up in perfect safety, the sails and rigging will be stored, and the boats, spars, and ballast can be protected from the weather if required.

The charge, including dock room, storage, and superintendence, £6 per yacht; coals, for airing the yachts when necessary, to be paid for by the owners.

If six or more yachts were placed under his care, the charge would be £5 per yacht.

John Griggs has had twenty-five years experience as master of yachts, and can give the most satisfactory references.
Brightlingsea, Colchester.
JUNE 1850.

It is interesting that John Griggs is credited with having been a yacht master as early as 1825, confirming Brightlingsea's early participation in the sport.

During the 1840's about half a dozen yachts are thought to have been laid up there and the numbers steadily increased to 70 in 1882 and to 170 around 1895, falling to but

20 in 1920 and rising again during the 1930's. Wivenhoe laid up 50 yachts in 1884 and Rowhedge about the same number. The boom in yachting brought the need for vast storage space to hold dismantled gear. Many yacht stores were built, not only in shipyards but on every waterfront and in skippers' back gardens. Most of them survive today, such as the big clench-built wooden sheds which dominate the creek sides along the Eastward at Brightlingsea, or Woodropes at Tollesbury, perched on piles to cheat the highest tides. Wivenhoe and Rowhedge preferred brick ones built along their more convenient quays or in skippers' gardens.

The 289 ft. American owned yacht *Nahma*, 1897. Commanded by Captain George Harvey of Wivenhoe with a Colne crew of seventy. She could steam at 18 knots and carried quick firing guns and searchlights for her voyaging in remote seas.

At the peak, between 1890 and 1914, the river was one of the world's largest yachting centres. Brightlingsea alone sent 800 seamen to man the 150 yachts of all sizes which each winter stretched over ¾ mile along Easterly, beyond Aldous' crowded yard, their masts like a leafless forest.

Upstream at Rowhedge, where almost every man in the village was either a yacht skipper or hand, fisherman or shipwright, a long line of some thirty laid up yachts wintered each year along the marsh wall above the village while, as if to balance the scene, a similar row of sleeping beauties lined the lower wall from Harris' yard round to the mouth of Mill creek. The photograph shows them secure in their soft mud berths, cutters and schooners, racers and cruisers, the fliers of that year and the one before; with a whole history of yachting, its fashions and follies, displayed by their fine bows and lean counters. Warps thick as a man's arm moored them head on to superannuated anchors buried deep in the marsh grass over the sea wall. Stern lines ran in a maze to stream kedges in the river's bed.

The now deserted Wivenhoe seawall below Cook's shipyard presented a similar appearance, with the accent on the large steam yachts of which that village's yachtsmen were so proud; while Husk's, Harvey's and, later, Forrestt's shipyards were always crammed with yachts, new and old.

Tollesbury chimed in during the 1890's and its creek and slipways soon presented a similar appearance, though nearby and now popular Mersea never wintered any yachts of consequence.

Yacht work followed successful skippers and village prosperity then depended, to an extent which we cannot now realise, on the reputation of these seamen. It was

Steam yachts laid up on the mud below Wivenhoe, about 1900.

Rowhedge in winter, 1900. Laid up yachts line the river wall above the village. Smacks at the quays and yachts on the slip in Houston's yard.

therefore natural that the winter's most important social event should be the "Yachts-man's and Tradesman's dinner", given for the yacht captains by local shipbuilders, sailmakers, chandlers, provisioners and others benefitting from the flood of work their commands brought. This notable evening usually needed the flag bedecked Wivenhoe shipyard mould loft to accommodate the gathering who enjoyed the best of good food, choice wines and cigars, and who became more expansive as the evening wore on, with toasts from the hosts to their guests bringing lengthy responses from the by this time well primed skippers. Quite a lot of business must have been sealed during these affairs which always ended with an uproarious sing-song to a tinkley piano, before the company broke up to roll off up Wivenhoe's narrow streets or along the wall towards Rowhedge ferry. As far as I can discover the dinner was discontinued some time before the First World War.

November the fifth brought another now forgotten waterside custom in the letting off of rockets, signal rockets of course, from the lines of laid up yachts on bonfire night.

Autumn generally found builders and designers with a rush of enquiries and orders for new yachts. Harvey, Harris, Aldous, Husk, Stone, and Wilkins, all burned the midnight oil over their drafting boards and cost sheets, and, as the days shortened, many a keel was laid in the dark echoing sheds. Others were busy too. Canvas was being overhauled and new sails cut in the lofts of Madder at Wivenhoe or Pattinson and Son at Brightlingsea, where Pannell and Hibbs would be working on boat covers, awnings and fenders for next season. The boatshops at Husks and Forrestts were repairing and building yachts dinghies, sailing cutters, and those beautifully modelled six and four oared gigs which were the owner's boat before motor launches came in.

At Brown's Wivenhoe ropery the puffing steam machinery teased long fibres and spun them into "fine yacht rope as supplied to Britannia, Ailsa, Valkyrie and Satanita", as their advertisements proudly read in the 'nineties.

The tremendous rush of painting in spring created a type of business peculiar to the Colne and Solent areas; Yacht Decorators, as they styled themselves, flourished locally until the 1930's. The Scofields of Wivenhoe were old established and rivalled by the Scuttons of Rowhedge, whose office door to this day proclaims their original trade. Robert Pearson of Rowhedge was another, and perhaps best known, of these specialists. An enterprising man, he also contracted for the painting of large yachts away from the village, for which purpose he often chartered the old yacht "Antelope" which, loaded with painters and paint, sailed round the coast; as in 1894 when the sailor painters fetched round to Tilbury to redecorate the big racers "Britannia", "Ailsa" and "Audrey" on their return from the Mediterranean winter regattas. Rowhedge even had its "Yachting Shoemakers", Mr. Everitt and Mr. Southgate, whose winters were busy making scores of pairs of strong, supple racing slippers, an important part of every racing man's outfit, as well as dozens of pairs of shining brown shoes, supplied by the owner to each hand for shoregoing wear during the season.

A few steps downstreet Mr. Cooper, the yachting tailor, was cutting dozens of pilot jackets and suits for skippers and mates, as well as racing outfits, overalls and shoregoing suits for the hands; all supplied by the owners.

By New Year many top flight racing skippers and mates would be away standing by new commands building at Gosport, Fairlie, Glasgow, or Southampton. A few months later saw their crews, each of perhaps thirty or so hands, shouldered seabags creasing best blue suits, mustering along to Wivenhoe or Brightlingsea stations to entrain for their new ships. What hopes they must have had as the old "Crab and Winkle" clanked out to the waves of relatives! A whole new season before them, with its prospects of hard sailing and the prize money that went with it. Perhaps the proudest of all were the Cup crews off to man the latest challenger for that elusive America's Cup, which the Colneside and Tollesbury skippers have striven to regain for so long.

Along Colneside, first days of spring found yacht masters picking crews and attending to the myriad details of fitting out. In the bars and captains' rooms of nearby pubs they gossiped on new commands, crew changes and the season's prospects; the racing skippers yarning with a friendliness which belied the ruthless tactics of the coming struggle around the coast. Slowly the laid up fleet awoke. Sounds of scraping and caulking came from the decks of some, and a man or two were aloft on others cleaning down the body-thick lowermasts. Nucleus crews aboard most prepared for hauling off when the top of springs lipped over the saltings. Occasionally one of the deeper draughted got be-neaped and the skipper held his temper as best he could while a gang of yard men squelched about under her stern, their shovels flinging out chunks of smelly mud, channelling a deep black groove down the river bank's glistening brown flank. Then it was up on the slipways for the hectic business of fitting out to begin in earnest, while the vacated mud berths rapidly filled with newly laid up smacks, their topsides hung with old sails against the hot suns of summer.

Colneside could beat the world in making a yacht ready for sea. There were men who did nothing else but work on yachts and smacks. They had the knowledge, long practice and traditions to guide them, and they worked rapidly and without skimping for long hours and a pitifully small wage. During these few weeks, hauled out hulls quite dominated the yards which rang with the urgent sounds of fitting out. Lines of caulking shipwrights crouched low over the sweeping curves of deck seams, their clicking mallets sounding unrhythmically, above the shouts of boys handing up kettles of glue to ladle, sizzling, over the clean smelling yellow pine and solidify in black squiggles awaiting the scraper.

Everywhere and in everyone's way worked the painters, their walrus moustaches and watchchains reflected in the perfection of enamelled topsides. The master painter crouched on the plank stage to cut in a boot topping or gold leaf the caveata, in between cursing the shipwright boys whenever a wind shift wafted smoke from their fires towards the wet glitter of the sacred topsides. The impatient rattle of clenching hammers echoed back from stores where processions of handcarts trundled by overalled yacht crews carried gear back aboard. Rigging, sails, blocks, cabin furniture, even saloon pianos; all shared the perils of this marine obstacle race through the boats and stagings, then out along the quays to encouraging shouts of "Keep her full!" from the hands sweating along with a particularly heavy load. Men swarmed under the bottoms scouring the dull green copper sheathing to bright metal. Under each bow stood monster hauling out capstans whose whelp-bound barrels, high as a man, were bought from Chatham dockyard when the Navy's wooden walls were thrown aside for iron. Now, instead of warping stately three deckers they hauled up the slipway cradles, their bars spun by noisy gangs of shipwrights and yachthands urged on, not by the Navy's fiddlers, but by a pail of beer placed on the flat crown, into which an old tin mug was dipped on the occasional fallout.

Strings of new varnished blocks hung like golden gooseberries beside lean to's where blistered hands scoured 'wet and dry' on spars which seemed miles long. Riggers spliced and fiddled at mastheads, scrapers squeaked, forges sparked and anvils rang. Colneside hands exchanged banter with some who had walked from Tollesbury or, perhaps, West Mersea, seeking a berth in the yachts. Dozens of others trooped by in a long line like a giant caterpillar, bent backs bearing the ton weight of a huge folded mainsail, fresh from the loft and ready for bending. Scores of renovated boats lay ready in the cool dark sheds, syrupy with the smell of varnish. Here and there sunlight shafts glinted on the bow badges of gigs and dinghies and the bright rectangle of rolled back doors might frame a graceful cutter warped under the nearby sheerlegs to receive her mast, the skipper squinting up the new-stepped spar for straightness, motioning at the hands setting up the shroud tackles, their cheesecutters canted against the sun glitter of high water lapping at the quays.

Striking over went on apace, the chuff and whine of steam saws rising and falling above the dull thudding of mauls setting up yachts for launch. Hammering echoed from the dark depths of steam yachts as engineers wrestled with crank pins or cursed at condenser tubes. Some, with a haze shimmering about their funnels, waited turn for dry docking at Forrestt's yard.

Each April day, yards echoed to the rumble of slipway carriages as hull after hull slid gracefully into the muddy Colne, curtseying clear in fresh glory for the summer's sailing. Somehow the last sail was bent, the last stores went aboard and the last boats swayed up in davits before, one by one, they sailed, sped on by the farewells of relatives and the shipyard workers. The watersides paused to wave in admiration as the graceful vessels slipped by each high water; the racers bound for Thames mouth and the opening matches of the season; and the cruisers, often, for the ends of the earth.

As each yacht's tall topmast or rakish funnel disappeared round Marriage's bight, or over the beach end, there were few in the villages who had not played some part in their refitting and who would not feel some pride in their voyagings and records of the coming season.

Winter work in the yacht store. Preparing the gear of the 100 ft. barge yacht *Thoma II*, built at Maldon by John Howard in 1909.

CHAPTER ELEVEN

The Flying Fish Sailors

A SPRING morning in 1876. The sun played cloud shadows over the slate roofs of Brightlingsea and along the sandy tongue of Colne beach; lighting the tan canvas of Brightlingsea bound smacks and a score of barges. A couple of brigs stood up as best they could amongst the half-hundred smacks dredging the Colne fishery grounds and made bold tacks clear of the big schooners and lithe racing cutters lying off East Mersea stone. All eyes were on Mr. Thomas Brassey's three masted, auxiliary schooner "Sunbeam", whose puffing windlass clattered her anchor home as the blue peter fluttered proudly from her foremast head. Smoke hazed above her squat buff funnel, half hidden by surrounding boats in davits.

From the flying bridge Captain Isiah Powell, a ring-bearded Rowhedger, acknowledged the mate's hail from forward and jerked the shining telegraph to bring answering gongs from below. Slowly she gathered way, white steam feathered from her whistle and the dredgermen straightened their backs to wave as the blasts echoed round the estuary. Butter-yellow spars and burnished brasswork winked in the sunshine as her Colneside crew catted the anchor and took a last look at home waters before "Sunbeam" glided out towards the Bar buoy on the first stage of her long and adventurous voyage around the world.

The outward bound schooner became perhaps the most famous cruising yacht of her times, and one which is recalled with reverence even now, if only for the extent of her 41 years of voyaging under Lord Brassey's ownership; during which she sailed and steamed half a million sea miles.

Today, with ocean sailing in yachts, often alone and in very small craft, becoming commonplace, many fail to realise that a century ago yachtsmen also sought the satisfaction of ocean passage making and numbers of auxiliary schooner and barquentine yachts were built for world cruising in all seasons. They were true floating homes carrying, in the owners' and guests' quarters, all the elaborate 'comforts' of the period. "Czarina", "Sunrise", "Waterlily", "Oceana", "Norseman", "St. George", "Sunbeam" and "Fedora" were some of their names, about which an atmosphere of tropic seas and trade winds still lingers. Essexmen served in them all, but the two last had an enduring connection with the Colne and were amongst the most imposing yachts ever manned from the district. Their wholesome rig and sea kindly proportions contrasted greatly with the lean and rakish steam yachts of those times, and there are now few vessels afloat which compare with them. The various sail training ships which compete in the 'races' held in recent summers make the best comparison; though a few large, modern auxiliary yachts of the size of these craft have a vogue amongst wealthy, foreign owners.

The "Sunbeam" was conceived by Thomas Brassey in 1872, after a rough passage of the Atlantic in the lean steam yacht "Eothen", which nearly drowned all aboard. He was determined to have a powerful sea boat and his new yacht was designed as a composite vessel of 531 tons by the Liverpool naval architect St. Clyre J. Byrne. She was launched at Seacombe, Cheshire, in January 1874.

Intended to perform equally well under sail or steam she was the forerunner of our modern motor-sailers. Her black hull swept 170 feet from clipper bow to counter stern and, with a graceful three masted, topsail schooner rig spreading 8,333 square feet above it, she made a fine picture roaring along at 15 knots, as she could on occasion, in a breeze. She looks a bit clumbungy to present tastes but the square topsails were ideal for trade wind passages and the fore and aft canvas made her handy on the wind, as she needed to be in some waters with a draught of 13' 4". Some sails were hoisted by steam but all were sheeted to the sound of a chantey and the tramp of feet. Her average sailing speed was 8 or 9 knots, but she steamed at 10.

The "Sunbeam" was built before the compact internal combustion engine, or even flash steam plants, were practical possibilities and was fitted with a 350 Indicated Horse Power steam engine driving a large Bevis patent propeller which "feathered" when under sail.

Her telescopic funnel was another feature typical of these craft. Lowered when sailing, it was hoisted up by tackles from the triatic stay on the order "Up funnel, out screw!", which brought an engineer scurrying aft with an enormous key, used to set the propeller to revolve.

To avoid going on deck in bad weather a passageway ran the length of the ship, through the engine and boiler room which could be observed in all its glory of polished steel and simmering power; a feature adding much to the novelty for guests. The large and airy deck saloon was designed for tropical use and, like all big yachts of the time, she carried a black gig, cutter, dinghy and a skiff in davits above the high bulwarks.

For long periods in many seas she was the Brassey family's floating home, a truly able and happy ship, beloved by them almost as a living creature. Lady Brassey shared her husband's passion for the sea, taking a keen and intelligent interest in the design and construction of the yacht and spending much time in the shipyard. Her interest in people and places was reflected in her descriptions of "Sunbeam's" voyages, which became Victorian best sellers.

A tireless champion of the Royal Navy and a first rate seaman, Lord Brassey was a practical yachtsman who eventually held a master's certificate. Stockily built, blunt of speech and side bewhiskered, he took the rough with the smooth and referred to his guests aboard as "the idlers". Rating himself as "Governor" he became a tough old sailor and enjoyed every minute the "Sunbeam" was under sail. Sometimes in a breeze he stood where the heaviest sprays dashed over, leaving him drenched and spluttering, but thoroughly enjoying it! He became one of the ablest self-taught navigators but on his first voyage to the Baltic in his earlier auxiliary steam yacht "Meteor" he acted as navigator with the result that she ran ashore in the Danish Islands and, when got off, had to ask the way of a passing Swedish cruiser, which hung overside a blackboard with the position chalked on it! There were plenty of similar incidents on passage back to the Colne to lay up. With this experience Lord Brassey thought highly of his skippers and crews and those of "Sunbeam", besides his earlier yachts "Cymba", "Albatross", "Eothen" and "Meteor" were, as he once wrote, "recruited as so many crews of yachts still are, from the shores of Essex. It is the general experience of my yachting brethren that they have seldom cause to complain of the men of Essex. They know their work and do it." The professionals could have no better tribute.

For the "Sunbeam's" voyage round the world in 1876 Captain Isiah Powell of Rowhedge shipped 14 of his neighbours in a total crew of 29. They always dressed man-o-war fashion and the owner's naval tastes were further reflected in their ratings which included such yachting curiosities as "signalman and gunner", "captain of the hold", "coxswain of the cutter", etc. They were paid for every mile she logged, more for sail than steam and extra for hoisting the funnel. Several of them were to become noted skippers in later life, such as Edward Ennew, and the legendary Tom Jay who would handle some of the largest and fastest racing yachts ever built. But on these voyagings they were just able seamen, standing their watches; maybe shivering, soaked at the wheel in the dew of a flaring tropic dawn, with wet decks and rigging sparkling rainbow colours in the fantastic sunrise or, perhaps, laying out on the footropes reefing a topsail as the schooner heeled to a freshening gale and the helmsman watched his luff with anxious eyes, the roaring wake dinning in his ears. Those were the sort of moments they recalled when their ocean wanderings were just memories, or souvenirs on the parlour walls.

There were amusing incidents. Lord Brassey loved making fast passages and the "Sunbeam" was fitted with studding sails; always fiddling bits of gear. The hands were aloft in a breeze one day struggling with the studding gear and complaining loudly "wish the old ... was up 'ere 'isself." "The old ... is up here," boomed a voice from the top and the startled hands turned to see the owner coming out along the footropes!

Shore trips for the crew were arranged in all countries visited. At Rome, one of them remarked that the Colosseum "wanted a tidy bit doin' to it to put it straight". In Greece another disgustedly dismissed the Parthenon as "nothing but a pile of old stones".

The "Sunbeam" was the first yacht to be built exceeding 500 tons Thames Measurement and the second to voyage round the world; a novel undertaking in 1876.

Outward bound through the Solent, she surprised everyone by beating out through the Needles in a light breeze which freshened to send her roaring south at a ten knot clip with the Brassey family lining the lee rail in the big sea running. Madeira and the Cape Verde's were soon astern, leaving memories as colourful as the dainty flying fish which slumped aboard.

As the yacht rolled south across the torrid equator Jim Allen, cox of the gig, donned an oakum beard and paper crown to come aboard as Father Neptune, attended by his 'doctor', in the shape of an engineer, to assist in the traditional ceremonies of "crossing the line".

Soon after, they spoke a whaling schooner under sail and, a week or two later, the "Sunbeam" raised Cape Frio, her Brazilian landfall, and a freshening gale sent her pitching in over Rio bar, with a raging sunset silhouetting the Sugar Loaf and the mountains beyond. On the fetch south to Montevideo the schooner scudded along the flat, treeless coasts, so like the crew's native Essex shore, under storm canvas but with bonito playing in the bow wave's phosphorescence and a fine, soaring albatross following her wake; this was real cruising! It took a day's steaming up the hundred mile wide River Plate to make Buenos Aires, where the sky darkened with clouds of locusts ravaging crops inland and the crew brought 70 parrots aboard.

Steaming and sailing south towards Sandy Point at the entrance to the Magellan Straits, the "Sunbeam" came up with a pillar of smoke which resolved into the British barque "Monkshaven", whose cargo of coal was blazing furiously. The yacht took off her crew who had lived on the deckhouse and in the rigging for four days and nights, despite signals to a distantly passing American steamer.

Off Cape Virgins the "Sunbeam" transferred the shipwrecked crew to a homeward bound Royal Mail Steamer and stood on past the low, sandy coast of Patagonia towards the rugged mountains of Tierra Del Fuego, to coal off Sandy Point.

Magellan Straits provided strange experiences; in English Reach a canoe load of natives came off to barter skins for beads and mirrors, and at night the flickering of their camp fires, alongshore, reminded "Sunbeam's" double watch of the origin of this weird and desolate land's name.

In Borja Bay the crew fixed a board bearing the yacht's name alongside the hundreds left there by passing vessels. The cold grew intense as they stood on, surrounded on every side by magnificent, snow capped peaks and stupendous glaciers which ran down into the sea and from which great masses of ice, large as a ship, broke off and thundered down into the water.

Topmasts were housed and yards cockbilled to steam through English Narrows where, despite a double-manned wheel, fierce currents swept the yacht close inshore until her bowsprit was over the land and stunted trees swept the rigging. With Cap Pilar astern they found fresh troubles with icebergs everywhere. The yacht put into Puerto Bueno to replenish her fresh water tanks by filling the gig under a handy waterfall and towing her off.

The "Sunbeam" visited the Chilean port of Valparaiso to provision for the first leg of the long Pacific passage. When the anchor came home the crew's chanteys were drowned by the bleating of 6 sheep, 60 chickens, 4 dozen pigeons and 30 ducks, penned on deck as consumable stores; great are the blessings of refrigeration!

Lord Brassey had been warned off unfriendly and unpronouncable Tatakotoroa Island in mid-Pacific, where the swell broke invitingly on milk white beaches shaded by feathery palms; but hostile natives ran out brandishing spears, as the yacht sailed by, close inshore. However, curiosity overcame the owner at Hao Harre Island and the gig's crew, with drawn revolvers, cautiously rowed the owner in, over underwater gardens of gorgeous coloured coral, to barter with surprisingly friendly natives and leave with a boatload of coconuts and a couple of pigs.

The dark foc'sle, with its tiers of cots, was the coolest part of the yacht in the tropics. Smoked hams and festoons of tobacco leaves swung from the beams, for the "Sunbeam's" crew rolled their own plugs, besides being ardent ship-modellers off-watch, when they were not practising for the sing-songs for which the yacht became famous.

But life was very different with the wind roaring as loud in the rigging as Captain Powell did on deck and the streaming decks plunged deep in the green seas of the Southern Ocean.

Five weeks in the South-East trades raised the French colony of Tahiti, since beloved of artists, adventurers and just honest-to-goodness loafers. There the "Sunbeam" let go her anchor off Papete, the capital, with its magnolias and yellow and scarlet hibiscus flowers overhanging the jumble of white, wooden houses along the waterfront. In common with most visiting seamen the Colnesiders had a riotous time, by all accounts, but in their more sober moments they took the cutter and gig off to view the exotic fish and pearl fisheries along the wonderfully coloured reef, pulling back at dusk guided by the native fishermen's torches, flaring like fireflies in the velvet tropic night.

They sang carols on the equator and Christmas day at Hawaii found "Sunbeam's" flower garlanded crew galloping along the beaches on borrowed horses; sailing in the quaint but fast local catamarans; or flirting with the native girls. The yacht, around which half the population seemed to foregather, was gaily decorated; her mastheads tipped with blooming sugar cane, the gangway topped by a triumphal arch, and the decks festooned with flowers; even the figurehead carried a bouquet. That evening the Hilo choir came alongside in boats and serenaded the seafarers, who enjoyed a party for all hands before turning in under the glow of the volcano, with the yacht gently swaying to the sound of seas on far off reefs.

At New Year the "Sunbeam" sailed in under Hawaii's Diamond Head and the crew rowed off the King of Oahu, who insisted on seeing over every part of the yacht; even the bilge and the heads.

"The Sunbeam" voyaged on across the Pacific where a 90° temperature started a 'flu epidemic on board, but the strong ocean winds soon blew it away. Who could be ill for long in a schooner sailing across the vast Pacific? The sea was that deep blue which only a tropic sea can have—almost purple. Occasionally a breaking crest capped one of the ridges of the long rollers and "Sunbeam" swung along with stun' sails set; the barefoot watch singing at work about the deck, while Captain Powell logged a steady and satisfying 10-11 knots, sometimes more, and once spun off 350 miles in 24 hours. Soon after they had the strange experience of sailing over an island. The island of Tarquin was marked on the charts but, though "Sunbeam" stood straight for it and passed over the position with lookouts at the mastheads, the island had vanished! A few nights later they passed the burning volcanic island of Vries, lighting the sky like a flare.

The lonely Pacific showed the Essexmen many more wonders before the junk infested waters of the coasts of Japan hove in sight with dropping temperatures and ice in the rigging.

"Sunbeam" was the first yacht to visit Japan, bringing up off Yokohama in January to find exotic flowers blooming amid the snow, and horses and cows all well wrapped in quilts and wearing bells on their tails, whilst their owners worked nearly naked in the fields. After sampling fried octopus and rickshaw rides at Kobe, and sailing through the picturesque Inland Sea, the "Sunbeam" squared away for Hong Kong, where the anchored yacht was so pestered by trade seeking bumboats and floating washerwomen, that it took the washdeck hoses to disperse them.

Cochin-China and Singapore were later visited and at Ceylon three coloured firemen joined to work the stokehold in the intense heat. They lived in a tent pitched on deck and seem to have got on well with the Colnesiders.

At Aden a gazelle was slung aboard to join the "zoo" which now numbered a hundred creatures, and the passage up the Red Sea was further enlivened by the crew's celebrated nigger minstrel show.

A beat up the Gulf of Suez, a steam through the canal and what must have seemed the almost familiar waters of the Mediterranean brought them rolling home to old England, and a tremendous welcome from yachts in the Solent which dipped their ensign and fired gun salutes to the circumnavigators who had sailed 37,000 sea miles.

The "Sunbeam" hove-to off Hastings, Sussex, to land the Brassey family in boats manned by the Royal Naval Artillery Volunteers. They were greeted by crowds at Hastings and at home, in Battle, the church bells pealed in welcome for these popular and humane public figures.

Born in 1836 and heir to a railway-building fortune, Lord Brassey was as active ashore as afloat. A statesman and author, he devoted much time to the Navy, economics and employment; later becoming a Civil Lord of the Admiralty and, afterwards, Secretary to the Admiralty. He was a member of Parliament for Hastings between 1868-1886 and became a peer in 1887. He was the first amateur yachtsman to obtain a Board of Trade Master's Certificate, in 1873.

Captain Powell left the yacht in 1878 and Charles Kindred, "Sunbeam's" bos'un, was appointed sailing master at the age of 34; a command he held for 36 years. Born at Framlingham, Suffolk, but resident at Rowhedge, he was a good, practical skipper of the old school, uncertified but wonderfully skilful at handling the "Sunbeam" under sail, and a popular ballad singer in the foc'sle concerts which were a feature of life aboard. That year they cruised through the Mediterranean and Dardenelles to the sea

Lord Brassey's 159ft. auxiliary topsail schooner *Sunbeam* in the trade winds during her circumnavigation of the world, 1876-1877. Captain Isiah Powell of Rowhedge was master of her Colne crew.

of Marmora and Constantinople. While seeking anchorage off Gallipoli the owner fell headlong from the bridge, but fortunately grabbed the ironwork and hauled himself back to Kindred's laconic order "pick up the Governor's cigar".

The "Sunbeam" was a success; as fit to entertain guests in Cowes Roads as she was for punching out to Australia. Her voyages were not all of trade wind variety and she spent several summers in home waters where leading personalities were frequently aboard, and the crew probably heard what Mr. Gladstone really said, weathering a gale during his trip to Norway in the yacht. The poet Tennyson spent all his time aboard smoking pipes, of which he carried one in each pocket! Another odd spectacle was a Home Secretary, impatient to get ashore to telephone, being ordered below after giving "orders" to the helmsman during a particularly anxious passage into Tobermory Bay. Liveliest guest was an Irish Duchess who insisted on dancing a hornpipe to the foc'sle accordian before going ashore.

During the next few years "Sunbeam" became a household word in many lands. She sailed to the West Indies and United States in 1883, to Norway in 1885 and made 11 voyages to the Mediterranean, 4 circumnavigations of Great Britain, and 2 of Ireland. Lord Brassey was founder of the Royal Naval Artillery Volunteers, forerunner of the Royal Naval Volunteer Reserve, and his naval interests led to "Sunbeam" accompanying the fleet to sea on manoeuvres, several times.

1887 found the "Sunbeam" bound for India, Ceylon, Singapore, Borneo, the Pacific Islands and Australia. To the great sorrow of all hands Lady Brassey contracted a fatal fever on a shore expedition and died on the homeward passage to the Cape, being buried at sea in the Indian Ocean. A few years later the owner remarried and the second Lady Brassey became almost as keen a sailor and skilled a navigator as her husband.

During 1888-1889 the "Sunbeam" sailed without auxiliary power; the screw aperture being filled in. She was originally painted black but, at Cowes during the '90s, her owner, tempted by the white hulls then becoming fashionable, had one side painted white but left the other black, and spent three days rowing round her in a state of indecision. After confounding the waterfront as she swung each tide, the "Sunbeam" was eventually painted white.

After voyaging to the West Indies and United States in 1892 and another to India in 1893-4, Lord Brassey was appointed Governor of Victoria, Australia, the following year and made the passage out in the "Sunbeam". Signing off at Melbourne with steamer fares paid home, many of the crew went on the spree. Three of them toured Eastern Australia on bicycles before sailing home before the mast. During the next five years the yacht cruised along the Australian coast, to New Zealand and Tasmania. A nucleus of the crew remained with her under Captain Kindred, and she came home in 1900. She slogged out to Canada in 1902 and to the West Indies and United States two years later.

Strangely enough, the worst weather she ever encountered in all her wanderings was when struck by a sudden North Sea gale off Flamborough Head. For two hours the "Sunbeam" laboured under short canvas, with topmasts housed, and her crew could not see one mast from the next in the flying spindrift. Her gig, dinghy and skiff hung smashed in the davits by sheer force of wind! The worst damage she suffered occurred in 1908 when Lord Brassey left her while he made an election tour of the West Country. Its climax was to be the "Sunbeam's" arrival at Saltash. Sailing round to Plymouth the old skipper would not take a licensed pilot, and the fisherman who conned her upstream assured him she would pass under Saltash bridge. The skipper wasn't so sure, but the answer soon came in a rain of spars and blocks as the graceful schooner emerged on the other side, "baldheaded", to commence her canvass. However, old Kindred didn't lose his berth and the owner paid up and looked as pleased as possible.

Although by no means a racer, the "Sunbeam" entered the transatlantic race of 1905 for the German Emperor's Cup. Matched against her were several ocean yachts evolved from her example, the largest being the Earl of Crawford's "Valhalla", a ship rigged, steam auxiliary of 1,490 tons, manned by 100 hands. Other competitors included the yawl "Ailsa" and the schooner "Hamburg" (ex "Rainbow"), two of Tom Jay's old racing commands. Propellers were of course, removed, but there was no handicap. The average size can be gauged from the smallest entry, the "Fleur-de-Lys", which was 108 ft. overall. The great American schooner "Atlantic" won, sailed by the Scots-American skipper Charles Barr. "Sunbeam" finished sixth, passing the Lizard light in 14 days, 6 hours from Sandy Hook, an average of 213 miles per day.

The old "Sunbeam" had by now become a legend in a yachting world at the peak of its splendour. She sailed to Canada in 1911, when Capt. J. R. Carter of Rowhedge was, at 33, appointed master; a position requiring much tact from this certificated Master Mariner who had to work with the old sailing master who had been with the yacht 37 years, not to mention an owner who still felt some responsibility in running her. Times were changing, as his crew of 36 included only 6 Essexmen; the remainder hailing from Hampshire and the West Country. Calling at Iceland and Newfoundland they steamed the "Sunbeam" up the St. Lawrence to Montreal, ending the passage with a visit to Grand Falls.

Baltic cruises became fashionable and in 1913 Kaiser Wilhelm visited the "Sunbeam" to discuss navies and politics over the owner's cigars, as "Sunbeam" swung to mooring amongst the glitter of Kiel Week, with its myriad sails set against the ominous background of the German High Seas Fleet.

With red crosses painted on her topsides "Sunbeam" became a hospital ship in the eastern Mediterranean early in the Great War. At Port Said, the flies became such a nuisance that the owner ordered Captain Carter to pay threepence for each dozen caught. By cunning use of condensed milk the resultant 'catch' was so large that the skipper withdrew payment before the crew became richer than the owner. Eventually she sailed to Bombay, where the now aged Lord Brassey presented her to the Indian government for use as an auxiliary. Lord Brassey died in 1918.

The old "Sunbeam" was afterwards sold to the shipowning Runciman family and was not broken up until 1929, when they replaced her with a fine new, steel hulled auxiliary yacht of the same name and size, and similar rig. After World War II she became the Swedish training ship "Flying Clipper" and is now barquentine rigged and owned by the Greek government, under the name "Eugene Eugenides".

The "Sunbeam's" success prompted the owner's younger brother, Albert Brassey, to order the very similar, three masted topsail schooner "Czarina" from Camper and Nicholson of Gosport, in 1877. This 564 tonner had dimensions of 152 feet 8 inches x 29 feet 3 inches x 14 feet 6 inches draught and was built without auxiliary power, but had an engine installed two years later. These yachts were almost sister ships in appearance, but the "Czarina" cruised mainly in European waters and to Iceland, Norway, the Baltic and Mediterranean. Her graceful black hull, with its Czarina figurehead, was well known in yacht anchorages, and her crew included many Colnesiders.

Due to the owner's parliamentary interests, she was laid up between 1895-1905, except during 1902. She was sold in 1914 to become a fish carrier, and was torpedoed when homeward bound across the Atlantic.

The steam barquentine yacht "Fedora", owned by Baron Newborough, was not so well known as the "Sunbeam", but made adventurous voyages. She sailed from Portsmouth in November 1897 on a two year voyage to the eastern and southern oceans, with a Colne crew under Captain Turner Barnard of Rowhedge.

This iron hulled, 141 footer was built and engined in 1881 by Henderson's of Glasgow, constructors of many large yachts. Although smaller and more heavily rigged than "Sunbeam" she was not quite as graceful, but performed better under steam and sported a tall "woodbine" funnel between main and mizzen masts. Her owner was amongst the greatest of newspaper magnates and decided on a long cruise. To get these voyages into perspective we must remember that ocean passages were more lonesome and perhaps more adventurous in those days before wireless and air mail, when the sea routes still swarmed with merchant sail and even ocean steamers still carried some canvas.

"Fedora" rolled out to Gibraltar and steamed on to Marseilles, Genoa and other Italian ports, before cruising the Adriatic coast up to Venice, then down through the Dalmatian islands and up the Dardenelles to lie off the mosques and minarets of Constantinople. The Black Sea was then a popular cruising ground and the "Fedora" spent some time there before sailing down through the eastern Mediterranean, standing over 600 miles on one tack! After Port Said, the cruise reads like something out of Kipling as the black barquentine winged her way east of Suez to Aden, Colombo, Trincomalee, to Rangoon; where she lay anchored in the chocolate coloured Irrawaddy, her yardarms brushed by the sails of grotesque native barges sailing down the steaming river.

Careful navigation was needed when "Fedora" sailed for the Andaman Islands in the vastness of the Indian ocean, then on to other remote groups, before refitting at Rangoon for a three months cruise around Borneo, then a home of headhunters. As she anchored in the Sarawak river, off Kuching, the famous white Rajah Brooke came off with his family and retainers, in dozens of gaily painted war canoes, each paddled by twenty fierce Dyak warriors. Soon the "Fedora" was the centre of scores of these craft, which also brought off the Rajah's band to play during his visit aboard. Later the Colnesiders went ashore to play the dyaks at cricket and football, and were treated to the spectacle of five hundred warriors competing in a canoe race. Athletics were popular too and one Rowhedger remarked he felt like running when a resident told him that his smiling opponent, whose scanty clothing was decorated with human hair, had only been cured of head hunting a few months before.

The "Fedora" stood south for the Philippines to anchor off Manila at the height of the Spanish-American war, finding the harbour crowded with cruisers of all nations and the remnants of the Spanish Pacific fleet. They were glad to leave this rather tense atmosphere, bound for the lonely island of Sula, then on to Java where the yacht lay in lagoons, moored fore and aft to coconut trees ashore, slowly lifting to the ground swell behind the creamy, offshore reefs. The crew sampled exotic fruits and saw land crabs the size of pigs stalking the jungle beach at night.

The *Sunbeam* completing her fitting out at Wivenhoe.

Christmas 1898 found the "Fedora" dressed with evergreens at the mastheads bound from Batavia to Singapore, then only partly reclaimed from swamp. Captain Barnard spent a few weeks recovering from fever on the heights of Penang and, on the Queen's birthday the crew dressed ship, manned the yards, and fired a loyal salute. Having completed several months beyond the original articles, 17 of them left, taking passage home to join yachts in home waters. For the others the muddy river Colne must have seemed very far away when they pulled the gig ashore for fresh fruit through the lines of surf creaming up the white shell beaches of the Seychelles islands, in the Indian Ocean; or held a sing-song in the tropic night, feeling the yacht lifting gently over long seas alive with phosphorescence, on her passage to Zanzibar. There, quayside scents of dhows loading cloves mingled with the babble and garishness of native markets to produce scenes from the Arabian nights.

Captain Hayzell Polley of Brightlingsea, one time master of the 224 ton schooner yacht *Heartsease*, demonstrates a sextant to the author's son, David, 1966.

Mombasa, Durban and Port Elizabeth saw the barquentine's topmasts, and she steamed into Cape Town to hear the first rumblings of the Boer war. From there she sailed for Ascencion Isle in the South Atlantic, where they enjoyed soup produced from the hundreds of thousands of turtles on the beaches. A few more long ocean boards brought the "Fedora" to St. Helena, where Napoleon spent his years of exile in isolated contemplation of the ocean. The Colnesiders visited Longwood house and saw Napoleon's grave before the yacht rolled on to the Cape Verde Islands, the Canaries and Madeira; the finish of one of Captain Barnard's earlier ocean racing successes.

The anchor came up to a homeward bound chantey and the "Fedora" scudded on to a landfall at Plymouth, then up channel to Ostende and Rotterdam, probably to stock up with cigars. A quick fetch across the North Sea raised the wink of the Sunk and in no time they were steaming up Colne to lay the "Fedora" in the homely Essex mud, on the buoys off Wivenhoe Ferry; almost two years to the day since leaving Portsmouth. Imagine the ostrich feathers, monkeys and parrots in cages which came ashore on Wivenhoe and Rowhedge hards, and the welcome the crew got from their families.

After a refit and overhaul the "Fedora" sailed for New York next year, to attend the America's Cup races. Unfortunately, Baron Newborough received severe head injuries during a gale off the Azores, so the barquentine returned to the Colne, where the crew paid off and she was berthed for a long time. After several more years of cruising the "Fedora" was sunk at sea on patrol service during the first world war.

After 1919 the auxiliary steam yachts were quickly superseded by equally large ocean going craft fitted with oil engines, such as the barque "Fantome" and the splendid auxiliary schooners "Creole" and "Sylvia", which had Brightlingsea captains and crews from the Colne.

CHAPTER TWELVE

A Lifetime Sailing

YACHTING achieved such importance in the economy of 19th and early 20th century Colneside, and later also Tollesbury, that it had a profound effect on the social development of the area.

Skill in yacht racing became the particular art and pride of local seafarers. In winter most of them manned the smacks, fishing under sail in the North Sea, down channel and, in earlier times, often far beyond. From this wonderful school of seamanship sprang their smartness under sail and even the greatest of the many racing skippers knew the feel of the dredge warp and the trawl before they held the tiller lines of the world's fastest yachts. Their crews were intelligent seamen, whose anticipation of the mate's and skipper's orders ensured smart sailing, so necessary when only seconds often separated many competitors after hours of racing.

Of the many thousands of smart local seamen who found a summer living in the racing yachts, one man's sea life has been selected as covering a considerable span of the finest period of the sport and indicating the variety of toil, challenge and success such a way of life demanded and presented to these superb fore and aft sailors, many of whom never owned a boat; spending their lives sailing those owned by others. Their private aspirations were usually a house of their own, pleasant family life and sufficient savings for old age security in an era indifferent to those without resources.

In the spring of 1889, young William Wadley shipped as 'boy' in the large racing cutter "Genesta", fitting out on the buoys at Wivenhoe ferry, under Captain Turner Ennew, with a crew of 20 men. William had been in and out of boats since a small child and, before leaving school, could row and scull a boat well. He had spent the previous two years as boy aboard a smack, spratting and fish trawling, and at sixteen years of age had the rudiments of seamanship. He wished to follow the traditional Colne seafaring of winters spent fishing in smacks and summers as a hand in yachts, particularly racing; at which his father was an experienced man.

The 80 ton "Genesta", owned by Sir Richard Sutton, had raced for the America's Cup four years previously under Captain John Carter of Rowhedge but, by 1889, only raced occasionally and was principally used for cruising. She was hauled up on the slip at Wivenhoe shipyard to have her coppered bottom cleaned before sailing for Lowestoft with the owner on board. She got ashore off the harbour entrance, which angered the owner, and the atmosphere on board was not a happy one.

Although it was reckoned a comparatively uneventful season for British yacht racing, William absorbed his surroundings eagerly and every passage made and every race, won or lost, confirmed his liking for this way of life as "Genesta" made the traditional round of racing and regattas between Harwich and the Clyde.

The owner was seldom on board, though his brother and a guest or two spent most of the summer enjoying the sailing, living in the elaborately fitted cabins amidships, waited on by the two stewards. The crew berthed in pipe cots which lined the sides of the long, dark foc'sle in two tiers. William, as the boy, had one of the foremost cots near the chain locker, where the motion at sea was most exaggerated. Captain Ennew had the privilege of a small cabin on the starboard side, abreast the mast, which came down through the crew space. All cooking and water heating was carried out on a black coal stove, which also dried the dozens of soaked clothes in bad weather. Everything on board, below, on deck or aloft, was incredibly clean, neat and shipshape, and the eagle eye of Charles Pudney, the mate, was everywhere.

When "Genesta" laid up at Rowhedge, William recalled his pride in walking up the High Street with the other hands, wearing his best blue guernsey with GENESTA. R.Y.S. in white letters on the front, soon to be as proudly worn, back to front in local custom, during the winter seafaring.

That winter he fished in John Cranfield's "Lily". John had ordered her to be built when he was away racing and his brother Lemon, the noted racing captain, visited the yard and discussed her plans with Harris, ordering one foot to be taken off the beam to make her faster!

Next season, through his father's influence, William was shipped by Captain William Cranfield of Rowhedge, as boy in the 90 footer "Yarana", a graceful, clipper-bowed racing cutter owned by Mr. Ralli, a banker, which had been crack boat of the big class for the previous two seasons. William had begun to get about easily aloft, encouraged by the mastheadsman, and besides tailing on to the sheets and helping about the deck under weigh, was sometimes allowed on the bowsprit in fine weather when a headsail was sent up or lowered, to accustom him to smart sail changing. The crew were kindly men, almost all Rowhedgers, and Captain Cranfield encouraged him as much as possible.

"Yarana's" competitors in the big class were the cutter "Thistle", which had raced for the America's Cup in 1887, sailed by Captain Duncan with a Clyde crew; the smaller "Valkyrie I", sailed by Captain Diaper of Itchen; and the new large cutter "Iverna", sailed by Captain William O'Neill and unusual in having a centreboard to extend her already great draught. She could not beat the "Yarana" which was second in the class, dominated by the big "Thistle".

At the season's end the "Yarana" sailed from Southampton Water to lay up at Rowhedge. She set off in company with the little 2½ rater "Heathen Chinee", a 25 foot waterline, centreboard racer setting 570 square feet in two fully battened lugsails. She was skippered and sailed by Edward Sycamore, then living at Harwich, who had as his sole hand young Roger Sparling of Wivenhoe.

The "Heathen Chinee" was a notably fast boat but Captain Cranfield felt safe when he accepted Captain Sycamore's challenge to beat the "Yarana" into Colne, the loser to stand the winner a good dinner.

Next day "Yarana" arrived in Colne to find the lugger had just beaten her. The "Heathen Chinee's" shallow draught enabled her to stand over shoals, shortening courses and cheating tides in a way the big, deep draught cutter could not, and Sycamore won his wager.

Captain Cranfield invited her crew aboard for a hot meal and two of "Yarana's" hands jumped aboard to dodge the rater about, meanwhile. Away they went, reaching down Colne, but when the helm was put down to return she refused to come about. Everything was tried in desperation but they did not know she had two centreboards, one at each end, and would not turn with them both lowered. Eventually the puzzled hands lowered all sail and "Yarana" sent her gig, with laughing Roger Sparling, to sail her back.

Another winter's fishing followed, in Lemon Cranfield's smack "Neva", and William recalled how she and James Carter's "Wonder" raised Stephen Cranfield's "Elizabeth Ann", run down and sunk in deep water by the steamboat "Essex", by dragging chains under her hull at low water and lifting her on the flood. Before the start of the winter spratting, the almost unbeatable "Neva" raced in the Rowhedge regatta smack race and, that year, Lemon and William Cranfield changed smacks for the race. As the smacks swept into the reach there was great excitement, for William's "Sunbeam" was leading; but it was Lemon at the tiller, waving his cap and shouting "That had you. Thought the old man was beaten at last!"

"Yarana's" owner retired from racing and she was sold. In 1891 Captain Cranfield and most of his crew, including William, joined Lord Dunraven's new 80 foot cutter "L'Esperance", designed by Arthur Payne and built by Nicholson as a fast cruiser. The owner referred to her as his "fishing yacht" because she occasionally towed a trawl for his pleasure and practical interest in fishing. She raced in the large handicap class mainly against the yawl "Columbine", sailed by Captain Garrard of Wivenhoe, and the German Emperor's cutter "Meteor", sailed by Captain Robert Gomes of Gosport, with an English crew. At that time the English yacht sailors reckoned the Emperor a "good sport", keen to further yachting in Germany.

At Plymouth regatta the yachts started just before the almost equally large local fishing smacks, and sailed the same course in heavy weather. To the locals' surprise, the "L'Esperance" and her competitors beat the hard weather trawlers very handsomely, despite shipping green seas and being hove in to the skylights turning to windward. They finished the season with only moderate success, winning £304 prize money, but William was satisfied in having developed into a racing hand on whom his fellow crew members could rely and felt he was worth his 23 shillings weekly pay.

That winter William fished in the deep-sea smacks, dredging down channel and in the North Sea. He recalled Jack Spitty losing a big cutter smack on the Sunk, when the old salvager and his crew burned paraffin soaked blankets as flares and were taken out of her by the Harwich lifeboat; ironically, as the lifeboats were the salvagers' greatest rivals.

William also remembered Captain Jabez Polley of the Brightlingsea 18 ton smack "Globe"; a tough seafarer and an ardent Methodist who always carried a top hat and frock coat on board and seldom missed an opportunity to preach on Sundays, at whatever port from which the Colne fleet happened to be working.

But yachting was always far more profitable and had more opportunities for advancement than fishing, and during 1892 William became a mastheadsman.

Mastheading, carried out in a big yacht by the first and second mastheadsman, was dangerous work and brought an extra few shillings each week to these young and daring hands who laced the topsails, cleared the head sails and spinnakers and checked and repaired rigging under way or at anchor.

William's father was appointed mate of the racing cutter "Valkyrie" under Captain William Cranfield. Her owner, Lord Dunraven, decided to spend the summer of 1892 racing in the Mediterranean and she was fitted out and launched from Harris' yard at Rowhedge.

William was shipped as second mastheadsman and they won many prizes in regattas on the French and Italian coasts, and in passage races. They met many other English and some foreign owned yachts manned by Colnesiders and the welcome "Give us your line, mate," echoed in broad Essex across exotic harbours. Ship visiting followed, with foc'sles crowded for a sing song, though the crews rarely wanted to go ashore. Thoughtful Lord Dunraven arranged shore visits to places of interest for his crew and, at Venice, he asked Captain Cranfield his opinion of St. Mark's: "Well sir," he replied, "what with all them domes and images I'd rather have our parish church, that I would."

Being true Essexmen, "Valkyrie's" crew thought little of foreigners and not to be able to speak English was, to them, equivalent to idiocy. "Would you come on deck a minute?" Captain Cranfield would call down the skylight to the owner. "Here's a feller a hollerin and shouting—I cannot understand a word he says."

The "Valkyrie" was sold to the Archduke Karl Stephan of Austria and was delivered at Pola, where her crew stayed on for a month to teach the Austrians racing drill, especially how to set the spinnaker. The Essexmen returned home across Europe by train, via Vienna. Well laden with the inevitable portraits of "Valkyrie", painted by Italian pier head artists, which would grace their 'front rooms' for the rest of their lives.

In the spring of 1893 Rowhedge went wild with delight for, of the four great, new style racers just launched, Rowhedge skippers were to command three of them; William Cranfield the "Valkyrie II"; John Carter the Royal "Britannia"; and Tom Jay the "Satanita".

William's ability gained him the second mastheadman's place aboard the "Valkyrie II", whose crew of 35 were Rowhedgers almost to a man. He worked aloft with Jack ("Pups") Cranfield, the first mastheadsman and most noted of all that daring breed.

There was wonderfully keen racing between these lovely craft which were joined by the Scotch "Calluna" and the American "Navahoe" to give added spice to a great season.

In one of the early races the "Britannia" put the "Valkyrie II" about when she was on the starboard tack. Lord Dunraven angrily asked Captain Cranfield his opinion. "Well sir," replied the skipper, "I'm sorry for that. I'm afraid I can't ask the Prince of Wales to tea next time he comes to our village."

William's father found the mate's duties in "Valkyrie II" exacting for an elderly man and stood down, being replaced by William Taylor of Rowhedge, an extremely able and fantastically quick seaman, and a good organiser; William remembered him as everything a racing mate should be. Racing in those days for all classes started in early May with the Thames matches, followed by the Down Swin to Harwich, for the regatta, after which commenced the summer's programme, proper. Every port and resort of consequence along the coast and across channel held regattas for the racers which worked their way week after week through the heavy fixture lists; along the South coast, round the land and up to the Clyde; then a long passage back for Cowes week, finishing with the West Country regattas in late August and September.

It was from this setting that "Valkyrie II" sailed early in the 1893 season to challenge for the America's Cup. Rigged down to a ketch for the voyage across, she took a rare hammering in the westerly gales, before making New York. In those days the "Cup" contests aroused much national feeling and were more keenly followed than a present day test match or the Olympic games, and the contestants' crews received the consequent publicity and feting. Many scores of thousands watched the racing from a great fleet of excursion vessels, ferries, and yachts gathered off the Sandy Hook course. In New York, business was at a standstill—everyone went to see the races! From his masthead perch William had a grandstand view of "Valkyrie's" efforts in one of the most hotly contested attempts ever. But despite superior starts, bad luck dogged the challenger. In one race she burst three spinnakers, one after the other, as quickly as they could be set, and the series went to the American "Vigilant".

"Valkyrie II" was hampered by the wash and blanketing of the large numbers of excursion steamers cluttering the course; enormous three decked vessels, crammed with Americans singing, shouting, drinking, with bands playing patriotic tunes; all totally ignoring the big canvas sign the English yachtsmen occasionally hung overside with "KEEP ASTERN" painted on it in bold letters.

The crew came home by liner and William shipped in a smack for the winter. Next spring he went out to America with some others of "Valkyrie's" crew, to sail her home for the British racing season with her racing mast stepped, which gave her a nasty motion in Atlantic seas.

The American "Vigilant" was coming to Britain that season and "Valkyrie's" crew looked forward to beating her in home waters, but fate intervened. The first race in which they would have met was the mudhook regatta on the Clyde, a feature of which was the one annual handling of the big boats by amateur helmsmen. Before the start the unfortunate "Valkyrie II" was rammed and sunk by the "Satanita". William witnessed this most spectacular of all yachting disasters from the "Valkyrie's" spreaders, one hundred feet above the deck. The first mastheadsman, seeing that collision was inevitable, shouted for him to make the deck and, as they slid down the

Crew of the racing cutter *Ailsa*, 1894. Captain Tom Jay seated in centre. William Wadley, third row, centre, immediately forward of ensign staff.

shrouds, they were flung clear into the water by the shock of impact as the flying "Satanita", her amateur helmsman aided by Captain Diaper, desperately trying to avoid a small yacht, crunched a gaping hole in "Valkyrie's" side.

They struck out and scrambled aboard the yacht which was slowly sinking. Lord Dunraven was at the tiller lines and Captain Cranfield sprang to help him.

When collision appeared inevitable the three lady guests on board were unceremoniously thrown down the companion hatch and were pulled up again and got off in a boat which quickly put off from a nearby yacht. She swung clear from the "Satanita" and drifted against the steam yacht "Hebe". As she swept alongside the crew scrambled aboard but William Brown of Rowhedge, one of "Valkyrie's" smartest hands, fell in the slowly closing gap between the yachts and was crushed. The "Valkyrie" slid clear, fouled the steam yacht "Vanduara" and sank with her masthead remaining above water.

They got William Brown out and rushed him ashore in one of the steam yachts' boats to Dunoon hospital on the shore of the Firth but, despite urgent attention, he died from terrible injuries and the incident cast a gloom over the whole season.

In the professional yachtsman's tradition, each member of "Valkyrie's" crew voluntarily subscribed a week's pay to Brown's dependents and his tombstone in Rowhedge churchyard still records his loss in the "Valkyrie II".

"Valkyrie II's" steward was the most indignant of her crew. "I was in me pantry," he said, "just clearing up, when in comes this here wessel right into me pantry." He had been almost killed when "Satanita's" bow tore into "Valkyrie II's" side, and was trapped there as the door jammed, but he burst it open and got on deck just before she sank. It was all over in eight minutes; "Valkyrie" lay at the bottom and "Satanita" was disabled for months. A few weeks later Captain Cranfield picked his crew to join him in the new "Valkyrie III" which Lord Dunraven had ordered on the Clyde to be built for the 1894 season, and William was included. However, that autumn he had opportunity to ship with Captain Tom Jay in the new large racing cutter "Ailsa", fitting out for the winter season of regattas in the Mediterranean, which had become such a feature of the yachting year, and Captain William released him from the engagement.

"Ailsa" won many prizes against the "Britannia" and returning from Nice for Southampton in the spring with a locker full of cups, the becalmed "Ailsa" was attacked by a galley load of armed Riffs near Gibraltar straits. Firing on the yacht, they were coming up with her to board, when a breeze sprang up, enabling her to escape. William always chuckled over the way the light weather kites were set in double quick time on that occasion by a crew armed with galley knives and deck scrubbers!

Apart from this excitement the passage home was tedious, with head winds, and the mainsheet was in all the way from Naples to Calshot Spit.

"Ailsa" went into dry dock at Tilbury in company with "Britannia" and "Satanita", preparing for the new season. Fife, her designer, prescribed alterations to her lead keel to increase sail carrying power but, afterwards, she did not win a prize in the season's opening matches on the Thames, the Down Swin, at Harwich, or in the Nore to Dover races. At Dover half the crew, Southampton men, started agitating for "losing money" as there seemed no prospect of her winning any prize money. To this the owner's representative would not agree. Things quietened after this until, after racing unsuccessfully at Cowes, they refused duty until losing money was paid. This was refused, so eight of "Ailsa's" crew, including William, packed their bags and left the yacht at Southampton, leaving Captain Jay stamping and raging on deck as some of his best hands stepped ashore.

William went home to Rowhedge to look for another berth. Captain William Cranfield, on a visit home from the Clyde, was surprised to meet him in Albion Street and William explained the reason. "Never mind" said the Captain, "I'll fix you in the new "Valkyrie III"." Two days afterwards a telegram arrived for William; "Join "Ailba" at Gourock. Cranfield." William thought the "Ailba" must be a houseboat which the "Valkyrie" crew were living aboard during fitting out, so, packing his gear, he entrained for Scotland. Walking along Gourock pier he met Steve Barbrook of Tollesbury, one of "Ailsa's" hands, who asked if William had returned to join. "No fear!" I'm shipping with Captain William in the new "Valkyrie", he replied.

"Valkyrie's" gig came ashore to fetch him and he stepped aboard the new America's Cup challenger to learn that he had been sent for to rejoin the "Ailsa", lying further up the anchorage. William refused, but Captain Cranfield and the mate tried to persuade him. He was adamant. After a conference in the cabin they said he could stay. However, when Lord Dunraven came aboard next day they tried again to get him to return to the "Ailsa". Eventually his stubborness won and they let him stay.

The giant "Valkyrie III" tuned up on the Clyde and had a light weather passage to America. Her crew anticipated transatlantic luxury travel by filling the boats on deck with water, as improvised swimming pools. She was in charge of Captain Cranfield, who had Captain Edward Sycamore of Brightlingsea to assist him when racing. At that time the most extreme yacht built in this country, the third "Valkyrie" had tremendous overhangs in her one hundred and thirty foot length; but despite her thirteen thousand square feet of canvas and wonderful handling by a crew specially picked for youth as well as ability, she lost the first race, won the second, and snubbed the Americans by merely coming to the line without starting, in the third. Her owner, the Earl of Dunraven, disgusted with the blundering interference of a hundred excursion steamers throughout the series, withdrew in what almost amounted to an atmosphere of international tension.

The crew suffered much discomfort from the summer heat of New York as they were kitted-out with the usual blue-serge trousers, guernseys and other clothes suitable for British weather and had to wear crew uniform when the yacht was sailing, and on deck when at anchor, for the eyes of America were on them and visitors and guests constantly on board.

After a season aboard the big yawl "Namara", handicap racing coastwise and across channel, William spent the winter spratting aboard the smack "Mary" and, in common with many of his contemporaries, studied hard at the Nottage Institute navigation classes, specially founded, at Wivenhoe, to assist local seamen to gain their Board·of Trade mates' and masters' certificates.

They realised the future might require a more versatile outlook for the Colne seafarers and, from about 1895, many of the young seamen kept a weather eye on the merchant service, though their love of sailing and skill in racing led most to continue spending the summer yachting and the winter either fishing under sail or seeking berths in merchant steamships making voyages which would return them to England, in the spring, for the following year's fitting out season. Many obtained their second mates' or mates' certificates and some went on to become masters of ocean going steam-ships.

In 1897 William went mastheadsman of the 110 ton cutter "Hester", with which Captain John Cranfield was thrashing the large handicap class, including the "Namara" and "Yarana" and the Wivenhoe-built "Creole". The skipper was a great man for perfection in sail trimming and his skill won a Queen's Cup. William shipped in her again the following season and recalled seeing the 331 ton racing schooner "Rainbow", thundering through Spithead at her 16 knot clip and leaving a wake fit to sink a ten tonner, with Captain Tom Jay at her tiller.

By then, William's younger brother Charlie had started in the racing yachts as a hand and they sometimes met as rivals in the crews of different craft.

With the temporary collapse of first class racing for several years, chief interest centred on the fifty-two foot class and in 1899 William joined the famous "Penitent" under Captain Dan Aldrige of Rowhedge. She was 75 feet long and set 3000 sq. feet of canvas. Her mate was Albert Turner of Wivenhoe and amongst her hands was Edward Heard, one of several young Tollesburymen who were beginning to be shipped and trained in the many racing yachts skippered from Rowhedge, as that village's capacity to provide sufficient hands from a total population of 1100 was fully extended. Mr. William Burton of Ipswich, "Penitent's" owner, was the foremost amateur racing yachtsman of those times and the boat came to the top of one of the keenest classes of yacht racing history. Her 7 man crew were as delighted as the owner, for in three seasons she never won less than £250 prize money. But it was hard-earned in extremely close racing where the yachts sometimes finished within 15 seconds of each other after sailing a 50 mile race, and the "Penitent" made many hard weather passages around the coast, including one from the Thames to the Clyde under double reefed trysail to fetch the Clyde regattas on time.

That winter William again fished in the big smacks and the fleet lay stormbound in Newhaven during a January blizzard. A nearby Brightlingsea smack got her cable foul of the bobstay clasp and one of her apprentice boys, with characteristic devilment, dived overboard, fully clothed, into the freezing water, to free it. When he clambered back aboard his clothes were frozen on him like armour and his furious skipper cut them from him with a knife, starting at the neck and finishing with his boots. There happened to be a big pan of boiling soup on the stove and the skipper poured it over the boy's head to "keep the blood a' circulatin"; they were hard seamen.

Only extreme bad weather kept the shellfish dredging smacks in port. Work aboard them often went on almost continuously for two or three days and nights, hauling dredges every hour or so in deep water, down channel. They slept briefly in their clothes and the youngest apprentice boy did the cooking. Sometimes an apprentice dozed off, tailing on to the warps as they were hauled; then it was usual for a man to smack him across the face with a wet, mittened fist to wake him up, not from cruelty or solely from desire to keep him at work, but to ensure no one went overboard through not being alert.

Their catches of scallops, often dredged off the French coast, fetched 6d to 1s a dozen and oysters 5s a hundred. But it was a hard and very unrewarding trade with the smack crews often ending weeks of work without having bettered themselves by a penny.

One big Brightlingsea smack was lost entering Newhaven through not setting his topsail and hustling-in before the onshore seas. Most smack skippers thought that, contrary to usual practice, vessels should be driven into that harbour before heavy seas; otherwise they were pooped, or pitchpoled at the entrance.

In 1901 William was selected as second mastheadsman in the 35 man crew of "Shamrock II", under two Captains; Robert Wringe and Edward Sycamore, both then living in Brightlingsea.

She did not win the cup but, during her tuning up in the Solent, with King Edward VII on board, this huge racing machine lost her mast. Ben Chaplin, the Brightlingsea first mastheadsman, was aloft when all hands heard the steel mast creaking. He was called down and just made the deck as 14,000 square feet of canvas went overboard; the mast buckling with its head in the mud, fathoms below, pinning the "Shamrock" until a gang of platers were sent out from a Cowes shipyard to cut the mast free. Several hands, including William, were swept over on the lee side, but scrambled back unhurt. The King enquired if anyone was hurt and coolly lit a cigar.

1902 saw William back in the 52 footers aboard Mr. Burton's new, Fife built, "Lucida", skippered by Albert Turner.

The fifty two footers were of the finest workmanship, but very lightly constructed, and were notorious for "working" when under way. Racing in the channel from Dover to Ostende, "Lucida's" cook was sent below from his racing station to prepare sandwiches for all hands, the mate intending to call him when they had to tack at the next mark. As "Lucida" neared the light vessel the cook came on deck and went to the jib topsail sheets. "I didn't call you, George," said the mate. "No," replied the cook, "I could see the lightship through the starboard seams!" The owner pretended not to hear.

In 1903 Sir Thomas Lipton tried again for the America's Cup with the third "Shamrock" and while she was building, Captain Sycamore, who was to sail in her, wrote asking if William would like to go in her as a mastheadsman. William wanted to but, in view of the £5 winter retainer Mr. Burton paid, discussed it with the owner, who tried to dissuade him. However, William wanted "to have another go at the Yanks", so he left the "Lucida" and shipped in this 135 foot light displacement boat by Fife, carrying the big sail spread of 14,000 square feet, with a draft of 20 feet and a set of lines which could not be bettered to-day. Her size can be gauged from the fact that her light weather balloon jib spread no less than 9,000 feet to the topmast head and needed all her crew of forty four to get the sheet in a freshening breeze. Mastheading in her was hard work as the jack-yarder had 2,000 square feet, in it and the topmast towered 185 feet above the waterline. The whole lot went overboard during a trial race at Weymouth, when one of her stewards, Mr. Collier of Wivenhoe, was drowned, despite the crew's efforts to save him, and another hand was injured by falling gear.

With Captain Wringe in charge she fared no better than her predecessors and was beaten by the huge American "Reliance", probably the most extreme racing machine ever built, setting 16,000 square feet and manned by 70 men.

In spring 1904 William signed on as mastheadsman in the crew of the large steel yawl "Navahoe", which had been designed and built in 1893 by Herreshoff as an American racer, but was then owned by George Watjen, one of the wealthy German merchants whom the Kaiser was attempting to inspire with a love of yachting and thus bolster support for his growing Navy and Imperial plans. The rapid development of German yachting created need for numbers of English racing skippers and crews as there were then no German yacht sailors. The "Navahoe" was commanded by Captain Edward Sycamore, whom William first remembered in the little rater "Heathen Chinee", and his crew were all Colnesiders, mainly from Rowhedge and Brightlingsea.

The "Navahoe" entered in the 308 mile Dover to Heligoland race for the German Emperor's Cup and a fleet of large racers went roaring and rolling away up the North Sea carrying Solent racing canvas in a strong wind. "Navahoe's" particular rival was the 122 foot American schooner "Ingomar", sailed by Scottish-American skipper, Charles Barr, who had beaten them in "Reliance". She crossed the line 35 hours out from Dover, but the race was won by the Brightlingsea manned ketch "Valdora".

The mastheadsman. William Wadley and Ben Chaplin lacing the luff of *Shamrock III's* topsail, 1903.

The fleet next raced off the German naval base of Cuxhaven, thrashing through the blustery dreariness of its North Sea approaches before towing through the Kiel Canal. As the "Navahoe" approached its high bridges, all hands looked apprehensively at the topmost head towering 130 odd feet above the waterline; but she slid beneath with a couple of feet to spare.

Then on to Kiel, whose 'week' was organised to be grander than Cowes. There were racing yachts by the score, German, British and American; warships of many nations, enormous British and American steam yachts; chartered liners acting as floating hotels for the hundreds of guests and, centre of it all the Emperor's giant steam yacht "Hohenzollern". Steam pinnaces rushed about the beautiful Kiel Fiord which was crowded with hundreds of small raters. Bands played, flags flew, sailors saluted, soldiers clicked heels and thousands thronged to see the Emperor and the yachts. All eight of the German-owned, large racers were built in either Britain or America and their captains and crews were almost all Englishmen, mainly from the Colne and Solent, with Captain Ben Parker from Itchen sailing the Emperor's new, American-built schooner "Meteor III" which precipitated a breath-taking incident.

The big yachts were beating down the Fiord, "Ingomar" on the starboard tack with "Navahoe" close astern. "Meteor III" loomed ahead on the port tack, attempting to cross "Ingomar's" bows. Closer, they thundered. William could see Captain Barr intent at "Ingomar's" wheel; her forty-man crew apprehensive as the bowsprit pointed at the German, who came on, apparently ignoring the rules, across their bows. "Navahoe" would go clear but her crew were alert to impending tragedy. If the schooners collided, masts and spars would go, lives might be lost and the Emperor was on board the "Meteor III". Surely Barr would give way, but he did not for he was in the right. "Ingomar's" bowsprit was almost stabbing at "Meteor's" shrouds when Barr's ringing "Lee oh!" sent the "Ingomar" shooting up into the wind and, at the same instant, "Meteor III" luffed head to wind, her canvas thundering, before each fell off on opposite tacks, without a word exchanged. But "Meteor III" knew she had broken the rules and down came her spread eagle racing flag, and a torpedo boat plucked her away to the anchorage.

Then they raced in the Green Baltic, from Travemunde, where the "Navahoe's" crew were roused one night by shouts of a man overboard from the "Ingomar", lying next ahead. William, and others, rushed up and fished out an indignant German admiral, still wearing his gold leaf cap.

Back at Kiel the "Navahoe" was visited by Kaiser Wilhelm who, characteristically, shook hands with every man of her English crew, congratulated them on their smartness and questioned Captain Sycamore on the yacht's racing performance before bluntly stating that he hoped all German yachts might soon be manned by Germans!

"Navahoe" continued her rivalry with "Ingomar" in the Channel races. For 60 miles, from Dover to the West Hinder, they beat to windward in heavy wind and sea and "Navahoe" held on to the big American.

As "Navahoe" entered Ostende harbour some fishermen had a line across the entrance. They were not quick enough in dropping it, and it caught in the yacht's rudder gudgeon. Sycamore said they would have a diver to clear it but William volunteered to go down. They gave him the cook's knife and he pulled himself down the rope with a lifeline round him. He sawed through the rope and cleared it after two attempts and bobbed up covered with the filthy harbour slime. Sycamore ordered him a tot of rum and gave him 10/-.

An incident in one of the later races in the Solent typified a mastheadsman's work. The "Navahoe" was racing the 166 ton cutter "Kariad", running with her spinnaker and large jib topsail set; a sail about 120 feet on the luff and 2500 square feet area. They hailed from forward that the spinnaker had fouled the jib topsail hanks and, as mastheadsman, William had to climb up the mast hoops; hand over hand up the masthead to the jumper strut, then up the topmast by the topsail halyard. He checked that the jib topsail halyard was clear in its block, then seized the topmast forestay, swung himself clear, and came down the wire stay, cutting the hanks off with his knife and kicking the spinnaker down with his feet a hundred feet above the bowsprit. The sails cleared away and he slid down the stay to the bowsprit end, where the grinning Brightlingsea bowspritendsman crouched, ready to help him. William swarmed inboard along the bowsprit and back to his station. Captain Sycamore said "Well done Bill."

That winter William had the exciting offer to become mate of the new 52 footer "Britomart" which was building on the Clyde for Mr. Burton. Albert Turner, who had been skipper of "Lucida", was in command and the class had reached a peak of racing perfection. "Britomart" was crack boat of 1905 and 1906, her closest rivals being the "Maymon", sailed by Captain Charles Bevis of Bursledon with a Hamble crew and the American designed "Sonya", sailed by Captain Fred Stokes of Tollesbury, and owned by a lady, Mrs. Turner-Farley.

Running hard for the line in a race at Harwich the leeward boat luffed "Britomart" hard and they had not time to get the spinnaker in, so William cut the tack and the halliard was let fly. The effect was tremendous, the spinnaker whisked out to leeward clear of everything and fell in the water like a great balloon. It won them the race.

In 1908 Sir Thomas Lipton ordered a large racing cutter to the then recently introduced 23 metre rule. Inevitably she was to be named "Shamrock", but was intended for racing round the coast with the British large class. Captain Edward Sycamore was skipper and William Wadley was her mate. The mate of a large racing yacht had much responsibility. The condition of the yacht's hull, mast, spars, rigging and sails were his care at all times, and he was constantly checking it all. In many ways he was harder worked than the captain from whom he received orders and saw they were carried out as quickly as was humanly possible, and in a racer those words had meaning. His usual racing station was on the foredeck, where he had special charge of the trim of headsails and spinnaker, and of their setting and lowering. On some points of sailing he advised the captain of competitors' tactics, when he had clearer vision than the skipper, at the helm. In large racers the second mate had charge of the backstays and mainsheet, and his racing station was aft.

The mate was frequently in charge of the yacht and her navigation at sea, on passage; and in harbour he was amongst the first on deck each morning and the last to turn in to his foc'sle cot. In large yachts he was often kept on all winter to superintend or carry out maintenance work.

"Shamrock, 23 metres" as she became known was a long-lived and successful racer and her class opponents were Miles Kennedy's "White Heather", sailed by Captain Charles Bevis of Burlesdon, on the Hamble, with a Solent crew; the "Brynhld", skippered by Captain Steven Barbrook of Tollesbury and the "Nyria" commanded by Captain Steven Ray, from Gosport.

Each yacht had a crew of 22 and set about 10,000 square feet of canvas, without the equally large spinnaker which set from the topmast head, 120 feet above deck. Fitted out they cost £12,000, and a season's racing cost the owner £5,000.

"Shamrock" was designed by Fife as a light weather boat, and her finest point of sailing was turning to windward in light or moderate breezes. In the Nore to Dover race they carried whole mainsails through a really heavy sea at the back of the Goodwins, which shook the yachts, straining them from stem to stern as they battled to windward through green seas for three hours, in clouds of spray. "Shamrock's" rigging slacked-up with the vibration and the mast was none too firm in its step. The boom drooped so low when she tacked that it almost swept the companion hatch off.

Though beautifully built and handled the racers had become extreme under the metre rules and the owners preferred more comfortable quarters. Sir Thomas Lipton and his guests lived in the large steam yacht "Erin" and Miles Kennedy, owner of "White Heather", chartered an ocean tug as her tender.

"Shamrock" finished that season as top boat with "White Heather" second and "Nyria" out of it.

"Brynhild" was dogged by bad luck from her launch, when the cradle killed a shipwright. During her first races in the Thames her mastheadsman fell from aloft and was killed, a hand was lost from her in the Solent, and there were other mishaps to make sailors growl she was ill-fated.

William finished that season with a good share of prize money, for which a structure of payment established by custom existed. In addition to his agreed wages the captain of a successful racer received 5% of the prize money won by the yacht and, usually, a substantial gratuity from the owner. The mates and hands each received varying proportions of the total.

Challenge cups were unpopular with all hands as little prize money went with them and, when these were raced for, owners paid each of the crew £1.

As mate of a first-class racer William was on full retainer all winter carrying out and supervising maintenance and fitting-out; another step forward, important for a married man with a young family.

At the start of the 1910 season, in the Orwell Corinthian Y.C. regatta off Harwich, "Shamrock", "White Heather" and "Brynhild" raced and, near the weather mark, the North Cutler Buoy, "Brynhild's" mast failed below deck, drove down through her bottom and sank her in fourteen minutes. William recalled all 25 of her crew clinging to her dinghy until her competitors quickly launched theirs and rescued them, aided by a destroyer. The prophecies had been fulfilled and "Brynhild's" shattered hull was eventually raised and broken-up on Brightlingsea hard.

With only "Shamrock" and "White Heather" remaining in the class they had a season of duelling all round the coast. In 40 races "Shamrock" won 21 first prizes and "White Heather" 19. They sailed without time allowance and usually finished within a boat's length.

The crew's work aboard a large racer, such as "Shamrock", followed a pattern evolved over generations of yachting. All hands turned out at 6 a.m. and shammied down the brightwork and decks, making the most of any dew to avoid scouring the varnish. The headsails and spinnakers were made up in stops or, if the weather was threatening, they put a reef in the mainsail. Breakfast was at 7.30 and after it the mainsail was set, followed by the headsails and topsail; ready for the start, which was usually about 9 o'clock, or a little later. With guests aboard and the yacht under weigh, all hands were at racing stations; the skipper at the wheel, mate and two hands in charge of the headsail sheets, two hands were on each side at the runner tackles and foresail sheets; the second mate and two hands at the jib topsail sheets, mainsheet and topmast backstay tackles. The mastheadsmen were aloft and the remainder of the crew were alert on deck to haul where required on sheets or halyards. In the "Shamrock", the cook and stewards had charge of the sails prepared below in the foc'sle, ready to send them up as required, through the forehatch.

The day's racing might be around a fifty mile course, sometimes longer, and after it, with the owner and guests gone and the yacht anchored, all hands lowered and stowed the sails carefully for the next day's racing. With everything checked and neatly stowed, minor repairs and maintenance carried out, and decks washed down, all hands had tea and tried to dry their almost invariably soaked clothes round the foc'sle stove or on the bowsprit shrouds, if it was fine. A smoke and a yarn and it was time to turn into the rows of pipe cots lining the foc'sle, ready for another day's racing.

At that time racing hands received 26 shillings per week basic pay. Men with special duties received additional pay; bowspritendsmen 2s. 6d. per day and mastheadsmen 5 shillings. Prize money was £1 per man for a first prize, 15 shillings for a second prize and, win or lose, there was "starting money" of 10 shillings per race. An allowance of 2s. 6d. per day was paid when racing as it was not desirable to cook or prepare meals aboard.

Though Sir Thomas spent a fortune on racing yachts he really knew very little about the sport and his crews eventually felt that, although at first the owner was keen to win the America's Cup, after the "Shamrock II" challenge he might have been disappointed if they succeeded, as his reputation in America as "the world's best loser" meant much to him, besides being wonderful publicity for his business. He appeared to be a great showman but was actually a bad loser in British racing, blaming everyone on board from the captain to the cook, when "Shamrock 23 metre" was beaten. But the "Shamrock" had a happy crew.

One autumn "Shamrock's" crew attended the Brightlingsea ploughing matches, as several Brightlingsea yacht captains had challenged the local farmers at furrow drawing. The field was crowded with a strange mixture of countrymen and serge-suited seamen, cheering their champions on. Irrepressible Captain Sycamore amused the farmers by turning out with a large compass lashed to his plough to help him steer a straight course!

The smack races remained keenly contested each autumn. William raced in Captain William Cranfield's "Sunbeam" at Tollesbury smack race and regatta, which she won, and they sailed her home after crossing the line, leaving Captain Stephen Cranfield, the owner's brother, to collect the cup and bring it back to a smoking concert to be held at Rowhedge. However, they waited in vain, for Stephen did not arrive for three days, and then with a terrific hangover!

The Tollesbury smack "Bertha" tried to rival the "Sunbeam" and "Neva", even going so far as racing with an enamelled bottom, one year, but still she was beaten.

In 1911 "Shamrock" was not fitted out and her crew took the 19 metre "Mariquita", one of the best of a class which were universally described as the finest in yachting history; 100 ton cutters, 95 feet long setting 6,200 square feet on the moderate draught of 12 feet. "Mariquita" started well by winning the King's Cup in the Nore to Dover race before the class sailed for Ostende, and Kiel regatta. After the Baltic they sailed for Scotland and the Clyde fortnight, meeting calms for several days until the wind came and rapidly freshened to a gale. "Mariquita" snugged down to small jib, foresail and trysail. Hatches were battened down and the long bow and counter pounded at the seas sweeping the canted deck, until the watch below were living in a drum. On deck the rig screamed in a flame of wind as the four racers turned 100 miles to windward through the gale, before bearing away for Aberdeen where, after a 430 mile passage, three of them entered the breaker-dashed piers abreast of each other. They sailed up to Inverness and the Caledonian Canal and William described the astonishment of the Scots people at the sight of four towering masts of the big racers towing through the quiet canal which had, hitherto, seen nothing large than a herring drifter or puffer.

They took a 'pilot' from Banavie to the Clyde but he later confessed he had last been there 20 years previously! So they piloted themselves and arrived in good trim for the Clyde racing.

The 19 metres were very evenly matched and competition was very keen. William recalled that "Mariquita" luffed the "Octavia", owned by Mr. Burton, and skippered by Captain Albert Turner of Wivenhoe, ashore on the Ryde sands, where she dried out and laid over at an alarming angle, but managed to pick up on the next tide.

William received much ribbing over this incident from his brother Charlie, who had become mate of the "Octavia". There was a similar incident near the No Man fort, in Spithead, when "Mariquita" forced the "Octavia" in, and she touched the outworks of the fort with her keel, bounding up and on, without stopping. She made no water and when slipped her keel was only dented, but that winter, when Charlie was painting through her bilges to earn his winter retainer, his paintbrush made a keelbolt nut revolve. He found it turned easily by hand and, to his astonishment, lifted up the 2 inch diameter bolt out of the keel, where it had been fractured with the shock of impact.

William raced again in "Shamrock" during 1912, when Sycamore and Bevis resumed their duties but next season Captain Sycamore and some of his crew left the "Shamrock" and stood by the new Nicholson-designed 15 metre "Paula III", building at Gosport for Herr Ludwig Sanders, a prominent German. A development of the famous "Istria" she stepped an incredibly tall mast and topmast in one and set 4,500 square feet on a 82 foot hull. They tuned her up in the Baltic and did not join the English 15 metre fleet until the racing off Havre where the combination of Sycamore's skill and a good boat won them most prizes.

They had terrific competition from a class of seven which included the new "Pamela", the "Maudrey", sailed by Captain Wallace Allen of Rowhedge, who had

The *Britomart*; champion 52 footer of 1905, wearing her prize flags. Captain Albert Turner of Wivenhoe and his Colne crew on deck. Mate William Wadley, forward.

been one of William's contemporaries in the "Valkyrie II", and the King of Spain's "Hispania", sailed by Captain Steven Barbrook of Tollesbury, whom William remembered as a hand in the "Ailsa". Then, on to Cowes week, where "Paula III" was equally succesful, winning the Commodore's Cup. At its presentation the owner stressed he was taking a cup back to Germany won with an English-built yacht, sailed by an English crew, and with an English helmsman.

Then it was back to the Baltic for more racing, before "Paula III" laid-up in a yard by beautiful Kiel Fiord.

War was in the air, everyone felt it but hoped it would disperse. That winter Captain Sycamore was asked to take charge of the German owned 15 metre "Sophie Elizabeth" which had been built by William Fife in 1911.

William went as mate and the pick of the hands went with them. The Essexmen fitted her out in a springtime oppressive with the shadow of war. She was a very fast boat and they raced with success in the Baltic, getting well tuned up by Cowes week, for which the English yachts racing in Germany had already sailed, closely followed by Krupp's giant schooner "Germania" and the English manned, German 15 metre "Paula III".

To save time, the "Sophie Elizabeth's" owner had arranged for her to be towed from Kiel to Cowes by the same torpedo boat which was towing the Kaiser's new racing schooner "Meteor IV". The little convoy hurriedly steamed through the Kiel canal and out into the North Sea, the towropes straining and the smoke blowing low over the tall-sparred racers. Suddenly, the torpedo boat slowed and much signalling followed between her and the "Meteor", then she turned and towed them at high speed back towards the Elbe. War was about to be declared between England and Germany and the Essexmens' spirits were very low indeed.

They berthed at Cuxhaven naval base and Captain Sycamore wired the owner but received no reply. The "Sophie Elizabeth" was laid on a buoy; a grim paradox of a crew of Englishmen, as yet unmolested and almost ignored, within the heart of a German North Sea base.

Later that day, when the hands were ashore for water, Captain Sycamore accompanying them in case of trouble, a launch came alongside and asked William if he was master, then left. Past midnight, with all hands asleep, there was a tap on deck and they fearfully turned out to find another launch alongside with an armed officer ordering them to leave the yacht with their personal belongings; war had been declared. They were taken ashore and marched to a prison, under armed guard. Each man was placed in a separate barred-windowed cell and meals were bread and black coffee. Later, they were searched, released and sent back aboard the "Sophie Elizabeth", but were not given back their personal effects.

Shortly after a large motor car arrived, sent by the owner to take them to Hamburg, where he met them. There was a Grimsby boat still lying at Hamburg, crowded with British refugees caught in Germany, and the "Sophie Elizabeth" crew tried to take passage in her but were stopped from sailing. Eventually, through the owner's influence, they were placed on a train for Denmark, intending to make for Esbjerg to get a ship for Harwich. However, the train was stopped and searched and the crew with other English refugee passengers were ordered off and jailed, Captain Sycamore being placed under guard. Again they were released, placed on another train and eventually reached Esbjerg where they took passage in a packet for Harwich and home. Their families were tremendously relieved at their safe return as many horrible rumours were circulating regarding the fate of Englishmen stranded in Germany. Like all their contemporaries the "Sophie Elizabeth's" crew either offered themselves for sea service as members of the Royal Naval Reserve or as volunteers, while others fished in the smacks.

Captain Sycamore applied for a naval commission and was given command of a motor launch. William spent the war at sea and returned to yachting by taking the ex-Kaiser's 400 ton "Meteor IV" out to Alexandria, with a Colneside crew. She had been bought by an Egyptian Prince who required her for cruising in the Mediterranean and Black Seas. However, a few months were sufficient to prove that the owner liked swinging round a buoy much better than seafaring, so skipper and crew left for England.

In the short Indian summer of fishing under sail during the early 1920's the Essex smack races combined into a week of events. In one of them William sailed in James Carter's "Wonder" at Clacton regatta in very light weather. The fleet crept slowly to the weather mark until the ebb ran and they kedged just downtide of it. A half hour passed and the smacks stood like statues in the tide. Aboard "Wonder" there was activity. The kedge warp was paid out and she slid astern but, before her astonished competitors could grasp the significance of the move, all hands were rousing in the warp, faster and faster, until her fine bows were slicing the tide and the dripping warp came home as "Wonder" surged to round the buoy and came sheering back, down tide, to certain victory past her enraged rivals.

Yacht racing recommenced in 1919, but post-war wages for experienced racing hands had risen to £3. 10s. per week; younger men and stewards receiving £3.

Despite rising expense the big class was re-established during the early 1920's and Sir Thomas Lipton had the 23 metre "Shamrock" fitted-out and racing under Captain Leavett of Tollesbury, then Captain Diaper from Itchen; soon superseded by Captain Sycamore whose post-war command had been the big schooner "Westward". William was quickly in her as mate and for the remaining summers of the 'twenties' the racing world seemed back to normal, with keen competition between "Shamrock" and the King's old "Britannia" skippered by Albert Turner with a Colne crew; "White Heather" sailed by Captain Ted Mountifield of Gosport; the newer "Lulworth", last of the big gaff racers and sailed by Sycamore's old rival Captain Bevis; the mighty "Westward", now sailed by Captain Alf Diaper who had difficulty in keeping a crew under the new ownership of excitable Mr. Davis. In 1928 these gaff rigged racers were challenged by new large yachts designed with bermudian rig which, at first, seemed reluctant to stay in them; particularly the Fife-built "Cambria" and the Nicholson "Astra", sailed by Captain Pound from Gosport, and in 1929 by the "Candida" sailed by Captain Gilbey of Bosham, with a Chichester Harbour crew.

This mixed fleet had good racing and to meet the challenge "Shamrock" was thoroughly refitted. As mate, William tackled this with enthusiasm and "Shamrock" emerged immaculate. When her designer, William Fife, spoke at a Clyde Yacht Club dinner of "Shamrock's" success he paid tribute to her wonderful condition at 18 years of age as being due to "Mr. Wadley, the best racing mate on the British coasts". It was a sincere compliment from a great designer, and William was proud of it, through life.

"The Rock", as her Colne crew affectionately knew her, seemed to go faster than ever, with Captain Sycamore characteristically getting the best starts. He had a biting sense of humour, snapping at a mainsheetman who eased the sheet a few seconds late; "When I was young we wouldn't have shipped you as ballast!" To another hand who fumbled with the backstay runner he observed; "You ain't no more use than a flea on a wooden leg!" Nevertheless, there was a twinkle in his eye and a great sense of leadership which welded a crew together.

By 1926 the safe limit of sail plan had been passed by the gaff rigged racers with Marconi masts. "Shamrock" was romping through the Solent during Cowes week when her 150 feet mast buckled and, with a tremendous report, fell over the lee side in a shower of splinters, fortunately clear of everyone aboard. During the same week "Britannia" became unmanageable in a breeze due to excess rig height, and the following season the powerful "Lulworth" lost her mast, which almost fell across a competitor, to leeward.

The big boats were, as usual, racing all round the coast and at the 1927 Bangor regatta, William recalled the whole class caught by a wind shift, rapidly rising to a gale, at anchor on a lee shore. All beat out except the "Shamrock", whose anchors were holding well, but the "White Heather" was almost driven ashore, plunging to windward in sheets of spray, well reefed, and touching bottom twice. Later, at the Royal Dorset regatta, "Shamrock" sailed a dead heat with "Britannia"; the only earlier instance being in 1892. That season she won her 100th first prize. When she raced the new "Astra" at Harwich there was a thunderous roar as all the slides on the 140 foot luff of the bermudian cutter's mainsail carried away and she was out of it. "Cambria" had little better luck and "Shamrock" and several of her contemporaries finished the season well ahead of the bermudian rigged cutters, with "Shamrock" top of the class by a considerable margin.

But bermudian rig needed a smaller crew to handle it and gradually improved its efficiency, aided by the vested interests of some designers who wanted the gaff rig racers' ratings amended to encourage building new boats.

During 1929 the old "Shamrock" sometimes continued to beat the new cutters "Candida", "Astra", and "Cambria", but Sir Thomas Lipton decided on a fifth attempt to win the America's Cup. He ordered a 120 ft. bermudian rigged racer from Camper and Nicholson. She was to be the pride of the racing fleet and it was expected that ageing Captain Sycamore and his smart crew would handle her, but fate intervened. Captain Sycamore died and was buried on the day the "Shamrock V" was launched. Tollesbury's Captain Edward Heard was appointed her skipper and brought many of his own racing crew with him.

William Wadley went mate of the powerful 120 foot racing cutter "Lulworth", under Scottish Captain Archie Hogarth, with a mixed Clyde and Colne crew. Launched in 1920, "Lulworth" was the last large racer built with gaff rig. She was by then out-classed in most conditions but was always keenly raced and gained a few places during 1930. On the Clyde she outsailed the new "Shamrock V" in light airs and kept the challenger neatly under her lee. Later in the season William witnessed another of the fortunately few serious yachting tragedies. The large class, including the "Lulworth", started one morning during Cowes week, to race westward in the Solent, to round the East Lepe buoy and set their giant spinnakers for a cracking, roaring run back past Cowes, towards the next mark. The yachts were well together, "Lulworth" being last. By then the 12 metre class were manœuvring for the start. The first gun had gone and they were standing inshore, close hauled on the starboard tack intending, at the gun, to come about close hauled for the beat to the west.

Aboard "Lulworth", her crew's forward vision was limited by the mass of sail carried by her competitors. Suddenly, the 12 metre "Lucilla" appeared between them and the next ahead, standing under the bow of "Lulworth", whose horrified crew shouted, leaping for the gybe as her Captain Hogarth spun the wheel to ease the shock of inevitable collision. As "Lulworth's" boom crashed over from port to starboard her bow bit deep into the "Lucilla's" starboard side. For moments the yachts were locked together while the dazed 12 metre crew scrambled aboard "Lulworth", frantically searching the water for signs of Saunders, one of her hands, who had been heavily struck by falling gear, knocked overboard and drowned.

"Lucilla" sank and "Lulworth" limped back to Cowes roads with a flag in her rigging. The incident shadowed the remainder of the season and the "Lulworth" was laid up; her crew quickly busy seeking other berths.

William's ability had long attracted notice and, that winter, Mr. Connell, a Clyde shipbuilder and noted owner of racing yachts, ordered the 12 metre "Zoraida" from Fife, and William Wadley was appointed captain. It was his first command and a good one. Arthur Connell was a clever amateur helmsman who had owned many racers and knew the worth of a Colne crew. His boats, including the "Zoraida" and his later 12 metres, were all tiller steered as he was convinced this gave the best touch for the helmsman. His 12 metres were also the last to use tackles on the headsail sheets, after the others had adopted sheet capstans.

William received much chaff from his contemporaries on the size of his command compared with the large racers; "Don't you take a big stride when you go aboard, Bill, do you'll step right over her," being typical, and he described the 12 metre class as "Fine little boats". Like all racing skippers he stood by the building of the yacht and particularly advised on deck layout and gear. These 70 foot sloops were allowed by the rules to set parachute spinnakers of 3,000 square feet area, which were difficult to handle with a crew of four.

During the 1930's the 12 metre class reached the height of its glory, racing at regattas all round the coast. The boats cost about £4,500 and provided owners with most of the thrills of big class racing at the expense of a modest crew of skipper and three hands. There were usually two or three amateurs aboard in addition, on race days.

Many of the amateurs were regarded as good racing men but they were naturally not as quick, nor could they pull their weight on a rope, like a professional. As most amateurs were unaccustomed to manual work their hands suffered terribly and, as William remarked, "You could always tell an amateur from a professional; the galvanised wire and the sheets took the skin off the amateur's hands, but the professional's hands took the galvanising off the wire."

When the "Sceptre" prepared for her America's Cup challenge in 1958 it was announced she would have a crew of eleven and one of William's ex-12 metre hands exclaimed "Eleven hands! Whatever they all going to do?"

William and Mr. Connell brought "Zoraida" out as top boat of the class against "Veronica", "Flica", "Moyana", "Doris" and "Vanity", winning 20 prizes in 26 starts.

During Harwich regatta the Scottish-crewed 12 metre "Iris" engaged in a furious luffing match with a competitor and, so fierce did it become, that they went roaring away into the North Sea, leaving the rest of the class to finish the race, sail home and stow up, long before they got back to the anchorage.

Next year "Moyana" was sold and, renamed "Morwenna", was put in charge of Captain Edward Heard of Tollesbury, with a smart crew from that village, but she was well beaten by the "Zoraida". However, the whole class was thrashed by Sir Richard Fairey's "Flica", skippered by Captain 'Grannie' Diaper of Itchen.

"Zoraida" was sold and William went north to stand by Mr. Connell's new

"Zelita" building at Fife's yard. She proved difficult to get into trim, did not come south from the Clyde until Cowes week, and was sold.

That winter Captain William had opportunity to skipper the "Flica" which had been bought by Hugh Goodson. She was a remarkable 12 metre, built in 1929 by Nicholson and of very advanced design.

William took his smart crew with him and the nine 12 metres in the class had a splendid season, notable for the intense rivalry between "Flica" and Arthur Connell's new Nicholson-built "Westra". "Flica" finished the season with 14 flags against "Westra's" 15.

The racing was so keen that all three boats were commonly rounding a mark within 4 seconds of each other, with the rest of the class only a few seconds astern. 1935 brought the full flowering of the large and the 12 metre classes in a splendid season's racing. With six boats in the class, "Flica" now had to contend with the new "Marina", sailed by a Colne crew under Captain George Francis of Brightlingsea and owned by Sir William Burton, who by now had owned more racing yachts than anyone else and was a great rival of John Payne of the "Vanity", who had owned almost as many. Both were very talented helmsmen in the class where Mr. Payne was known as "Fiddler" for his ability on the violin when the day's sailing was done.

"Flica" won the first race of the season at Harwich, but was second to "Marina" next day. In the following races off Southend, "Flica" won in a hard wind which brought disaster to the large class; "Endeavour" lost her mast, "Velsheda" sprung her boom and "Astra" lost a hand overboard, drowned. The American visitor "Yankee" won. She roared past the 12 metres, well reefed and with a small staysail, swept from end to end and shining with spray.

One morning "Flica's" crew noticed a stranger in the 12 metre fleet, with the letter "X" in her mainsail to designate nationality. All hands racked their brains over this mysterious letter. "Perhaps she's a Russian?" said one...... "X for excitement" laughed another. It was the Fife built "Miquette" owned by a Chilean Ambassador and hard sailed, particularly in the west country regattas where she and "Flica" were tack and tack off Fowey until "Flica's" staysail sheets burst and the Chilean went on to win.

Yachts of all sizes entered the round the Isle of Wight race in 1935 and the 12 metres easily saved their time on the larger yachts in light airs. In the tradition of British yacht racing, at the finish the losing crews "cheered the winner" and were cheered in return; a custom which intrigued the crew of the visiting American racer "Yankee".

The big class and the 12's raced at Havre regatta for three days each July, maintaining an old association. That year there was dense mist during one race and William's careful and quick navigation enabled them to win a prize.

William always considered that yacht racing in the grand tradition, around the coast, really ended on the last day of August 1935, at the culminating regatta at Dartmouth, where the big class, with the 12 metres, cruiser classes and smaller fry, lay in the pool flying their prize flags; the towering masts dwarfed by the green hills of Devon, dark clouds scattering rain showers before a blustering west wind, with intense bursts of sun glinting on the brasswork. Owners' launches scudded amongst the racers against a backdrop of white motor yachts, and boats and flags were everywhere.

"Flica" had 26 replicas of her racing flag aloft and was third in the class, having sailed 39 races, "Marina" and "Westra" narrowly beating her.

Mr. Goodson was so pleased with "Flica's" success that she had a complete new suit of sails for the 1936 season, when "Flica" started in 31 races out of 40, winning 6 firsts, but was becoming outclassed. The 12 metres were then the biggest class sailing around the coast and racing without time allowance. They commenced at the end of May and raced until the end of August, round the east, south and south-west coasts of England.

She did little better in 1937 with 9 prizes in 31 starts, but her owner thoroughly enjoyed racing in a class now swollen by the new 12 metres "Little Astra", "Trivia" and "Alanna".

About this time, as a small boy, I remember the arrival of "Flica" at Rowhedge in September, to lay up at the lower yard. Her tall mast moved slowly up-river against the trees. There were quiet orders from Captain Wadley at the wheel as the long, sleek hull turned, under tow, in the narrow tideway and came gently alongside the quay where crews' relatives and onlookers greeted her return from another successful season. The beautiful contours of her deck planking were complemented by gleaming brass and glistening varnish. The lofty rig then seemed enormous and her form, when she was hauled out on the slip, had beauty which even a child could appreciate.

In 1938 "Flica" and the other 12 metres made their last full round of the British regatta season during June, July and August; sailing and racing from Harwich, Southend, Ramsgate, Dover, then down channel to Fowey and Falmouth, round Lands End and up to the Clyde for the fortnight, and to Belfast Lough. After this they had five days to get back to the Solent races, followed by Ryde and then Cowes week. Afterwards they sailed west again for Plymouth week, finishing with Torbay, Dartmouth and Weymouth.

The collapse of big class racing brought Mr. Sopwith back into the class with "Blue Marlin" but, despite starting 32 times, she did not win a single first prize and only got eleven flags against "Flica's" nine. Mr. Goodson pondered ordering a new 12 metre for 1939 and went to J. Laurent Giles for her design. She was built by Fife for a season exciting for the visit of the American 12 metre "Vim" to challenge the English class in their home waters.

Racing the 23 metre *Shamrock*, 1928. First mate William Wadley of Rowhedge in foreground with peaked cap. The spinnaker is being hoisted from the forehatch. A good impression of the speed and power of a large racing yacht.

William recalled "Vim" as a racing machine which had streamlined steel rods for standing rigging, a mast made of duraluminium and an enormous wardrobe of headsails, often carrying a large genoa to windward with a reefed mainsail.

The new British 12 metres, including "Flica II", "Tomahawk", "Oronsay" and "Jenetta", could do little against her and she won 19 first prizes in 28 starts.

War clouds hung heavily over that season which was to be the last spent afloat for many of William's generation. When the racing fleet dispersed from Torbay he knew he would never race again.

Like many of his contemporaries, William found work in the village shipyards during the war, and amongst the chaos of that time, a minor sadness was the dry-docking at Wivenhoe of the old 19 metre "Mariquita" for removal of her 80 ton lead keel; then worth far more than her beautiful Fife hull, which became a houseboat and now lies at Pin Mill.

For some years William had lived in Parkfield, a secluded part of Rowhedge, near the playing fields where he could cheer the village football team on Saturdays for, like most of the sailing professionals, he had always been a keen footballer and supporter.

Every day he walked by a Rowhedge waterside greatly changed from that of his youth but still actively maritime with its busy shipyards. Sometimes he visited West Mersea where, in saltings by the Coast road, lay houseboats whose mutilated hulls bore proud names; "Genesta", "Hispania", and "L'Esperance" amongst them, and the old hands could recall the hopes of youth.

William died in 1958 aged 85, respected in his day as an experienced racing yachtsman, navigator and skipper; a Colnesider would wish no better tribute.

CHAPTER THIRTEEN

"The King's Britannia"

THE OLD Royal racing cutter "Britannia" held a special place in local yachting history as, throughout her 43 years' career, she was skippered and almost totally manned from the Colne and Tollesbury. Probably no yacht was more famous or more fully captured the hearts of her owners, skippers, crews or the general public than the "Old Britty" as she became affectionately known.

Her story really began on a May morning in 1893. Gravesend presented its grimy face to the Thames tideway where tugs with strings of lighters butted up on the flood avoiding scores of barges sailing amongst the heavily sparred steamers whose wash rocked hundreds of spectator craft eager to see the year's first major yacht race. Crowds ashore and afloat had eyes only for the big yachts whose towering canvas filled the reach and dwarfed the anchored liners, as they manoeuvred for the start. Centre of attraction was Prince Edward of Wales' new racer "Britannia" with Captain John Carter at her long white tiller sparing a glance under her immense boom at his principal rival, the great "Valkyrie II" which slid past shaving the royal yacht's counter as Captain William Cranfield, Carter's near neighbour from Rowhedge, eased the Earl of Dunraven's prospective America's Cup challenger round on "Britannia's" weather. "Lee oh!" Thirty hands aboard each obeyed the order to tack and the rattle of gear and calls of the mates carried downward as the gun sent them roaring over the line in company with the "Calluna" and "Iverna". The 50 mile course led down to the Thames Estuary's Mouse Light Vessel and back, and the Prince wedged his bulky figure in "Britannia's" main hatch, puffing a cigar and eager to see how his new yacht would compare with the well tried old "Iverna" and the new Scottish "Calluna". No-one could be certain, for "Valkyrie II", "Britannia" and "Calluna" were the first large British yachts of a then radical new type which we now accept as classic, but whose origin needs explanation.

By 1892, big yacht racing was at a very low ebb and four distinguished owners tried to rejuvenate the sport by ordering new boats. The mighty "Satanita" was laid down at Southampton, the unlucky "Calluna" at Fairlie, and the near-sisters "Valkyrie II" and "Britannia" at Glasgow. At that time, Rowhedge skippers reigned supreme in the racing world and command of all four yachts was offered to captains from that village. William Cranfield took "Valkyrie II", Tom Jay "Satanita" and John Carter was offered both "Calluna" and "Britannia" which he naturally chose. Commissioning her designer, the Prince told the Scotch yacht architect George Watson to produce an ideal racing yacht within the limits of the length and sail area rule then current. His one stipulation was that he should be able to enjoy a hot lunch on board when racing. D. and W. Henderson, the Glasgow shipbuilders, constructed her at their Partick yard almost alongside "Valkyrie II" and in April, 1893 Mrs. Henderson christened

"Britannia" as she slid into the narrow Clyde. Perhaps the proudest man on that occasion was Captain John Carter who had spent the winter consulting with designer and builders. Born at Wivenhoe in 1851 he had resided at Rowhedge throughout his racing career and his crew was largely drawn from those places. He was at that time one of the foremost international racing skippers, fresh from his success with the 40 rater "Thalia" and having previously skippered many noted racers, amongst them the unsuccessful America's Cup challenger "Genesta", with which he won the Cape May and Breton Reef cups. Apart from his seamanship, John Carter was a fortunate choice for, like many skippers of his generation, he possessed a polished manner essential aboard a yacht frequently entertaining distinguished guests.

In these days of smaller yachts, "Britannia's" vital statistics are interesting and typical of her contemporaries. Composite built of wood on steel frames, her black hull, with its coppered bottom, was 121 foot 6 inches overall, 87 foot 8 inches on the water-line and 23 foot 3 inch beam. She drew 15 feet and displaced 154 tons, being 212 tons Thames Measurement. Her sail plan was drafted in the heyday of long booms and hers measured 92 feet, reaching 16 feet outboard. Aloft, her gaff cutter rig of 10,327 square feet soared 142 feet above deck and reached 172 feet from bowsprit end to boom end, but such size was typical of the first class racers of the time, and would be surpassed later. Decks were uncluttered except for a couple of skylights, hatches and the stowage for the spinnaker boom, and of course there were no guardrails. All handling and sheet-ing of sails was carried out by hand, winches were unheard of, and a 400 foot mainsheet took some overhauling and a 1½ ton mainsail some hoisting!

Below decks the Royal yacht provided plain but comfortable accommodation for owner and guests; though it was seldom used. For the crew it was different. Only the captain had a cabin, and cots and hammocks for 30 men were crammed into a foc'sle 30 feet long and overflowed into the sail locker aft. However, such conditions were inevitably part of a racing man's life, though what it was like below after a few days' hard racing with everyone's clothing drying round the single cooking stove is hard to imagine. The dark mahogany and white enamelled saloon had a piano, and the Royal cabin a bathroom—an unheard of luxury in a racer. "The ladies" had a separate cabin aft and all lighting was by oil lamps or candles. The mast heel came down in the foc'sle and Captain Carter would comment to visitors "How would you like to be shipmates with that chap? Four tons if he's a pound!" But, despite its size, the yacht's hard driving was to spring three of them before the first season ended.

Naturally, "Britannia" was beautifully finished and her Royal owner, who had previously owned a succession of cruising and racing yachts, was delighted with his fine racer which had handled so well on her shakedown sail from the Clyde to the Thames.

Now the testing time had come and with quarter waves breaking white on the tidelines, the yachts reached away to the Mouse which "Britannia" rounded first, closely followed by "Valkyrie II" and "Calluna". The old "Iverna" was close on their heels and the older "Mabel", in a different class, not far behind to the delight of old croakers who had condemned the new boats as "hideously ugly, overcanvassed racing machines". Once round the Mouse it was a different story. Tack by tack the new yachts drew ahead from the old, until it became a race between "Valkyrie II" and "Britannia". A terrific maiden struggle between yachts whose names were to become legends. The wind eased and William Cranfield, that amazing light weather helmsman, began to make "Valkyrie II" sing to windward and crept up on "Britannia". Tack and tack with only 30 seconds between them. In the Lower Hope and three miles to go with the breeze hardening to squalls, setting the badly stayed bowsprits soaring upwards until suddenly "Valkyrie's" jib crumpled and the whole rig shook, her bowsprit was gone and cleared as quickly, but "Britannia" had swept over the line to win her first race to the cheers and syrens of every ship in sight. The delighted Prince took his scarf ring from his necktie and gave it to John Carter.

A few days later in the Southend to Harwich race down Swin with the Prince aboard, the racers were joined by the mighty new "Satanita", 300 tons of speed with Tom Jay in command. "Calluna" was proving a dud but competition between the others was intense as, race after race, they battled it out at the various regattas from Harwich to the Clyde and back to the Solent, lifting seamen's hearts with their new beauty and power, and exciting public interest to a test match intensity. The new cutters were faster and more weatherly than anything which had gone before, averaging $12\frac{1}{2}$ knots, a speed never since equalled in large yacht racing, and tacking in 12 seconds.

In America, also, four large new sloops were built that year and one of them, the "Navahoe", arrived here in August to be beaten in her first race by "Britannia", despite

Captain John Carter of Rowhedge and the crew of the Royal racing cutter *Britannia*, 1893.

clever piloting by Tom Diaper and use of a huge red spinnaker. "Britannia's" victory was repeated in the later match sailing between the two boats but the real test was yet to come. A prime object of the "Navahoe's" visit was to regain the two cups won by "Genesta" during her America's Cup visit in 1885. Both races were to be sailed from the Needles, round Cherbourg breakwater and back; a 120 mile course. In mid-September they started for the Brenton Reef Cup in a strong easterly wind giving a reach out and home in a heavy sea. Under single reefs, jib headed topsails, reefed staysails and small jibs they handed staysails off St. Catherine's Point and thrashed across channel at $12\frac{1}{4}$ knots, housing their 60 foot topmasts when nearing the French coast—a feat in itself under the conditions and one rarely executed when racing. "Navahoe" stormed through the western entrance of Cherbourg breakwater in the lead but when they emerged to the eastward John Carter had beaten the American to windward and "Britannia" came surging back across channel with seas thundering up her lee deck, to round the Needles in darkness and half a gale, finishing 300 yards and 3 seconds ahead of the "Navahoe" which was awarded the cup on protest that the markboat had shifted. However, next day John Carter had his revenge and beat the Yankee by 30 minutes over the same course in light weather, in a 24 hour race for the Cape May Cup.

So "Britannia" ended her first season in triumph and the following spring found her bound out to the Mediterranean to race in the regattas of the southern French resorts of which her owner was so fond. Arriving at Marseilles the evening before the first race at Cannes with her saloon full of stores, Captain Carter cracked on and berthed at Cannes next morning in time to embark the Prince and cross the line to win the first race and all six others she entered. She returned to English waters to meet the challenge of the bronze hulled "Vigilant", which was crack of her class in America and had beaten "Valkyrie II" for the America's Cup the previous autumn.

"Vigilant" first met the British yachts on the Clyde in a race attracting 100,000 spectators but marred at the start by the tragic sinking of the "Valkyrie II" by the "Satanita" when avoiding running down a small sailing boat. Unaware of the accident, "Britannia" and "Vigilant" carried on and, after a hard race, John Carter beat the Yankee; a performance repeated 12 times in their 17 encounters which took place all round the coast at Belfast Lough, Dublin Bay, Cork Harbour, Penzance, Cowes, round the Isle of Wight, Ryde, Dartmouth and Start Bay; all part of the annual round of old style yacht racing. Although "Vigilant" carried 2,000 square feet more canvas than "Britannia", it did not set well and her owners approached Ratsey for a new racing suit. His reply was characteristic—let the Americans supply their own and keep the contest truly international! A shadow on the season for "Britannia's" crew was the loss of a hand off Portland Bill when on passage in hard weather, followed by the drowning of her mate, Jim Simons, a tragedy met in the fashion typical of those days of personal insecurity by each of his shipmates voluntarily subscribing a week's pay for his dependents.

The "Ailsa" came out next season with Tom Jay in charge in an attempt to beat "Britannia". They first met at the Riviera regattas where "Ailsa" proved the better boat but, as if to console Captain Carter, on the 2,200 mile passage home under trysail gear in April, "Britannia" logged 27¾ nautical miles in two hours, her highest ever recorded speed. With only "Ailsa" and "Britannia" racing in the big class the excitement of 1895 was provided by the truly gigantic America's Cup challenger, "Valkyrie III" skippered by William Cranfield. In one race against her "Britannia" set a sail of John Carter's own design which was identical with the genoa jibs supposed to have been "invented" in the 1920's. Its success helped "Britannia" to win 32 first prizes in 39 starts and she remained top of the big class.

Next year "Britannia" made her customary spring pilgrimage to the Riviera with "Satanita" and "Ailsa", who beat her once again. The yachts came home to meet a change of rating rule and trouble in the shape of the Kaiser's new Watson-designed "Meteor II"; a giant, light displacement cutter of immense sail area, specially built to beat "Britannia" and impress the yachting superiority of the German Emperor on his uncle, the Prince of Wales, who was becoming increasingly disgusted with his nephew's arrogant rivalry and rudeness when sailing in British waters. Also, the rule was stretched to allow the little 60 rater "Caress" into the big class, and these two extremes began to break up what had been well balanced competition. "Meteor II" was British in everything but flag for there were then no German yacht skippers, hands or yards, and few yachts, but the Kaiser was striving to arouse his country's maritime interests. Clyde built, with a Solent crew under Captain Bob Gomes of Gosport, she beat "Britannia" by sheer size in most of their meetings. The class's decline was hastened by a Solent fatality caused by "Meteor's" 98 foot mainboom accidentally sweeping across the rig of the German 52 footer, "Isolde", whipping the gear clean out of her and killing her owner, Baron von Zedwitz. The Royal cutters raced no more that season and "Ailsa's" owner declared that, due to the handicapping, he would not race again in British waters so she and the evenly matched "Britannia" sailed off to the Mediterranean for the spring. In one of their races there "Britannia" gybed accidentally, slashing "Ailsa's" mainsail with her boom-end and crippling her. Both yachts berthed and sailmakers were summoned from Toulon but, before they arrived, the yachts' crews, guests and owners took the damaged sail ashore, laid it out on a villa's ballroom floor and had the 90 foot rent repaired before the Frenchmen appeared next day. Queen Victoria took a good deal of interest in her son's yacht and visited her when the racer lay at Nice to decorate Captain Carter with the M.V.O. for his yacht racing services to the Prince.

The time-allowance success of the "Caress" inspired the small new "Bona", skippered by Captain Sycamore, which finally killed the class in 1897. It became too much of a mixed bag with "Caress" and the new cruiser-racer "Hester" successfully skippered by John Cranfield of Rowhedge, and with "Meteor II", "Satanita" and "Britannia" which won 10 races. But the Prince was tired of sport-killing handicaps and, after five years of racing, the "Britannia" was put up for sale. During that period she won £10,172 in prize money, but crew's wages and maintenance accounted for about £3,000 per annum. In December, 1897, "Britannia" was sold for about £4,000 and, passing through two owners' hands without fitting out, she was purchased by Sir Richard Williams-Bulkely who appointed Captain Jack Carter, John Carter's son, as master. He had served aboard "Britannia" as ordinary seaman, able seaman and mate, before going deep sea to obtain his square rigged master's certificate and under him "Britannia" spent much time cruising about the Irish sea.

In 1899 the America's Cup challenge of "Shamrock I" again brought "Britannia" back to the Prince's ownership to race as a trial horse against the challenger, and Jack Carter handed command back to his father, who also enjoyed a few races against "Meteor", "Bona" and the enormous schooner "Rainbow", which he had skippered when new but was now handled by his old rival Tom Jay. The Prince sold her again but still loved the old yacht, chartering her for Cowes Week 1901 and eventually re-purchasing her the following year. By now big class racing was almost extinct and the "Britannia", with John Carter again in charge, was generally seen cruising leisurely about the South Coast with the now King Edward and his queen aboard, often accompanied by foreign royalty such as Alfonso, the sail loving King of Spain.

Britannia reefing while racing during the early 1930's. Note short boom and boom struts of her bermudian rig.

1910 was a sad year in "Britannia's" career for then her Royal owner and her skipper died. However, it was but the beginning of a new chapter, for King George V, the sailor King, took over his father's old ship and re-appointed Captain Jack Carter to her helm. Nevertheless "Britannia's" racing days seemed over for the big class was again in the doldrums, Sycamore in "Shamrock" and Bevis in "White Heather" having duelled themselves to a standstill under a new but stagnant rule. With her long tiller replaced by a wheel, bulwarks raised and a sunk deckhouse fitted, "Britannia" seemed destined for a premature old age, cruising about the South Coast with the Royal family aboard quietly enjoying themselves but, in 1913, the King decided to enter her for handicap racing and Jack Carter started putting her through her paces. A new owner's representative was appointed at this time; Major Philip Hunloke was a wealthy courtier and old personal friend of the new King, besides having been an enthusiastic amateur helmsman in the Solent small classes. After learning something of the handling of big yachts from captain Carter he held strong views on the duties of an owner's representative which normally consisted of checking the starting times and signing the racing declaration, and began to insist on handling the yacht when racing. It took unusual skill, nerve and judgement to handle a big class racer at close quarters and whilst sailing the Solent a few years ago I was fortunate enough to meet the late Captain Carter, then in retirement at Cowes, and hear at first hand what it meant to be the man at the helm of a really big racer with a crack crew. Major Hunloke's decision was something of a risk but, with the Captain's guidance, he succeeded in acquiring sufficient ability to race her in the large handicap class. Her opponents were a heterogeneous collection ranging from the little 23 ton "Bingo" to the 135 ton "Cariad" and including such fine yachts as "Julnar". Whilst there was nothing of her mettle in the class she enjoyed some good sport especially against the rejuvenated old 40 tonner "Bloodhound", a flier of the 1870's which made a wonderful comeback under Captain Ben Chaplin of Brightlingsea. However, "Britannia's" presence at the round the coast regattas kept alive some semblance of a big class and encouraged entry of "Harbinger" and "Sumurun" in 1914 when the European applecart was upset on the very eve of Cowes Week. With the declaration of war, "Britannia" was towed up the Medina to lie in a mud berth for four war years while her crew served afloat, scattered on the seas.

Yachting in 1919 was a poor shadow of its pre-war glory, but for 1920 the King decided to fit "Britannia" out for racing. It was in some ways a courageous decision for she was, even then, an old yacht whose contemporaries had all been scrapped long before. However, his decision was justified for "Moonbeam" was ordered from Fife, for Brightlingsea's Captain Skeats to command; the great cutter "Terpsichore" was building at White's, and "Nyria" converted to bermudian rig, the first large yacht to do so. These joined other cruisers and racers including the great 385 ton schooner "Westward", which fitted out at Brightlingsea under Captain Sycamore. Here, almost unexpectedly, was a big handicap class once again. Major Hunloke, who had once more taken up his duties as the King's sailing master, intended to continue handling

"Britannia" himself and had to find a professional skipper, for Captain Carter was on longer available. Captain Charles Leavett of Tollesbury, who had skippered Colonel Bagot's famous old Wivenhoe built 40 rater "Creole" for many years, was lent by his owner as "Britannia's" skipper. For the first few races of her post war revival the Royal yacht failed to win a flag but improved as the season progressed. She was still in cruising rig, the equivalent of one reef, and did well to be third in the class, which encouraged the King to order her rig to be altered and modernised and, with bowsprit and boom shortened and bulwarks renewed under Alfred Mylne's direction, she became a true racer again for 1921. An incident occurred that year which led to another change of skipper for the Royal cutter. In one race the captain gave the order "In spinnaker!" which was instantly countermanded by Major Hunloke who ordered it to be reset. Captain Leavett, who was an experienced racing skipper, properly regarding himself as the man to give orders, went below and shortly afterwards Major Hunloke was looking for another skipper.

That winter "Britannia" was thoroughly refitted at Cowes but there was no racing in 1922 for economy reasons and she lay in her mud berth all that year. However, Hunloke was successful in obtaining a professional skipper from the Colne. He approached his contemporary, Sir William Burton of Ipswich, who had for many years steered his own large yachts when racing and was a noted amateur with his heart thoroughly in the sport. His professional skipper was Captain Albert Turner of Wivenhoe who had originally served under Captain William Cranfield before taking charge of the Solent 2½ rater "Papoose", going on to skipper the 20 rater "Luna" successfully. He had skippered Sir William's 52 footers "Lucida" and "Britomart", the 15 metre "Ostara", and 19 metre "Octavia" and, in 1914, took Lipton's "Shamrock IV" to the States for the challenge interrupted by war. In 1920 he sailed in her, with Sir William, for the Cup and had thoroughly adapted himself to the then quite unusual position of being skipper to an owner who steered large yachts when racing. He was, therefore, well fitted to join Hunloke in "Britannia" and accepted the appointment. During the years 1923-35 they were together beside "Britannia's" wheel for every race except one, when Captain Turner took the responsibility alone.

This partnership resulted in 23 flags in 26 starts, 11 of them firsts. "Nyria" ran her close, but the Royal racer was in good form and King George was pleased for he was intensely fond of his yacht and thoroughly enjoyed being aboard, where he could relax from state formality. But, even there, he could not totally escape officialdom for the Admiralty, who were responsible for his safety afloat, that year detailed the destroyer "Vesper" to attend "Britannia" through the racing season. "Vesper's" best service was in providing drying facilities for the racer's crew whose clothing was soaked in anything of a breeze and who were, of course, expected to appear in neat rig for the next day's racing. All the subsequent years of "Britannia's" racing saw a fleet minesweeper assigned to this duty and she often provided a welcome tow when becalmed on passage.

The class altered in 1924. "Terpsichore" changed owners and "Shamrock" joined the class with "White Heather" who headed it with "Britannia" second. A prime reason for the old yacht's continued success was that during her years of absence from racing the big class had departed from the wholesome form of the '90's to pass through a period of extremes before returning to saner hulls not unlike "Britannia's," though able to sail faster in light weather for "Britannia" revelled in a breeze, which also suited the now Sir Philip Hunloke's helmsmanship. Next year the racing evened out with T. B. Davis, the South African stevedore millionaire and his skipper, Captain Alf Diaper of Itchen, bringing "Westward" back to her original winning form. "Britannia" was at the tail of the fleet with "Lulworth", gaining a flag for every race sailed. This season emphasised "Britannia" as a heavy weather boat and, during the

Setting *Britannia's* spinnaker, 1894. Note crew's stocking hats and ratlines to shrouds.

winter, Will Fife III, the Scottish designer, was commissioned to alter her sail plan for increased light weather performance. The Royal yacht changed to the then fashionable Marconi rig in which the topmast was socketed into the head of the lowermast. With a new suit of sails, more ballast on her keel, and topside planking lightened, she emerged as a fair weather flier and the old yacht did not like it. This was proved during Cowes Week 1926 when a squall whipped down and caught the big ones all standing. "Shamrock" heeled over to bury her decks before Captain Sycamore brought her on the wind. "Britannia" went wild and ran off her helm before Philip Hunloke could control her and go on to win. This was repeated a few days later when "Shamrock's" mast went overboard and "Britannia" stood by until assistance arrived, when she thrashed on with "Westward" and "Lulworth" to finish under mainsail and jib alone—a very rare combination in big class racing. That year the "Old Britty" had only 11 flags to show for 23 starts and her future began to be questioned with the whole future of the class which came under review. They were beginning to get oversparred in 1926, five years before Britain adopted the American "J" rule which is often quoted as the start of their excess. Further alterations brought more expense which the King deplored in those times of national want and industrial unrest. Of course, "Britannia" was his personal property to do with as he wished, unlike the unstable old Royal steam yacht "Victoria and Albert", designed, built and manned by the Admiralty for use by the head of state and which was usually in attendance to give accommodation when His Majesty raced aboard "Britannia". Occasionally the King took the wheel when racing and especially loved leading his crew in giving three cheers for the winner when they crossed the line second to some rival.

Although throughout her life the majority of "Britannia's" crew hailed from Colneside or Tollesbury, with a few from Pin Mill; during the 1920's and 30's a proportion from Looe, Polperro, and similar West Country ports served aboard her by the King's wish. By this time her professional crew was reduced to 23, with a further 6 or 7 extra hands for general pulley-hauley recruited for the day from the fleet minesweeper or the "Victoria and Albert". Even so there were none too many for smart handling of a big racer's sail plan whose power had to be seen to be believed. There was, in addition, the local racing pilot for the particular area sailed and the bearded Joe Giles and his predecessor Paskins gave their expert advice culled from years of fishing, when "Britannia" raced in the waters of the Wight. A good mate was essential to a racer and, during the 1920's, Arthur Barnard was first mate, followed by "Monkey" Byford; once probably the most celebrated mastheadsman of all time. As in all racers of that era only the orders of skipper and mates were heard, the crew did their work in silence and did it instantly and well for the discipline of a racing yacht was absolute, yet the crew had to anticipate orders and think fast for themselves, a unique form of sailoring.

In 1927 "Britannia" emerged with sail plan lowered 4 feet and its base shortened. With 16 flags in 24 starts she finished second to "White Heather" in the class to which the following year brought a boost. Fife built the "Cambria" and Nicholson "Astra", and the season started with 7 big yachts on the line ranging from the "Little Astra" of 23 metres to the big "Lulworth" and "Westward" of 25.7 metres. "Britannia" now rated 24.2 metres and sailed 34 races for 19 flags, being beaten only by "Shamrock". Perhaps the highlight of that season was the Harwich - Southend race when "Shamrock" led "Britannia" by a bare 150 yards at the Gunfleet and Captains Sycamore and Turner fought it out in their home waters knowing every minute trick of the tideways and using every wrinkle of their experience with the result that after 6 hours of short tacking up Swin "Shamrock" finished 15 seconds ahead.

During 1929 "Britannia" lay in her mud berth during her owner's illness and Hunloke bought the barge yacht "St. Michael" which, with Captain Turner and a steward, he sailed to the West Country on a glorious holiday from yacht racing. Next year the King had "Britannia" fitted out to meet 7 competitors, including the "Shamrock V", the first British built J class yacht and Lipton's last Cup challenger. Skippered by Captain Edward Heard, she made a wonderful showing before leaving for the States and the old "Britannia" lagged fifth in a class now increasingly adopting the bermudian rig. At the season's end she laid her gaff ashore for the last time and yet another rig, this time by Nicholson, was fitted to her, for that winter Britain adopted the J class rule for the big boats, encouraging a type of yacht penalised in sail area and forced to an extreme height of rig quite unsuited to British conditions.

Next year "Britannia" came out with a 175 foot stick and a 20% reduction in sail area. Her ballasting was altered too, and the old yacht felt unhappy, yet she won 13 flags in 20 starts but could not outsail the "Shamrock V". 1932 saw a further reduction in her canvas to rate level with "Astra" and "Candida" and she finished top of the fleet in the first season of big class racing with all amateur helmsmen, though the skippers remained at their elbows to give instructions and aid, and Captain Turner was invested with the M.V.O. for his services. The new "Velsheda" put "Britannia" into second place for 1933 and the following season the old yacht seemed to really tire, winning only 3 races despite further minor lightening.

Although they did not know it, "Britannia's" crew fitted her out for the last time in 1935 when she prepared to meet all her old competitors and the American racer "Yankee". Quadrilateral jibs had come in with "Endeavour" and rigging had to be reinforced. She also had a "Park Avenue" boom and all her copper stripped off in an attempt to smooth her bottom. But it was "mutton dressed as lamb" in vain, for she never won a place and there was no prize money for her crew. However, King George had so enjoyed his season that he ordered them to be paid as if she had won. The "Britannia" was at last really outclassed to windward and the centreboards of the new J's had a lot to do with it, though their speeds were nothing like those attained by the old yachts of the 'nineties. During the second period of her racing career, "Britannia" won £9,910 which seems a vast sum but was in fact small when compared with the costs of ownership during that time. Throughout her life she sailed 635 races, won

231 first prizes (far more than any other yacht before or since) and gained 129 places; a remarkable record.

In January, 1936 King George died. As his sailing master said of him; "aboard "Britannia" the King was like a schoolboy on holiday. He loved the old yacht, enjoyed winning, but was a splendid loser". What better could be said of a yachtsman? By the King's wish, "Britannia" should have been broken up and, later that year, her gear was sold by auction, but it was decided to give her a sea burial and she was launched off Marvin's slip with a wreath of flowers at her stem. At midnight on July 9th, the destroyers "Winchester" and "Amazon" towed her out from the memory crowded Solent to a position well south of the Isle of Wight where, in the early morning and in the presence of Sir Philip Hunloke and Captain Turner, an explosive charge rent her hull and the old yacht sank quickly to the bottom of the channel.

Although it is many years since her end, the fame of "Britannia" lives on and she has become a legend of all a racing yacht should be.

The *Britannia* fitting out on the slip at Marvin's yard, Cowes, about 1928. Crew on deck in fitting-out rig, with Captain Albert Turner of Wivenhoe, amidships.

CHAPTER FOURTEEN

Essex Yachtsmen and the America's Cup

THE AMERICA'S Cup is yacht racing's premier trophy and professional yachtsmen from the Colne and Blackwater districts of Essex have been intimately connected with it from the initial race of 1851, through fifteen of the subsequent twenty unsuccessful challenges to regain it.

The Cup takes its name from the schooner yacht "America" built in 1851 for a syndicate of New York Yacht Club members to represent the American nation in English waters during that year of the International Exhibition. George Steers designed the rakish 100 footer, modelling her after his speedy New York pilot boats, and the excellent proportions of hull and well setting sails contributed largely to her success. After the transatlantic passage to Cowes she found English yachtsmen welcoming but, at first, unwilling to race. However, eventually a race was arranged over the Royal Yacht Squadron course round the Isle of Wight for a £100 Cup presented by the Squadron. The "America" started, without handicap, against seventeen English yachts ranging from the 393 ton schooner "Brilliant" to the little 47 ton cutter "Aurora", and including such fliers as "Alarm" and the sleek cutter "Volante", fresh from John Harvey's Wivenhoe yard, manned by a Colneside crew under Captain George Pittuck, and England's pride, "Volante" and other leading yachts rounded the Nab Light as was customary and stated in the sailing directions, but the race programme made no mention of it and the "America", accompanied by several English yachts, stood inshore and to windward emerging with a clear lead. In turning to windward along the island's south shore, "America" was overhauled by the leading English yachts until "Arrow" got ashore and "Alarm" stood by to assist. Shortly afterwards the crack "Volante" was fouled by "Freak" and lost her bowsprit, leaving the "America" to win by eight minutes from the "Aurora".

Although protested for not rounding the Nab, "America" was awarded the Cup and, after winning a match against the small schooner "Titania", was sold to an English owner. The Cup she had won was eventually presented by her owners to the New York Yacht Club as a trophy for international competition.

Interest in it lagged until Mr. Ashbury, a member of the Royal Harwich Yacht Club, challenged for it in 1870. His 188 ton schooner "Cambria" beat the American "Dauntless" in a race across the Atlantic, only to lose the Cup Race held on what was to become its traditional course off Sandy Hook, at the approaches to New York.

The Royal Harwich Yacht Club challenged again for Ashbury in the following year when he had built the schooner "Livonia" for another try, skippered by Captain John Woods of Brightlingsea. She lost under conditions which permitted the defenders to substitute a light or heavy weather boat on the day of the race. It was a great disap-

Crew of the America's Cup challenger *Valkyrie III*, 1895. Captain William Cranfield of Rowhedge centre, middle row. Captain Edward Sycamore, third from left, middle row. Most of her crew of 40 were Rowhedge men; the remainder from Wivenhoe, Brightlingsea and the Clyde.

pointment for her Essex crew and today few can realise the importance of these contests to a district whose life and economy, afloat and ashore, was based on yachting and fishing; with the former's expansion bringing an improving standard of living to the villages of Rowhedge, Wivenhoe, Brightlingsea and Tollesbury, which were the homes of the racing men, though few present-day residents may realise the esteem in which their seamen were held in the yachting world.

Just what qualities did these men possess which enabled them to better their rivals from the Solent and Clyde? It was no mere chance which gained Colnesiders and Tollesburymen their reputation. Their subtle skill in racing stemmed originally from sailing the weatherly North Sea smacks—and the dream of most young smack's boys was to be serving in a crack racer, perhaps some day to command one of these great vessels. That dream came true for many of them for some of the finest skippers this country, and for that matter any other, ever knew hailed from these little Essex ports.

These great Essex sailing masters were above all fine helmsmen, having a natural ability to windward, using excellent judgement, and were more than mere sail trimmers; they possessed the faculty of taking in hand and tuning up the whole fabric of hull and rig, besides concerting the efforts of a crew numbering anything up to fifty hands.

To succeed they had to act more quickly than their opponents, themselves equally experienced men, must know the rules thoroughly and have iron nerves when stretching them to their limits—for a major error of judgement at the helm would not only shatter a reputation but, worse, might cost the lives of several men.

Such a seaman was Captain John Carter, Wivenhoe born but hailing from Rowhedge, skipper of Sir Richard Sutton's cutter "Genesta", the challenger of 1885; and later "Britannia" in the heyday of her career. "Genesta" was something of a international effort, being from the board of the Irish designer Beavour-Webb, built on the Clyde, and manned from Rowhedge and Wivenhoe.

Dapper Captain Carter soon had the lean 90 footer tuned up and made a fast passage of twenty-four days to New York, where she was to meet the "Puritan", a traditionally American broad-beamed centreboarder of the type which had successfully defended the Cup against the two Canadian challenges of 1876 and 1881. At the start of the first race, the Yankee skipper tried to bluff "Genesta", who had right of way, into going about, but the unruffled John Carter held course and "Genesta's" long bowsprit poked clean through "Puritan's" mainsail! It was a clear case of foul but captain and owner waved the committee aside with "we came here for a race, not a

Valkyrie III, America's Cup challenger of 1895. Captain William Cranfield of Rowhedge. 187ft. from bowsprit end to boom end. Sail area as shown; 13,028 square feet.

sail over!" "Puritan" won the other races but John Carter had his revenge by winning the Cape May and Breton Reef Cups in offshore races before "Genesta" sailed home.

Next to try was the steel cutter "Galatea" of 1886; owned by Lieutenant and Mrs. Henn, she was nicknamed the "Tin Frigate". Clyde built, she was a typical British cutter, and proved a duffer in the light winds of the Cup course.*

Scotland tried in 1887 with the cutter "Thistle", designed by G. L. Watson with hull form largely influenced by the success of the yawl "Jullanar", designed by John Harvey of Wivenhoe and E. H. Bentall of Heybridge, where she had been built 13 years previously. "Thistle" was slow and Skipper John Barr of Gourock failed to beat the "Volunteer".

The Earl of Dunraven challenged in 1893 and genial William Cranfield of Row-hedge, one of Britain's foremost professionals, was given command of the new Watson-designed "Valkyrie II"—perhaps the most perfectly proportioned of the many sweet-lined challengers. This 117 footer carried 10,000 square feet of canvas and formed, with her near sisters, "Britannia", "Satanita" and "Calluna", that lovely quartet which at a stroke broke from tradition and established the form of yacht hull we use today. Captain William believed in young crews, and they certainly had reason to believe in him. One of six brothers, all of whom became famous in international racing, he had a terrific reputation for getting a big boat along in light weather; a most difficult aspect of racing. There was something very colourful and adventurous about these racing skippers and the thousands of pounds prize money they won; almost an air of the dandy in their choice of fine cigars and smartly cut pilot jackets; but they were tough seamen, in sole charge of these big yachts, and their orders were carried out with an unquestioning smartness far exceeding the discipline of a man-of-war.

"Valkyrie II" made a twenty-two day, fine weather passage out, during which her crew of young Rowhedgers and a few Wivenhoe and Tollesburymen anticipated transatlantic luxury travel by several years by filling the lifeboat on deck with sea water to improvise a bathing pool. Off New York she met the "Vigilant", designed by Nathaniel Herreshoff, the most ingenious yacht builder of all time, who was to produce the five successive defenders. "Vigilant" was plated in bronze, regardless of expense, and carried a crew of no less than seventy men! "Valkyrie II" led her in the first race until she was left becalmed while the American finished with a favourable slant. She lost the second race and had the very worst of bad luck on the last day which was not only Friday, but the 13th! Having beaten "Vigilant" all round the course she turned the last mark and blossomed a giant spinnaker which split in tatters; another lighter one was set in seconds by the sweating crew, but it soon went to pieces in the freshening wind. Undaunted, the bowsprit spinnaker was set as a last resort but "Vigilant" had come up and just beat her. There was great enthusiasm for this series and the boats and their crews received greater publicity than is nowadays accorded to test cricket. Post offices on Colneside displayed telegrams telling how the racing was

*Her original skipper, Capt. Lemon Cranfield of Rowhedge, renowned as the cleverest racing helmsman of all time, left her after trials from which he foretold her certain defeat, and in the Cup races she was sailed by Capt. Dan Bradford of Dartmouth, Devon.

Valkyrie III in dry-dock at New York, 1895, after her transatlantic passage. Note 22ft. draught, size of mainboom and mast.

going while in New York a huge hoarding in Times Square indicated who was leading by two yachts moving in accordance with messages semaphored from the course.

The Earl tried again a couple of years later and in "Valkyrie III" Captain Cranfield had a craft which "out-Yanked" the Americans for she was, at that time, the most extreme yacht built in this country, having tremendous overhangs in her 130 foot length and spreading 13,000 square feet of working sail, stretching over 180 feet from the bowsprit end to the end of her boom! Still tiller steered, these great racing yachts were becoming too complex for one man to handle alone so William had to assist him Captain Edward Sycamore, born at Rowhedge but better known at Harwich whence he had risen to skipper small raters in the keen Solent classes before moving up to 40 raters and settling at Brightlingsea. Sycamore stood at the commencement of a thirty year career in big-class racing and shared with Captain William the thrill of this fine yacht giving proof of her speed on the Clyde where, in squally weather, she travelled at such speed that her roaring wash swamped and sank a ferryboat.

Ketch-rigged for the passage, she took a hammering in the Atlantic gales giving her crew some anxious days as she drove westward under snug canvas. But alas for the hopes of her young crew! She lost the first race to "Defender", won the second but was protested, and snubbed the Americans by merely crossing the line in the third when her owner, disgusted with the blundering interference of spectator craft and a difference of opinion with the New York Yacht Club, withdrew in what almost amounted to an atmosphere of international tension! It took a few years for things to calm down but others were willing to continue the quest for the £100 Cup, which by now had swallowed up several million pounds.

In those far-off days owners maintained their yachts regardless of expense, much as racehorses are kept today, and the fabulous Sir Thomas Lipton, the next challenger, is reputed to have told the designer when ordering "Shamrock" in 1899: "Now, Fife, I haven't money to burn, but if it will make her a second faster—shovel on the notes!" Clydeside skipper Archie Hogarth was put in charge of this, the first of the green-hulled cutters which were to become so much a feature of the yachting scene during the following thirty years, and her afterdeck must have been rather crowded for he had Brightlingsea's Captain Robert Wringe and Southampton's Captain Ben Parker to help him, backed by a large crew from all three places. Despite hard sailing the part aluminium built "Columbia" beat her British competitor handsomely, as she lacked power in her rather narrow hull. Sir Thomas took his defeat in good part and his next boat, "Shamrock II" of 1901, by Watson, had an Essex crew under Captains Sycamore and Wringe, but she fared no better than her sister.

Launch of Sir Thomas Lipton's America's Cup challenger *Shamrock IV* at City Island, New York, 1920. Captain Albert Turner of Wivenhoe and first mate Edward Heard of Tollesbury amidships.

Sir Thomas Lipton and some of the crew of the America's Cup challenger *Shamrock IV*, at Gosport, 1914. Captain Albert Turner of Wivenhoe and first mate Edward Heard of Tollesbury, to left and right of owner.

1903 found Lipton preparing yet another "Shamrock" which had a predominantly Essex crew of forty-one under Captain Wringe, who had Captain Beavis of Hamble to advise when racing. This Fife-designed third "Shamrock" was a 135 foot light displacement boat carrying the whopping sail spread of 14,000 square feet with a draught of twenty feet and an astonishingly modern set of lines. Notable as being the first wheel steered challenger, she lost her rig during trials when several hands were injured and one, Mr. Collier of Wivenhoe, a steward, was drowned. Towed across the Atlantic, she raced against the more extreme "Reliance" an even more gigantic yacht setting 16,000 square feet of working sail with a seventy-man crew under the Scottish-American Captain Charles Barr, victor of the series.

In 1914 the undaunted Lipton challenged yet again and Nicholson of Gosport produced the radical but small "Shamrock IV", the command of Wivenhoe's Captain Albert Turner, widely known as Sir William Burton's professional skipper who, like Sycamore, had commenced racing in the Solent raters. This was the last gaff rigged challenger, having very tall sail plan and many surprisingly modern features. The triple-planked hull was aluminium framed and the plywood deck rippled when walked on. America-bound "Shamrock IV" suffered from the first World War. In tow of the steam yacht "Erin" when hostilities broke out, she was hauled out on arrival at New York and laid up awaiting more tranquil times while her crew, most of them naval reservists, found themselves manning a cruiser instead of a yacht. There she remained until 1919 when the quest was resumed, but a shock was in store. It was found that her cradle had buckled and her enormously long ends, left almost unsupported, had sagged and distorted the hull. However, she raced against "Resolute" the next year with Sir William

Burton of Ipswich in charge, with Captain Turner to relieve him at the wheel. A member of the Royal Harwich Yacht Club and a notable racing yacht owner, Sir William was England's finest amateur helmsman and in present times, when all yacht racing is done by amateurs, it is interesting to note that until that time none but professionals had handled Cup challengers. Despite her troubles "Shamrock IV" came nearer to winning the Cup than any of her predecessors.

1930 brought "Shamrock V", last of the line and first British J Class yacht and bermudian rigged challenger. Carrying but half the sail area of previous competitors she was a more rational yacht which could be handled by a smaller crew and Captain Edward Heard of Tollesbury, who had been a hand in "Shamrock III" and first mate of "Shamrock IV", was master of her score of hands hailing from Tollesbury, Mersea, Colneside and the West Country. The skipper was fresh from his successes with the 12 metre "Noresca" and prospects seemed bright, but alas for their hopes! It seemed that Nicholson had designed her to the spirit of the rules, rather than the letter, and her heavy rig and elaborately fitted interior gave her little chance against the scantily furnished but gadget crammed "Enterprise", whose larger dimensions but lighter displacement told heavily against the well handled challenger.

There were many local professionals amongst the officers and crew of T. O. M. Sopwith's beautiful 1934 challenger "Endeavour" which, sailed by her owner, lost to the American "Rainbow" after crew troubles just prior to sailing from England led to the substitution of amateurs for part of her professionals. Handled by her original crew she might well have brought back the Cup as she was acknowledged to be the faster yacht and won one race of the series.

Three years later under Captain Heard with a perfectly drilled all professional crew from Essex, the West Country and Southampton, she accompanied the new "Endeavour II" to America as trial boat for the last pre-war challenge. There she achieved distinction by beating both the defending "Ranger" and the previous defender "Rainbow" in trial races before the start of the Cup matches in which the owner-sailed "Endeavour II" lost to the superior "Ranger". The homeward-bound "Endeavour" caused a press sensation when heavy weather made her break from the motor yacht towing her across when only 200 miles out. After searching, the "Viva" put back reporting her as missing but, after riding it out to a sea anchor and mizzen of the ocean ketch rig, Captain Heard and his crew set sail and arrived in good spirits after a fifteen day passage.

After a 21 year lapse, interest in the Cup revived in 1958 when alterations to the deed permitted the comparatively small yachts of the 12 metre class to sail for it. The British "Sceptre" challenged with amateur Grahame Mann at the helm, and Stanley Bishop of Brightlingsea as professional skipper of an amateur crew. Her failure against the superb "Columbia" reflected lack of preparation. In 1962 Australia challenged, after experience gained with the chartered American 12 metre "Vim". The "Gretel" and her all amateur crew gave the defending "Weatherly" a keenly contested series, but the Cup remained in America.

It continues to do so despite subsequent 12 metre challenges by the British "Sovereign" (1964) and Australia's "Dame Pattie" (1967) and "Gretel II" in 1970.

The day of the professional racing yachtsman has gone and few now hail from these waters, but the Colneside and Tollesburymen's past skill and seamanship in the great days of yacht racing has earned them an honoured place in the sport's history.

Shamrock V rounding the Cork light vessel off Harwich, 1930. Sir Thomas Lipton's last America's Cup challenger, sailed by Captain Edward Heard of Tollesbury.

CHAPTER FIFTEEN

The Brave Old Days

BRIGHTLINGSEA, with Leigh and Harwich, was amongst the earliest of Essex ports to build its own seagoing vessels. In 1301 King Edward 1 commanded Brightlingsea and St. Osyth to build a forty oared barge for use in the war against Scotland and there were, even then, many locally owned crayers trading coastwise and cross sea from Colne; many of them probably built there. These were small, three masted craft of about 60 feet length, having a single square sail on the fore and main masts and a lateen on the mizzen; with sometimes another squaresail set under the bowsprit. The whole rig would go to windward about as well as a paper bag. Smaller vessels called cogs or nefs had a single square sail, and about 54 of these types were owned at Brightlingsea then; when such unlikely places as Salcote, Fingringhoe and East Mersea owned coastal shipping and were the homes of many hardy seamen.

Organised fighting fleets did not then exist and the reigning monarch commandeered sufficient merchant ships of over thirty tons to act as warships, transports and supply vessels for the various campaigns; the owners receiving compensation for loss of trade. During the 14th and 15th centuries, Brightlingsea ships were often impressed for service in expeditions such as those against Calais, Crecy and Brittany. It would be such a ship for which Thomas Hale bought materials in 1518 and had the keel laid at Brightlingsea.

Around 1500 Henry the Seventh laid the foundations of the British navy, and Brightlingsea took a part in the building, maintaining and manning of the Tudor fleet. Several ships were built there including, probably, the "Barbara of Brightlingsea" of 1512, whose 140 tons must have been crowded as there were seventy mariners, ten gunners and forty five soldiers on board under Captain William West. She carried her 48 guns in Sir Edward Howard's fleet and the green and white uniformed crew seem to have been fairly well fed on a daily diet of one pound of biscuit, a quarter pound of butter and half a pound of beef; all washed down by three quarts of beer.

Shipwrights were then subject to impressment, as well as ships and seamen. In 1513 John Seriaunt (Sergent), William Seriaunt, and John Heret of Brightlingsea were amongst those packed off on foot to Woolwich, Kent, where King Henry VIII's first dockyard was building the largest warship in the world, the "Harry Grace a Dieu", to rival the King of Scotland's "Great Michael". There they worked, with scores from other parts, under the direction of James Baker, the master shipwright of the dockyards at Woolwich and Deptford, who was advised by Genoaese and Venetian shipbuilders, brought in as consultants by the King. The Brightlingseamen earned 16d. a week and received 2½d. a day lodging allowance in addition. Indeed, the whole project with its direction of labour, travel allowances, the workmen living in a hutted camp at the yard and eating in a canteen, is all reminiscent of a large civil engineering enterprise of the present.

One of the first English ships built from plans, the "Great Harry", as she became known, was as bluff and cumbersome as her royal namesake, but her specification contains many references and materials familiar in the shipwright's trade today. No-one knows her exact size but she was at least 180 feet in length and about 1200 tons burden, exceeding by 200 tons the largest ship of the later Spanish Armada. Built entirely of oak she cost £15,000 and was the first ship to carry her guns on two decks and, as she sprouted 21 big bronze cannon and 231 smaller pieces, her topsides looked like a pincushion. She was 4 masted and some idea of her size can be gauged from the two great trees felled from the woods of the Abbot of St. Osyth for her mainmast. Each of these weighed seven tons and was hauled to the creek for shipment by crayer to Deptford. When launched before the King and Queen the "Great Harry" was the most powerful warship afloat and carried the King on his famous voyage to the Field of the Cloth of Gold, but much of her time was spent in Colne, where she must have made a fine sight fetching in with her huge silk banner stretching 120 feet from the mainmast head, besides scores of other flags snapping in the breeze; though however she worked through the Knoll channel I can't imagine; for these cumbersome craft were incapable of sailing very close to the wind and made a good deal of leeway. The yardarms were fitted with sickles to cut an enemy's rigging when boarding and her high poop was decorated with rows of gaily painted shields which contrasted with the black, oiled oak hull which had messsdecks for 700 men. She was burned out at Woolwich in 1552.

The impressment of these Brightlingsea shipwrights for naval service is not surprising for King Henry VIII was keen on the Colne becoming a haven for the ships of his growing navy; even preferring it to nearby Harwich, on his visit to both places in 1543.

Armies were often quartered in the district before embarkation and large quantities of timber from local woods were being shipped to the Thames dockyards.

It is hard to imagine Brightlingsea rivalling Portsmouth as a naval harbour but such was its standing by 1562, when the waters where the Hornets and Flying Dutchmen now skim on Saturdays, often saw the fleet of England riding at anchor under the guns of forts at St. Osyth and Mersea Stone. Warships berthed there regularly and the town boasted a dockyard, equipped with a crane, storehouses, and timberyards for their maintenance. It even had a dry dock, formed from a small creek into which these ungainly ships were floated and a mud bank thrown across the mouth; after which a primitive pump discharged what water remained at low tide before the shipwrights got to work. It must have been a joyous business slopping about in a mud creek to clean and caulk a ship's bottom, but they managed somehow and when repairs were complete the bank was dug away and the ship floated out. Its site is anybody's guess, mine is on the site of James and Stone's yard.* Wherever it was it must have been of fair size for one of the ships repaired there, the "Trinity Henry", was of 240 tons.

*A Creek which ran into the West Marsh.

Naval activities in northern waters were then similar to present day yachting in that warships laid up in autumn and fitted out again in spring. When they were not fishing, trading, or being nabbed by the press gang for naval service, many locals were employed in maintaining these ships or serving as watchmen aboard them. Much time was also spent in dragging for anchors lost by the fleet in Colne. Most of the King's 85 ships were built at Deptford or Woolwich, but the tall framing of a ship on the stocks would have been a familiar sight in Brightlingsea, towering above the huddled cottages of its waterside, especially between 1564-1568 when it was described as "a place meet for building the Queen's ships". In 1559 Brightlingsea owned the largest ships in Essex; the 140 ton "Bark" and the 100 ton "Mary Flower". By 1565 it was the home port of 21 ship masters and owners, and 59 fishermen, in a population of 504. Its 13 ships sported robust Elizabethan names, such as "Mary Fortune", "Ann Gallant" and "Michael Bonaventure"; and odd ones such as "Green Lettuce" and "Mary Sweepstake". These merchantmen were not the begilded, banner flaunting ships of artists' imagination, but well tarred, leaking little tubs, whose bulging sails needed a good breeze to set a wave frothing about their bluff bows.

Wool provided many of their outward cargoes to the Flemish ports, and salt for Lisbon appears as many foreign bound freights. The coal trade flourished as an inward cargo with ships discharging it on the hard, alongside Mediterranean traders bringing figs, prunes, currants, raisins and lemons.

At that period Brightlingsea owned one tenth of the ships employed in the wine trade from Bordeaux, and in 1572 seven Brightlingsea vessels brought the first vintage to England.

During the Armada scare Brightlingsea and Colchester assisted with ships forming the fleet which defeated the Spaniards. The Brightlingsea "William" served at the battle of Gravelines, when it was recorded that the port's fleet numbered 22 ships of which the largest was the 80 ton "Pernell Bark", skippered by Francis Hay. The 80 ton "John Evangelist" was Colchester's largest, at a period when Essex possessed 9 ships of over 100 tons, 7 of them owned at Harwich where the "Tobyas", a proud 140 tonner, lorded it over the slightly smaller vessels from Leigh. The Colne owners had nothing to compare with them, generally trading with 40 tonners, which was also the average size then sailing from Manningtree, on the Stour.

The Colne's importance as a naval station declined as quickly as that of Harwich rose, and during the 17th century Brightlingsea's merchant shipping was affected when the colonisation of North America brought a shift of trade to the West Country ports. Some enterprising local mariners went out themselves, such as Captain John Seamen, who in 1680 sailed from Brightlingsea in his own ship, bound for the new world. He took possession of a great part of Long Island (now part of New York state), which he did his best to populate with 23 sons. Those left behind shunned blue water voyaging for the more profitable fisheries then expanding, and a bold era of the Colne's seafaring was ended.

CHAPTER SIXTEEN

Colneside and The Wooden Walls

THE WOODEN walls of old England are a legend familiar to most of us but few local people realise the part the Colne and Blackwater shipbuilders played in the construction of the sailing men of war.

Recently I acquired copies of old plans which piece together parts of the story of the days when Essex woods rang to the axes of the felling gangs and the huge, pink wheeled timber jims cut rutted ways towards watersides throbbing to the clump of adzes and the chup of mauls. These drawings bring to mind the lives of the bygone fighting seamen; conjuring up pictures of sail and the flicker of gun flashes in the smoke clouds; of desperate fighting with boarding pike and cutlass; of spars and masts shot away; of floggings and messdecks which ran with rats; and all the other grim realities of sea war under sail which history has since glamourised.

Wivenhoe was one building centre for these craft. Ships must have been built there from very early times but the trade is poorly recorded before the beginning of the nineteenth century. It was well established when the 6th rate, 262 ton ship of war "Fagons" or "Fagans" was launched in 1654, probably from the site of the later Wivenhoe Shipyard. This 82 footer, approximating to a frigate, was well armed with 28 muzzle loading cannon and, though the name of her builder is beyond discovery, her captain was Thomas Elliot of Aldeburgh, Suffolk, who was given a poor send off to his commission by surveyor Humphrey White who came down to pass the ship at Wivenhoe quay. Marine surveyors have much to try their temper, even now; but White seems to have completely lost his when, in answer to a chance remark, he called Elliot a "rogue, a knave, and a malignant dog"! Ending with the offer to fight him on the quay!

After six years' service around the world the ship was renamed "Milford" and her spectacular end came when she accidentally caught fire and burned out at Leghorn, Italy, in 1673. She was one of a number of warships coming off Wivenhoe ways at that time. In March 1656 Captain Richard Country sailed from Harwich in the Wivenhoe built "Hind", probably another 6th rate, under orders to join the "Kent" and search for Dutch ships in the North Sea. There is no suggestion that this Wivenhoe enterprise was a naval yard; most likely the need for warships, which strained the capacity of the Royal dockyards, was met, as it has been ever since, by private builders contracting to deliver ships designed by the Admiralty. These ships cost around ten guineas a ton and were built in the open on piled berths which launched them bow first, then a common practice with such full bowed craft. The yard's sole equipment would comprise a shed to house tools; a covered floor to run the lines and make templates; scrieve boards recording the shape of each frame stood near the sawpits where all timber was cut from the trees by hand; a forge; and a quay where the ships could be completed, for, in the scramble to build as many as possible, most were merely planked to the main deck before launch and the topsides finished afloat.

Not all the ships coming off the yard were of such size, as in 1666 the 59 foot ketch "Wivenhoe" of 100 tons was completed for scout work in the North Sea under Captain William Berry. On patrol she encountered Dutch warships off the Shetlands and was chased for seven hours before superior speed enabled her to escape. Privateers may also have been built, for in 1659 the Flushing trader "Fortuna", bound for Dunkirk with lime, encountered a fast ketch wearing English colours off the Goodwins. A shot brought the Dutchman to and Captain Robert Walker of Wivenhoe ordered her skipper to strike his colours and come aboard the ketch, after which his crew plundered the "Fortuna", though I should like to have seen their faces when they discovered the freight was only lime! Captain Walker's command may have been one of the two "nimble ketches" built in 1650 to guard the Essex and Kent coasts against the pirates from Dunkirk and Ostende. If so her action was excusable.

The largest local contribution to the fleet of that day was the Blackwater built, 50 gun 4th rate "Jersey", which took the water from Mr. Starline's yard at Maldon in 1654. This fine 500 tonner was 101 feet long and 32 feet in beam. Captain Terry took her to sea but in 1669 Samuel Pepys was appointed her captain; though he never set foot aboard her! Admiralty red tape is nothing new as in those times only captains could attend court martials and Pepys, who was directly concerned in one, was given 'command' of a ship he never saw! The site of Starline's yard is unknown but it was probably where Dan Webb's yacht yard now stands. It must have been well established to contract for a ship of "Jersey's" size and probably built several others. Maldon was the only Blackwater port to build ships, as distinct from the smacks and other small craft constructed at Tollesbury, West Mersea and, possibly, Salcote.

Shipbuilding, then as now, suffered from terrific booms followed by dismal slumps and, after the 17th century outburst, I can find no record of ships built at Wivenhoe for over one hundred years. The Harwich naval yard suffered a similar fate in 1695 when, after turning out 17 warships, six of them over 1000 tons, its berths lay idle for about sixty years until Barnard and Turner took them over as a private venture. It was not until the 18th century wars with France that warships again reared their frames on Colneside stocks and the shipwrights, sawyers, riggers, sail, rope and block makers prospered as never before on £17 a ton earned on the new Admiralty contracts. Moses Game was the Wivenhoe shipbuilder of those times. He built vessels of some size, the earliest of which I have found record was the quaintly named "Inspector", a ship rigged sloop of 16 guns, launched in 1782. This three masted, 97 footer was of 306 tons burden and had what was obviously an experimental hull form; the after bottom being flattened into a chine and a curious bulbous sole built out from this making her after sections literally of wineglass shape. I can find nothing relating to the origin

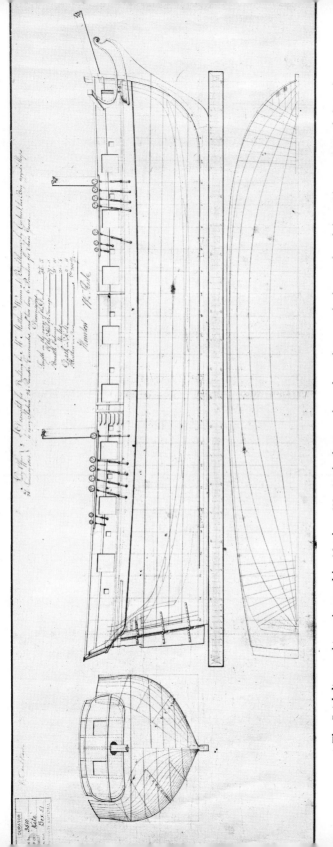

The Brightlingsea shipyard owned by Matthew Warren built several naval gun brigs at the beginning of the 19th century including the 16 gun KITE, a brig rigged sloop 96ft long on deck, 25ft 10in beam and 11ft 8in depth in the hold. She was launched in 1805.

or efficiency of this feature but should not think it was ever repeated in other ships. Her plans are superbly detailed and show the double wheel on the quarterdeck and the elaborately carved surrounds to the stern windows. The "Inspector" would have been employed on escort duties as well as at sea with the fleet. She may have been the ship in which a Brightlingsea smuggler was serving his sentence, as was the custom then. His ship was anchored in the Downs off Deal during a gale of wind when her cable parted in the jump of sea and there was nothing to do but set some sail and hope to run clear through the maze of shoals and across the Thames estuary. No pilot was aboard and volunteers were asked for, the Brightlingsea seaman stepping forward to pilot her safely through the intricate channels until she could lay-to till it moderated. For this, we are told, he received "substantial promotion".

In 1783 Game launched a most spectacular vessel in the ship rigged fireship "Comet". Fireships played a great part in the blockade tactics against the French fleets and were armed with sixteen 32 pounders and several smaller pieces. In addition to guns her topsides probably mounted several mortars which would fire explosive rockets. On operations, fireships were loaded with barrels of tar, oil, and other combustibles and were manned by crews of 120 daredevils, the equivalent of today's 'human torpedoes', who left them only after having made sure the ships were headed amongst the enemy fleet, usually at night and when they were at anchor. As the skipper left, in the last boat, he fired trains timed for the whole ship to burst into flames when she drifted amongst the enemy. Tremendous destruction was achieved with these craft which burnt like torches and set fire to everything they fouled. Of course, being expendable, they were good for trade!

The 424 ton "Comet" was, by contrast with the "Inspector", of rather conservative hull form, even for those times, but sported an exceptionally handsome stern decorated with carvings of cherubs, mermaids, and, of all things, horse drawn chariots! Her male figurehead was set off with trail boards decorated with rising suns, and the whole design seems lavish if she was intended for eventual burning. The snub black muzzles of twenty carronades sprouted from her gun deck ports and she probably proved a very handy unit of the fleet, and a smart sailer as her underwater lines show promise of speed under canvas.

These ships built by Game approximated in size to the wooden minesweepers built at Wivenhoe during the last war; but were, of course, of more striking appearance due to the rig. The plans of both ships are masterpieces of the designer's art with a wealth of artistic detail which has no place on our present day vessels. "Comet" must have fulfilled her fiery purpose somewhere as another warship of the same name and type was built in the West Country in 1807.

The remainder of Game's career is unknown. He may have been one of the many builders bankrupted at the time by shortage and delays in the delivery of timber, for, by the middle 1700s, the woods and forests of Britain were almost stripped and the

Admiralty timber buyers were scouring the whole country for compass timbers for frames, stems, crooks and knees. It takes one hundred years for an oak tree to reach useful proportions before felling and good timber was to these men what steel is now. As it took forty acres of sound oaks to build a frigate the shortage is not really surprising. Foreign substitutes were introduced and many ships were built from fir and white oak imported from North America. Shipwrights and yachtsmen of today who sigh for the sound stuff that went into Nelson's ships should remember that the whole ship-building scene at that time was of ships constructed with wonderful skill but from timber so green that most of the fleet were rotting before they left the ways. The most extreme example being the battleship "Queen Charlotte" of 1810, which was completely rotted before ever putting to sea!

Downstream at Brightlingsea Philip Sainty, that most colourful of Essex ship-builders, was building ships before 1800 on the site of what became Aldous Successors' shipyard. In that year the yard came into the ownership of Matthew Warren and Sainty moved to a Colchester yard. Matthew Warren seems to have had a thorough knowledge of his trade, and good connections. In common with many builders he contracted for numbers of warships designed by the Admiralty and in 1804 launched the gun brigs "Sparkler", "Thrasher" and "Tickler", each of around 150 tons and 80 feet length. To build these he employed 12 shipwrights, 1 joiner, 1 boatbuilder, and 10 sawyers (the timber was still cut by hand); all these men were protected from the pressgang—a very necessary precaution as all trades and walks of life were pressed for men to man the fleet which needed a seaman for every two hundred men, women and children in the population.

Matthew had other troubles too, for these ships were built under contracts which contained penalties for delay in delivery. "Tickler" was 28 days late and a £179 penalty was exacted but afterwards repaid as he pleaded default in the delivery of some copper bolts—times change but the excuses, never! The Brightlingsea built ships saw plenty of action, though they formed but a minute part in a British Navy then at the height of its fame and composed of 191 line of battle ships, 245 frigates and several hundreds of smaller craft, such as these ships. The "Tickler" had the most adventurous career. After salving the American ship "Lone Star" in 1807 she was captured in the Baltic the following year when four Danish gunboats crept up on her under oars during a calm in the Great Belt. For four hours they battered at the unmanoeuvrable brig, killing fourteen and wounding twentytwo of her crew of fifty. With her skipper dead and sails and rigging shot to pieces, "Tickler" finally hauled down her flag. "Sparkler's" luck was just as bad. After blockade operations against Heligoland she was driven ashore and wrecked on the Dutch coast in 1808, where the survivors of her crew were captured. "Thrasher's" record is unknown but she was sold out of the service in 1814.

1805 saw the brig rigged 16 gun sloops "Sharpshooter", "Protector", "Raven" and "Kite" leave the ways. The last pair, designed by Sir William Rule, would look cumbersome to our modern tastes; but the plans show their underwater lines to have been wonderfully easy and fair by any standards. They were units of a numerous class which gained a great reputation for rolling, if nothing else; though they saw hard service. The 178 ton "Sharpshooter" proved true to her name in operations against the French coast and in 1810 her boats, with those of the gunbrigs "Surly" and "Foam", captured the French ship "Alcide" which was driven ashore in the mouth of the river Piroir to be covered by the guns of 400 French troops who kept up an incessant fire as she was got off and taken as a prize by the British boarding parties. "Protector" was in the British fleet covering the landings of troops at Table Bay, South Africa.

The 201 ton "Raven" was blockading off Oporto in 1807 and assisted in the disastrous Walcheren expedition of 1809. Three years later her boats took part in an action off Norderny island on the North German coast and next year she drove three French brigs ashore near Flushing. The "Kite" almost suffered the same fate as the "Tickler" when she was reduced to a wreck by Danish gunboats, but was saved at the last minute by a breeze. By 1813 she was battering at Turkish forts in the eastern Mediterranean and, later, was in action with the fleet against Marseilles and Toulon. She was sold in 1815.

The 383 ton brigs "Ringdove" and "Redwing" were launched by Warren in 1806. The labour force had grown in keeping with the larger tonnage and several shipwrights were brought in from Yarmouth and Ipswich, then a noted shipbuilding centre, swelling the total to 28 shipwrights; with 4 joiners, 2 smiths, 5 labourers and 10 sawyers—a fair picture of how they built them in those days. "Redwing" spent most of her time in the Mediterranean whilst "Ringdove" fared far afield to Newfoundland and the West Indies, where she assisted in the boarding and capture of two French ships and the destruction of two more at Guadaloupe. These rather shallow, tiller steered 80 footers were hardly ideal for this work but, deep laden with sea stores, their messdecks crowded and their bulwarks cluttered with spare spars, these salt rimed little ships were used for shepherding straggling convoys across the rolling Atlantic; always going in fear of the powerful French, and later American, frigates which occasionally pounced on them. The navy seemed loath to part with "Ringdove" as she was not sold till 1828.

By this time the 384 ton brigantines "Sparrowhawk" and "Eclair" were in frame and glided into the creek in 1807. They were very much economy jobs with plain bows not even boasting the 'beak' fitted in the others in lieu of a figurehead; though the helmsman had an easier time with the wheel steering gear. The crews of both ships did well for prize money as "Eclair" captured the French ship "L'Algire" in 1811 and, three years later, the "Revance"; she also fought in the Gulf of Venice and was on ocean convoy duty to the West Indies. "Sparrowhawk" captured a Dutch gunboat in 1808 and, later, the French "L'Intrepid".

Warren's admiralty contracts seem to have stopped with "Eclair" but the yard continued to build other craft until sold to the Aldous family who were to bring it such fame with yachts.

The last plan takes us back upstream to Philip Sainty, the doyen of Colneside yachtbuilders whose later career is outlined in another chapter. His grandson, Mr. Charles J. Sainty, brought to light the interesting fact that many of the ships turned out by this builder were designed by his brother and business partner, Mosely Sainty. In 1828 their Wivenhoe yard built the 558 ton ship rigged sloop-of-war "Pearl"; which I believe to have been the last sailing warship built on Colneside. I do not know what other warships the Sainty's built, apart from the revenue cutters of which they were such masters; but the "Pearl" was almost certainly designed by them and her plans show a wonderfully slippery set of lines, reminiscent of the fast French frigates of Nelson's war. The print shows her to have been a handsome looking ship carrying a generous sail spread which probably totalled 10,000 square feet without the studding-sails, whose booms can be seen bent to the ends of the yards. "Pearl's" stern was finely proportioned like a yacht's, and the otherwise plainly decorated hull was relieved by a graceful female figurehead. They must have had quite a time getting her downstream when completed, as she drew 15 feet 8 inches. The draught records that her upper deck was "Arranged to carry sixteen 24 pounder carronades and two long six pounders for chase guns"; these last were brought to bear from bow and stern ports and were used to pepper an enemy when pursuing or fleeing him; though I doubt if "Pearl" ever saw much action in the navy of those comparatively peaceful times.

Although "Pearl" was the last of the Colne built sailing men-of-war, the yards at Wivenhoe, Brightlingsea and Rowhedge were already busy with the beginnings of yachting which would make them famous and prosperous, and the long tradition of Colneside shipbuilding was being carried into a new and more graceful era.

The 558 ton ship-rigged sloop of war *Pearl*. Designed and built at Wivenhoe by Philip John Sainty 1837.
National Maritime Museum

CHAPTER SEVENTEEN

Wood and Iron

COLNESIDERS tend to take the river's shipyards for granted. They are utilitarian, noisy places, full of grim-looking, rusty hulls, yet behind them lies a tradition of enterprise which few may realise.

While never able to compete with the bigger centres in the matter of size, local builders have always enjoyed a reputation for turning out a sound ship, and the story of shipbuilding on the river is a long one of continual development. What hopes and ambitions were bound up in those old yards, whose greatest period of expansion and change began just 150 years ago!

After the long Napoleonic wars, British shipbuilding was far less centralised or specialised than it is today, and the small ports and their yards, Colneside among them, enjoyed a greater importance in the shipping world. The largest merchant ships were still constructed on the Thames, which was not to lose this supremacy to the Tyne and Clyde until the coming of the first iron ships some decades later. Aberdeen was a rising rival, but the age of its famous clippers had yet to dawn.

Everywhere wooden ships were still supreme and the postwar slackening of naval construction released most of the oak which had, for years past, been hauled, still green, into the dockyards. With the seas free again overseas trade picked up and expanded rapidly at a pace which was to accelerate with the coming industrial revolution.

In the matter of materials the old ports and their yards were almost self-supporting. Shortages were unknown, large quantities of locally grown timber going into the ships. The finest oak in Essex was reckoned to come from St. Osyth Priory, and a vessel built with timber from this neighbourhood was a strong ship.

Power driven yard machinery was non-existent. Rope tackles swung the heavy ships' timbers into position and sheerlegs were used to step the lowermasts, for many of these old ships were launched fully rigged.

All the smithwork was beaten out in the yard forge, and the sails were locally made, while spar, block and ropemakers thrived on the Colne and Blackwater.

Philip John Sainty, born at Wivenhoe, was undoubtedly the Colne's most colourful shipbuilder. He lived to a great age, reputedly had many children, and was not above a bit of smuggling.

He started in the shipbuilding trade about 1789, eventually becoming foreman of a shipyard at Brightlingsea before 1800, and afterwards at a Colchester shipyard; probably that of William Stuttle, who built ships at the Hythe from about 1778 to 1808. Sainty is believed to have started in business on his own as a shipbuilder at Wiven-

Shipbuilding at Colchester Hythe, 1853. The 120 foot fast cutter *Margaret* in frame at J. Mann's yard. Built to the design of G. Tovell of Mistley. Craft of this size were launched broadside at Colchester.
K. Clubb

hoe in 1805 but was back at Colchester Hythe by 1809, probably taking Stuttle's yard above the lock gate at the New Quay, which was for sale in November 1808.

Some account of the yachts Sainty built there is given in chapter 7. He was equally famous for his fast commercial, revenue and, paradoxically, smuggling cutters and luggers; which were sometimes built side by side to the puzzled annoyance of the authorities.

The "Wasp" was one of Sainty's fastest revenue cutters, which proved disastrous to his family's fortunes. About 1825 Philip designed the fast lugger "Wolverine" which his brother Robert and a man named Grinyer had built at Old Shoreham, ostensibly for the channel mackerel and herring fishery. For seven profitable years she smuggled cargoes between Dieppe and a cave near Beachy Head, until two revenue cutters caught her between Newhaven and Beachy Head. The "Wolverine" soon shook off the Newhaven cutter but the other, which proved to be the "Wasp", out sailed her and forced Hobden, the "Wolverine's" skipper, to run her ashore on Worthing flats, setting fire to lugger and cargo; before escaping with Robert and the crew, inland; after Robert had blown up the cave.

In 1819 the carriage of mails from Holyhead to Howth, the port of Dublin, was subject to a Government inquiry seeking improvement in the speed of the mail and passenger carrying cutters operating this service across the stormy Irish Sea.

The foremost British designers of fast craft were invited to submit designs for new cutters; the Surveyor of the Navy; Peter Hedderwick, who specialised in design of the fast Leith to London packets; and Philip Sainty, who produced a beautifully formed, 70 foot cutter, superbly draughted. He stated that he had designed a 76 ton

263

cutter which could beat to windward across the English Channel, under a three reefed mainsail, at an average speed of 5.4 knots. At that time Sainty stated he had built "almost all descriptions of vessels from ships of 400 tons down to cutters of 6 tons." Most of these were "Smacks and Cutters" (his distinction is interesting) and most of them were designed for fast sailing, though he had also built "vessels of great burden". Sainty had been at sea at various times during his shipbuilding career, "backwards and forwards in the North Sea, to the Baltic, and from London to Colchester". The board inquired if he had personal experience of bad sea conditions and, characteristically, Sainty replied; "The North Sea is not very pleasant!"

Sainty moved downstream to a shipyard at Wivenhoe by 1823, probably to take advantage of the less restricted launching facilities and increased yard space. There he continued to design and build fast and also burdensome vessels up to 400 tons, some of which are described in chapter 3.

Philip Sainty sold the Wivenhoe yard to Thomas Harvey in 1832 and died in 1844. His tombstone, still to be seen in Wivenhoe churchyard, bears the legend "Builder of the Marquis of Anglesey's Yacht 'Pearl'."

Philip's son, Philip M. Sainty junior, carried on the family tradition, though not in the same yard. He seems to have been a designer and builder of some ability, but very little is known of either his yard or the craft constructed there. In fact as a personality he seems to have been overshadowed by his father.

It seems feasible that, with the old yard in other hands, he set up his own business on a site which is reputed to have been on the Fingringhoe bank of the river, though where it would have been is difficult to imagine. The present sea walls are of some antiquity and show no signs of it and surely some traces would remain of the piling which the marshy ground would need to build vessels of any size. As no one in his senses would have tried to build up the creek at the mill the only possibility seems the ferry hard.

There was of course a ballast quay and a road down to it opposite to where Cook's Shipyard now stands (part of the structure remains), but no sign of a building berth. One does not know what there was at the sandworks quay before this was started just after the first World War. A possibility is that Sainty was legally debarred from competing with Harvey at Wivenhoe and went across the river for a site.

But all this is supposition. What we do know is that as late as 1856 the barque "Leading Star" was designed by him and launched from his yard for William Cross. Of 210 registered tons and 130 feet overall she was classed at Lloyds and her dimensions indicate that she was probably intended for the then booming colonial trade to New Zealand. Described as "built upon a new principle", she had perfectly flat floors which were a novelty in those days of fine-bottomed, heavily ballasted hulls. From this it would seem that Sainty had early mastered the problem of designing a ship to sail without ballast, though this feature may equally well have been the result of changes in the tonnage rules, then current.

Launches then, as now, seem to have been festive occasions, for we are told "About noon the company began to arrive, and by 2 p.m. the shipyard was well nigh filled". A cabinet minister, local squires, and a military band from the barracks attended. With such a send-off "Leading Star" could hardly have failed to be successfully set afloat, after which she was moored alongside the shipyard and a reception was held aboard. They did themselves well, as "about three o'clock the attack commenced and fowls, tongues, pigeon pies, ale and stout, port and sherry, speedily vanished!" What a picture of activity existing a hundred years ago on the now almost deserted Fingringhoe shore!

The previous year the Fingringhoe yard launched the 59 ton billyboy ketch "Excelsior" for Goole owners, and it must have survived until 1864 when the 59 ton Grimsby smack "Gauntlet" was built there.

Philip Mosely Sainty also built merchant ships at Rowhedge, where his main berth was on the site of what is now Ian Brown Ltd.'s big slip. There, the oak framing of ships reared high against cottages and trees and on launch day the village rang with cheers of shipwrights and spectators.

In 1861 the 205 ton barque "Caroline Sainty" slid into the Colne fully rigged and dressed overall, which was then the custom. Three years later the 176 ton barquentine

Harris Brothers' yacht yard at Rowhedge, 1893. A cruising yawl fitted out, alongside. The Rowhedge smack *Wonder*, on slipway in centre, being lengthened six feet amidships. Yacht building under roof, to right. Daniell's brewery in background.

Shipwrights and other workmen of John Houston's yacht yard at Rowhedge, 1895.

"Maid of Honour" was launched from the same berth for London owners. Sainty also owned merchantmen, including the barque "Velocipide", the 204 ton brig "Patience", built at St. Malo in 1857, and the 188 ton barquentine "Conqueror", built in Denmark in 1839. In October 1866 the schooner "Hero" of Whitby was advertised for sale lying at "Mr. Saintys Wharf", Rowhedge.

First record of shipbuilding at Rowhedge is given by the bill of sale for the 25 ton smack "Neptune", dated 1770. The customer, a West Mersea oysterman, paid £120 for her. Next reference is another bill of sale dated 1789, for a 16 ton smack costing £100. Her inventory reads very like that of a modern yacht and included those vital seafaring utensils; "One frying pan and one kettle".

In 1839 Susannah Cole owned a shipyard "Up Street", where William Cheek built various types of vessels, probably mostly smacks. The cottage where William Cheek lived still stands at Shipyard Corner. He closed his yard in bankruptcy in December 1866.

James Harris is recorded as a Master Shipwright at Rowhedge in 1848, though the site of his shipyard is unknown but, "Down Street" Sainty's yard must have been absorbed shortly after 1865 when Peter T. Harris and his sons Enos and, later, John, commenced building in what is now the Lower Yard of Ian Brown Ltd.

They built up a considerable reputation for yacht work in the following half century.

At first P. T. and Enos Harris appear to have designed and built craft independently in the same yard, but by 1886 were amalgamated, and the firm known as P. T. Harris, though Enos continued as an active partner.

They constructed 54 yachts, the largest being the quaintly named 50 ton yawl "Cushie Doo"; but the best known was the 42 ton cutter "Thanet", built for Lord Gort in 1914 and still sailing in the Mediterranean.

Photographs show Harris' yard crammed with every type and size of yacht from 100 foot racing cutters, such as "Valkyrie", "Genesta" and "Yarana", to steam yachts and smart little raters, many hauled up for repair; others laid in the mud berths awaiting fitting out. Long lines of them stretched up and down the sea walls above and below the village.

Besides building and repairing yachts, the energetic Harrises found time to turn out over 40 smacks of all sizes from big, deep sea cutters and ketches to such lovely clippers as the Rowhedge "Neva", crack smack of the Essex fleets for thirty years.

P. T. Harris and Enos P. Harris designed almost all the yachts and smacks their yard built, but in 1879 they launched the 27 ton cutter "Vivandiere" to one of the earliest designs of George Watson, and a few other yachts were built from designs by Fife and Shepherd; besides the 10 ton cutter "Firecrest", designed by Dixon Kemp as a racer-cruiser for Canon Norman of Mistley. She became noted, in her old age, as having been sailed single-handed from France to New York by a Frenchman Alain Gerbault, who afterwards sailed her to the South Seas.

The yard mould loft is still in use for its original purpose, in a sylvan setting adjacent to the characterful house traditionally occupied by the owner of the shipyard and now, appropriately, the home of Mr. Ian Brown.

In the 1890's Harris dug a big new slipway to cope with increasing yacht tonnage and excavated the site of Sainty's old, wood bottomed building berth, which was laboriously dug out by one old man with a spade and a wheelbarrow!

Hitherto, all the slipways had been hauled up by big hand capstans but for the "big slip" the ingenious Harris installed a windlass engine removed from the steam yacht "Walrus", driven by the same traction engine boiler which by then provided steam for the sawmill.

To step and unstep the tall masts of the large yachts using the yard, Harris erected a pair of 90 feet sheerlegs at the end of Cat Island Quay and, just upstream from the big slipway, laid a gridiron, used chiefly for bottom cleaning and painting of steam yachts too large to go on the slip. Another pair of large sheerlegs were built to serve this berth, to lift boilers and heavy machinery.

A steam driven saw was not installed at Harris' yard until about 1898 and previously all timber was hand sawn. Mr. James Theobald of Rowhedge, my wife's grandfather, recalled spending much of one winter with another young shipwright, pit-sawing great baulks of clear grained, yellow pine into deck planking for the racing cutter "Genesta".

In 1903 the yard's name was changed again to Harris Brothers and its business continued to increase until it was sold to become part of the Rowhedge Ironworks Co. in 1915.

"Up Street", W. Puxley occupied Cheek's old yard and built vessels, including yachts, in the 1870's and 1880's. In 1875 he launched the 14 ton cutter yacht "New Belle" and in 1888 built the steam yacht "Sunmaid", to a design by John A. Houston, who was believed to have been yard manager. She was the first composite craft built at Rowhedge, with pitch pine planking on iron frames, and her 6 nominal horse power engine was by Mumford, the Colchester engineers who built machinery for many locally owned steam vessels.

About 1890 Houston purchased the Upper Yard from Puxley's widow and expanded the business of building, repairing and slipping yachts, steam launches and other craft.

Many steam yachts were also refitted there and considerable marine engineering carried out. The yard also advertised as builders of iron yachts but I cannot discover that any were built by them.

John Houston was a member of the Institution of Naval Architects and designed numbers of yachts, besides building to those of other designers. The estimating, business and general management of this enterprising yard was carried out by Houston and one clerk, while the shipwrights, joiners, painters and riggers were under foreman shipwright James Pryke. The yard had a slipway and a 130 foot gridiron, served by lifting sheers.

The clipper-bowed, 80 foot cutter yacht "Thele", designed by Arthur Payne of Southampton, was the most notable yacht of the seven built by Houston, who also constructed many other craft such as Government ammunition barges and foreign service steam launches. In 1897 Houston built the Walton Volunteer Life Boat "True to the Core"; a 40 foot pulling and sailing craft which cost £437. She was to the order of an independent group who rivalled the Walton R.N.L.I. boat, but were also supported by voluntary contributions.

Most of Houston's building was carried out in the "Big Shed", which was burned down in 1898 in the largest fire Rowhedge has experienced, an event which landmarked others in the village for many years.

The shed was rebuilt and was still referred to as the "New Big Shed" when I started my apprenticeship at Rowhedge Ironworks, 46 years later!

John Houston had a great reputation for good work when his yard closed in 1900. He went to Africa to manage a yard building and maintaining river craft and was drowned early in the First World War when the ship in which he was returning to Africa was torpedoed and sunk.

The Upper Yard lay empty for a time until local people, including Ernest Beard, owner of the steam yacht "Alexandra", reopened it as Donyland Shipyards Ltd., managed by Mr. Reid, a Scotsman, formerly a draughtsman at Forrestt's.

They appear to have built only one vessel, the wooden steam yacht "Imogen", which was unusual in having steam turbine machinery, then still experimental and only recently fitted to destroyers. She was designed in 1902 by Cox and King, who were also shareholders in the shipyard, and had the extreme dimensions of 52 feet x 8 feet 6 inches beam x 3 feet 7 inches depth of hull. Her speed is not recorded but she is the only steam turbine vessel ever built, or likely to be built in the area.

In 1904 the Donyland Shipyard was bought by the newly formed Rowhedge Ironworks Co. Ltd., who were to transform it into a steel shipbuilding yard.

Shipbuilding revived at Colchester Hythe during the 1850's under J. Mann, who is believed to have moved there from Mistley. The fact that at least two vessels built by him were designed by Captain G. R. Tovell, also of Mistley, supports this.

In 1853 Mann built the 265 ton, 120 foot cutter "Margaret" on Tovell's patented principle in which the lines were developed mathematically, with the hull profile

Rusk's boatyard, Wivenhoe, about 1930. From right; John Smith, Stanley Cook (foreman), extreme left; James Theobald.

resembling that of a modern yacht and every frame being a segment of a circle. Her model was exhibited in the Great Exhibition of 1851 and a similar form was later patented by Dr. Frederick Ljungstrom of Sweden, in 1937, who claimed "quite astonishing results".

Mann built the "Margaret" as a speculation for either the fruit trade (she was coppered) or as a passenger packet, as her hold was fitted with seats to accommodate 170 passengers. She had 24 foot beam and was 9 foot 10 inches deep in the hold, but her slack-bilge hull form made her tender and the cutter rig, with its 88 foot lower-mast almost amidships, setting 7200 square feet of working canvas, made her wet at sea and hard on her Mistley crew.

She went well to windward and was credited with beating the large yachts at a contemporary Harwich regatta, despite the refusal of her entry on grounds of her being a merchant vessel. This triumphant sail round brought a reward for the shipwrights who built her and their foreman, John Martin of Rowhedge. When no buyer came forward Mann ran her himself in the fruit trade between Ipswich, London and the Mediterranean; often loading at Smyrna.

From contemporary photographs of the "Margaret" on the stocks it appears that she was launched broadside; a practice which must have been common at the Hythe if the restricted width of the river is considered.

Some owners had faith in Tovell's patent for, in 1856, Mann launched the barque "Minnehaha" for the far east trade. In letters to her designer her master reported fast passages to and from Hong Kong, compared with other ships.

In 1857 the 25 ton schooner yacht "Silver Star" was built of iron at Colchester, for Peter Bruff, the colourful civil engineer of the Eastern Counties railway and many other East Coast projects. She was designed by Tovell and was built under his name, probably on leased premises, possibly in part of Mann's yard.

The "Silver Star" is believed to have been the first iron vessel built on the Colne or Blackwater and her construction presented unique problems, as shipwrights shunned ironwork as an unclean material threatening their craftsmanship and, everywhere, iron ships were being built by boilermakers, who were the only tradesmen skilled in shaping iron plates and sections. There were then few boilermakers in the area but no doubt Bruff's engineering connections supplied the men.

The 54.7 foot "Silver Star" had only 10.3 foot beam. She appears to have been used for cruising and was in Bruff's ownership until 1886.

In 1860 Tovell patented a fin keel hull form for sailing craft and became associated with Thomas C. Gibson, shipbuilders of Ramsey, Isle of Man; who built a series of commercial craft and yachts on Tovell's principle. These included the pilot cutter "Guide"; the 35 ton yacht "Wren" for Ernest Thelluson; the three-masted merchant schooner "Jane" for trade between England and Philadelphia, U.S.A.; the 230 ton yacht "Eagle"; and the 600 ton, iron sailing ship "Ramsey", which might have been another builder's speculation. It appears that Tovell's interest ended with the patented principle of hull form as P. M'Nidder from Glasgow was employed by Gibsons to prepare the individual designs and detail plans, and to lay-off the lines.

In 1845, a Tovell was a member of the Royal Harwich Yacht Club, owning the 7 ton cutter "Symmetry"; a name suggesting that he was the Mistley designer. The reputed speed of Tovell's designs is at variance with the reported performance of the 7 ton cutter yacht "Blanche", racing in the small class of the Royal West of England Yacht Club regatta at Plymouth in 1866. She was just launched and built on "Tovell's principle" but "Cannot apparently do much to windward, which is just the fault that all vessels built on this concentric circle principle have exhibited".

Fishing vessels have been built at Wivenhoe over many centuries. In 1690 a yard there was building craft of between 20-40 tons for the oyster trade.

At the end of the 18th century, shipbuilder Moses Game built a hundred oyster smacks in 20 years, and others were built, around 1800, by a Mr. Cole. George Wyatt of Wivenhoe was a shipbuilding contemporary of Moses Game. Little is now known of his career, or his yard site. He died in 1770 aged 64 and his tomb near Wivenhoe church tower is inscribed "Shipbuilder of this parish", indicating that his business was of importance.

Choice of a site mattered little to some builders. At Fingringhoe, a fishing smack is reputed to have been built on Pigs Foot Green, in the rural centre of the village and, on completion, was transported two miles, drawn by horses to her launch at the ferry. During the mid-nineteenth century some large smacks were built on the hard at Brightlingsea, including the "Equity", by Polley, and the 28 ton "Volunteer", in 1860.

Barr of Wivenhoe built the 60 foot Rowhedge smack "First Fruits" behind the Greyhound Inn—an unusual choice for a berth, unless it was to encourage the thirsty shipwrights. When completed she was towed down the High Street on a carriage and launched from the town hard. In addition to smacks, Barr turned out a number of yachts, largest of which was the yawl "Snowflek", 28 tons, but the lean cutter "Senorita" is the best remembered from the writings of her owner, Harvey Reynolds. Barr seems to have gone out of business in the 1890's.

Somewhere along Wivenhoe's quays G. R. Lardner built his one and only yacht, the 16 ton yawl "Silver Spray". That was in 1882 and is the only record of him as a builder. One wonders how his enterprise ended?

In 1720 Messrs. Browne moved their rope manufacturing works from Nacton, in Suffolk, to Wivenhoe Cross; where much new housing was built for the great number of employees. At one period it was the only ropery between Maldon and Great

John James' yard at Brightlingsea. Building small smacks, on a site now the car park of the 'Yachtsmen's Arms'.

Yarmouth, and served a great number of shipyards and ships. Steam power was installed in 1847 but in 1855 a boiler explosion killed men and wrecked the works. It employed 70 men in 1900 when "Browne's fine yacht ropes" were in demand. The works closed about 1905.

Joseph Edwin Wilkins was a pupil of John Harvey at Wivenhoe shipyard, which had closed in 1881. Wilkins partly reopened the yard in 1882, being backed financially by Edmund Round.

Wilkins was a trained naval architect of considerable ability and in 1883 was building yachts, and large smacks for the Great Yarmouth Steam Carrying Company including the "Jolly Tar" and "Blue Jacket", launched in September 1885, which were 70 foot on the keel x 19 foot beam and 9 foot draught. A few months later Wilkins launched the similar smacks "Irex" and "Tara", which were towed to Great Yarmouth for fitting out.

In 1881 Wilkins designed the 70 foot ketch "Kara", the only yacht built at Wivenhoe by E. J. Gardiner. She was designed specially for Arctic cruising, exploration and natural observation; being strengthened and sheathed to resist ice pressure. Each spring she fitted out at Wivenhoe under Captain Ashley with a local crew, who were supplemented by skilled whalers when she arrived at Peterhead, and later at the Shetlands, before sailing for the Arctic with her owner Sir H. W. Gore-Booth, on board.

With the harpoon gun rigged and trying-pots on deck, she frequently cruised for whales before sailing as far north as possible, sometimes being locked in the ice for long periods. She invariably returned to Wivenhoe with polar bear skins and other rarities shot by the owner's party.

The yard built several yachts ranging from the 3 tonner "Dwarf" to the beautiful 130 ton yawl "Elfreda", a 100 footer designed and built in 1886 for Theodore Pim, also well known on the Colne for his series of yachts named "Rosabelle".

Wilkins closed his Wivenhoe yard in 1887 and moved to London, opening offices as a yacht architect. He afterwards designed the large steam yachts "Malikah", 328 tons, 155 feet, in 1887; and "Gundreda", 386 tons, 171 feet, in 1893; both built by Ramage and Ferguson of Leith. He also designed small cutters and steam yachts, including the novel, 30 foot gunning launch "Tyche", built by Forrestts at Wivenhoe in 1894 for Col R. P. Davis of New House Farm, Walton-on-Naze, who enjoyed wildfowling on a grand scale, manning her with two professional Brightlingsea sailor-fowlers.

Wilkins' business failed in 1894 and he returned from London to carry on a designing consultancy at rented accommodation within Wivenhoe shipyard until about 1904.

Douglas Stone's Brightlingsea yard, about 1903. A smack building under roof. Large smacks, barges and a bawley repairing. A yacht's steam launch waits off the waterside lined with smacks' boats.

James Husk commenced yachtbuilding during the late 1840's in a yard at the downstream end of Wivenhoe, on a site now part of James W. Cook's shipyard. He took readily to innovations and introduced much use of iron members in his construction. Husk was credited with the invention of the piece of rigging gear known as "sister hooks" and in the little cutter "Polka", introduced a novel form of stern which became sufficiently well known to bear her name. Yacht repairing and building the smaller smacks kept his yard busy, and he contrived a small dry-dock from the hull of an old barge.

James Husk built at least 10 yachts between 1873 and 1898, largest being the 70 foot yawl "Crusoe", and all except one were to his design. The exception, the 28 ton yawl "Wild Wave" launched in 1882, was draughted by her barrister owner, Dr. Stuart Bruce. The 13 ton cutter "Surge" was Husk's most noted racer which in 1873 won the Challenge Cup of the Thames Corinthian Yacht Club against the best designs of Fife and Hatcher.

James Husk, junior, seceded from the business about 1892 to found his own two storey boatbuilding shop adjacent to his father's yard. He became noted for building beautifully finished yachts' boats, gigs, galleys, cutters and dinghies. His gigs were champion rowers and a regatta success usually saw the victorious crew drinking champagne from the cup in the builder's boatshop.

In those times most big steam yachts carried a 20 foot sailing cutter which competed against those of other yachts when together in an anchorage. Husk was noted for fast cutters which rivalled those of Fife and Mylne, who also designed them as competition increased.

Husk also built a few small yachts, such as the 5 ton yawl "Verven" of 1900, which I believe to be the first local craft built with a motor auxiliary; a three quarter horse power engine! He was succeeded in business by his son who, trained as an engineer, expanded the firm's construction of motor propelled craft during the 1920's and 1930's by initiating a series building of popularly-sized motor cruisers, besides constructing several wooden passenger craft for Southend-on-Sea and the Broads.

Husk and Son's largest yacht was the 60 foot "Margaret Mary III", built in 1930 for George T. Morris of the Colne Yacht Club, who also designed her. She regularly competed in pre-war motor yacht races and meets, and was so highly regarded by George Morris that he willed his ashes to be scattered from her by his friends at the mouth of Colne, and thoughtfully left money for them to drink a toast to his memory in champagne, afterwards.

In 1941 Husk's yard was absorbed by Vosper Ltd. of Portsmouth who established a "shadow" yard at Wivenhoe for expanding their building of fast, light warships. Large sheds were erected to house this important work but the first motor torpedo boat was laid down in Husk's old boatshop in July 1941 and was launched 12 months later; a considerable feat when the complexity of these 70 foot thirty knot boats is considered.

Fourteen other M.T.B.s followed her off the ways and thirty five other coastal force craft were repaired at this yard, which employed 225 local men until it closed in 1945. The premises were taken by James W. Cook Ltd. in 1946 and were developed as a thriving steel shipyard.

One of John Harvey's premium apprentices was Douglas Stone, of Erith, Kent, who absorbed much of Harvey's artistry of design and afterwards became a partner in the successful shipyard of Stone Brothers at Erith; building sailing barges, fishing bawleys and small yachts. The Stone family also owned spritsail barges, including the racer "Anglo-Norman", the first barge to be fitted with wheel steering gear in 1882.

Douglas Stone was a member of the Institution of Naval Architects and was an accomplished draughtsman. He sought expansion in yacht building and in 1892 moved the firm to Brightlingsea, occupying the site of the present James and Stone shipyard.

That year Stone designed and built the "Eva" for the Corinthian Yacht Club 21 foot class and she soundly beat the "Tottie", champion for five years and designed by G. L. Watson.

The 64 foot cutter "Gwyneth", launched in 1901 was the largest yacht designed and built by Stone Brothers, who produced many small racers, besides continuing to build bawleys and small smacks, and four sailing barges; the "Millie" and "Freda" for Hibbs and Jarvis of Brightlingsea, who were also ship chandlers and sailmakers, previously Panell and Hibbs; and the "British Empire" and "Federation" for Howe of Colchester.

In 1903 Stone's built two yachts of the South Coast One-design class, designed by Alfred Mylne of Glasgow. These elegant 50 footers were "gentlemen's day racing boats" of the period, setting a 2,000 square feet cutter rig and having a skipper and three hands.

Mylne complimented Douglas Stone on the superior finish his yard had achieved on the "L'Amoureuse" and "Harmony", later renamed "Eilun", which, 45 years later, was winning offshore races rigged as a bermudian ketch.

The 110 foot racing schooner "Susanne" was the largest yacht to lay up at the yard, whose shareholders included some noted Brightlingsea racing captains.

In 1931 Douglas Stone bought the old, Wivenhoe-built, 40 rater "Creole" for breaking up, as her owner wished her to be destroyed so that no-one else had the pleasure of sailing in her!

In 1930 the yard's title changed to Douglas Stone and Sons and Mr. Robert N. Stone carried on the business which increasingly specialised in laying up and refitting

yachts and building small class racing dinghies. "Robbie" Stone designed many successful one-designs including the Brightlingsea 18 footer, West Mersea "Sprite", the
"Jewel" and the "Firecrest". Until his recent death he maintained a keen interest in
racing craft design and rig development and, typically, I last chatted to him on the beach
at Thorpe Bay where he was examining the latest wingsail masts of the British and
American 'C' class catamaran contenders for the international trophy.

As with nearby Aldous Successors, Stone's were extremely busy during the 1939-45
war, maintaining the large numbers of naval small craft using Brightlingsea as a base,
and building others.

Stone's were linked to John James and Co. in 1942 under joint managership and
over 500 craft were slipped for repair by the war's end; besides building 132 ships'
boats and eight steam and two diesel harbour launches. The yard maintained M.T.B.
flotillas, including that commanded by the famous Lt. Commander Hichens, converted
trawlers for minesweeping, and yachts for patrol duties; and repaired 130 landing craft.

Yachtbuilding and refitting was revived after 1945 but a few years later the firm
commenced building small steel and aluminium vessels, particularly fast launches for
foreign service. In 1958 the business assumed its present name of James and Stone
(Brightlingsea) Ltd., and continues to build commercial craft of widely differing types,
including ferries, trawlers, launches, tugs and special shallow draught vessels.

John James was a Brightlingsea contemporary of Douglas Stone and built
numbers of small smacks for the oyster trade, smacks' boats and small yachts. His first
smacks were built on ground now forming the car park of the "Yachtsmen's Arms",
but he later occupied what is now the eastern end of James and Stone's Shipyard,
adjacent to Brightlingsea Hard.

Space precludes mention of other small yards such as Carrington, the Colchester
barge builder, or the Brightlingsea smack and yachtbuilders Root and Diaper, or
Rashbrook; who contributed to the artistry of the adze and the maul.

CHAPTER EIGHTEEN

The Harvey Story

THOMAS Harvey and his son John were amongst the most notable of the Colne's builders of fast sailing craft and their influence in yachtbuilding became international.

Thomas Harvey was born at Wivenhoe in 1803 and began life as a joiner and carpenter in conjunction with a Mr. Todd. For several years he kept the Black Buoy public house in Wivenhoe and apparently worked in the village shipyards. It is not now possible to ascertain the depth of knowledge he initially possessed of the specialised wooden shipbuilding trade but, in 1832, he took over the Wivenhoe shipyard when Philip John Sainty retired, and in a very few years earned a reputation for building fast and sound ships. It is not certain who was responsible for the design of these craft but early orders included fast schooners for the fruit and other perishable food trades, in which a growing fleet of east-coasters were sailing to ports in Spain and the eastern Mediterranean. First off the stocks were the 86 ton "Lady Rebow" of 1836; "Gurdon Rebow", 59 tons, of 1839; "Slater Rebow" and "General Rebow"; all named after the family then occupying Wivenhoe Hall. The last was a 90 tonner which was launched fully rigged, ready to sail next day for Lisbon on her first charter.

Harvey also built the bulkier brigs for general trade and the 212 ton "Essex", launched in 1837, was typical of the type. In 1840 the prosaically named schooner "Invoice" was built for the Chinese silk trade and, soon afterwards, the 350 ton "Lady de Crespigny" sailed on her maiden voyage to the West Indies. Next winter the fruit schooner "Prospero" was laid down after the 220 ton "Jane" had been delivered to owners in the Scilly Isles. In 1845 Thomas Harvey launched the 120 ton schooner "Hero" in which his second son, Edward, sailed on her maiden voyage to Malaga, Spain, for a cargo of oranges. She was struck by a severe gale in the Bay of Biscay, which shifted her ballast and she lay on her beam ends for two days and nights. The crew cut away her masts in an attempt to right her, but could not cut through the tough, new shroud lanyards, and were in grave danger when sighted by a homeward bound East Indiaman, which took them off and landed them at Portsmouth.

Brigs were also used in the fruit trade and in 1845 Harvey launched the "Dart" for the Azores run. Many early 19th century fruiters were also cutter rigged. In 1853 Harvey hauled up the fast cutter "Providence", built by Sainty in 1806, cut her in two, and lengthened her amidships, increasing her tonnage to 59. She was commanded by Captain Turff of Rowhedge, in the fruit trade between London and Teneriffe.

Thomas Harvey also continued and expanded Sainty's yachtbuilding tradition. The 25 ton cutter "Prima Donna", launched in 1845, was one of his early racers which did little at first, but rapidly improved to beat the Lord Paget's iron cutter "Belvedere" and the Rowhedge manned "Ino"; the crack yachts of the spirited 25 ton class, in the "finest season even known", according to contemporary reports.

The quest for lightness in racers is nothing new. Harvey constructed his fliers with English elm keels, Dantzic fir hull planking, garboards of English or Canadian elm, deck shelves and beams of fir and the deck of crown deal. All ballast was then inside, usually of iron, though this rapidly changed to lead. By contrast, Harvey's cruising yachts were planked in oak and all his craft were noted for longevity; the 39 ton cutter "Avalon" was still winning prizes thirty-five years after her launch in 1850.

The business thrived and in 1849 Harvey reopened Read and Page's old shipyard at Ipswich, where he supplemented the Wivenhoe output by also building merchant ships, yachts, and fishing vessels. This expansion may have been motivated by Harvey's increasing need for shipbuilding timber as, with existing transport, it would be easier to open a branch of the business adjacent to timber supplies than to haul it to the home yard.

Thomas' son John Harvey, born in 1830, showed early aptitude for everything pertaining to the shipyards; particularly regarding the design of fast craft. He was apprenticed at the Wivenhoe yard and at the age of 15 was, remarkably, a member of the Royal Harwich Yacht Club. When only 19 years old he was closely associated with the design of the noted racing cutter "Volante"; a lean and deep 48 tonner launched at the Ipswich yard in 1849. She was one of the fastest British yachts racing against the schooner "America" in 1851, for the Cup which has since become famous as the America's Cup. Captain George Pittuck of Wivenhoe sailed the "Volante" with a Colne crew and she was lying second to the "America" (which had sailed a shorter course due to faulty instructions) when the yacht "Freak" collided with her, springing "Volante's" bowsprit and disabling her, to the crew's bitter disappointment.

In 1852 the "Volante" raced the equally noted iron yacht "Mosquito" at Plymouth and the records give authentic proof of the speed of these mid-Victorian racing cutters. They started in a gale with topmasts housed and a reef in their mainsails. The course totalled 50 sea miles in four rounds which they covered in 4 hours, 18 minutes, 15 seconds; an average speed of 11.61 knots. The "Mosquito" won by 3 minutes 8 seconds. Captain Pittuck sailed the "Volante" and Captain John Nicholls, of Southampton, the "Mosquito".

In 1861 the outclassed "Volante" was bought by H. C. Maudslay who, with her old skipper George Pittuck again in command, sailed her until 1869 when, with the owner and his bride on their honeymoon cruise, she dragged ashore on the Ryde sand in a gale and all hands had just got aboard the Ryde lifeboat when "Volante's" bottom was stove in and she instantly filled to the deck and sank. Raised and refitted, she continued racing for several years. A tragic accident occurred on board her at Harwich

Regatta in 1871 when she gybed heavily and the boom broke against the lee runner. Its after end flew to windward and pinned a man to the bulwark, clean through his chest, killing him instantly.

In 1852 John Harvey designed the 10 ton racing cutter "Kitten", which was built at Wivenhoe for his own use, to gain experience in class racing. With dimensions of 43 foot overall, 37 foot 4 inches waterline x 8 foot 9 inches beam x 6 foot 8 inches draught, she illustrated her designer's early originality. Twenty four years later, speaking of the noted yacht "Jullanar", of which he was co-designer, Harvey said of the "Kitten"; "Then recent experience induced us to construct a boat for ourselves of the type and nearly of the proportions of the . . . . 'Jullanar'". The "Kitten" had a radical forward end which was cut away boldly to reduce wetted surface and her keel was heavily raked. In 1898 the noted yacht designer George Watson wrote "the 'Kitten' was as much an epoch making vessel as the "Jullanar" was later on when, in conjunction with Mr. Bentall, Mr. Harvey put the famous yawl afloat".

The "Kitten" raced with moderate success against yachts of similar size. In 1870 she was sold to George F. Clarke of Boston, Massachusetts and, renamed "Saxon", was amongst the earliest examples of the later popular English cutter type owned by American yachtsmen. She later reverted to her original name and was still sailing in the 1880's.

The Harveys' most noted yacht of 1852 was the racing cutter "Thought", a radically shaped 25 tonner having a heavily raked sternpost to cheat the tonnage rule for rating, and extremely "veed" sections. Her dimensions were 52 foot 9 inches x 11 feet 3 inches and, unfortunately she was a comparative failure. Two years later her owner took her to Dan Hatcher, at Northam, Southampton, where she was almost completely dismembered and rebuilt, to race with distinction for many years afterwards. My uncle, George Barnard, worked on the "Thought" as a shipwright apprentice shortly before she was broken up in 1899 and recalled the tremendous size of her deadwoods, necessitated by the incredibly fine shape of her bow and stern.

George Pittuck left the "Volante" to skipper the "Thought" which, under his skilled helmsmanship, eventually soundly beat the Poole-built "Phantom", which had been crack yacht of the second class racers. Although the Thames measurement tonnage rating rule is thought to have been the principal influence restricting beam in mid-19th century racing yachts, John Harvey was always in favour of narrow boats of great displacement, because of their weatherliness and supposed superior qualities in choppy waters, and the "Thought" was an early example of his theory.

The "Esk" was another Harvey-built 10 tonner, launched in 1852, which proved her seaworthiness by beating in over Exmouth bar in a gale, with the loss of her dinghy. By then yachts from John Harvey's board were determinedly challenging those by older, established builders in all classes, and orders flowed in to the Wivenhoe yard office.

The Crimean War brought a demand for shallow draught warships to carry out bombardment work in the Black Sea, and in October 1855 Thomas Harvey contracted to build four 170 ton mortar vessels to be ready the following spring. Two were built at the Wivenhoe yard and two at Ipswich. The Harvey family's honesty bordered on the unbusinesslike as the gunboats were completed to contract date and, shortly afterwards, during a business visit to London, Thomas Harvey was hailed on London Bridge by a fellow shipbuilder who had also just handed over several gunboats. He enquired if Thomas was pleased with the Admiralty bonus payment for completion on time and was astonished when Harvey replied that he had not thought to claim it!

These craft appear to have been the only warships built by the firm, but they evidently maintained government cutters, as the 44 ton "coastguard cutter cruiser" "Frances" was advertised for sale at the Wivenhoe yard in 1866, and Mr. Welch, a naval constructor responsible for "Her Majesty's cruisers", was frequently at the shipyard.

Many merchant ships and numbers of large smacks for Yarmouth and Lowestoft were coming off the ways as well as dozens of rakish cutters for the fishing fleets of Colne and Blackwater. Fast schooners for the foreign butter trade were also built by the Harveys, including the John Harvey designed "Peri" of 1858. She was built at Wivenhoe and had typical dimensions of 95 foot overall hull length, 85 foot waterline x 19 foot 3 inches beam x 11 foot draught. Her two masted schooner rig set a boomless gaff foresail, a loose-footed boom and gaff mainsail, staysail and four jibs, a large square topsail, with a topgallant and a royal above it, two main topmast staysails, and a very large main gaff topsail with luff laced to the topmast and a topsail yard setting its head well above the main topmast. These heavily rigged schooners loaded with butter, cheese and eggs at Guernsey, in the Channel Islands, and sailed as fast as possible for London, racing all the way; the first to berth getting the best prices.

About 1857 John Harvey was taken into partnership and the firm became Harvey and Son. Personally, John Harvey appears to have been a clear thinking man of great character and integrity, with charming manners and a powerful voice accustomed to summoning men from the far corners of the shipyard, above the noise of shipwrighting. He lived for some years in a house which was part of the yard, later moving to Quay House on Wivenhoe quay, which has since altered little in appearance. His wife suffered much illness and died when her children were young. One of them, John Martin Harvey, born in 1863, though apprenticed in the shipyard with his father's hopes on him as a successor, spent much of his time there studying books from the library of W. S. Gilbert's yacht, which that literary genius permitted him to read. His father realised young John's heart was not in shipbuilding and soon after allowed him to be trained for acting, in which he rose to prominence.

By 1860 the Harvey shipyards were at the height of their fame for yachtbuilding; leading the world in quality and quantity. A contemporary description of a launch

The Harveys of Wivenhoe. Left Thomas, 1803-1885 and right, John, 1830-1901.

typifies the buoyant spirit of that time; "On September 4th, 1860, the handsome pleasure yacht "Ione", built by Harvey and Sons, shipbuilders, Wivenhoe, for Richard Blanchard Esq., Walton-on-Naze, was launched with the usual ceremony, in the presence of numerous spectators. The yacht is 120 tons burden, her keel and fore rake is 84 feet long, length overall 99 feet, main breadth 18 feet 2 inches, height under beam 6 feet 6 inches, draught 9 feet 6 inches aft, 6 feet 6 inches forward. She is built completely of oak, timber and plank, copper fastened with the exception of the floors which are of cast iron, thereby promoting her stability and power of carrying canvas. She is handsomely fitted up, with three cabins, the ladies, main, and owner's; and her total cost was upwards of £3,500. The 'christening' was performed by Mrs. Blanchard, and at the close of the ceremony a sumptuous champagne dejeuner by Salter of the "Cups", Colchester, was served in Harvey's spacious moulding loft. It is understood the firm have received an order for the construction of a yacht for Lord Alfred Paget".

Born in 1816, Lord Alfred was the fifth son of the Marquis of Anglesey, for whom the famous "Pearl" had been built. He became the most prolific yacht owner of the nineteenth century, with over forty yachts, several of them designed and built by the Harveys who produced the best racer he ever owned; the 138 ton yawl "Xantha", launched in 1865 and later renamed "Gertrude". The following season John Harvey designed and built the 107 ton cruising yawl "Waterlily" for Lord Alfred, who in 1867 sold her and commissioned John Harvey to design a 116 foot steam yacht which was built and engined at Palmers' Tyne shipyard, and also named "Xantha". Such rapid change was typical of this Victorian sportsman's outlook.

His skippers and crews were principally Rowhedge men and, in appreciation of their services and skill, he founded a number of almshouses at Rowhedge for their old age, and these are still occupied by descendants of the men who sailed the Paget family's yachts.

The cutter "Audax", launched in 1861, was a failure at first, but next winter, Harvey altered her ballast, including in it some lead from Wivenhoe church, then under restoration, and next season she was reckoned to "Goo like a trine". Shortly afterwards the "Audax" was ordered to Colne instead of competing in the Channel race, which greatly disappointed her Colne crew, as the first prize was a gold cup and a hundred sovereigns, which she stood a good chance of winning. Captain Rayner ignored the owner's instructions and entered the yacht for the race, which she won. The owner's first news of it was in the next day's paper, but he was so pleased that his skipper's impetuous and unparalleled action was quickly forgiven.

In 1864 a Mr. Sneddon, owner of the yachts "Astarte" and "Phryne", challenged Mr. Jones, owner of the yawl "Banshee" and the racing cutter "Thought", to race the latter against a new iron yacht of 28 tons which Sneddon was to have specially built; the winner of the best of three races to become owner of both "Torpid", as the new yacht was named, and "Thought", besides a money stake. The match was sensational and John Harvey and Dan Hatcher were requested to act as umpires. The "Thought" was sailed by Captain Herbert of Brightlingsea and the "Torpid" by Captain Will Penny of Southampton, whose crew of 20 included seven other yacht skippers.

"Torpid" won the first race by 20 minutes and the second by 48 seconds, which was not surprising as, despite their close similarity in Thames tonnage, the "Torpid" was a much larger and more powerful yacht. After the race the victorious owner's steam yacht towed both the racers up Southampton water, in triumph.

The 80 ton yawl "Druid" of 1868 was designed and built by Harvey as a cruiser, but two seasons later her owner entered, for fun, in the class for schooners and yawls against such cracks as the schooners "Flying Cloud" and the America's Cup challenger "Cambria"; both of which she beat handsomely in light weather, to the delight of Captain Forsgate and his Wivenhoe crew, who were even more jubilant when she roared into Harwich a few days later, neck and neck with the big, Brightlingsea manned schooner "Gloriana", and beat her also.

The young Prince of Wales, later King Edward VII, caught his lifelong love of yacht racing as a spectator at many of the Thames matches, following the fleet in his 39 ton steam yacht "Alexandra", built for him by John Harvey at Wivenhoe in 1869 and believed to be the firm's first steamer. She later had local owners, including Wilson Marriage of Colchester and Ernest Beard.

Other Harvey-designed and built steam yachts were the 18 ton "Fairy" of 1872, which was unusual in having twin screws, probably the first such installation made on the Colne; the 55 ton "Gazelle" of 1872 and the 38 ton "Lorna Doone" of 1880, whose engines were by Plenty, of Newbury, Berkshire.

Between 1866 and 1869 the Prince of Wales owned the 37 ton cutter "Dagmar", built by John Harvey in 1865, and was taught the rudiments of sailing by her Colne skipper and crew, aided by Lord Alfred Paget, then the principal equerry to Queen Victoria.

About 1865 Thomas Harvey retired from the shipyard, which he transferred to John, and went to live at Brightlingsea where he bought land extensively and speculated in building houses on it. He also built the Brightlingsea public hall, before his death in 1885.

In later life Thomas Harvey was a regular visitor to Wivenhoe, scorning the railway to walk the seven miles journey carrying, as a walking aid, a 5 foot spline, once a measuring staff for timber. Like many contemporary local people Thomas had become an ardent follower of the Swedish mystic Swedenborg (there was a Swedenborg church in Wivenhoe) and sometimes told his family of his visions of paradise. The ageing shipbuilder particularly stressed the avenue of grand elms he had seen in his dreams of heaven.

The firm became John Harvey and Company and was progressively organised, being one of the earliest in the district equipped with steam saws. Harvey was an advanced designer, constantly seeking lighter construction for yachts and, although he did not originate double-skin planking, he extended and improved its use, besides developing the use of sawn main frames with intermediate bent timbers, combining lightness with strength.

In the "Sea Belle", built in 1874, the floors were the size and shape of those usually fitted in wood, but were made of cast lead with iron cores, and the keelson and bilge stringers were similarly constructed. The famous schooner "Miranda" of 1876 had her internal lead ballast cast in strips to fit the bottom, and these were suspended from the bilge stringers to evenly distribute weight. Like all his contemporaries Harvey fought shy of putting the greater part of a sailing yacht's ballast outside, on her keel, largely because the deep draught engendered by the rating rules encouraged retention of internal weight.

He patented several rig improvements and a form of construction for hollow masts and spars, which were fitted in several noted yachts.

In 1874 a severe fire damaged and destroyed the shipyard buildings, stock and craft under construction, but undaunted, John Harvey rebuilt his workshops, mould loft and offices, and the prodigious production of yachts continued, almost without check. But Harvey's genius did not extend to finance and the yard appears to have suffered from shortage of capital at various times after about 1870. George Pryer, who was also a naval architect, entered partnership about that time and was actively associated with the firm which was then building many of its most notable yachts.

In 1874 Harvey designed and built the schooner "Sea Belle" as a great performer to windward and in hopes of beating the Ratsey schooner "Pantomime", then crack boat of the flourishing class of racing schooners. "Sea Belle's" hull had double skin planking and a powerful rig. She had considerable success, sailed by Captain Harry Harlow of Wivenhoe, and later by Captain John Downes of Brightlingsea.

Two years later Harvey launched the racing schooner "Miranda", his most noted yacht, built for G. E. Lampson. She was designed to reach much faster than the "Sea Belle" and her graceful, moderate displacement hull was set off by a clipper bow. But "Miranda's" principal feature was her rig; the mainmast being so far forward and close to the foremast that she was nicknamed "The cutter rigged schooner". Clever sailing by Captain John Downes brought her to the top of the hotly contested schooner class, followed by Captain Barnes, but her greatest success came later, when Captain Lemon Cranfield of Rowhedge took charge and she beat the big schooner class so often that, after he won £1,415 prize money in 1882, they refused to sail against her, and "Miranda" had to race with the cutters, which she also frequently beat.

Harvey yawls of this period were popular. In 1875 he designed and built the 89 ton "Rosabelle" for Theodore Pim; first of a line of five yachts of that name, all of which have had Colne connections. She seldom raced, but Captain Harry Harlow was fond of getting the best out of her beautifully shaped hull.

In 1869 Harvey launched the 148 ton yawl "Rose of Devon" as a fast cruiser having wholesome proportions, which did not stop her from becoming a prizewinner whenever her owner felt like a race. During the 1880s she sailed an unusual one from Lands End to Plymouth against the naval steam gunboat "Cromer", which was under both sail and steam. The "Rose of Devon" won by four hours, which delighted her crew. She later won a race from Weymouth to Ryde by 6 minutes 8 seconds.

During the 1870s John Harvey was at the peak of his career and, from the several papers which he read before the Institution of Naval Architects, of which in 1860 he was a founder member, we realise that he ranked with Fife, Benjamin Nicholson, Dan Hatcher and Michael Ratsey as one of the world's leading yacht designers and builders. However, he appears to have excelled them in theoretical reasoning and scientific approach to the design of sailing craft, evolving his designs from sound mathematical principles of naval architecture, with detailed design analysis, much of which was published.

In 1875, with this reputation, it was natural that Mr. Ernest H. Bentall of Heybridge, near Maldon, should call John Harvey in when his active fancy ranged to a new yacht of radical form. Principal object of the design was to obtain speed by reducing the area of wetted surface, and its consequent friction, by cutting away her ends. W. P. Stephens, a contemporary yachting authority, wrote of her design; "Mr. Bentall's part went no further than to sketch out the general dimensions and some novel features; the final design, including alterations to the midship section, all calculations, and the adjustment of centres being done by Mr. Harvey". Thus the famous "Jullanar" was the joint product of John Harvey and E. H. Bentall, and was recorded as such in the design credits of contemporary yacht registers.

Harvey anticipated her sailing performance from his design analysis, but also knew she would have been faster in lighter weather had his original and more extreme design been built. Her form had in fact been anticipated by at least two other vessels; the yacht "Austrailia", built at Sydney in 1858, and the fruit cutter "Margaret". John Harvey exhibited "Jullanar's" design in the shipwrights' exhibition of 1875, in competition with those of other yachts. The judging committee's decision was that she was fit for neither cruising nor racing, Harvey and his partner, George Pryer, being the only two naval architects with complete faith in her windward ability.

Fruit schooners and yachts building at Harvey and Son's Halifax shipyard, Ipswich, during the 1850's.
Suffolk Photo Survey

She was originally designed with schooner rig, but this was altered to yawl in the design stage. Her mainmast was well aft and a short bowsprit complemented her clipper bow. Principal dimensions were 110 feet 6 inches overall, 99 foot waterline x 16 feet 8 inches x 13 foot draught aft. Her vertical sternpost, comparatively small rudder tucked well under the hull, and immersed canoe stern, were reminiscent of trends in modern racing yachts. The "Jullanar" was built by direct labour at Heybridge on the Blackwater, where she was launched and towed to Harvey's yard for completion. After a season's use as a cruiser she was fitted out for racing in 1877, under Captain John Downes of Brightlingsea, who sailed her to the top of the yawl class and surpassed it next season by coming into Colne to lay up with prize flags almost dressed overall, and with the best record of any racing yacht that year.

When the "Kitten" was sold to America in 1870, John Harvey designed and built himself a ten ton cruising cutter, resembling a smack, which he whimsically named "Who'd a thought it?". She was later sold to fish from Wivenhoe, where she became known as "the old Hooda".

In 1874 John Harvey was the twentythird amateur yachtsman to obtain his Board of Trade master's certificate and the following year he was actively promoting the formation of the influential Yacht Racing Association, which in recent years has become the Royal Yachting Association. But the most durable of Harvey's achievements was the origination of scantling rules to govern yacht construction. In 1876 he wrote to Dixon Kemp, the sport's chronicler, expressing the opinion that, as owners and insurers of commercial craft were safeguarded by the classification of their vessels by Lloyds Register of Shipping, it would be a good plan to do the same for yachts. The scantlings of trading craft being necessarily heavier than those required for yachts, and the unsatisfactory system of building under no special survey continuing, he submitted that rules be drawn up for this purpose and put forward his own detailed proposals. These were approved by yachting personalities, owners and builders, and a committee was formed; Harvey and Nicholson representing the builders. The rules were framed and Lloyds Register took over the whole scheme, resulting in the establishment of Lloyds Register of yachts and yacht classification as we know it today.

In 1878 John Harvey designed the extreme racing cutter "Muriel" to be built in the U.S.A. where many yachtsmen were rebelling against the traditional, beamy, centreboard type of American yacht in favour of the lean, deep English cutter; a movement aided by the racing success of Harvey's old cutter "Kitten" which was sold to Boston, Massachusetts. The "Muriel's" success brought Harvey several notable design commissions for racing cutters to be built in America, in addition to the continued high output of yachts and smacks at the Wivenhoe yard. However, by 1881 the business appeared to be headed for financial embarrassment and, after thoroughly assessing the situation with George Pryer, John Harvey decided to put the company into voluntary liquidation to ensure that all shareholders and creditors could be paid in full. This was done and the yard closed that year, to the great sorrow of the Harvey family and with severe effects on local employment.

Despite this setback Harvey's great international reputation as a yacht designer was undimmed and, during 1881 he visited New York in connection with the building there of the cutters "Bedouin", "Oriva" and "Wenonah", to his designs. The "cutter craze" was at its height in America and the big, black first class racer "Bedouin" had dimensions of 83 feet overall x 70 feet 2 inches waterline x 15 feet 8 inches beam x 12 feet 2 inches draught. She set 5,795 square feet of canvas and typified in every way John Harvey's ideals for windward ability, but achieved only moderate success in racing, probably due to indifferent handling by her American crew, unaccustomed to the type. Her best year was 1884 when she won eight first prizes in nine starts. The "Bedouin" was a contender in the 1885 trials to select a defender for the America's Cup, against the British "Genesta". Thus, the same Englishman who assisted in designing the "Volante", which bad luck robbed of beating the "America" in 1851, also designed a possible defender of the America's Cup.

With the shipyard closed Harvey decided to emigrate to the U.S.A. and continued supervision of yachts to his design, besides acting as yachting editor of the "Forest and Stream" magazine for a short time. In 1883 he designed the 43 foot cutter "Surf" as a fast cruiser for two American owners; Rathbone and Zerega. She was built by George Byles of City Island and was contemporarily recorded as "Remarkable for exceptional dryness, buoyancy and ease in her behaviour". With dimensions of 35 feet 3 inches waterline x 7 feet 4 inches beam x 7 feet 4 inches draught she, typically, set 985 square feet in mainsail, staysail and jib, without her various sized topsails, and heeled to 35-40 degrees in strong winds, despite 6 tons of lead and three tons of inside ballast.

John Harvey was later associated with William Gardner, a U.S. citizen who had been privileged to study naval architecture at the Royal Naval College, Greenwich. In 1888 Gardner opened a design office in New York and Harvey appears to have been a partner for several years. He was still working there in 1892 and was remembered as retaining his Essex accent.

They had early success with the 60 foot racing cutter "Liris" for Colgate Hoyt and Charles Whetmore, noted New York yachtsmen. The orders came steadily after that and the design office worked long hours; Harvey draughting far into the night with wax candles fixed all round his board. The last craft he designed in America was a miniature cutter for Edward M. Padleford, which was only 14 feet 9 inches overall x 11 feet 11 inches waterline x 3 feet 6 inches beam x 3 feet 4 inches draught.

John Harvey returned to England in May 1898 to retire, although he proposed to continue research into the construction of double skin vessels. G. L. Watson, then at the height of his career, wrote letters to the "Field" and "Yachtsman" magazines proposing a presentation fund for John Harvey in recognition of his many services to yachting; Watson heading the list with 50 guineas, followed by leading yachting personalities including William Fife, Edwin Lapthorn and E. H. Bentall.

John Harvey died in England in 1901, in obscurity, unmarked by comment in the yachting press. However, his name should be recalled with pride on the Colne as one of the world's greatest yacht designers and builders, a pioneer in the development of fast sailing craft, and the connecting link between the old type of designer—yacht-builder and the competent professional naval architect.

John Harvey's Wivenhoe Shipyard, 1878.

CHAPTER NINETEEN

Steel and Steam

STEEL shipbuilding combined with marine engineering was introduced to the Colne by Forrestt and Son, who moved from the Thames to Wivenhoe in 1888 and founded a tradition of building small ships and special service vessels which inspired other local shipbuilders, and survives in yards at Wivenhoe and Brightlingsea.

The business was founded in 1788 by Thomas Forrestt, who built ships and boats at various small, Thames-side yards. After his death the firm passed to his sons, Thomas and W. A. Forrestt who expanded the firm, which settled in yards at Blackwall, and Norway yard, Limehouse. The sons died in 1875 and a limited company was formed named Forrestt and Sons, Ltd. Restriction of space at Limehouse and the high cost of Thames labour, coupled with the desire to build steel ships, made a move desirable and, in 1888, the company took over the Wivenhoe shipyard site, then experiencing one of the unused periods of its centuries of shipbuilding; J. Edwin Wilkins having vacated it the previous year.

Forrestt's, as the firm quickly became known on the Colne, reconstructed the shipyard in the most efficient manner, leading a railway spur into the premises and its shops, to facilitate materials handling and the despatch of small craft. In 1889 they constructed a dry dock 205 foot long and having 14 foot 6 inches of water on its sill, unique in being the only one between Lowestoft and the Thames. The patent slip was renovated and plate, anglesmiths, engineers and galvanising shops were erected to cope with a wide variety of work. A range of vessels were soon on the stocks, overshadowed by the wooden, 131 foot steam barquentine "Southern Cross", building for the Melanesian Mission Society, for welfare and educational work amongst the Pacific Islands.

She was similar to the yacht "Sunbeam", but her rig was fitted with patent reefing gear, enabling sail to be shortened from the deck. The "Southern Cross" could accommodate 78 people, including six missionaries, and was fitted with class-rooms and recreation spaces. Her 130 horsepower steam engine drove a feathering propeller and she made the 15,112 mile passage out to New Zealand in 109 days. Her best day's run was 230 miles under sail alone.

In 1890 Forrestts built the 40 rater racing cutter "Creole" for Col. Villiers Bagot, to designs by G. L. Watson. She was composite-built and raced with great success for several years under Captain Tom Skeats of Brightlingsea, with a Colne crew, and was later regularly racing in the handicap class under Captain Leavitt of Tollesbury.

But Forrestt's ambition was to build the more profitable steel craft and their first steel order, and the first steel vessel built on the Colne, was the steam oyster boat

The Shipbuilder. Edward Pullen, shipwright foreman at Forrestt's shipyard. Standing inside the framing of the wood steam tug *Penguin*, built at Wivenhoe for Callao, Peru, 1903.

"Surprise", for Heath of Wivenhoe; a beamy, tug-like craft engined by Mumford of Colchester, who built steam sets for many locally built vessels. Forrestts also quickly became prolific builders of marine steam engines, and much other marine equipment, and their engineering side was always particularly able.

Forrestt's reputation was founded on building specialised craft quickly and at attractive prices; business they developed to an astonishing variety at Wivenhoe, setting the pattern for Colneside shipbuilding which has lasted to the present.

It is only possible to briefly survey their large output which, in even that era of callous industrial relations, made the yard workmen really proud of the vessels designed and built there. There were steel, wood and composite craft; including steam launches of all sorts and sizes, surf boats, cargo barges, bucket dredgers, firefighting steamers, the early oil tank steamer "Homelight", shallow draught gunboats, mining launches, the 50 foot paddle dredger "Pyefleet" for the Colchester oyster fishery, small boats of all kinds, hopper barges, grab dredgers, the 185 foot steam lighthouse tender "Beacon", target towing craft, steam and sailing yachts, lifeboats, pontoons, and sternwheel, side wheel and tunnel screw steamers for foreign service.

During the winter of 1891-92 Forrestt's built a number of torpedo boats for the Belgian government's Congo forces and solved the problem of taking these complex little craft of limited seaworthiness out, by the novel method of purchasing the three-masted barque "Moira", which was towed up to Wivenhoe and the warships were lifted on board to voyage to Africa under sail.

Soon after, they laid down the 140 foot passenger steamer "Tern" for the Furness Railway services on Lake Windermere. She was one of Forrestt's earliest "re-erection" jobs; a type of work which became commonplace on the Colne and which is still occasionally built, usually for service abroad. The vessel was constructed in the usual way but was not riveted up, being bolted together on the berth. When complete, each plate and angle, piece and part, was numbered to key with specially prepared plans and also, often, coloured bands were painted on hull and decks to aid identification when the craft was reassembled. After dismantling, the pieces were packed in crates and secured in bundles for transport to destination, where she was "re-erected", to be riveted up and launched on site, often under the superintendence of a man from the builders. The "Tern" was launched in 1891 to carry 700 passengers and it is a tribute to Forrestt's workmanship that, 79 years later, she is still at work on the lake, having been re-engined with diesels.

The 74 foot steamer "Cecil Rhodes" was a re-erection job which was different, being launched and running a trial trip before being dismantled into pieces not exceeding 70 pounds weight, which were carried overland between Lake Nyassa and Lake Tanganyika, where she worked on laying the Cairo to Cape Town telegraph cable.

Portable boats for exploring expeditions were an unusual speciality of Forrestt's. The 28 foot lugsail boat "Advance", immortalised in H. M. Stanley's explorations of Africa, was built by them in 13 days and earned high praise from the explorer. Similar sectional boats of aluminium were also built, notably for Major Gibbon's trans-African expedition in 1898, when Forrestt's produced a series of boats, each section of which could be carried by two bearers. The sections could be put together in various ways "Forming three separate boats of such sizes as may be most convenient".

Amphibious boats were built for many countries, particularly Sweden. Many had railway type wheels driven from the boat's engine by clutches, enabling them to traverse small lakes as a normal boat and emerge to mount rails when the propeller stopped and proceed ashore like a narrow gauge train.

In 1896 Forrestt's boatshop constructed 35 ships' boats for Chilean cruisers then building at Vickers of Elswick, where a special train carried them from Wivenhoe station.

The Admiralty ordered an 85 ft. diving bell barge for laying and inspecting battleship and cruiser moorings at Gibraltar; an intricate craft equipped with air compressors, elaborate pumps and a lowering tube, fitted with air locks, leading to the cylindrical diving bell which was complete with pneumatic drills, electric light and telephones.

Soon after, the contrasting spritsail barges "Niagara", "Atrato" and "Wyvenhoe" were built in steel, and the 85 foot pointed-stern ketch barge "Lady of the Lake" was a re-erection job for service on Lake Nyassa. She was one of several similar leeboard barges Forrestt's built for Africa, and elsewhere.

In 1897 the Spanish government ordered seven steam gunboats from Forrestt's for service in Cuba, then on the brink of revolution, and all these 70 foot steamers were designed and delivered within three months of date of order.

Forrestt's introduced the building of shallow draught river steamers for foreign service to the Colne and the chunking paddles and tall funnels of these two and three deckers became familiar sights on the stocks or running trials down the river. Their

Launch of Thames firefloat *Beta* at Forrestt's Wivenhoe shipyard, 1903. A typical Edwardian launching group.

Platers and hand rivetters at Forrestt's Wivenhoe shipyard about 1900. Typical tradesmen who founded the Colne's tradition of steel shipbuilding.

very shallow hulls lacked longitudinal strength and were braced at the sides, fore and aft, by trussing; often steel wires passing over kingposts which were sometimes incorporated in the spindly superstructures which carried the cabins and the helmsman's position, right forward. The boiler was placed forward, usually with a wood burning furnace, and the main steam pipe ran along the deck to the horizontal engine cylinders on each quarter sponson, where whirring cranks drove the great wheel with its wooden floats kicking a smother of foam.

Dozens of these craft were built at Wivenhoe shipyard in many sizes too varied to detail. The 100 foot "Raven" for the Niger was typical in having a beam of 19 feet and a hull depth of only 4 feet. Fully loaded with passengers and cargo she would float in only 22 inches of water, yet could steam at 10 miles per hour; the units in which all sternwheeler speeds were reckoned.

Almost all the sternwheelers were re-erection jobs but some were sent out in sections. Forrestt's built the steel sternwheelers "Killock" and "Selenga" for service on the river Amour, in connection with the building of the Trans-Siberian railway. They were designed in 16 sections for shipment to Vladivostock, and the completed dimensions were 140 foot x 28 foot x 4 foot x 30 inch draught, and they made 11 miles per hour on trials down Colne. Their design was developed for the similar sternwheel gunboats "El-Fateh", "En-Naser" and "Ez-Zafeh", which Forrestt's built rapidly for Lord Kitchener's Nile expedition in 1896, but the speed increased to 14 m.p.h.

The 160 foot steel shallow draught steamer "Corona" was the most spectacular of this type of craft built at Wivenhoe. She was fitted out as the Nigerian Governor-General's yacht; the most practical method of touring that vast country being by water, and her accommodation was on three decks. The twin propellers worked in "tunnels" or depressions in the hull at the stern, and with full crew, stores and fuel she drew only 24 inches. She steamed at $10\frac{1}{2}$ m.p.h. and was one of the first locally built craft fitted with refrigerators. The "Corona" ran trials down Colne with shipwrights still working on her sun deck. After acceptance her sides were boarded up and she was prepared for the long tow out to Nigeria astern of a big Dutch tug which picked her up off Mersea Stone on a calm summer morning.

But clouds were gathering at Wivenhoe; for Forrestt's made a loss between 1892-1898, and only a very small profit in the three following years. By 1903 the company was in liquidation, due principally to the loss sustained by having continued to build small boats at the Norway yard, and lack of working capital. A winding-up order was made against them by the Zambesi Traffic Co., for whom Forrestt's had contracted to build several craft. However, in 1904 the company was reconstructed as Forrestt and Co. and concentrated on steel vessels, but also built in wood. The drydock was lengthened to 237 feet to accommodate the longer ships and yachts building and repairing at the yard. The considerable numbers of large yachts, especially steamers, manned from and regularly laying up at Wivenhoe, Rowhedge and Brightlingsea were often beyond the capacity of local slips and made busy demands on this one local dock, particularly in spring, when additional tradesmen were needed to ensure their refit in time for the summer season. Many were also fitted out in autumn for the winter season in the Mediterranean. The dock was built with a heavily "veed" floor to suit the sharp bottoms of such craft and this proved a disadvantage with the flat bottomed ships of later years.

The labour force fluctuated but Forrestt's became a splendid nursery for shipbuilding craftsmen, turning out the very best type of skilled apprentice in all trades. I was fortunate enough to work under many of these men in later life, while serving my apprenticeship, and have never met their equals elsewhere.

To cope with the increasing and profitable steelwork the management imported a number of North Country platers and blacksmiths, who gradually mellowed into the local scene and whose descendants still live locally. Traditionally, shell platers are kingpins of steel shipbuilding, more especially in those days of all riveted construction. One of these northcountrymen emphasised this by regularly appearing for work in a hard hat, and when cambering a plate indicating where his perspiring helpers should strike with their hammers by tapping the spot with a piece of rod: rounding off the performance by smoking a cigar in defiance of works regulations. However, in view of his excellent workmanship little was said to him. Smoking was forbidden in local shipyards until the 1939 war, but the rule was often surreptitiously broken.

Although much beer was consumed at the Shipwrights Arms during breakfast and dinner time, drinking in the yard was almost unknown; an exception being an old spar maker who always kept a bottle of rum in his tool box where, if the foreman found him grovelling over it, the old man complained fiercely of stomach cramp!

A continuous run of employment was then uncommon and skilled and unskilled labour was engaged and sacked as work demanded. Though this seems callous by today's standards it was the only way the industry could survive on the small profits and frequent losses made by building a such wide variety of specialised craft. The day's work commenced with clocking-on at 6 a.m. Between 8-30 a.m. and 9-0 a.m. all hands took breakfast, many in the welcoming doors of the Shipwrights Arms, where trestle tables were loaded with piles of sandwiches and pots of beer. Dinner was between 1-2 p.m. and for Rowhedge employees meant a trudge to the ferry and return within the hour. The day ended at 5-30 p.m. and on Saturdays at 1-0 p.m., making a 56½ hour week for which a shipwright received 31/6d. As ever, the boilermakers earned more—how much more the shipwrights never discovered. The ironworkers also received a bonus and the wage differential between these trades has always caused dissatisfaction to the highly skilled shipwrights. Piecework, with its often cut-throat prices and "squad" systems of payment sharing earnings, often brought trouble and, sometimes, hardship. Probably the riveters earned most from this system in both senses of the term as "knocking down" up to 700 rivets each day was expected of a good riveter in the days before "the machines".

The only holidays then recognised by employers were Christmas day and the bank holidays—all taken without pay, as was any longer break such as if a rare week's holiday was desired. Under these circumstances trade unions flourished; not the extreme variety of the industrial areas but a restless movement amongst skilled men respectfully seeking a better living standard, recognition of their skills and, most of all, some security for families dependent, in sickness, on whatever savings they could scrape together, or on charity. The trade union sick clubs were then of benefit beyond present appreciation.

Forrestt's most brilliant versatility was displayed in 1904 when they built the submarine "Volta" for the British Submarine Company under conditions of great secrecy, in a corner of the main building shed, during the Russian-Japanese war. Extremely few practical submarines were then in service and the 34 ft. "Volta" was designed by A. Hilliard Atteridge to be carried into action by a parent ship or to be used for harbour defence. She was powered solely by electric batteries, which restricted her endurance to about 40 miles. There was one main ballast tank and she was trimmed for diving or surfacing by a movable weight running on rails, fore and aft. A pump maintained equilibrium for running at various depths. The crew of three comprised captain, engineer and a torpedo man, and she first ran submerged trials in the dry dock. Later, in the Colne, she dropped her emergency ballast weight which, when released, allowed her to rise like a cork, in case of breakdown.

The government were suspicious of the Wivenhoe submarine's final destination and on the day she was due to leave drydock a customs officer boarded her and refused to leave until Forrestt's gave written undertaking that the "Volta" would not leave the country unless notice was given to the authorities. But the "Volta" was to have no dramatic adventures; her compass would not work properly due to the complex electrics on board and, with money running short, she left the yard for a now undiscoverable fate.

Forrestt's also constructed steel steam yachts including the 82 foot "Cysne" and the larger "Cysne II", both specially designed for cruising the Dutch waterways; the rakish 91 foot "Sado" for the King of Portugal, and the luxurious "Mansa Kil Ba", built for the Governor of Gambia and unusual in having triple screws. The 146 foot "Sea King", built in 1910, was probably the ugliest craft launched at the yard and unusual in being a luxurious, self-propelled houseboat, owned by Baron Barreto, who later took her to Austrian waters. Several yachts of galvanised steel construction were built, such as the steamers "Paladin" and "Alabama", and the yawl "Coryphée". The steam yachts "Elfin" (65 feet) and "Pearl" (48 feet) were built as re-erection jobs for Lake Windermere.

In 1913 the 80 foot wood motor yacht "Brabo" was built on the Railway Quay, for Belgian owners. She was propelled by twin, 90 horse power heavy oil engines and was amongst the earliest diesel yachts built in the world.

Forrestts also continued to build, and lose money on, wood sailing yachts. The South Coast one-design racers "Jean", "Gracie" and "Heroine" were launched in 1903 to designs by Alfred Mylne, who called these 24 tonners "Gentlemen's day sailing boats". The fine yawls "Aline" and "Alia" were also built from Fred Shepherd's designs.

The yard also built many steel steam tugs of all types and sizes up to 105 feet ship-handling giants, such as the "Sun VII", fitted with a 650 Indicated Horse Power engine. To assist at launching, and for docking and trials attendance work, Forrestt's owned, in succession, the small steam tugs "Enterprise", "Wyvern" and "Forrester"; known to the yard as "creeping Jenny" for her slowness. Later they built themselves the "Girl Guide".

Scores of Admiralty small craft were built in wood; 40 feet pinnaces and 52 foot vedette boats predominating. Before 1907 Forrestt's were installing diesel engines in the 52 footers, but vibration troubles brought a reversion to the smoothness of steam.

In May 1906 the yard commenced the 115 foot wood steam tug "Penguin" for Callao, Peru, probably the most heavily constructed wood vessel launched on the river.

Her oak framing was enormous and dwarfed conventional commercial construction. Shipwright foreman Edward Pullen and his men revelled in building what was to be the most powerful tug in South America.

Two years later Forrestt's constructed a steel "salvage tube", 90 feet long by 6 feet in diameter, for a syndicate proposing to recover the gold lost in the frigate "Lutine", wrecked off the Dutch coast. The tube was tried in the Colne off Brightlingsea, being suspended between two sailing barges, and its lower end, fitted with a working chamber, was lowered to the bottom. Shortly afterwards the tube was abandoned after being hauled up in John James' Brightlingsea yard, where it was broken up for scrap in 1939.

Financial troubles led to negotiations for a merger and in 1912 the shipyard came largely under the control of G. Rennie and Company of Greenwich who, like many Thames-side steel shipbuilders, were then being forced out of London by labour difficulties and costs. They transferred their steelworkers and foremen, with much machinery, to Wivenhoe and the firm became the Rennie, Forrestt Shipbuilding, Engineering and Dry Dock Co. Ltd.

The variety of work continued. In 1913 the 162 foot three masted, auxiliary steam, training schooner "Exmouth II" was built for the Metropolitan Asylums Board, to provide sea training for orphans and waifs to enter the merchant service and the

Ships lying at Wivenhoe for repair and conversion by Rennie, Forrestt's shipyard, 1920.

steam trawling industry. She was one of the noblest looking ships built at the yard, and was based at Grays, Essex. In appearance and arrangement she greatly resembled the present sail training schooners "Sir Winston Churchill" and "Malcolm Miller", except that she was more heavily rigged. Her steam engine was by Mumford of Colchester and she attained 8 knots.

The new company maintained Forrestt's lifeboat building traditions and constructed two copies of the Royal National Lifeboat Institution Hunstanton boat for the Turkish government lifeboat service, immediately before the 1914 war. At its outbreak, Rennie, Forrestt's, like many British shipyards, were left with many foreign contracts cancelled and a second pair of these lifeboats were stopped, the inverted hull of one of them eventually becoming a chicken house.

Steel lifeboats were also built at Wivenhoe for Russia, and one for Nigeria which was named "Mosely" and served with distinction as a gunboat in the Cameroons campaign against the German forces.

The contract for one Turkish vessel named "Reched Pasha" was taken over by the Admiralty and she was launched as H.M.S. "Wave" but the shipyard closed for a short time after the outbreak of war. It reopened in 1916 to cope with the increasing demands for small ships. Armed trawlers quickly proved invaluable for minesweeping and patrol work and the Admiralty placed many orders for the standard "Strath" type. Rennie, Forrestt built nineteen of these 115 foot x 22 foot x 13 foot steel ships, which could steam at 10 knots.

Improved minesweeping techniques and operations off the Belgian coast required shallow draught minesweepers and the Wivenhoe yard was naturally chosen to build several of the "Dance" class, including the "Pirouette" which, on dimensions of 130 feet x 26 feet x 7 feet, drew only 3 foot 6 inches. Although the propellers were in tunnels they could steam at 10 knots in a seaway, and were amongst the most unusual Colne built warships.

81 foot 6 inch steel, shallow draught tugs were also built for the Tigris and Euphrates service and the Mesopotamia Expeditionary Force. Developing 300 horse power on only 36 inch draught, they were of great value in that hard fought but now almost forgotten campaign.

The dry dock was an asset of national importance (as it was also to be during the second world war) in being the only one between Sheerness and Lowestoft. It was hardly ever empty of naval and merchant vessels under repair or fitting out.

The "Strath" trawler programme continued after the armistice and several were not launched until late in 1919 or early 1920. These were completed as fishing vessels, for which purpose Rennie, Forrestt's were busy reconverting many minesweeping trawlers at that time.

Several ex-German merchant steamers were brought up to the yard to be refitted for service under new owners and these 250 footers moored in the river, causing considerable congestion, worsened when the 250 foot American, four masted merchant schooner "Gloria" arrived for conversion to twin auxiliary diesel power. Rennie, Forrestt's were also pioneer builders of motor coasters and launched the 89 foot "Cristo", fitted with a 120 horse power Bolinder engine.

The company became associated with other shipbuilders; Ritchie, Graham and Milne Ltd. of Whiteinch, Glasgow, and William Chalmers and Co. Ltd. of Rutherglen, Glasgow; the consortium being known as the Rennie, Ritchie and Newport Shipbuilding Co. Ltd. with yards at Wivenhoe, Rutherglen and Newport, Monmouthshire, the head office being in London. The yard underwent considerable post-war reorganisation and laid down three new berths capable of building steel ships up to 250 feet in length. A large new engine shop was erected and the firm built standard triple expansion marine steam engines of 100, 200, 300, 430 and 660 Indicated Horse Power. They undertook the complete installation of all the craft built and a fitting out wharf was built with a 40 ton lift sheerlegs and a 9 ton crane. A self-contained yard for building re-erection vessels had been laid out adjacent to the railway quay, on a site now occupied by Harbourmaster Ltd. This had its own platers' and anglesmiths' shops.

Rennie's introduced a type of standard cargo steamship with machinery aft, 207 foot length B.P. x 35 feet x 15 feet 9 inches depth and drawing 14 foot 8 inches when loaded to 1,425 tons deadweight. Two boilers supplied steam to the triple expansion engines which were built by the shipyard. These were the largest ships ever launched from a Colne shipyard, and were a considerable enterprise.

The "Maindy Transport" and "Maindy Tower" were built in 1920, the "Maindy Keep" in 1921 and the "Maindy Cottage" in 1922, completed after the yard had closed for a short period. A fifth ship of the type was laid down but remained incomplete, for the slump in shipping had begun and, as the dole queues lengthened, her rusting hull lay in the quieter yard. Eventually she was launched for Dutch owners who towed her to Holland for completion.

By then the yard had so few men that, to set her up for launch, the foreman shipwright had to walk round Wivenhoe calling in sufficient ex-employees for the day.

In 1925 the yard changed names again, becoming Otto Andersen and Co. (London) Ltd., who struggled on into the deepening depression, even commencing to build semi-diesel engines.

The shipyard closed in 1930, having been bought by Shipbuilder's Securities Ltd.; a group then actively purchasing and closing various British shipyards to rationalise the industry's capacity. A forty year embargo on steel shipbuilding was laid on the shipyard which stood, echoing and empty, with grass growing on the berths and mud filling the dry dock, until it was reopened by Wivenhoe Shipyard Ltd., a company associated with the Rowhedge Ironworks Co. Ltd., in November 1939.

The *Maindy Transport* sailing from the builders' yard at Wivenhoe on her maiden voyage, 1920.

CHAPTER TWENTY

Aldous of Brightlingsea

DECEMBER 1962 brought closure of the Brightlingsea Shipyard of Aldous Successors Ltd., ending 129 years of enterprise in yacht and small ship building.

In 1833 James Aldous, a local builder and contractor, acquired the creekside site, believed to have been previously used for shipbuilding by Matthew Warren during the Napoleonic Wars, and earlier by Philip John Sainty, prior to his removal to Colchester Hythe around 1800. Aldous seems to have continued his contracting interests, building St. James' Chapel of Ease in Brightlingsea's High Street during 1835, besides many rows of houses. Gradually the shipyard claimed all his attention and ability, founding its reputation on fishing vessels and yachts. The cutter "Fawn" built by Aldous in 1846 is reputed to be the first yacht built at Brightlingsea, though I suspect there were several before her as some were built at Colchester and Wivenhoe over 40 years previously and had frequented the river from that time.

By 1855 racing yachts designed and built by Aldous were attracting attention, especially the 9 tonner "Violet", first of a series of that name built at Brightlingsea for J. R. Kirby of Ramsgate. In her maiden race on the Thames, she worked completely to windward of the whole class, beating them by over a mile after an hour's sailing. She enjoyed great success until beaten by the radical 10 tonner "Kitten" designed by the youthful John Harvey of Wivenhoe, who was to offer an increasingly strong challenge to Aldous.

In 1858 another "Violet" left the ways to become perhaps the most notable of all the Aldous yachts. She did little for three years until sold to H. Kennard and renamed "Christabel", commencing a splendid racing career after being lengthened and improved by Aldous, to emerge as a fast boat in sheltered waters, winning races all round the coast against the Harvey designed "Audax" and "Volante", and the "Thought" by Hatcher. Eventually she was beaten by the new "Phryne" and "Phosphorus" but her successes continued during 1863 when she won the 'Ocean Race' from Cherbourg to Ryde against 20 starters, including the crack "Glance" sailed by George Bartlett of Wivenhoe, and several other Harvey designed yachts.

It was an era of rapid development and during the following season "Christabel" remained laid-up as outclassed. However, such was the faith of owner and builder in the old cutter that she was hauled up at Brightlingsea, sawn in two, and again lengthened to 65 feet, a common practice at that time. But now they had gilded the lily as she was long, low, and wet in heavy weather and although she beat the new Poole-built "Hirondelle" and won the Southampton Town Cup in a gale with the loss of her bowsprit and dinghy, she could not match Hatcher's new "Niobe" sailed by old Tom Diaper of Itchen. The Scottish cutter "Surf" and her old rival "Volante", sailed by Wivenhoe's George Pittuck, also snatched a few prizes from her. Even so, she entered Brightlingsea creek wearing flags for 15 first and 4 second prizes, with £115 as her crew's share of the £5,718 paid that year for the racing fleet's 112 matches. I have not discovered the name of "Christabel's" skipper but it may have been Brightlingsea's Jack Downes or Southampton's Will Penny, prominent at the time.

1866 was the high water mark of "Christabel's" career. She stormed into Harwich to win the Down Swin match, and in the boisterous Nore to Dover race led a fleet of 17 schooners and cutters, and the enormous 209 ton lugger yacht "New Moon". The little "Christabel" sailed magnificently through a heavy channel sea, only to be beaten by the beautiful schooner "Egeria" when within a few hundred yards of Dover harbour, where 10,000 spectators cheered her gallant effort. At the Mersey regattas, "Christabel" at last really met her match in the new Fife boat "Fiona", pride of the Clyde and, although she beat the "Vanguard", sailed by Ben Harris of Itchen, she could not catch the flying Scot, who won by a bare 40 seconds after a terrific struggle, but was protested by the "Christabel" for "bearing out" her headsails, then prohibited although sail area remained unrestricted.

After that season the new creations of Fife and Harvey proved too much for the gallant "Christabel" which settled back for a long and useful life as a cruiser but, even then, they could not leave her hull alone, for it was again almost completely rebuilt in 1883 and, soon afterwards, re-rigged as a ketch. The old yacht finally ended her career by being broken up in 1908.

The 1860's saw Aldous at the height of his fame and activity as the designer and builder of racing yachts. His creations rivalled those of the five other notable designers of the period: John Harvey of Wivenhoe, Wanhill of Poole, Dan Hatcher of Southampton, Inman of Lymington and Will Fife II of Fairlie. These well-whiskered old timers liked racing aboard their productions and Aldous spent some time aboard the fleet little "Satanella" which he built in 1865 for the then popular 15 ton class to meet Hatcher's "Octoroon", which she beat easily. Hatcher replied with the "Queen", cock of the Solent, which challenged "Satanella" on the Thames in a hard fought race from Erith, round the Chapman and back. The respective designers were aboard urging their craft on and the Aldous boat won by a short margin.

There is a fine robust atmosphere about the races of those times, when yachts started at anchor with headsails down and carried, besides their large racing crews, many hands below deck to hump the bags of shot ballast from bilge to bilge when turning to windward; for all their ballast was inside.

The little "Satanella" made the rounds of the coastal regattas, to the Clyde and back to the East Coast to beat yet another Hatcher boat, the "Vampire", in the Yorkshire and Great Yarmouth regattas. "Satanella" won £70 that season and was still racing with success in the Solent 16 years later. The 7 tonner

Robert Aldous, with foreman Rashbrook, making the daily round of his Brightlingsea yard.

"Rifleman" and the 80 ton schooner "Fleur-de-Lys" were other noted Aldous racers of the time, when the yard was coming into the charge of Edwin Aldous, eldest son of the founder.

Building racing yachts is never a very profitable business and, rather than continue the growing struggle against Hatcher, Harvey and Fife, Aldous chose to concentrate on refitting and repairing the increasing numbers of yachts which Colneside skippers were bringing to lay up there each winter. In 1867 the shipyard launched the 25 ton steam yacht "Christine", which I believe to be the first powered craft built at Brightlingsea, though her engines were supplied by Saberton of Norwich.

Although Aldous had lost interest in building racers he continued to produce a number of fine cruisers of all sizes. "Peregrine", "Stork", "Folly", and "Mabel" are still remembered and one of them, the 52 foot yawl "Mignonette" built in 1867, featured in one of the most gruesome incidents ever recorded at sea. In May, 1884, she was sold to Australian owners and sailed with a professional crew comprising the skipper, two hands, one of them Edward Brookes of Brightlingsea, and the boy,

Richard Parker of Itchen. Around the Equator, she ran into heavy weather and the battered yacht leaked so badly that she sank on the 4th July. All hands abandoned her in the 14 foot dinghy (also built by Aldous) which was so damaged in launching that a jersey had to be stuffed into her holed planking and they baled continually in the heavy sea. As provisions they had two tins of preserved turnips, but not drinking water, though they caught some rain. After drifting four days without food a turtle was caught which sustained them for eight days, after which they finished the second tin of food. By now all were desperately hungry and thirsty, and the boy Parker drank sea water and collapsed, after which one man proposed that they should survive by killing the boy and eating him, casting lots to determine the killer. Brookes did not agree and went into the bow while the skipper prayed for forgiveness before cutting the boy's throat. The three men ate his flesh and lived until, after 24 days adrift in the tropics, they were picked up by a German steamer and landed at Falmouth. There the killers were charged with murder, but Brookes was cleared. After a long trial at Exeter, the skipper and hand received the death sentence which was shortly afterwards commuted to six months' imprisonment in view of the circumstances.

From his start as a shipbuilder, Aldous was well known for his fishing vessels and completion of the Brightlingsea branch line in the mid 1860's brought larger landings

The 48 ton cutter *Christabel* racing in 1862. Designed and built by Aldous in 1858, and the pride of Brightlingsea.

in rail contact with Billingsgate and gave terrific impetus to the ordering of larger smacks by Colne fishermen. The shipwrights' trade boomed against a background of daylight to dark labour. Keel after keel was laid in Aldous' yard and the graceful hulls, in frame, planked or fitting out, dominated an optimistic waterside alive with the clump of adze and click of caulking mallets. Those fine cutters fared all round the British Isles and far beyond in search of shellfish, their grace and ability catching the eye of fishermen in many parts, resulting in further orders for Aldous from places as widely separated as Liverpool, Hull, Bosham, Anglesey, Skibereen and Mumbles, whence a delegation travelled to Colneside to place orders for cutters similar to those from Colne which had almost stripped their own oyster grounds yet had excited their envy! At this period the yard became almost a "smack factory", building no less than 36 twenty to forty tonners between 1857-1866, besides many smaller smacks and other vessels, all of them, of course, by hand; heavy and shaped timber being pit sawn.

Aldous always strove for perfection in hull form, rig, and gear, whether it was a bold 40 tonner for the North Sea and Channel fisheries, a dashing 15 tonner for spratting or fish trawling, or a beamy, shoal draught dredger for the local oyster fisheries; into the design and construction of each went all his artistry of form and faithfulness of construction, for speed under sail meant profit for the fisherman, and careful building minimised repairs in a hard trade. From his draughted lines a section and ribband model was often made to confirm the judgement of his eye, and decorate the walls of the mould loft. After laying off and scrieving the shipwrights soon had the oak frames rising on the keel and before long were spiling the clear pine planking. Launch day might see a simple ceremony, the bottle broken by the owner's wife or child and, pe haps a garland of flowers at the stem head as the black hull slid into the creek before warping under the sheers to receive her mast, with a silver shilling under it for good luck. Always religous, Aldous provided a bible in a box for the cabin of each smack built, and he must have thrilled when each weighed for the first time and the lofty rig drove the bold hull out of Colne to the greetings of her sisters, for there is a unique atmosphere about the building and maiden trip of any fishing vessel, which carried the hopes and labours of men in their greatest speculation against the sea.

Often the origins and owner-builder relationship of these Aldous built smacks are delightful examples of local lore. The little "Deerhound" built for a West Mersea fisherman/yachtsman in 1889, is one. Her owner was serving in the crew of Captain Nottage's 40 rater "Deerhound", under the Rowhedge racing skipper Tom Jay. While the yacht was on passage down the Irish Sea at night, in heavy weather, the skipper, who always steered from the lee side, was swept overboard and only saved by the quick-witted Merseaman grabbing him by the hair and dragging back aboard. In thanks, Captain Jay is said to have presented his rescuer with £100, which he promptly decided to invest in a new smack for his favourite trade of winkling on the Dengie flats. Writing his family to order a new smack from Aldous for his return from the racing season, they sailed round to Brightlingsea (the quickest way of getting there in those days) and duly placed the order. Robert Aldous, bearing in mind that the owner was a racing man, designed a delightfully dainty, but sharp bottomed little cutter which, though a joy to sail, was practically useless for the frequent grounding of the winkling trade and was eventually sold by her despairing owner! The "Deerhound" is still in service as a yacht.

The longevity of Aldous-built smacks is astonishing. Only the other day I was admiring the sleek, hauled-out hull of one of them, the swift sailing Tollesbury "Bertha", a 15 tonner reputed to have once beaten the champion Rowhedge "Neva" in a smack race—itself sufficient tribute to the ability of her builder and crew. Strangely enough, probably the most travelled of all the smaller smacks built by Aldous, the West Mersea "Daisy", started life in 1884 as a Blackwater oyster dredger. After over 50 years spent mainly inside the bar buoy, she was bought by Douglas Dixon for use as a cruising yacht, renamed "Dusmarie" and sailed about the North Sea and to the Baltic, where she became the H.Q. ship for his pre-war Manno schoolboy adventure expeditions. Caught laid up in Lapland by Hitler's war, she weathered ice and snow until peace came and her owner returned to find her still serviceable, but needing repairs in which the Baltic shipwrights superimposed the flaring topsides of their native craft on to her low Essex hull, with startling, though pleasing effect. No Colne or Blackwater mariner would now readily recognise "Daisy" the dredgerman in the high-sided yawl which nevertheless returned home to win the Mersea smack race in 1954, before leaving to continue her wanderings in the Mediterranean.

The Brightlingsea ketch "Excellent" was perhaps the most successful of all the North Sea smacks built by Aldous, and has been described as the smartest ketch smack known to local seamen, turning to windward almost like a cutter. She ended her days in the scallop fishery.

Aldous also lengthened many smacks, including the 18 ton Brightlingsea "Globe", built at Wivenhoe in 1805, which had 8 feet put into her abaft the mast at a cost of £64.

Robert Aldous loved to get afloat. When the original Brightlingsea Sailing Club was formed in 1885, he designed and built a small racer for the club matches. Named the "Aha"! she competed four times without success and her owner broke her up in disgust. Three years later, he tried again with a 22 footer of the same name but strangely enough, she too was unsuccessful and by about 1907 she shared the same fate. However, the interest of members of the Aldous firm in local racing has been well maintained in modern times with the two Brightlingsea one-designs, "Mike" and "Bidi", which have been prominent in the class.

In 1889, the shipyard, then known simply as "Robert Aldous", became Aldous & Son, with yacht refitting continuing to expand the firm's activities, which were still guided by the bowler hatted Robert's daily inspection of every part of his flourishing yard, sometimes, it is said, snatching off his bowler to chalk on it some detail needing

Launch of the 99 ft. wood steam yacht *Anemone V*, built by Aldous in 1906. Smack and racing yacht under repair at right.

explanation to a shipwright! By 1870, fifty yachts were laying up at Brightlingsea, by 1882 this increased to 70, and during the early nineties, over 100 were cramming the yard and the mud berths for half a mile to the eastward, their masts thick as a wood and their bowsprits soaring over the sea wall, where specially constructed sheds stored their gear. The yard was filled with the lean hulls of racers such as the crack 40 raters "Lias", "Creole", "Varuna" and "Vendetta", all skippered from the town which then provided about 500 hands for the yachting fleet. The turn of the century saw some of the largest racers such as the German owned "Navahoe" or the Italian "Bona" hauled out, their long ends well shored against sag.

During this period Aldous produced some very fast little cutters for the Colne River Police of which the "Prince of Wales" and "Colne" still survive as yachts. I believe these were designed by Mr. Polley, the shipyard's draughtsman-loftsman, and the lesser known "Raven" and "Alexandra" were also by him, doing good service with a force formed to keep watch over the then extensive Colne oyster fishery. They were skilfully handled by the seabooted "Coppers", recruited mostly from Lowestoft for obvious reasons, who regulated the fishery and kept watch for pilfering by other vessels.

In 1912, the shipyard was reorganised as a limited company which commenced building steel craft for the then rapidly expanding colonial markets which were to become the shipyard's principal trade, although a tremendous amount of yacht refitting and occasional building continued until 1914, when Robert Aldous died.

During the first World War, Brightlingsea became a naval repair base and Aldous were busy maintaining mine-sweeping drifters, trawlers, and minor war vessels from that hot spot of naval service, the Dover Patrol. In one year they slipped over 300 of them and still managed to build various service craft, including the wooden hulls of flying boats to design by Linton Hope, the yacht architect.

Yachting revived slowly after the war and few yachts graced a Colne filled with redundant Admiralty fishing vessels, whose reconversion to fishing kept Aldous busy. Gradually, the long neglected yachts commenced fitting out. In 1921, the company undertook conversion of the 177 foot, four masted schooner "Elizabeth Ruth", which arrived as an American built wartime auxiliary cargo vessel and emerged as the Duke of Westminster's "Flying Cloud", 1807 tons of cruising comfort with an immaculate new suit of locally made sails.

Between the wars, many of the steam yachts which had previously been maintained at Wivenhoe or Rowhedge began to refit at the yard and the buff funnels and clipper bows of "Elfreda", "Elsie", "Rosabelle", "Lorna" and "Vanessa" were familiar sights on Aldous slips which held noted yachts of all sorts from great schooners such as "Altair", "Tamesis" or "Creole", fine fast cruisers like "Valdora", "Sumurun", and "Rendezvous" to the 12 metres "Vanity", "Veronica", "Marina" and "Jenetta".

The form and draught of racers often presents unique hauling-out problems for even the most experienced shipwrights and Sir Thomas Lipton's 23 metre cutter "Shamrock" aroused tremendous interest and caused a few heartburnings before she was safely "got up" on Aldous' slip during the 1920's.

In 1934 the firm became Aldous Successors Ltd. and also increasingly specialized in the construction of craft for re-erection abroad. Sternwheelers, cargo barges, tunnel vessels, ferries, dredging equipment and tugs reared rusty shells on berths in and before the great black sheds along the waterside. The boatbuilding shops produced numbers of wooden launches and special service craft besides small yachts such as "Jumbo"; and a 12 tonner was offered as a stock boat. Marine and general engineering and sail making completed the comprehensive service the shipyard offered to any class of vessel under 200 ft., and in 1939 the Admiralty were quick to take advantage of Aldous facilities when Brightlingsea again became a base for naval small craft.

The yard's impressive war record included building motor launches, harbour pinnaces and 129 landing craft, besides 82 service launches and fast motor boats. 547 craft ranging from trawlers to M.T.B's and landing craft were converted or reconditioned, and 4,700 bridging pontoons built, the yard employing approximately 600 men during this period.

After the war, Aldous built large numbers of commercial craft including tugs for the Ministry of Supply, alloy boats for B.O.A.C., pontoons, water and oil barges for Africa, lighters for the Cameroons, launches for Spain, Burma, Suez and Nigeria, vehicle ferries for West Africa, oyster skiffs for the Colne fishery, outboard pontoons, and, largest of all, a 170 foot Customs cruiser, the first ship of the new Nigerian Navy. None of these exceeded 170 feet in length, but in numbers, quality, and complexity were an impressive achievement, for the extremely high standards of workmanship needed to build small vessels are not generally realised outside the industry.

The long story ended with one Nigerian Government launch completing in the well equipped shops of the 15 acre yard. Aldous were not alone in their decision. All over Britain, small shipbuilders were feeling the drastic effects of contracting colonial rule, and the rapid establishment of on-site shipyards in the emergent countries, often with foreign aid.

The closing of a shipyard is a sad thing for once its labour force is scattered the team spirit built up over the years is hard to re-kindle. However, one thing is certain, the name of Aldous will always be remembered in the trade for enterprise and ingenuity in designing, building and repairing craft of many types faithfully and well and, as a nursery of good craftsmen, the firm will be sadly missed on Colneside.

Launch of the small yacht *Dawn*, built by Aldous of Brightlingsea. Owner's party and crew on deck. Robert Aldous in bowler hat on quay, at left.

CHAPTER TWENTY ONE

Sixty Years of Shipbuilding

ON A GREY November day in 1904, three young shipbuilders hopefully surveyed the derelict looking shipyard they had just bought at Rowhedge with money borrowed from their fathers. The narrow, wooded Colne, lined with the towering spars of laid-up yachts and the bustling fleet of smacks at Rowhedge quays, presented great contrast to the grime and clamour of Swan, Hunters and Wigham Richardson's great Tyneside shipyard which they had just left to set up on their own in Essex, at the yard vacated by Donyland Shipyards Ltd.

Their spirit of enterprise was backed by specialised knowledge. F. E. Maslin was to be naval architect and secretary, Walter Oxton designed steam engines, and L. P. Foster became works manager as the contract came in for ship number one; the 45 foot steel launch "Desterro" for Brazil, an order typical of the foreign service vessels in which the yard was to specialise. Designed, built, and engined by the new company she achieved 9 knots on trials and her success brought repeat orders. The firm was incorporated as the Rowhedge Ironworks Co. Ltd. in February, 1905 and those unfamiliar with the industry are often puzzled by the title 'Ironworks'. The building of iron ships had ceased in favour of steel long before the firm's founding and, of course, no iron was ever smelted there, but 'Ironworks' was then a favoured way of indicating that a company was willing to undertake steam and general engineering, besides the building of steel ships.

Rowhedge Ironworks inherited a tradition of shipbuilding at the yard by the enterprising John Houston who, besides designing and building some launches and barges, continued and expanded the village's long tradition of building and repairing wood yachts and other craft, a trade carried on earlier at the same site by Mrs. Puxley, a woman shipbuilder who succeeded shipwright James Harris, who took over from William Cheek, the earliest known tenant of the yard which was then (1839) owned by Susannah Cole. His cottage still stands as part of the upper shipyard stores.

Houston's business closed in 1902 and was succeeded by Donyland Shipyards Ltd., whose career was short lived. At the beginning, the Rowhedge Ironworks' total employees, including apprentices, only numbered 20 with a weekly wage bill of £19 but, despite its small size, enquiries for foreign service craft came in steadily in those days of booming colonialism. Many such contracts were placed at Rowhedge by London agents, James Pollock, who later established themselves as rival shipbuilders at Faversham, Kent. The sternwheeler "Sultan", built in 1906 for the Governor-General of Nigeria as Rowhedge's 21st order, was an early example of the firm's increasing specialisation in craft for re-erection abroad. Like most of her kind, the 80 foot "Sultan" could float on a dew pond with her 22 inch draught, but was unique in being amongst the few sternwheelers to run full trials on the Colne where her flimsy awnings, "Wood-bine" funnel and churning paddles made bizarre contrast with the stout smacks and graceful yachts.

The firm were also obtaining orders for harbour service and estuary craft and the steamer "Prince of Wales", launched in 1908 for the channel pilots' Thames service typified the sturdy, tug-like workboats of the day. There was fierce competition for orders and times were not easy. The young firm lost heavily until, in 1909, the company considered closing. However, the directors decided that if two of them sold out to the third, the firm would survive. Accordingly, Mr. Oxton's father bought the share-holdings of Maslin and Foster and in June, 1909, Walter Oxton, aged 41, became sole managing director. Gradually he expanded the firm's production and reputation and, by 1912, the wage bill had soared to £140.

The largest vessels built at that time were around 80 feet in length; a size favoured by a yard having little lifting equipment for erection, and needing rapid turnover of orders.

A 60 foot sternwheeler for an expedition exploring the Upper Orinoco was designed and built in 6 weeks, including machinery, and sent out to South America in 7 pieces. Speedy construction gained them work and by 1911 the keel was laid of ship No. 99, the side-wheeler "America". Designed to be shipped out to Brazil as deck cargo, she was steamed round from Colne to London Dock in wild March weather, giving her the worst dusting she would endure in a life of placid paddling among the mangroves.

Much of Rowhedge's output for abroad has gone out in the form of worked plates and sections for re-erection and riveting-up on site, usually in Africa and S. America. The craft are constructed in the ordinary way except that everything is bolted together. When steel work is completed each plate, section and fitting, however small, is allotted a combination of letters and numbers corresponding to those shown on detail plans and the plating is further located by various coloured lines painted diagonally across hull and decks. When dismantled, plates and sections are boxed and bundled for ship-ment with sufficient rivets and bolts to re-erect on site, usually supervised by a European who, on a large contract, is often a shipwright or plater from the builder's yard. Re-erection work has been a great part of the Colne's shipbuilding and requires fine and fair workmanship. The double erection and shipment are expensive but it is often preferable to attempts made to build on site. Probably the most exacting re-erection job of all was completed by Rowhedge Ironworks in 1912 when the 40 foot steel passenger launch "Carolina" for service on lake Titicaca, 4,000 feet up in the Andes, was sent out in parts each weighing not more than 84 lbs, dictated by the load a llama could carry up the mountains! Fortunately all the beasts survived the journey and she was duly launched and is still working amid the snow-capped mountains.

The yard maintained its interest in repair work and each winter before 1914 laid-up yachts of large size lined the mud berths above the yard to the "first stile", as a

Launch of a wooden minesweeper at Wivenhoe Shipyard Ltd., 1943. Frank H. Butcher, managing director of Rowhedge Ironworks chats with service officers and the Home Guard provides a guard of honour. Another minesweeper building on the next berth, and others fitting out alongside quay. A sailing barge sweeps by in the background.

background and reminder that their refit provided much useful work for the yard, though not on the same scale as at Harris Brothers shipyard "downstreet" where some of the most noted British yachts had wintered and been built.

Rowhedge Ironworks were engaged on Admiralty contracts in 1909 and naval preparations for the Great War brought many orders. In 1912, the firm were commissioned to build numbers of $52\frac{1}{2}$ foot wood steam pinnaces to be carried aboard battleships and for harbour service. Batches of these continued to be a feature of Rowhedge's production for the next forty years during which they altered only slightly in appearance. Their early machinery was by Mumford of Colchester but Rowhedge were also soon producing the beautiful little compound sets. Numbers of warships' motor boats and a few Admirals' barges were built, one for service aboard the battle-cruiser "Repulse". An odd wartime contract was an 80 foot Belgian canal tug for the War Office, but the bulk of steelwork comprised sternwheel tugs and barges for the Mesopotamia and other campaigns. The concentration of minesweeping drifters, trawlers and barrage vessels in the Swin, and at the Nore and Dover created much repair work for the Colne yards, and Rowhedge Ironworks did its share, leasing the Harris Brothers' shipyard in 1915 to improve the firm's facilities for slipping, repair and construction of wooden craft. In later years this part of the Rowhedge Ironworks became known as the "lower yard", and during the 1914-18 war it built several of the 50 knot coastal motor boats, the early motor torpedo and smoke-laying launches, some of which are reputed to have engaged in the glorious but futile Zeebrugge raid in 1918. Surprising as it now seems the yard also built flying-boat fuselages which, in those days of "sticks and string" aircraft, had triple-skinned wooden hulls, copper clenched and finished like a boat in bright varnish! Other yards, such as Camper and Nicholsons of Gosport, also engaged in this work which went away by road to be fitted out, often at Felixstowe.

During the post-war period the now well-established company secured a wide variety of contracts and its versatility placed Rowhedge amongst the dozen or so British yards specialising in "problem" craft under 150 feet in length; the most exacting branch of steel shipbuilding. The platers were well led by foreman Pullen, who was succeeded by Frank Mumford. Craft were built for Egypt, Nigeria, the Congo, Brazil, Argentina, and the Sudan, with which strong ties were established leading to considerable work over the next 30 years. An early Sudan contract was the most unusual, calling for a 60 foot, lateen-rigged "Gyassa", or shallow-draught Nile trading vessel which was shipped out in 1926. Two years later the Sudan ordered four 139 foot Nile sternwheelers one of which, the "Rejaf", later featured on a Sudan postage stamp and another, the "Omdurman II" carried the then Prince of Wales to Khartoum during his African tour. These were the largest vessels then built at Rowhedge which was also building passenger craft like the 103 foot "Putney", beloved by followers of the boat race, and the wooden "Brightlingsea", still running in the Harwich-Felixstowe ferry service.

In 1930 things looked black for Rowhedge Ironworks. Throughout Britain shipyards were closing and those remaining were fighting for the few orders out to tender, usually against severe Dutch competition. At this most trying time, when foremen in some yards were to be found red-leading stock plate to justify their retention on the staff, Rowhedge secured the order for the coasting tanker "Ben Sadler" a name honoured in the firm's history as the first of a series built for the National Benzole Co. over the next quarter century. The 289 ton "Ben Sadler" was built in the "big shed" in record time and her owners were so pleased with the ship that eight of their subsequent tankers were built at Rowhedge. These sturdy coasters were described by a Benzole director as "some of the finest little tankers built in the British Isles". The 129 foot tar tanker "Target" completed in 1936 for Dorman Long, Middlesborough, was unique for the times in being propelled by steam machinery. She needed steam in large quantities for the heating coils which kept the heavy cargo fluid.

By now the company was widely known simply as "Rowhedge", appropriately for, straddling the High Street, the shipyards were an integral part of the village which has generally been as proudly conscious of their achievements as of its seafaring past, which ship-building skills largely replaced as a livelihood. Rowhedge boys became shipbuilders and engineers as readily as their forebears became racing yachtsmen and fishermen, for they saw ships on the stocks every day as a commonplace background to life. Children have always been attracted to the doors of the "big shed" opposite the office, where vessels took dim shape in sunlight filtering through the high skylights. Often the road to school was blocked by a great baulk protruding from the whining sawmill, or by sections of a sternwheeler going to Africa. When an especially notable ship was launched, such as a Benzole tanker, Rowhedge school children of the 1930's were invited to see the village's latest and greatest go down the ways. Because of tides, launches at Rowhedge always occur around midday and anything of importance merited the High Street dressed with flags and brought excitement as important guests arrived for cocktails served in the big shed, before the launching party mounted the improvised platform under the bow. The village turned out and crowded the yard, where unattended machinery accentuated an expectant atmosphere. A blessing by the vicar contrasted with muffled comments of shipwrights getting the last blocks out, while painters gave finishing bottom touches. The shipwright foreman, most important man of the day whose responsibility the launch was, signalled ready; the lady sponsor said her piece and activity burst with the pop and fizz of the bottle spraying champagne down the bow. A whistle blast, a rally of mauls and the dogshores dropped. "There she goo" from the crowd as she started, the 240 ton "Ben Johnson" looking large as the "Queen Mary" to young eyes, gathering speed down the smoking ways to rush into the river amid cheers from the launching party. As the backwash subsided and she rode to anchor in midstream the crowd dispersed in the strangely empty yard, while the men who built her criticised her trim and appearance afloat. That little scene has been enacted at Rowhedge hundreds of times, yet never lost its appeal.

Quick delivery was a feature of the 1930s. In 1935 the passenger vessel "Royal Princess" was built in 17 weeks for Thames service, where the entire employees of Rowhedge Ironworks have several times enjoyed annual outings on her—a typical example of a busman's holiday. Shortly afterwards the firm launched the smaller "Wroxham Belle" for the Broads, which later saw service at Freetown as a wartime liberty boat.

Of course Rowhedge continued to repair and build yachts and two of them were of exceptional interest. The 25 foot sloop "Buttercup", designed by Robert Clark, was a superb and prophetic piece of boatbuilding having twin keels, heavily cambered deck and rounded deck edge, and a deep steering cockpit: all features incorporated in modern boats such as the Fairey "Atalantas". After giving years of pleasure to Mr. Foster, who sailed her round England, she was sold to Major Major who, in 1956, sailed her across the Atlantic. For this voyage she was, appropriately, fitted out at the Rowhedge Lower yard where Gerbault's world-girdling "Firecrest" had been built 60 years previously. The steel motor yacht "Essex Maid" was a seaworthy craft built at Rowhedge in 1938 for Mr. John Blott, whose interest in sea fishing led him to have her designed on the lines of a drifter, but finished and fitted out in true yacht style.

Large numbers of passenger and cargo barges were built, and launches for refuelling aircraft, police work, medical dispensing, and towing. They even built one with a glass bottom! An unusual feature fitted in a boat for coral observation in the Caribbean. Connections were made with Thames lighterage interests and some powerful tugs were built for John Hawkins, the Rotherhithe firm whose contracts with Rowhedge were always sealed by the passing of a penny between owners and builders, an informal bond typical of the good faith which existed between Rowhedge and their clients.

Centre of this activity was Mr. McGhee, the yard manager. Shipyard legend has it that when he left the towering cranes and complex shipyards of his native Clyde to join Rowhedge Ironworks (which was then very small) he was met at Wivenhoe station by an employee who explained the prospect of Rowhedge unfolding over the marsh. "Where's the shipyard!" McGhee asked and, when it was indicated, exploded into violent Scottish and turned about! Nevertheless, he stayed for the remainder of his life, to appreciate the quality of its labour and to further the firm's reputation by his adroit management. He was backed by good foremen. William Tabor, a master plater, Arthur Simons of the shipwrights, and Richard Munson of the engineers, who were leading a team of craftsmen keen to produce vessels to designs by Mr. Street, the chief ship draughtsman, later followed by Mr. Crowte. Engine draughting was under Mr. Frank Jones, whose diesel experience never displaced his love of steam engines. In 1937 the firm suffered a setback in the death of its founder Mr. I. Walter Oxton, succeeded as managing director by Mr. Frank Butcher, who joined the firm in 1907 as a young engineer. "F.H.B.", as he became widely and respectfully known, was a

The Thames tug *John Hawkins* ready to launch at the Rowhedge Ironworks Company, 1946. Centre, right, Donald Oxton, managing director. Frank Jones, chief engine draughtsman. Jack Butcher, engineer manager, Robert Buckingham, director. Albert Cork, shipyard manager.

dynamic character in the best shipbuilding tradition and it fell to him to guide the firm through the busy wartime period.

Like most yards in 1939, Rowhedge Ironworks were full of work, much of which was immediately converted for Admiralty use. An 83 foot Nigerian Customs cruiser had her fortunes changed when she was fitted out as H.M.S. "Umbriel", for use as H.Q. ship at Lowestoft, and three mine recovery vessels for the Turkish Navy were also caught fitting out, but were allowed to proceed to Turkey, whose mining service was important in closing the Dardenelles during hostilities. Many locally manned motor yachts, including the "Caleta" and "Essex Maid", were converted to boarding and examination vessels. The R.N.L.I. lifeboat "Guide" subscribed for by the Girl Guides of Britain was completing for the St. Ives station at the time of Dunkirk and hastily sailed to Ramsgate with a village crew. Taken to the beaches by naval ratings she was returned riddled with bullets, to the despair of the shipwrights who had built her immaculate hull.

With the magnetic mine menace, wooden ships suddenly assumed new importance and Rowhedge's directors negotiated the lease of the derelict Wivenhoe shipyard from Shipbuilders Securities, Ltd., and drafted in staff to commence a programme of mine-sweeper and drifter construction, besides reopening the drydock for repair of naval and merchant ships. Wivenhoe turned out 55 craft for the Admiralty, including the famous "wooden submarines", decoy dummies for use in anchorages. Some naval netlayers were commenced there which had the heaviest scantlings remembered in Colne built ships; their total thickness of side being about 22 inches! At the war's end they were stopped and dismantled, to the relief of those working on their exaggeratedly shaped sterns. Eventually pressure on this yard became so great that berths to build 90 foot wood drifters were laid out on Rowhedge Brewery Quay at the Lower Yard where all kinds of vessels were built and repaired during the war, including landing craft fresh from Normandy.

Most tragic of all the Rowhedge war-built ships was the Benzole tanker "Ben Hann" lost with all hands on her maiden voyage. After her the "tanker berth", largest in the yard, was filled with the Ministry of War Transport ships "Empire Homestead", "Empire Lad", "Empire Boxer" and "Empire Barkis". Their skippers were delighted with the high standard of workmanship maintained at Rowhedge and the stand-by crews became almost part of the village community. Torpedo carrying, armament, heavy oil and victualling coasters were also built for the fleet, the latter having vertical coal fired boilers and lofty funnels which merited (and received) "frying tonight" chalked on them. Dozens of $52\frac{1}{2}$ foot steam pinnaces were built, reverting to steam propulsion to the joy of the fitting shop, which was again filled with gleaming compound engines in course of erection. With their long experience of these craft Rowhedge acted as "parent firm" for these launches, providing templates, engines and experience to other builders around the coast.

316

At the war's end almost all contracts were suspended and this, coupled with the death of Mr. Frank Butcher, brought temporary fears for the yard's future, happily resolved when Mr. Donald Oxton assumed managing directorship. Eventually most of the ships were completed, though some lingered, especially a naval tanker known as H.M.S. "Odd Moments", which a wag chalked on her bow. The management was reorganised with Mr. A. Corke becoming responsible for shipbuilding and Mr. J. Butcher in charge of engineering.

Despite shortages and power cuts the post-war boom was soon filling the yard with all the old variety of types, which fascinated me as an apprentice. The Thames tugs "John Hawkings" and "Express", the Southampton ferry "Hotspur VI", a missionary launch for Africa, barges for Lake Victoria, the tanker "Ben Hebden", barges for the Sudan, a passenger boat for London, the superbly plated yacht "Umbrina".

Traditionally shipbuilding is a restless industry, fluctuating in its prospects and movement of labour but, as in some similar yards, Rowhedge seemed to go forward fairly steadily and many of its employees spent almost their whole working lives in its service and were justly proud of its products in the manner of accomplished craftsmen whose skills had wrought and continued its reputation for sound ships. Except for a few national stoppages, strikes were unknown at Rowhedge. Although higher pay could often be had elsewhere most workers preferred local employment and the wide variety of work ensured interest in the job and brought a satisfying sense of creation to skilled tradesmen who were often still discussing a constructional problem on the way home to dinner. From a kaleidoscope of apprenticeship experience one remembers most the personalities which made shipyard life the colourful thing it remains. The noisy activity of Jim Gould and his merry men on the rattling punch and shears known as "Silent Sue" and their cussing of heavily shaped platework. The sheer artistry of Fred Firmin, a shell plater whose equal I have never met in any yard. He

The 76 ft. steel motor yacht *Umbrina* built by the Rowhedge Ironworks Company for an American owner, 1949.

had a scorn of welding and love of a fair line only equalled by Mr. Fookes, his opposite number in the plate shop. The rattling gusto of Bob Payne and Jim Saws, surely one of the last hand rivetting squads to exist? Mr. Govan the anglesmith whose north country accent persisted despite years in Essex and could be heard above the furnace roar and clanging hammers forming a background to his thirsty squad who bent glowing metal into the ever-changing shape of ships. The patient craftsmanship of shipwrights Turner Springett, James Theobald and Richard Spinks; masters at building R.N.L.I. lifeboats, that most exacting test of boatbuilding skill. The quiet efficiency of Mr. Lee the loftsman, meticulously penning battens round ship's lines and gently reminding the drawing office that the tuck wasn't quite fair, again! The superb joinery which emerged from Mr. Day's shop, Tom Prior's cheerful whistling at the fitting shop marking table, the painting and rigging squads yachting yarns which fascinated apprentices interested in sail, and Orlando Lay's unassuming efficiency in slipping and striking over the most awkwardly shaped yachts.

These were some of the 180 or so men under foremen Robert Tabor (platers), Stanley Cook (shipwrights), Edgar Warner (fitters), Fred Day (joiners) and Gibson Schofield (painters), who built over 300 craft between 1945-1964; and during its last ten years the yard launched probably its greatest variety of types. Vehicle ferries, pontoons, ferries for Bermuda, canal barges, dredgers and hoppers, a shallow draught tug, the yard's last sternwheeler, oil, cargo and passenger barges for the Sudan; launches for Lake Maracaibo, customs duty at Freetown, pilot work at Aden, hydrographic work, war office transport, and for oil refinery service. Tugs, dredgers, surf boats, yachts, a passenger vessel for New Zealand, H.M. patrol vessels "Kingsford" and "Ickford", two R.N.L.I. lifeboats and two Benzole tankers. Even an icebreaker—for the Heybridge canal. Considerable repairs and conversion work were undertaken and non-marine work for power station screens and filters produced.

The Wivenhoe shipyard, purchased from Shipbuilders Securities in 1945, continued to repair wooden and other craft and built three 150 foot minesweepers of the "Coastal" programme before finally closing in 1962.

At the end of 1962 Rowhedge Ironworks booked substantial orders for new tonnage, the shipyard administration of management and foremen was reorganised and new berths laid out for prefabrication to speed production. The following year the firm built the largest ship ever launched at Rowhedge; the 200 foot tanker "Mahtab" for Pakistan. A 90 foot Admiralty tug was the last ship on the berths before the yard was sold to become a scrapyard.

Apart from the loss of employment and character to Rowhedge village, it is sad to see the end of a yard which, over 60 years, achieved a splendid reputation and built 947 vessels. I have met people from many parts of the world, concerned with the building and operation of small ships to whom "Rowhedge Ironworks" on the builder's nameplate meant a craft well designed and built for its work.

Some of the staff of the Rowhedge Ironworks Company Limited at the time of the firm's Golden Jubilee 1904-1954. The author as a ship draughtsman, is seated on chair on the extreme left of the front row.

GLOSSARY

An explanation of some of the terms used in this book. The definitions are not exhaustive and have been restricted to clarification of terms in the sense and period covered by this history.

Barge .... In this book the term generally refers to the spritsail, cargo carrying barges of the east coast.

Belay .... To make a rope fast to a cleat, pin, bollard, cavil, etc. An order; "Belay the jib sheets".

Bermudian .... Bermudian rig. A main or mizzen sail, or the foresail of a schooner; of triangular shape set from the mast by slides running on a track, or by the luff rope fitting in a mast groove. Bermudian rig was revived for small racing yachts about 1911 and spread to the large racing yachts after 1919. The rig has since become predominant in sailing yachts, which were previously principally gaff rigged. Bermudian rig was commonly used by sailing craft in the West Indies at least 170 years ago. The rig as set by modern yachts is very efficient to windward and in large racers enabled the number of crew to be reduced.

Berth .... In shipbuilding a place on which a ship is built. "Building berth". A vessel is said to be "berthed" when she is moored alongside a quay or in a dock. i.e. "In her berth". To sailors, "getting a berth" meant obtaining a place in the crew of a vessel. In accommodation on board ship a berth meant a sleeping place for one man.

Board .... Making a tack to windward. "Making a board" (to windward). A term widely used but of obscure origin. The term may have been a survival from use of the "Traverse Board" for course plotting in seagoing ships.

Bobstay .... The chain or wire staying the end of the bowsprit to the stem.

Brig .... A small, square rigged cargo vessel or sailing warship. Brigs were much used on the east coast, particularly in the coal trade from the north-east coast to London.

Cable .... The anchor cable. Substantial chain or rope attached to an anchor and from which a vessel "rides" or lies at anchor.

Capstan .... A mechanical device for hauling ropes or tackles. A cylindrical barrel mounted on a spindle is turned by capstan bars thrust into slots in its top, which are pushed round by men. Alternatively, it may be turned by one or two handles, via gearing to the capstan barrel.

Cheesecutter .... A peaked, close fitting seafaring cap worn by captains, mates and others in yachts and smacks during the period covered by this book.

Clipper bow .... A form of stem which rises from the water in a graceful, forward curving line; in yachts usually ending with a small decorative emblem at deck level. The bowsprit protruded forward extending the outreach of this stem. The mid-19th century clipper ships generally had this type of bow.

Counter .... A counter stern. A usually graceful shape. In profile the under part of the vessel's stern rises at a gentle angle from the water and ends in a shapely and short, upward raking line. Counter sterns were used in most types of craft mentioned in this book.

Culch .... The clean shell, often oyster shell, laid broadcast over oyster layings before spring "spatfall"; the period of birth for young oysters which cling to the clean culch to commence their life cycle. Culch was often dredged from the sea bottom by sailing smacks who sold it to owners of layings.

Cutter .... A single masted sailing craft usually setting a gaff mainsail, staysail (or foresail), jib and a topsail set above the mainsail. A jib topsail is also often set above the jib. This is a most speedy, seaworthy rig and was usual for the Essex fishing smacks and for racing yachts. Yacht's cutter; the principal small sailing boat carried by a large yacht as one of her tenders.

Draughting .... Drawing. Usually refers to drawing plans. Draughtsman.

Dredging .... Oyster dredging. A form of fishing by smacks towing oyster dredges along the sea bottom by dredge warps to gather oysters.

Fetch .... To sail towards and arrive at a certain position despite the wind and weather. e.g. "to fetch a mark", "to fetch a port".

Fish .... To catch fish. Quantity of fish. Alternatively, to repair a broken spar or mast by supporting it with spare spars or other improvised items such as hand-spikes, etc., which are bound to it with rope, like splints.

Fo'csle, or forecastle .... The forward compartment of a sailing vessel's hull. In yachts, small smacks and traditional merchant ships this was the space where the crew lived. In large smacks the crew usually lived aft and the fo'csle was used as a store.

Foresail .... More fully: "Forestaysail". An alternative term commonly used for the "staysail" in sailing vessels, (see staysail). In a schooner the large fore and aft sail set on the foremast is termed the foresail.

Gaff .... The spar supporting the head of a gaff sail. Hoisted and lowered by the throat and peak halyards.

Gig .... A long, clencher built rowing boat pulled by four to eight men and usually between 22 - 32 feet in length. Carried by large yachts for the owner's use before small steam and later motor launches became common.

Gun punt .... A small, low, pointed stern boat used by wildfowlers and generally mounting a long barrelled, fixed gun.

Headsails .... Staysails, jibs and jib-topsails are frequently referred to as "Headsails". i.e. sails at the "head" or forward end of a vessel.

Jackyard topsail .... A large topsail in gaff rigged craft, principally used by racing yachts. The luff (forward end) was extended above the masthead by the topsail yard and the clew (after, upper corner) was extended beyond the end of the gaff by a "jackyard". Jackyard topsails were also sometimes set in light weather by working craft.

Jib topsail .... A triangular sail set from the topmast head, down the fore topmast stay above the jib. Racing yachts usually set three types of jib topsail; the "Long roper" (large), the "Baby" (small) and the "Yankee".

Ketch .... A two masted sailing vessel with gaff or bermudian sails on each mast. The after or mizzen mast is shorter than the mainmast (the forward mast) and is stepped forward of the vessel's sternpost or rudder stock.

Lift .... More correctly "Topping lift". The item of running rigging used to raise or "top" (lift) a boom. In small craft a single rope. In smacks and yachts usually also fitted with a purchase to give adequate power.

Luff .... The forward edge of a sail. In a gaff or bermudian sail the edge abaft the mast. To luff; the act of steering a craft closer or into the wind.

Mastheadsman .... A sailor with special duties aloft, particularly in a racing yacht. Large yachts had a first and second mastheadsman; positions of extra pay and advancement.

Mingle .... A wooden or iron instrument used to discharge sprats from a stowboat net. Mingles were placed under the after end of a net and parted off the desired amount of its contents for discharge on deck or down the fish hatch. This quantity was termed a 'cod' (about four bushels).

Mizzen .... The after mast or sail set on the after mast, in a ketch or yawl rigged vessel. The after mast of a square rigged vessel, other than a brig or brigantine.

"One-design" .... When all the craft of a racing class are built and equipped exactly alike to ensure that skill in handling decides the result of a race they are termed "One-design". Originally more fully; "One class—one design".

Oyster Dredge .... A triangular shaped iron frame with a cross bar and hoeing edge, having a rectangular shaped net with an iron mesh bottom and fibre net upper part or back, and tapering sides. The net is held parallel to the hoeing edge at its rear end by a cross stick laced to it. Dredges were generally of two sizes; small ones about three feet across the hoe and large or deep sea dredges often six feet or rather more, across the hoe or "scythe". Dredges were towed by bass rope warps from the smack, in varying numbers depending on the work.

Oyster dredgers .... Fishermen cultivating or gathering oysters with dredges towed by smacks or oyster skiffs. Alternatively, smacks engaged in an oyster fishery.

Oyster layings .... Areas of a river or creek noted for the good growth of oysters. Usually clearly marked by withies (saplings driven into the bottom with their heads above water). Layings were frequently owned by individuals; oyster dredgers and merchants.

Oyster skiff .... A beamy, shallow draught, clench-built open boat about 18 - 25 feet in length, used for transporting oysters from smacks to shore, or to oyster layings. Usually rowed or sculled by an oar over the stern.

Plater .... A tradesman skilled in iron or steel shipbuilding. Platers commonly style themselves "Boilermakers" after the origins of their trade.

Prize money .... Paid to crews of racing yachts, or smacks racing in regattas, from the money given as a prize. In racing yachts prize money formed a substantial supplement to the crew's wages, which for a hand in a fast yacht might be almost be doubled thereby. Racing yachts' captains and mates received a larger proportion of the prize money than the hands.

Quarter .... The sides of a vessel's stern. i.e. the port and starboard quarters.

Raking .... Rake. As applied to a vessel's rig this means at an angle to the vertical. e.g. "raking masts"; masts sloping aft. "Rakish"; with much rake or speedy looking.

Ratlines .... Ropes secured at vertical intervals between the shrouds supporting a mast to provide a "ladder" for climbing the shrouds to the mast heads.

Reef .... To reduce the area of a sail by reefing. The position line of a reef across a sail. To reef; act of reefing. Reefed. Reef points; short lengths of rope sewn to a sail at the line of a reef. The sail below the reef points is bunched up after the reef pendants have been hauled taut (see reef pendants) and the points tied under the sail in a knot, reducing the sail area.

Reef pendants .... Stout ropes which are rove through "cringles" (reinforced holes) at the luff and leech (forward and after edges) of a sail and which are hauled down taut to the boom before tying the reef points. e.g. "Hauling down a reef". "Shake out a reef"; to untie the reef points and release the pendants to restore sail area.

Rigger .... A skilled man usually employed by a shipyard or yachtyard to make and overhaul rigging. Often an ex-seaman with exceptional skill in working with fibre or steel rope.

Ruck, rucked .... When the peak or upper end of a gaff sail is lowered by its halyard to swing freely, while the luff remained set up taut, the peak is said to be "rucked", rendering the sail less powerful in driving effect. A manoeuvre much used to regulate a vessel's speed when fishing, coming to anchor or moorings, or to ease her in bad weather. An alternative term for ruck is to "scandalise" a gaff sail.

"Runners" or running backstays .... Stays supporting a mast at the "hounds" and leading aft. These were usually of wire (the runner pendant), the windward of which was set up by a tackle (the runner tackle).

Salvager .... A seaman or a smack engaged in giving assistance to a stranded or wrecked vessel, particularly in winter: helping to save life or remove cargo and equipment from wrecks.

Schooner .... A two or more masted sailing vessel with the masts of equal, or almost equal, height and fore and aft sails, either gaff or bermudian, set on each mast, also having headsails forward of the foremast. Schooners fitted with square topsails were termed "topsail schooners".

Scope .... The amount of cable let out and to which a vessel lays at anchor. e.g. "Give her more scope; pay out more cable.

Set .... A fore and aft sail is set when it is hoisted. A square sail may be set when it is loosed from the yard and sheeted.

Sheer .... The line of a vessel's profile at deck or the top of the bulwarks; usually a gentle curve. "A sweeping sheer". Alternatively, sheer; to move obliquely through the water, commonly against the tide: "to take a sheer".

"Shifters" or shifting backstays. .... Stays supporting a topmast head and leading aft. These were usually of wire (the shifter pendant) which was set up by a tackle (the shifter tackle). They were called "Shifters" because, unlike the runners, they had to be "shifted" i.e. slacked right off and the windward one set up, at each tack the vessel made.

Shrouds .... Wire rope rigging transversely supporting a mast and set taut with rigging screws or "deadeyes and lanyards". Before c. 1870 shrouds were usually of hemp rope, which stretched badly.

Smack .. A cutter or ketch rigged sailing vessel used for fishing. These craft were developed to near perfection by the Essex fishermen and shipbuilders.

Spit .... The point of a shoal.

Spitfire .... A small storm jib.

Spreaders .... A pair of struts supporting topmast shrouds on a mast. An earlier term was "Crosstrees".

Staysail .... The triangular sail immediately forward of the mainmast or foremast in fore and aft rigged craft. More fully, forestaysail (see foresail).

Stem .... The forward member or edge of a vessel's bow.

Stowboat net. (Stow net) .... The large, close-meshed, funnel-shaped sprat net of the Essex and Hampshire fisheries. It is now obsolete. Dating from the Middle Ages this was earlier known as the "stall net" from the smack setting it lying at anchor with the net beneath her, when fishing.

Topmast .... An addition to the head of the lowermast usually attached to its forward side and arranged to "house" or lower when required either for relieving strain on the vessel in bad weather or for repair. Most of the Essex smacks and the gaff rigged yachts were fitted with topmasts which could be housed.

Topsail .... The sail set from a topmast above a gaff main or mizzen sail, or above the gaff foresail in a schooner. Also a "square topsail" in square rigged vessels such as brigs, barques, etc., or in a topsail schooner.

Trawl .... A fishing net and associated gear for catching bottom-swimming fish and shrimps. The "beam trawl" was the type used by the sailing smacks. A triangular shaped net spread behind a wooden beam which might be 25 - 35 feet long. This was towed astern of the smack, along the sea bottom, by a rope warp which passed through a large block attached to the trawl heads at each end of the beam by a rope bridle. The net was attached at the upper forward edge to the beam by lacings, and at the bottom forward edge to a ground rope between the heads, which might be weighted to seek out fish lying close to the bottom. At each end of the beam an iron trawl head carried it above the bottom in a sledge-like manner. The trawl nets mesh varied with the type of fish to be caught. The smallest mesh being used for shrimps. When trawling, fish entered the net's mouth and were trapped in its apex called the "cod end". Those attempting to escape back towards the mouth along the net were caught in pockets in the wings or sides. The trawl was hauled up by the trawl warp by hand, or with the aid of a hand capstan in the Essex smacks.

Trim .... The adjustment of a vessel's floating disposition longitudinally or transversely. e.g. "Trimmed by the stern"; a vessel drawing more water aft than forward. To trim sheets (of sails); to adjust the sheets. To trim cargo; to level or adjust it for the best seaworthiness.

Truss, trice-up .... When the tack of a gaff sail is lifted part way up the mast by a tricing line (truss) or tackle, the tack is said to be "triced up".

Trysail .... A sail of moderate area usually set as a substitute for the mainsail in storms, or in case of accident to the mainsail. Large racing yachts set a trysail for passagemaking to preserve the set of the racing mainsail. A storm trysail was of much smaller area than a mainsail and was made of stouter sailcloth. Until about 1914 trysails were usually quadrilateral and were set by a trysail gaff. In later years they were increasingly triangular.

Ways .... Long wooden timbers of rectangular section placed under a vessel to be launched. There were two sets; the fixed or "ground ways" and the upper or "sliding ways". The surface between them was well greased to permit easy movement when the time came for the launch. Similar ways were sometimes used in small yards to haul vessels out of the water. They were also commonly used to "strike over" craft of all sizes and types which needed to be moved about in a ship or yacht yard.

Windlass .... The mechanism for raising an anchor. The Essex smacks were fitted with a primitive wooden windlass, the barrel of which was rotated by two handspikes fitting into slots and turned by one or more men. Several turns of the chain cable were taken round the barrel which could be retained by a ratchet pawl. After about 1850 most yachts had a compact iron windlass of patent design, or an iron capstan.

Yawl .... A two masted sailing vessel with gaff or bermudian sails on each mast. The after or mizzen mast is considerably shorter than the mainmast and is stepped aft of the sternpost or rudder stock.

INDEX

F

Fairey, Sir Richard, 227.
Fenn, Capt. Ben, 163.
15 meter, 164, 168-170, 222, 223, 238.
52 foot Class, 163, 172.
Fingringhoe, 16, 40, 43, 44, 57, 61, 70, 252, 264, 265, 271.
Firmin, Fred, 317.
First Class racer, 101, 171.
Fisher, Ephraim, 70.
Fitzclarence, Lord, 90.
Florio, Ignazio, 145.
Forrestt—built/yards, 128, 186, 190, 269, 273, 289-300; and Co. 294; Rennie, 298, 299; and Son, 289; Thomas, 289; W. A., 289.
Forsgate, Capt., 118, 282.
40 rater, 136, 138, 139, 148, 149, 162, 232, 238, 307.
40 Ton Class, 120.
Fountain Inn, 86.
Francis—family, 71; Capt. George, 179, 227.
French, Capt. I., 127-129, 132.
Frost, Capt. William, 152.
Fruit trade, 90, 270, 277, 286.

G

Gaff rigged bumkins, 70.
Game, Moses, 256, 258, 259, 271.
Gampton, Jack, 175.
Gardiner, E. J., 272.
Garrard, Capt., 136.
Geeton Creeks, 70.
Geirbault, Alain, 267, 314.
George V, 171, 174, 237, 238, 240-242.
German Emperor's Cup, 155, 157, 160, 161, 214.
Glozier—family, 67; Mr., 66.
Goff, Capt. William, 162.
Goldmer Gat, 64.
Gomes, Capt. Robert, 149, 150, 206, 235.
Gorbills (or Guardfish), 70.
Gorey, 33.
Gould—Capt. Edward, 138, 157, 160; J. 146; Jim, 317; Capt. 128, 136, 138.
Govan, Mr. E., 317.
Greyhound Inn, 271.
Griggs—family, 72; John, 184.
Gunfleet, 46, 68, 241.
Gunn, Mr., 66.
Gurten, Capt., 172.

H

Half raters, 140.
Ham—Capt. James, 118; Capt. William, 90.
Hamble, 146, 158, 217, 218, 249.
Handicap classes, 136, 148, 150, 152, 154, 157, 158, 163.
Harlow—Capt. Harry, 112, 118, 284; Thomas, 40.
Harris—67, 205; Capt. Ben, 118, 120, 132, 133, 137, 302; Brothers, 113, 170, 312; 268; E.P.,

154; Enos, 266, 267; Enos P., 267; James, 310; John, 266; of Rowhedge, 29, 124; Peter T., 266, 267; yard etc., 29, 134, 147, 156, 168, 186, 187, 207, 267, 268.
Harvey—98, 264, 303; and Son, 280, 281; design, 108, 283, 301; Edward, 277; John, 100, 109, 112, 243, 246, 272, 275, 277-280, 282-288, 301, 302; John and Co., 283; John Martin, 280, 281; Nathaniel, 44; Robert, 40; Thomas, 99, 101, 264, 277, 278, 280, 283; Thomas (Carpenter) 44; Yard/built etc., 96, 106, 118, 121, 125, 186, 187, 243, 277-288.
Harwich, 16, 28, 46, 52, 57-59, 64, 65, 68, 92, 104, 112, 113, 116, 124, 137, 139, 145, 149, 150, 165, 169, 173, 204-208, 211, 218, 223, 224, 226, 227, 228, 233, 241, 247, 252-256, 270, 278, 282, 302, 313.
Hatcher—301, 303; Dan, 108, 109, 279, 282, 284, 302.
Heard, Capt. Edward, 172-175, 212, 225, 227, 241, 250.
Heath—38; James, 40; William, 40; of Wivenhoe, 290.
Heave away on the trawl, Song, 83.
Henry VII, 184, 252.
Henry VIII, 252, 253.
Henry of Prussia, Prince, 136ff, 139.
Herbert, Capt. John, 107, 125, 282.
Heret, John, 252.
Hewes—Fan, 680; and Son, 68.
Heybridge, 61, 246, 285, 286, 318.
Hogarth, Capt. Archie, 140, 149, 152, 154, 225, 248.
Hope, Linton, 308.
Houston, Capt. John, 112, 113, 118, 122, 268, 310.
Howe of Colchester, 275.
Hunloke, Capt., 238-242; Major Philip, 172, 237.
Husk—James, 274; James Jnr., 274; & Son, 274; yard, 186, 187, 274.
Hythe, The, 102, 121, 122, 124, 131, 270.

I

Imperial Yacht Squadron, 128.
Ipswich, 42, 61, 86, 92, 97, 101, 158, 174, 213, 238, 240, 260, 270, 278.
Isle of Wight, 87, 91, 95, 106, 110, 123, 140, 150, 164, 227, 234, 242, 243.
Itchen, 102, 107, 109, 117, 118, 120, 121, 124, 134, 136-138, 145, 149, 150, 152, 157, 163, 169-171, 175, 205, 224, 227, 239, 301, 302.

J

J Class, 173, 240, 241, 242, 250.
James—John, 276, 297; and Stones' yard, 253, 275, 276.
Jay, Capt. Tom, 128, 136, 137, 140, 145, 148, 150, 151, 193, 199, 208, 210, 212, 233, 235, 236, 305.

INDEX OF VESSELS

Vindex, 109.
Viola, 114.
Violet (1855), 109, 301.
Violet (became Christabel), 109.
Virginia, 152.
Viva II, 176, 177, 178, 250.
Vivandiere, 267.
Volante, 101, 105, 106, 243, 278, 279, 287, 301.
Vol-au-Vent, 124, 129, 133.
Volcanic, 90.
Volta, 295, 296.
Volunteer—smack, 271; American yacht, 246.

W

Walrus, 267.
War Hawk, 106.
Wasp, 263.
Waterlily—yawl, 282; Auxy. steam yacht, 191.
Water Witch, 44.
Waterwitch, 94.
Wave, 298.
Weatherly, 251.
Wendur, 132.
Wenonah, 287.
Westra, 227, 228.
Westward, 170, 171, 223, 224, 237, 239, 241.
White Heather, 161, 164, 165, 166, 171, 217, 218, 223, 224, 237, 239, 240.
White Heather I, 160.
White Slave, 136.
Who'd A Thought It, 286.
Wildfire, 107.
Wild Irish Girl, 95.

Wild Wave, 274.
William—43; of Brightlingsea, 254.
Winchester, 242.
Witch, 93.
Wivenhoe, Ketch, 256.
Wolverine, 263.
Wonder, 18, 25, 74, 75, 206, 223.
Wonderful, 109.
Wren, 270.
Wroxham Belle, 314.
Wyvenhoe, sailing barge, 292.
Wyvern, 296.

X

Xantha (became Gertrude), 281.
Xanthe—154, 155; smack, 74, 155.
X-anthe (nickname for Xanthe), 155.
Xarifa, 97.

Y

Yankee—152; visited England, 1935, 175, 176, 227, 229, 241.
Yarana (became Maid Marion), 134, 136, 145, 205, 206, 212, 267.
Young Paddy, 95.
Young Pheasant, 37.

Z

Zelita, 179, 226.
Zephyr, 118.
Zinita, 146.
Zoraida, 174, 179, 225, 226.

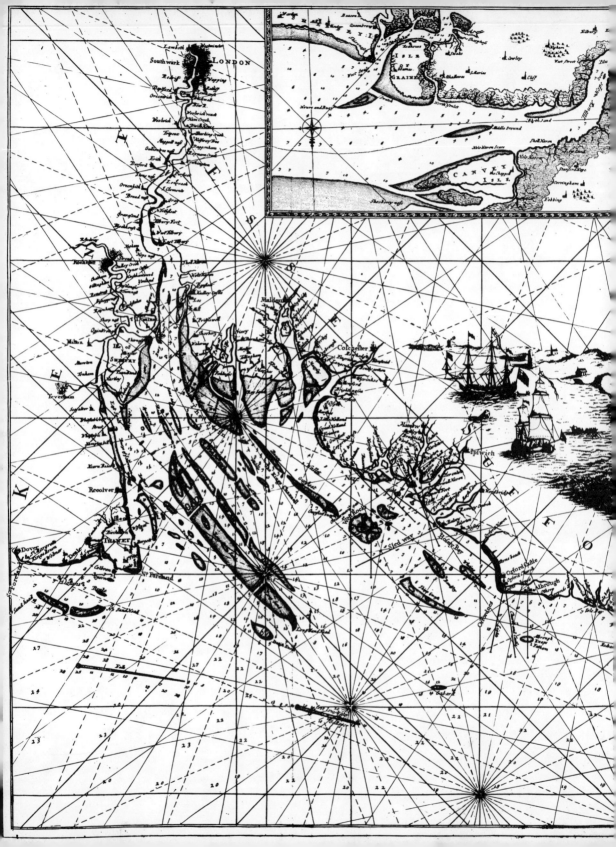